INFORMATION SYSTEMS ASSESSMENT:

Issues and Challenges

IFIP WG 8.2 Working Conference on
Information Systems Assessment
Noordwijkerhout, The Netherlands, 27–29 August, 1986

NORTH-HOLLAND
AMSTERDAM · NEW YORK · OXFORD · TOKYO

INFORMATION SYSTEMS ASSESSMENT:

Issues and Challenges

Proceedings of the IFIP WG 8.2 Working Conference on
Information Systems Assessment
Noordwijkerhout, The Netherlands, 27–29 August, 1986

edited by

Niels BJØRN-ANDERSEN
Copenhagen Business School
Copenhagen, Denmark

Gordon B. DAVIS
Carlson School of Management
University of Minnesota
Minneapolis, U.S.A.

1988

NORTH-HOLLAND
AMSTERDAM · NEW YORK · OXFORD · TOKYO

ISBN: 0 444 70335 7

Published by:
ELSEVIER SCIENCE PUBLISHERS B.V.
P.O. Box 1991
1000 BZ Amsterdam
The Netherlands

Sole distributors for the U.S.A. and Canada:
ELSEVIER SCIENCE PUBLISHING COMPANY, INC.
52 Vanderbilt Avenue
New York, N.Y. 10017
U.S.A.

Original artwork introducing each article by Riitta Kalmi

Library of Congress Cataloging-in-Publication Data

IFIP WG 8.2 Working Conference on Information Systems Assessment (1986
   : Noordwijkerhout, Netherlands)
   Information systems assessment : issues and challenges :
proceedings of the IFIP WG 8.2 Working Conference on Information
Systems Assessment, Noordwijkerhout, The Netherlands, 27-29 August
1986 / edited by Niels Bjørn-Andersen, Gordon B. Davis.
     p.   cm.
   Includes bibliographies.
   ISBN 0-444-70335-7 (U.S.)
   1. Information resources management--Congresses. 2. Information
technology--Congresses.   I. Bjørn-Andersen, Niels. II. Davis,
Gordon Bitter. III. Title.
T58.64.I35 1986
658.4'038--dc19   87-27178
                                                             CIP

PRINTED IN THE NETHERLANDS

PREFACE

This volume is the proceedings from an IFIP Working Group 8.2 international conference titled: "Information Systems Assessment", held in the Netherlands, August 27-29, 1986. There were 80 participants from Europe, North America, and other parts of the world. Papers were accepted for the conference and included in this book based on a scholarly review process. Authors revised the papers from comments and suggestions at the conference.

The 21 articles address crucial issues in assessing costs and benefits of information systems both in organizations and at the societal level. The topics include both the *ex ante* assessment of the consequences of alternative information system designs as well as the *ex post* evaluation of implemented information systems. Assessment includes technical, economic, organizational, and social dimensions; these are relevant both prior to decisions about acquisition or design (in order to select the best from the possible alternatives) and after the organizational implementation (in order to modify the systems and learn from the successes and failures). This book should make a significant long-term contribution to the field of information systems assessment. The articles are likely to be relevant for a long period due to the high level of theoretical content.

Assessment is not a simple task because the relationship between technical solutions and organizational consequences is not well understood. Successes are frequently sheer luck, and failures are often due to our lack of ability to foresee all the organizational consequences of technical solutions and/or because the chosen technical solutions do not have the anticipated results.

The articles in this volume should have an increasing relevance over time because the potential of information technology to result in changes for the better or for the worse will increase as more complex systems are implemented. Accordingly, it will become even more pertinent to understand and assess the likely consequences of the information systems we are designing and implementing before taking irreversible steps.

The articles are grouped (sometimes somewhat arbitrarily) into three sets:

1. *The Nature of Technology Assessment*

   The major emphasis of these articles is on the rationale, problems, and taxonomies that are useful in understanding the nature of the information systems assessment task.

2. *Theoretical Frameworks for Information Systems Assessment*

   The focus of these papers is on underlying theory, logical design of assessment and conceptual dimensions.

3. *Empirical Investigations*

   These articles include reports of assessments. However, these are not merely descriptions; they tie the assessment work to conceptual frameworks and organizational theories.

This working conference was the first major international conference on assessment of information systems; this report from the conference should encourage further research (there are research suggestions from working groups at the conference) and lead to improvements in our ability to perform both *ex ante* and *ex post* assessment.

The preparation of the report reflects not only the work of the authors and editors but also the invaluable assistance of Benedicte Due-Thomsen of the Institut for Informatik & Okonomistyring. She applied information technology to convert author articles submitted on diskettes into a common book-style format. Janice DeGross, Executive Assistant in the MIS Area in the Carlson School of Management at the University of Minnesota, assisted with editing of manuscripts and prepared the final camera-ready copy.

Finally, our thanks go to Assistant Professor Riitta Kalmi, Computer and Information Sciences, University of Turku, Finland, for the absolutely delightful illustrations introducing each paper.

Niels Bjørn-Andersen
Gordon B. Davis

TABLE OF CONTENTS

PART IV
WORK GROUP REPORTS

PART I
THE NATURE OF TECHNOLOGY ASSESSMENT

A Post-Modernistic Essay on Technology Assessment
Niels Bjørn-Andersen

"The truth is not hidden --
it is all in what you see."

INFORMATION SYSTEMS ASSESSMENT
N. Bjørn-Andersen, G.B. Davis (Editors)
Elsevier Science Publishers B.V. (North-Holland)
© IFIP, 1988

A POST-MODERNISTIC ESSAY ON
TECHNOLOGY ASSESSMENT*

Niels BJØRN-ANDERSEN
Informatics and Management Accounting
Copenhagen Business School
Howitzvej 60
2000 Frederiksberg
Denmark

This essay gives a somewhat academic account of
post-modernism (PM) in order to explore this
development of technology assessment (TA) in
general and information systems assessment (ISA) in
particular. The account of PM is given in a
kaleidoscopic way, aiming at giving a first answer
to the questions of whether there are elements in
TA/ISA which could be called post-modernistic and
whether PM is a potentially useful paradigm in
technology assessment research.

However, those two objectives would put the paper
clearly into the realm of modernism. As such it
would be part of the "great story." Instead it is
written in a PM fashion as a number of small
stories, where the main objective is to create an
experience in the mind of the reader. The emphasis
is on form instead of content, acting instead of
thinking, and play instead of work.

1. INTRODUCTION

Modernism is running wild. Control of the development does not exist, and the great triumph in the
form of the victory of culture over nature has been
superceded with the post modern chaos.   [Movin,
1986]

Technological developments have given us control over nature --
even though it sometimes fights back, e.g., Bopal, Chernobyl,
Sandoz, acid rain. "In the 60s and 70s we wanted more than we
could accomplish -- today it is the big problem that we can
accomplish more than we want" (Töjner, 1986, p. 113). We are
developing technologies at a speed and with such far reaching
implications that large groups of our population are becoming
alienated, as Jungk (1958, 1968) and Ellul (1980) have already
pointed out.

---

*The idea to write this essay was provoked by Erik Wallin,
Lund, who asked me on May 26, 1986, "whether the PM discussion in
the media in Denmark had had any impact on information systems
thinking." At that time, I did not know what PM stood for. But I
have had invaluable help from Lars Ginnerup, who assisted me in my
inquiry into PM, and from Dian Kjærgaard, who has provided many
valuable comments on the paper.

This alienation is due to the cultural schizophrenia between what Snow (1964) called the two cultures, humanities and science. But this schizophrenia can not be sustained. Today, it is as useless as scholasticism in the 17th century (Hoffmeyer, 1985, p. 48). Or, to use a more modern example, as useless as Per Flensburg without his Mackintosh. Accordingly, technology assessment in the widest sense of the word becomes important and even mandatory.

At the same time, TA gets even more complicated because of the far reaching first, second, and third order consequences which often do not occur until after a long period of time. The underlying structures and relationships are almost impossible to grasp and, when we do, it is often too late.

So, in order to give advice on the redirection of (parts of) the development of new technologies, we have to concentrate our energy on developing still better theories, methods and tools in order to define, perceive, map, and diagnose the different implications. To do anything less would be to resort to escapism.

Over the past years, a large number of useful attempts have been made to develop strategies, methods, tools and procedures for doing TA in ways that solve some of the problems. The state of the art described in this volume (Bjørn-Andersen and Davis, 1987) gives evidence that major breakthroughs are achieved in bridging the gap between the two cultures by

- enriching the evaluation basis to include social science evaluation criteria

- integrating humanities into the technological development process

However, the basic questions remain. Even if we extend TA in these two directions, do we achieve the objective? Do we get a real understanding of the implications or the technological developments, and do we get a basis for actively influencing the technological development?

Is it not true that "TA has a large risk of becoming a true child of the technocratic plan ideology" (Quortrup, 1985), as already pointed out by Hoos (1972)? Similarly, Allpass (Fischer, 1985, p. 109) concludes that solution oriented planning in reality often is preventing problem solution due to its narrow and contrasting effect on creativity.

In spite of our efforts to humanize the technology, are we still applying the engineering paradigm to legitimize the decisions and the results which are there already? Are we asking the fox to guard the hens? Is it not so that if we include TA as part of the planning and .development process of new technology, we have capitulated in favor of the technocratic planning universe, and have restricted our choices to actions within that universe (Fischer, 1985, p. 101)?

Perhaps one ought to take a different view and challenge the underlying assumptions of TA by confronting TA with its deadly enemy (Churchman, 1968). The most pertinent place to look for inspiration to such a challenge is within the human/cultural sphere. Here the newest and most fiercly debated development is called post-modernism. Even though it is far from providing an integrated normative approach, it might provide an alternative to the modernist approach to information systems assessment.

2. AGE OF POST-MODERNISM

If we are to believe the intellectuals, we are now in a typical post-era. The architects talk about post-functional, the cultural avant-gardists talk about post-structuralism, post-critique and post-semeiotic, the economists talk about post-Keynesian and post-industrial society, and the British historian Stephen Toulmin even claims to be able to identify something called a post-modern natural science (Jensen, 1986).

It is evident that society is undergoing dramatic changes and a large number of suggestions have been offered to characterize the essence of the society after modernism. Information society, computopia, nuclear age, space age, service society, third wave society, leisure society, etc. But most of these terms turn out to be too specific or too contemporary, and none of them have gained general acceptance. So, until any concept gains a general acceptance, we shall characterize the future society as post-modernistic, even though some will argue that a more precise concept would be late modernistic (Wievel, 1985).

Galtung (Fischer, 1985, p. 114) defines the following periods

Antique period	500 bc	- 500 ad
Middle age	500 ad	- 1500 ad
Modernism	1500 ad	- 1970 ad
Post-modernism	1970 ad	-

To avoid confusion, I might point out that modernism is sometimes used in a much more narrow sense as categorizing a number of experimental developments within literature, art and music (e.g., an author like Rimbaud in the last century or Kafka in this century). Furthermore, we find the concept of modernism used in a narrow sense within the Catholic church around 1900 for the (albeit fruitless) movement to change the Catholic religion to conform to the latest developments within natural science and the existing social conditions. However, with Galtung we use the concept of modernism in its broadest sense as covering the technological, cultural and social developments over almost a 500 year period from 1500.

2.1 Where Did Post-Modernism Come From?

As with many other developments, PM started in art. Actually, one might argue that there is a straight line of development from the American minimal-art, post-painting and pop-art of the 50s and 60s to the post-modernistic ideas of the 80s (Wievel, 1986, p 96). Many similarities can be found in the paintings and sculptures which are characteristic of these developments, especially in their reaction against the traditional ideal of beauty, style, and the notion about what constitutes a "proper" piece of art. Where modernism believed in progress, the vertical Ikaros line, the ideal of PM lies in the maze or the labyrinth -- "the labyrinth as a sensuous and spiritual symbol of richness" (Fischer, 1986 p. 115).

Figure 1. A Beautiful Example of Post-Modernistic Architecture
(The University Extension, University of California,
Irvine. Architect Charles W. Moore.)

Together with the so-called New Age, PM represents perhaps the
most potent answer to the breakdown of modernism or the industrial
age. The main difference is that the former has a utopia, i.e., a
certain set of defined, agreed upon values, while the latter has
not. There are no underlying truths or ethics that are universally agreed upon in PM. It might be argued that the labyrinth is
an ideal, but it is an ideal which is qualitatively different from
a utopia.

Within architecture, the last part of modernism was/is characterized by concepts such as functionalism, rationalism and puritan-
ism. These developments are now contrasted with the PM development, sometimes referred to as "scene architecture," where styles
are copied and mixed in orgies of color and form without any
regard to so called "good taste" or an expressed utilitarian
request for optimal functionality. This is done to create an
experience or an absolute presence, where the "on-looker" changes
from a role as outsider to a role as being part of the architecture. The truth is not hidden -- it is all in what you see.

Similar developments are found within other areas such as literature and movies. Perhaps the most obvious example of PM is the
music video produced to introduce new pop melodies.

Why is it that PM is coming now? Movin (1986) expresses it in
the following way:

> The ideals of modernism have met [their] Wall
> Street crash, and we are now desperately playing
> Monopoly with worthless pictures in a world which
> is more modern than the people living in it.
> Everything suggests that "we are on the road to
> no-where" at full speed, as the pop-group Talking
> Heads are singing.

2.2 Definition of Post-Modernism

The philosophical roots are unmistakably traceable to Nietzsche
in his later years. In *Ecce Homo* (1967) he writes:

> We are at the same time on the first and the last
> step on the life ladder, decadent and virginal.
> This explains something of the neutrality (freedom
> to choose in relationship to problems of life)
> which characterizes me.

When Nietzsche writes that "God is dead," it provides an enormous
liberation, an absence of moral quality. There can be no self-
actualization in relation to societal norms (based on generally
accepted ethics), because there are no such basic societal norms.
Instead, each and every one of us has to create and administer a
morality in accordance with his/her own internal voice and
consciousness.

Lyotard (1979) defines the post-modern as a breakdown of the
existing philosophical, political thinking. It is a breakdown of
"the great story," as he calls it. The existing meta-theories
which put everything into one single historical context are
becoming untrustworthy. Marxism, Freudism, Islamic fundamen-
talism, Fascism, and most other "isms" have that in common; the
definition of the right order of things. Everyone who does not
conform will be treated as traitor, outcast, dissident, heretic,
physically ill, etc. The idea that there is one explanation and
one way to live is moralizing. It corresponds to the world spirit
of Hegel, *Das Kapital* of Marx, or even "*the* technological development" (Kemp, 1986). The result of such a dominant rationality is
well known in the form of concentration camps, terror, or surren-
der to the technological development. As a bank clerk once
responded to me, when questioned about whether she was against a
new system: "How can I be against the new computer system -- it
is progress, isn't it?"

The message of PM is that modern science and modern technology
have given us a plurality of stories. We do not need the great
story any more. PCs and modern communication technology hold a
promise (not often a fulfilled promise -- but still a promise) for
each individual of amplification and augmentation of his/her
personal capabilities for identifying proper moral behavior.
Accordingly, relativism becomes a fundamental cornerstone. Total
liberation is the promise.

Critics sometimes interpret this as indifference. It is not. It
does not mean that everything is allowed. Wanton destruction of
property, destruction of the environment or a nuclear holocaust
can never be defended, because they are fundamentally destructive
of human values. Accordingly, after the liberation from the great
story with its straight-jacket, we have to rely on some underlying
ethic (Kemp, 1986) about the integrity and sacred nature of each

individual.   This fundamental ethic is not or should not be
questioned.   But within this ethic, almost everything is allowed.

Perhaps the biggest provocation of post-modernism is not that it
is a "new style"; it is the (relative) absence of style (Töjner,
1985, p. 112), or rather the-one-right-style.   The right to
explore different kinds of rationality, i.e., freedom from the
straight-jackets of Stalin, Taylor, Friedman, and Freud.   The
absence of one unifying set of ideals or criteria by which to
evaluate quality applies both to quality in any kind of process
(such as an information systems assessment process or a systems
development process) *or* to the resulting piece of art (the TA
report or a computer program).

In this way, PM is a nihilistic, non-directed protest against the
attempts at giving final solutions and fundamental truths about
underlying patterns for everything (Wievel, 1985, p. 101).   It
focusses on the hidden forms which legitimize scientific truth and
is, as such, without normative reasoning.

Finally, a major characteristic of PM is illustrated in the song
by the Danish pop group, Gangway, "Rhythm's our business/we're
stealing every sound," and the group Naive, who are singing, "You
know we are in business -- stealing is the name."   The slogan is
the same in PM and in pop-music -- citations, references, borrowing, patch-working, theft, re-use, and recycling.

3.   POST-MODERNISTIC TRAITS IN TA RESEARCH

The overwhelming characteristic of TA research is that it is
firmly grounded in modernism.   We do not normally think of it as
modernism, but the whole notion of ("scientific") research is
oriented towards discovering underlying structures and relationships in order that we may even better control nature.   Are there
any signs of a post-modernistic development?   I should like to
point to a few examples.

First, it seems that the traditional research breaks down, because
the research results are deficient in meeting the external demands
on information systems assessment research.   In spite of an
obvious increase in volume of research (and as such presumably an
increase in knowledge about the field), practice seems to rely
almost exclusively on rules of thumb.

Second, we search other disciplines for inspiration to complement
our research theories (Mumford, et al., 1985).   Realizing the
inadequacies of our existing field, we expand our perspective by
introducing theories from organizational behavior, work group
sociology, psychology, etc.   But having done that, we have left
the safe harbor of our traditional discipline for a rougher sea
where the islands of truth are even further apart.

Third, there are frequent criticisms voiced by prominent researchers within the information systems research discipline in
general about the political implications of our research (Kling,
1980; Weizenbaum, 1975).   What is the research really being used
for?   Who are we serving?   We have also seen a prominent member
of the research community, David L. Parnas, resign from the SDI
Organization's Panel on Computing in Support of Battle Management.

Finally, there is some research which exhibits clear PM characteristics; e.g., in the doctoral dissertation by Flensburg (1986),
the traditional characteristics of a dissertation are kept at a
minimum to explore certain issues and provide an assessment of the
phenomenon of "experimental systems design." This is done without
following the "golden rules of research." Rather, it is through a
phenomenological process where the concepts and the phenomenon
have an absolute presence. The reader is invited to become part
of the story, and the experience of the reader is, to a large
extent, outside the control of the author. In this way, his work
is an attempt to provide a different inroad to an understanding of
the phenomenon in its social reality.

4. WHAT CAN WE LEARN FROM POST-MODERNISM?

Originally this was not part of the paper, but having given the
talk I was asked from the audience, "What does this mean for
information systems evaluation?"

The quick answer is that my presentation (in a true PM sense) does
not serve any utilitarian purpose. The value of it, if any, is in
the experience it creates in the mind of the listener. The longer
answer is more complicated because we might need to learn it from
post-modernism itself. But how can a field of research and a
related set of practices which is so heavily based on natural
sciences and pure logic learn anything from post-modernism? Movin
(1986, p. 2) writes,

> If we can learn anything from post modernism, it is
> that the world is just as disorderly as it looks.
> We can not systematize or explain ourselves out of
> our own deficiencies. Any scientific project which
> aims at identifying the system, the truth, the
> logic behind the chaotic and meaningless surface,
> is doomed to failure.

If we were to take this statement at face value, there would be
very little left. How can any science progress or even exist if
there is no underlying structure, and all the structures we
"discover" are either just elements of our own imagination or
results of joint seductions based on self fulfilling prophecies?
For obvious reasons, we cannot ourselves falsify the above
proposition, because doing that would just confirm that we are
subject to the seduction of modernism. However, post-modernism
might perhaps give us some insight for IS assessment in the
following ways:

1. The attack on "the great story" and the liberation from that
    is probably the most important message in post-modernism.
    However convincing, we should never allow ourselves or anyone
    else to canonize any single solution, any single behavior,
    any single overriding ideal. We should be much more open to
    alternative perspectives and be prepared to let "the thousand
    flowers bloom."

2. Post-modernism should also warn us that the "significant"
    results of assessment findings through extensive data
    analysis might be accidental and not based on an underlying
    structure. There might be no underlying truth or pattern.
    What we learn could be a result of superstitious learning.

3. Post-modernism could also inspire us with its emphasis on the experience that an artifact creates in the mind of the spectator. When we are designing systems and introducing users to our "new wonderful system" or performing an information systems assessment, it is not enough to be concerned with whether the system satisfies the expressed information requirements. We should also be concerned with the experience that the system creates in the mind of the user. We should contribute toward creating an absolute presence of the system for the user.

4. Furthermore, post-modernism might inspire us to experiment with different scientific approaches to information systems assessment from outside our own field research and to look for metaphors and illustrations from art to enrich our understanding and broadcast our results. When researchers and practitioners within our field have indulged in the social and organizational aspects in order to get a "holistic picture," it has so often been an example of social engineering or positivist/reductionist methods of enquiry. What is warranted would be humanistic approaches and/or critical social inquiry.

5. Finally, in the design of an assessment enquiry and in writing up the final TA report, we might find encouragement (or consolation) in the proposition in post-modernism of recycling, re-use, patch-working, and borrowing!

5. POST SCRIPT

The title of this paper should be taken seriously, much more seriously than the paper itself. It is written with a somewhat academic bias in that it provides (some) references and pretends to have a clear logic. If the logic is clear to the reader, it is important to remember the risk of self seduction! The essay has been written to create an experience. It has been written to stimulate some thoughts in the mind of the reader. It has not been written to convince the reader to adopt my thoughts. Why should my thoughts be better than yours? If I have contributed to a process of reflection over and above the initial surprise, the objective of this essay is fulfilled.

REFERENCES

Bjørn-Andersen, N. and Davis, G. B. (eds.), *Challenges of Information Systems Assessment*, North-Holland, Amsterdam, 1987.

Churchman, C. W., *The Systems Approach*, Delta Books, 1968.

Ellul, J., *The Technological System*, translated by C. Edward Hopkin, Pilgrim Press, 1980.

Fischer, J., "Fremtidsbilleder (Pictures of the future)," in Soderquist, T. (ed.), *Informationssamfundet (The Information Society)*, Philosophia, 1985.

Flensburg, P., "Eksperimentel systemutvekling (Experimental Systems Design)," *Studentlitteratur*, 1986.

Hoffmeyer, J., "Tvedelingen mellem kultur og natur (The Division between Culture and Nature)," in Söderquist, T. (ed.), *Informationssamfundet (The Information Society)*, Philosophia, 1985.

Hoos, I., *Systems Analysis, A Critique*, New York, 1972.

Jensen, I. J., "Post-modernismens rum (The Space of Post Modernism)," *Lousiana Revy*, Vol. 26, March 1986.

Jungk, R., *The Big Machine*, translated by G. Mamor Spruch and T. Wess, Schribner, New York, 1968.

Jungk, R., *Brighter Than a Thousand Suns: The Story of the Men Who Made the Bomb*, translated by J. Cleugh, Grove Press, New York, 1958.

Kemp, P., "Frigørelse eller sort reaktion (Liberation or Reactionary Behavior)," *Lousiana Revy*, Vol. 26, March 1986.

Kling, R., "Social Analyses of Computing: Theoretical Orientations in Resent Empirical Research," *Computing Surveys*, Vol. 12, pp 61-110.

Lyotard, J. F., *Viden om det post moderne samfund (Knowledge About the Post Modern Society)*, in Danish by F. Fransen, København 1982.

Movin, L., "Æd verden med sultne øjne (Eat the World with Hungry Eyes)," *Politikken*, 3rd July, 1986.

Mumford, E., Hirschheim, R., and Wood-Harper, T. (eds.), *Research Methods in Information Systems*, North-Holland, Amsterdam, 1985.

Quortrup, L., "Informationssamfundet: samfund eller ikke-samfund (Information Society: Society or Non-society)," in Söderquist, T. (ed.), *Informationssamfundet (Information Society)*, Philosophia, 1985.

Snow, C. P., *The Two Cultures: A Second Look*, University Press, 1964.

Töjner, P. E., "Det uomtvistelige (The Irrefutable)," in Behrendt, P., et al., *Kritik 72 (Critique 72)*, 1986.

Weizenbaum, J., *Computer Power and Human Reason*, New York, 1975.

Wievel, H., "Sidste skrig -- om post-modernismens narreværk (The Last Yell -- About the Fuzzyness of Post-modernism)," in Behrendt, P., et al., *Kritik 72 (Critique 72)*, 1986.

A Critical Analysis of Information Systems Evaluation
R. Hirschheim and S. Smithson

" Unfortunately, as will be argued in this paper, much
of what has been done under the umbrella of
information systems evaluation has been ill-conceived."

INFORMATION SYSTEMS ASSESSMENT
N. Bjørn-Andersen, G.B. Davis (Editors)
Elsevier Science Publishers B.V. (North-Holland)
© IFIP, 1988

A CRITICAL ANALYSIS OF INFORMATION SYSTEMS
EVALUATION

R. HIRSCHHEIM

Templeton College
Oxford OX1 5NY England

S. SMITHSON

London School of Economics
London WC2A 2AE England

Although the information systems literature appears
to be in widespread agreement regarding the need to
evaluate the product and process of systems
development, the vehicle for undertaking such an
evaluation is far from clear. Numerous platitudes
have been offered about what should be done, and
there have been various attempts to define how it
should be done. Unfortunately, as will be argued
in this paper, much of what has been done under the
umbrella of information systems evaluation has been
ill-conceived. The social dimension of evaluation
has largely been ignored in the drive to provide a
rigorous interpretation and vehicle for evaluation.
This, it is argued, is misguided and inevitably
leads to an overly rational, simplistic notion of
evaluation which is dysfunctional in the long run
due to the inherent unintended consequences it invariably brings about.

1. INTRODUCTION: THE FUNDAMENTAL NATURE OF EVALUATION

Evaluation is endemic to human existence. Whether consciously or
not, people evaluate the products and processes of their labor.
Food, drink, appearance, social interactions, etc., are constantly
being evaluated by someone or something (cf. Legge, 1984, p. 3).
Evaluation is undertaken as a matter of course in the attempt to
gauge how well something meets a particular expectation, objective
or need.

People, it seems, have an insatiable appetite or curiosity for
such things. Consumer products are assessed to see if they meet
market demands; academics, as a matter of course, tend to evaluate
the intellectual faculties of colleagues through discussions;
political ideologies are evaluated on the policies adopted and
their expected societal implications; and so forth. Evaluation is
apparently an important and intrinsic property of the process of
understanding, which in turn is a prerequisite for, or a prelude
to, a carefully considered action.

It is only natural, therefore, that people have sought mechanisms
to help in the process of evaluation. Various tools, methods, and

techniques have been developed to aid this process. Criteria such as bouquet and clarity are used to judge the quality of wine; hardware monitors are used in computers to assess their efficiency; econometric models are used to evaluate the state of a nation's economy; formal methods are used to evaluate the correctness of a computer program. As was noted by Mason and Swanson (1981), underlying these tools and methods is a more basic concept -- that of measurement. They called measurement the "sine qua non" of decision. In fact, measurement is the link between evaluation and tools. In order for something to be evaluated it has to initially be measured, which is normally undertaken through the application of tools and techniques. Moreover, it must first be decided exactly what to measure and why;[1] unfortunately, parts of this simple relationship appear to have been forgotten in the desire to create ever more powerful techniques for evaluation.

It is our contention -- at least within the information systems area -- that in the drive for better tool creation (to improve the process of evaluation), there has been a concentration on the "means" to the detriment of the "ends." That is, the function and substance of evaluation[2] has been given too little attention, while the mechanisms for carrying out evaluation have been given too much attention.

2. SOCIAL NATURE OF EVALUATION: FORMAL/INFORMAL ASPECTS

The strong urge to evaluate everything has resulted in the development of many tools and techniques but, particularly in the light of their doubtful effectiveness (discussed in more detail below) and their vulnerability to organizational hijacking by a strong interest group, they are unlikely to satisfy the need to evaluate. Inevitably much informal evaluation remains, outside of the official evaluation procedures. And there may be considerable tension between formal and informal evaluations. Formal evaluations may appear to be unnecessary, unwieldy and often largely political compared to the apparently effective, non-bureaucratic expressions of what the users really feel, that may be found in informal evaluation. Alternatively, one may take the position that formal evaluations are objective, rational mechanisms aimed at improving the communication and learning within the organization whereas informal evaluations are ill-informed, hasty and largely subjective judgments.

Formal evaluation studies take place within an organizational environment characterized by much political activity as interest groups jockey for power and status. The results of formal evaluation studies have a considerable legitimacy that can form a sizeable political prize. Where an evaluation team approach is used, comprising members from various organizational groups, the ground is laid for the type of political manoeuvres associated

---

[1]As Strassman (1985, p. 100) notes: "You cannot measure what is not defined. You also cannot tell whether you have improved something if you have not measured its performance."

[2]When we speak of "evaluation" in this paper, we refer specifically to post-implementation evaluation.

with formal committees. In any case, the questions of who carries
out the evaluation, when it is carried out and what criteria are
used, are important tactical positions to be grabbed en route to
the final prize. The political nature of IS development has been
emphasized by such writers as Keen (1981), Markus (1983), and
Wynne and Otway (1982) and such a high-profile activity as a
formal evaluation study is unlikely to escape political activity.

The urge to evaluate everything, felt by all individuals, results
in informal evaluations but these evaluations are unlikely to be
performed in isolation. New information systems will be discussed
informally by groups who are affected, to varying degrees, by the
new system. Particularly where the group has borne the brunt of
the impact of the new system in terms of changes to working
practice or redundancies, or where the group is near the beginning
of the learning curve, experiencing much uncertainty and anxiety,
such discussions are unlikely to be either brief or ill-informed.
The behavior of work groups has been studied in some detail by
organization theorists (see for example Smith, 1973) and much is
known, or hypothesized, about the formation of groups, their
maintenance, the development of group norms and the sanctions
applied to deviants within the group. Where the group feels
itself threatened, in particular if traditional norms are under
pressure, by a new information system, then clearly much interaction within the group may take place. New group norms may have to
be developed or old ones reinforced as the group adjusts to the
new situation. Thus the process of informal evaluation may be
subject to very considerable social pressures; they differ from
those surrounding formal evaluation, being perhaps more subtle and
more or less ritualistic, depending on circumstances.

Thus on the one hand we have formal evaluation studies which
although technical on the surface may contain much intergroup
political activity underneath, and on the other hand we have
informal evaluations subject to intragroup pressures. Clearly the
common factor is the social nature of evaluation, however it is
carried out. Since it is argued that information systems should
be regarded more as social systems and less as technical systems
(Hirschheim, et al., 1984), similar reasoning can be applied to
the notion of evaluation itself.[3]

3. THE INFORMATION SYSTEMS EVALUATION LITERATURE

The human desire to evaluate ostensibly everything they come in
contact with -- particularly those elements which are time consuming to make, expensive to purchase and/or likely to have
important consequences -- leads to a strongly felt need to assess
all forms of technological intervention; for example, computer-
based information system (IS) implementation. The literature
abounds with examples of IS evaluations; in fact, until very
recently, there was an entire journal devoted to IS successes and
failures: *Systems, Objectives, Solutions.*

Evaluation per se can be treated as a very wide area indeed,
encompassing many processes that take place during project

---

[3]An interesting parallel may be drawn between formal and
informal evaluation and formal and informal information systems
themselves (cf. Earl and Hopwood, 1980).

selection, procurement, system testing prior to implementation, and post-implementation evaluation studies. For reasons of space, this paper concentrates on the last area and where the term evaluation is unqualified, it should be taken to refer to post-implementation evaluation.

Approaches to IS evaluation have been frequently compared (see for example, Ein-Dor and Segev [1981] and more recently Sanders [1984] and Srinivasan [1985]), but fewer attempts have been made to classify the approaches, and those that have (e.g., Orman, 1983; Sanders, 1984) seem to neglect the social nature of information systems and of evaluation.

3.1 Literature Framework

The method of classifying approaches to IS evaluation adopted here recognizes two rudimentary dimensions. The first reflects the assumptions underlining any particular evaluation approach, and can be thought of as a continuum ranging from the highly objective or rational approaches to evaluation at one end, to those which regard evaluation as very subjective or political at the other. Unlike the classification of Sanders (1984), who saw evaluation in terms of the impact of an information system upon the organization and individual, this continuum represents the (often unspoken) assumptions underlying the approach.

The second dimension, which is not a continuum, depicts the relationship between IS evaluation approaches and their counter-parts in other disciplines. By presenting the IS evaluation literature in this fashion, starting with the most "objective/ rational" and moving along the continuum to the more "subjective/ political," while paying attention to the origins of the ap-proaches, insight into the nature of evaluation can be gained.

3.2 Literature Review

Starting at the highly rational/objective end of the continuum, it is possible to detail an area of evaluation literature which might broadly be defined as an efficiency zone. Here, one can find the approaches based on the notion of quality assurance, as it is known in production management. These approaches assume that the function and goals of evaluation are non-controversial and that the overall aim is to achieve more precise measures of perfor-mance, efficiency or reliability. Much work has taken place in this area in the field of computer systems. There are many books on performance (e.g., Ferrari, 1978) which discuss the use of hardware monitors, software monitors and simulation as techniques to more accurately measure the operational performance of computer systems. A similar rationale underlies the huge effort put into testing the correctness and efficiency of programs (see for example Myers, 1979; Van Tassel, 1978). This has directly led to significant improvements in programming through techniques such as structured programming (Dahl, et al., 1972). This firm notion of quality assurance appears in the "product assurance" approach to software reliability of Bryan and Siegel (1984) and Spencer (1983); they emphasize conforming with accepted standards, verification and validation. The key assumption here is that computer systems (as opposed to information systems) should be more efficient in terms of speed, reliability, etc., and that they should match the requirements as specified; the further, often hidden, assumption being that the specification is correct. Further evidence of this perspective exists in the traditional design criteria such as efficiency, compatibility, reliability, etc. that are to be found in most textbooks of computer systems design (e.g., Waters, 1974). They are usually seen as non-controversial general goals that all systems should subscribe to. Evaluation measures connected with them (e.g., mean time between failures) are similarly non-contentious.

These approaches are almost solely concerned with efficiency, defined as performing a particular task well in relation to given criteria, compared with effectiveness, which is related to deciding which tasks should be done ("doing things right" versus "doing the right things" -- Drucker [1971]). This distinction has been much emphasized by, for example, Keen and Scott Morton (1978). Moreover, the limits of concentrating on aspects of efficiency (e.g., small savings in a meaningless task) are clear and, in the view of Bjørn-Andersen (1984): "we have overemphasized efficiency at the expense of effectiveness."

However, the desire to evaluate information systems in terms of effectiveness raises many problems. Whereas, in the case of efficiency, it is relatively easy to arrive at criteria and measures to determine the worth of a system, as we leave the confines of the efficiency of a computer system to tackle the effectiveness of an information system one tends to hit the real problems of evaluation. The difficulty of IS evaluation has been noted by numerous writers. Keen and Scott Morton (1978), for example, offer four reasons why evaluation is so problematic.

(1) Systems do not have an initial adequate definition of objectives and criteria for "success" and "failure."

(2) Evaluation must take into account social (qualitative) aspects, yet most attempts at assessment only include efficiency oriented and easily quantifiable aspects, i.e., technical objectives.

(3) Because of what evaluation must embrace, it is intrinsically subjective, based on individual value judgments which will differ from one person to the next.

(4) Even if initial system objectives could be set, they would be considerably different from the final objectives due to the fact that user requirements evolve and change over time.

Moreover, as Curran and Mitchell (1982) point out, often the aspects that are measured are those that are easy to measure rather than those that are important.

Moving along the continuum from the "efficiency" zone at the objective/rational extreme, the first measure of effectiveness would seem to be that of usage or utilization. These measures are widely used in other fields, for example average seat occupancy rate may be used to evaluate the success of an airline service. The choice of usage as a measure rests on the notion that the more a system is used the more successful/effective it is, this approach being supported by Ein-Dor and Segev (1978). There can be problems in determining precisely how to measure usage (e.g., connect hours versus proportion of enquiries answered through the system) but the tools (e.g., system log) are fairly simple. It is criticized by Ginzberg (1978) and Keen (1975) on the grounds that such a system may be poor but there is no alternative means of performing the task, plus the fact that this measure ignores the importance or value of the individual task, e.g., the system may be used infrequently but, when it is, its use is crucial. Many studies have tried to correlate usage with satisfaction to determine whether the former is a good indicator of the latter. These have been summarized by Zmud (1979) and more recently by Srinivasan (1985). For example, Lucas (1975) found a positive association generally, but Schewe (1976) found no significant relationship. Robey (1979) discerned a strong relationship, but Srinivasan (1985) found that the relationship was not always positive.

A slightly less objectively-based approach is cost benefit analysis (CBA) (King and Schrems, 1978). Originating in the area of economics (see for example Layard, 1980), this is one of the standard approaches in project selection and procurement as well as in evaluation.[4] Where costs and benefits are easy to identify and quantify, this technique has many advantages in terms of acceptability and comprehensibility although many writers (e.g., Keen, 1975; Hogue and Watson, 1983) argue that in most MIS/DSS developments the benefits are largely qualitative. The determination of costs may be relatively straightforward, although Strassmann (1985) criticizes the frequent failure in practice to include all the true costs. The calculation of benefits, however, is fraught with difficulties (Land, 1976). The problem of accounting for qualitative benefits is usually surmounted by attributing to them some quantitative value, treating them as a side issue or ignoring them altogether (Keen, 1975). It is not surprising therefore that many writers have been critical of CBA. Tapscott (1982), for example, criticizes CBA on the following grounds:

1)   the frequently quoted benefit of increased productivity is problematic when there is no widely accepted theory or measure of office/management productivity (see also Bitran and Chang, 1984; Strassmann, 1985),

2)   it is often far from easy to predict reliably the exact impact of a new information system,

3)   savings in, for example, time are not necessarily additive,

4)   it is difficult to show causality, i.e., to prove that a particular benefit is directly/solely due to the new information system.

Canning (1985) asserts that management are more interested in "hard" benefits than vague promises of increased productivity but Keen (1975) suggests that, although the formal justification may be in hard terms, the actual planning of the system is often based upon the recognized qualitative benefits. This point is echoed by Tapscott (1982) who quotes "The First Law of Cost-Justifying Office Systems":

the probability of a chooser accepting a cost-benefit analysis is directly proportional to the

---

[4]Closely related to CBA is utility theory, again originating in the field of economics, and put forward for use in information systems evaluation by Kleijnen (1980).

degree to which s/he is favorably inclined to the technology anyway.

An alternative approach to effectiveness which steers clear of the difficulties inherent in trying to precisely measure costs and benefits is to examine the information system with respect to either the organization's, or the system's, objectives. The notion of critical success factors (Rockart, 1979) is an example of management thinking transferred to IS evaluation. Here one could evaluate a system with regard to the key functions of the users. Boynton and Zmud (1984) discuss the problems this may cause through bias or over-simplification but find the technique still useful in many cases. As far as the system's objectives are concerned, it is widely recognized (Keen, 1975; Mumford, et al., 1983) that if clear objectives, evaluation criteria and a monitoring mechanism are agreed in a project's early stages, then evaluation becomes much simpler but, as mentioned above, the difficulties of setting precise objectives and predicting the likely impact, in a climate of uncertainty, are not trivial. Furthermore, senior management's aversion to clear objectives have been noted by, for example, Isenberg (1984).

Instead of relying on the quasi-objective measures produced by CBA or a comparison with some objectives, one can adopt the position that success is a more subjective notion which is best measured in terms of user satisfaction; the intention being to take the answers of a questionnaire completed by the users and manipulate them according to some weighting scheme to arrive at a numerical value. This approach, supported by Hamilton and Chervany (1981) can be thought to have its roots in social surveys (cf. Bulmer [1977], particularly in relation to the use of social surveys by Charles Booth in the late 19th century) from a methodological perspective, and in the socio-technical school of organization theory (Mumford and Banks, 1967) in its regard to the satisfaction of the user. However, the measurement of satisfaction is not easy; Ives, et al. (1983), discuss the various measures concluding in favor of the 39-point questionnaire and weighting scheme from Bailey and Pearson (1983).

The survey may be made more specific: Sanders (1984), in addressing decision support systems, measures satisfaction in terms of both overall satisfaction and also decision-making satisfaction. The specificity may be brought down a further level of functional detail, as in the questionnaire used by Francis (1981) in evaluating statistical software packages, which contained 61 items under the headings of capabilities, portability, ease of learning and use, and reliability. The evaluation of a proposed system through an examination of how well it is able to perform particular tasks is widely recommended at the procurement stage of a project (see Gullo [1985] on office systems, Reimann and Waren [1985] on DSS, and Brownstein and Lerner [1982] on software packages).

While the approach has much to commend it, the imprecision and unreliability of the measuring tools (as with most questionnaires) reduces its credibility somewhat. In addition, Ginzberg (1981) emphasizes the role of expectations in user satisfaction, both in regard to realistic/unrealistic and positive/negative expectations, finding that unrealistic expectations are often associated with system failures.

The shortcomings of the above approaches to measuring effectiveness (usage, CBA, comparison with objectives, user satisfaction) have led some researchers to adopt combinations of these measures (e.g., Bruwer, 1984). Whether this ameliorates or compounds the problem is a matter for discussion.

Moving along the continuum towards the subjective/political extreme, we emerge from the "effectiveness" zone into a qualitatively different area, which might be called the understanding zone. By this it is meant an understanding (or appreciation) of the functions and nature of evaluation, as well as the limitations and problems inherent in the process of evaluation. This should not be confused with an understanding of the particular information system, its environment, and the people involved in it. Unlike the two other zones, measurement is not attempted; rather, the understanding of evaluation is the aim.

The first approach here is still concerned with individual users and their satisfaction, but is based upon Personal Construct Theory from the field of psychology (Kelly, 1955). This theory attempts to show how people construct personal mental models of the world using "personal constructs" as filters:

> Man looks at his world through transparent templets
> which he creates and then attempts to fit over the
> realities of which the world is composed. [Kelly,
> 1955, pp. 8-9]

According to Kelly, these constructs are bipolar in nature (e.g., "black-white," "kind-cruel"), each having a particular range of application. This theory is clearly relevant in seeking to explain the process of informal evaluation, as the user applies his personal constructs to a new information system. The usefulness of this approach has been recognized by some researchers in the area of man-machine interfaces (Gaines and Shaw, 1980) and information requirements analysis (Grudnitski, 1984) but, as far as we are aware, it has not been discussed to any degree within the IS evaluation literature.[5]

Moving from the consideration of how an individual user might evaluate a particular system -- if left to his own devices -- we arrive at the extreme point of the continuum, the highly "subjective/political" area where one considers how evaluations are performed within the political-social environment of an organization. As remarked above, evaluation is a largely social activity, whether formal or informal, and the object being evaluated -- an information system -- is equally a social entity. The existence of political forces in the development and evaluation of IS has been noted by various writers. Land (1976) and Mendelow (1984), for example, explore the conflicting evaluation criteria of the various groups of stakeholders; Land proposes that a consensus regarding the objectives and criteria should be arrived at by negotiation between the parties at an early stage of system development. A similar theme is adopted by Carnall (1982), who states that the evaluation of any organizational change, such as the introduction of an information system, poses problems because of conflicting interests and differing views.

---

[5]The choice of Personal Construct Theory for IS evaluation does not rule out the use and/or appropriateness of other personality theories.

The relationship between the rational tools and political behavior is reflected in the writings of a number of writers. Boland and Pondy (1983), for example, suggest that there is a rational myth in the foreground and political manoeuvres in the background. This was supported in an empirical study by Franz and Robey (1984), who assert that:

> The rational elements are tools used by participants to gain new ground or to protect ground already won. They also serve as "facades" to mask political motives and legitimize self-interest.

Laudon (1985) found that environmental (objective/rational) factors were used during project selection as a legitimizing tool whereas institutional (political) factors determined the utilization and management of new systems.

On a similar theme, Kling and Iacono (1984) noted that "key actors used the language of efficiency to push the CBIS in a direction that increased their own power and control in the organization."

These empirical studies, while not specifically concerned with evaluation, highlight the political behavior within organizations. An overlapping area which seems to have been overlooked in the IS evaluation literature is that of "evaluation research" (cf. Weiss, 1972). According to Legge (1984), it specifically addresses the difficulties associated with formal evaluation studies (in particular those concerned with social change) within the political environment of an organization. She discusses positivistic and interpretive approaches to evaluation in the light of what she sees as the three crises of evaluation:

1) utilization (whether the results are used),

2) verification (the methodological validity),

3) accreditation (the values underlying the evaluation).

Of these, she regards the third as being the key factor. Kling (1985) attempts to incorporate social values through a "social impact analysis" at various points within the information systems development cycle. He agrees that there are no simple formulae for such evaluation. However, evaluation to be meaningful must take into account the values intrinsic to the process of evaluation. These often conflict, are unspoken, and are the source of considerable confusion.

The political nature of evaluation has led many writers to conclude that evaluation is meaningless. Beer (1981) suggests the result of evaluation can often be made to show whatever is desired simply by choosing a technique which supports the underlying value position. According to Suchman (1970) this can be effected through the use of one of two types of evaluation: "eye wash" or "white wash." The former refers to evaluation as a way of justifying or supporting a weak system by choosing to look at only those aspects which show the system in a favorable light. The latter is used to conceal the truth by avoiding any objective appraisal. Gowler and Legge (1978) hold a similar perspective. They postulate two types of goals associated with an organizational intervention: overt and covert. They state "real" success is often seen in terms of achieving covert goals. All that is required from the success criteria of the overt goals is that they

are sufficiently broad to allow room for politically advantageous
interpretation.

Using, in particular, the "underlying assumptions" continuum, it
is possible to depict in diagrammatic form the different approaches to evaluation.   They can be represented between the two
poles of objective/rational and subjective/political (see Figure
1).   What is most interesting is that clearly the approaches from
the "efficiency" zone have received the most attention to date.
The approaches from the "effectiveness" zone are becoming more
fashionable than before and receiving more attention, but little
information system evaluation research has taken place in the
"understanding" zone.

The historical reasons for this bias may be found in practical
pressures: the technical imperative of getting computer systems
to work properly was followed by the rational economic imperative
of information systems supporting commercial organizations.   The
important (and some might say academic) step of understanding
evaluation has yet to be made.

4.   CRITICAL ANALYSIS OF THE ASSUMPTIONS INHERENT IN THE INFORMATION SYSTEMS EVALUATION LITERATURE

It can be noted from the above literature review that IS evaluation has largely been based on an objective/rational grounding.
Very little exists which is of a more subjectivist or political
nature.   Given that evaluation is by its very nature subjective,
then it might seem appropriate to question the value of an
approach which is entirely objective and rational.   How effective
and valuable are these objectivist approaches?   And while the
objectivist is likely to argue that such approaches are valuable
because they bring into the open the criteria used in evaluation,
as well as providing a "logical" vehicle for assessing an information system, there are some nagging doubts about the validity of
these arguments as hinted to above in regards to formal versus
informal evaluation.   Moreover, there are a number of underlying
assumptions and beliefs which have apparently gone unchallenged.
In particular, the following seem to us to require closer scrutiny:

(1)   that a concentration on the development of tools and techni-
      ques is a meaningful basis by which to advance the state of
      IS evaluation knowledge;

(2)   that the "scientific" approach is a meaningful basis by which
      to develop tools and techniques for evaluation;

(3)   that information systems are themselves inherently objective
      and rational and thus capable of being evaluated in an
      objective/rational fashion.

4.1   The Concentration on Tools and Techniques

From an examination of the literature, it seems to us that
research on evaluation has been misdirected toward tools and
techniques for measurement and away from understanding the process
of evaluation itself.   It is likely that this is a major reason
why there continues to exist so much consternation and confusion
over evaluation.   Instead of concentrating on developing a rich

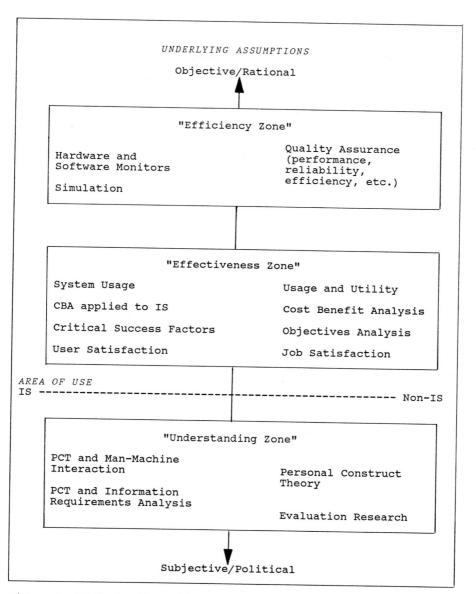

UNDERLYING ASSUMPTIONS

Objective/Rational

"Efficiency Zone"

Hardware and
Software Monitors

Simulation

Quality Assurance
(performance,
reliability,
efficiency, etc.)

"Effectiveness Zone"

System Usage

CBA applied to IS

Critical Success Factors

User Satisfaction

Usage and Utility

Cost Benefit Analysis

Objectives Analysis

Job Satisfaction

AREA OF USE
IS --- Non-IS

"Understanding Zone"

PCT and Man-Machine
Interaction

PCT and Information
Requirements Analysis

Personal Construct
Theory

Evaluation Research

Subjective/Political

Figure 1. IS Evaluation Literature Framework

understanding of the subject of study, man has sought to apply
more formal tools, techniques and methods. This appears to be
consistent with man's desire to structure and formalize ever
greater amounts of what he does. Through formalization, quantification can occur which allows more "scientific" approaches to be
applied. Evaluation is hence enhanced because the methods are
grounded in science. Unfortunately, in the drive to develop
better and better tools and techniques (particularly more formal
ones), the basic reason for, and goals of, the research (i.e.,
understanding the process of evaluation) has been forgotten. The
"means" have ostensibly taken over the "ends."

A similar misdirection has been said to have occurred in the
Operational Research field, particularly among the OR academics.
Here, the techniques of Operational Research have attained primacy
while the problems which led to their formulation appear now to be
neglected. Many have argued that the concentration on the means
(OR techniques) has virtually totally displaced the ends (problem
formulation and solution) which has led to the perception of OR
being irrelevant. For further information on this subject, see
the recent debate which occurred within the Operational Research
Society (Ackoff, 1979a, 1979b).

The same "irrelevance" may be thought to exist within IS evaluation. Clearly there is more to evaluation than simply the
application of a particular objective methodology. Evaluation
must contain a large measure of subjectivity; it must consider the
political and social domain. Rationalizing these processes such
that they can be dealt with through the application of some formal
and objective tools and techniques must surely be suspect. This
is not to suggest that a structured approach to evaluation is not
feasible nor desirable, rather that the emphasis of evaluation
should be brought back to understanding the subject of inquiry.
This is an epistemological issue and leads directly into the
second challenged assumption.

4.2 The Adoption of the "Scientific" Paradigm for IS Evaluation

The general belief appears to be that by adopting a more "scientific" approach, better evaluation can be obtained. In fact it is
the belief in a "scientific" approach which is largely responsible
for the IS community's misplaced concentration on the tools and
techniques for evaluation rather than the nature of evaluation
itself. Fundamentally, it is the uncritical adoption of the
so-called "scientific method" which is at the root of the problems
with IS evaluation.

The notion of evaluation is inextricably bound up with the
scientific community's strong predilection towards positivism.
(McCarthy [1982] refers to this as "scientism" -- the adopting of
positivism and its associated research methods irrespective of its
appropriateness for the subject matter of study. For a further
treatment of this subject see Klein and Lyytinen [1985].) The
adoption of this paradigm ostensibly leads to the rejection of
subjective data (except for the case of conjecture development)
and thus the large-scale dismissal of social criteria in evaluation. The alternative is to "objectivise" the subjective data so
that analysis techniques appropriate for objective data can be
applied. However, this is likely to be unsound in most cases and
lead to questionable conclusions (cf. Legge, 1984).

The fundamental difficulty here is an epistemological and ontological one. Positivism searches for regularities and causal relationships and treats individuals as though they are deterministic, that they "respond to events in predictable and determinate ways" (Morgan and Smircich, 1980, p. 495). Whilst a positivistic approach may be appropriate and acceptable for dealing with a subject of study which does not possess free will, information systems are not of this kind. As information systems are fundamentally human and social entities, positivism is felt to be an inappropriate basis for inquiry and hence evaluation. This is a theme which is well discussed in the social science literature (cf. Halfpenny, 1979; Van Maanen, 1979; Lessnoff, 1974; Fay, 1975; Garfinkel, 1967; Burrell and Morgan, 1979; Reason and Rowan, 1981; and Morgan, 1983) and is gaining prominence in the information systems literature (cf. Mumford, et al., 1985). The emergence of alternative research approaches based on hermeneutics (Klein and Hirschhiem, 1983) and phenomenology (Boland and Day, 1982) are responses to the uneasiness many individuals conducting research within the domain of information systems feel toward positivistic methods.

Irrespective of its appropriateness, positivism has been the basis of IS evaluation but not necessarily because it has been successful. Legge (1984) for example, notes its ritualistic value:

> Positivistic [evaluation] designs prosper largely through acting as a rhetoric for an evaluation ritual whereby the lack of rationality of actual decision making and the accountability and responsibility demanded of the idealized decision maker, are reconciled. [p.112]

Basically, positivism has been adopted because it is widely believed to be the only "right" way to undertake inquiry. Alternative approaches adopting a more interpretive and subjectivist stance are considered "unscientific" and an unacceptable basis for evaluation. This, it is felt, is a mistake, and can only lead to a furthering of quantitative tools and techniques which assume individuals are deterministic and behave in a rational and objective manner. With such a conception, IS evaluation is likely to continue down the path of irrelevancy.

4.3 Information Systems are Inherently Objective and Rational

Existing IS evaluation approaches have assumed that information systems are objective and rational, and thus capable of being evaluated by the use of objective/rational tools and techniques. The adoption of positivism reflects and cements this belief. It is possible, however, to conceive of two alternative positions about the nature or ontology of information systems, of which the objective/rational is only one. The second is subjective and political. The former ontological position we will refer to as the analytic perspective, the latter as the interpretivist perspective.

The perspectives differ on a number of dimensions. For example, the former sees information systems functions and activities as largely deterministic, rational and overt whereas the latter conceives of them as mostly nondeterministic, political and covert. The analytic perspective metaphorically conceives of the organiza-

tion as "structure;" the interpretivist, organization as "agent"
or "culture." This metaphorical difference (based on Argyris and
Schon's [1978] "theories of organizational learning") reflects two
alternative views of organizations. The "structure" view sees
organizations as "an ordered array of role-boxes connected by
lines which represent flows of information, work, and authority"
(Argyris and Schon, 1978, p. 324). The "agent" or "culture" view
notes that organizations are both instruments for achieving social
purposes and small, restricted societies where "people create for
themselves shared meanings, symbols, rituals, and cognitive
schemas which allow them to create and maintain meaningful interactions among themselves and in relation to the world beyond their
small society" (p. 327).

The analytic perspective sees organization action in terms of
manifest behavior; the interpretivist, in terms of the shared
social meaning of the actors. The former is observable and empirical, the latter is symbolic and largely nonempirical. It
follows, therefore, that the appropriate measurement instruments
and research paradigms must also differ. The analytic perspective
adopts formal models using empirical methods as the appropriate
measurement instrument, while the interpretivist uses phenomenological study. The former embraces a quantitative research paradigm; the latter, a more qualitative one. This is similar to the
Burrell and Morgan (1979) dichotomy of "objectivism" versus "sub-
jectivism." Lastly, the two perspectives differ in their focus:
for the analytic, the focus is on analysis; for the interpretivist, it is understanding. The former seeks to analyze organizational operations and functions by breaking them down into their
constituent parts. Knowledge is acquired through the scientific
endeavour of reductionism. The latter is less concerned with
analysis and more concerned with understanding. Knowledge is
available only in the context of understanding the social actions
and meanings of the participating actors in a social setting. The
focus is on understanding these social actions and meanings.
Table 1 summarizes the differences of the two ontological positions.

	ANALYTIC	INTERPRETIVIST
IS Functions	Largely deterministic, rational, overt	Largely nondetermin- istic, political, covert
Metaphor	Organization as "structure"	Organization as "agent" or "culture"
Action as:	Manifest behavior	Social meaning
Appropriate Measurement Instrument	Formal models	Phenomenological study
Research Paradigm	Quantitative	Qualitative
Focus	Analysis	Understanding

Table 1: Comparison of the Analytic and
Interpretivist Perspectives

It is our belief that the ontological position adopted in current IS evaluation, i.e., the analytic perspective, is misguided and does not reflect the reality of organizational life. Information systems cannot be treated as objective and rational as this is too simplistic a conception. Organizations are complex social and political entities which defy purely objective analysis. As information systems form part of organizational reality (i.e., a gestalt), they cannot be viewed in isolation. To do so simply perpetuates the naive and technical notion of information systems and leads to unintended and deleterious consequences (cf. Klein and Hirschheim, 1983, 1985).

5. CONCLUSION

The concentration on tools and techniques, the adoption of the values, beliefs and methods of positivistic science, and the objectivist/rational conception of organizations and information systems, have provided the foundation and inspiration for current IS evaluation. The result has been a more "technical" interpretation of evaluation: not only in terms of the mechanisms used, but also the substance being evaluated. Most IS evaluation has concentrated on the technical rather than the human or social aspects of the system. Part of the reason for this lies in the ontological beliefs of the evaluators -- that information systems are fundamentally technical systems (although they may have behavioral consequences). With such a belief, it is not surprising that only the technical aspects of IS are evaluated, especially considering the difficulty of evaluating social aspects. Bjørn-Andersen (1984) captures this succinctly: "we tend to spend more and more time and use even more refined technological tools for solving the wrong problem more precisely."

Unfortunately, such "technical" evaluation, with its omission of the social domain, is unlikely to produce a true or meaningful evaluative picture. Worse, it could have unintended and deleterious consequences. It is, in fact, these unanticipated consequences which are perhaps the most worrying aspect of current IS evaluation. For example, an IS which is technically elegant, and evaluated highly because of it, may have a negative influence on its users' job satisfaction and social environment. The worsening of job satisfaction could lead to high staff turnover, absenteeism and the like. Systems which score poorly using technical criteria may be strong on the social side. IS evaluation must therefore take into account both the technical and social aspects of a system. In order to incorporate the latter, more problematic, aspects into the evaluation, a deeper understanding of the nature and the process of evaluation itself is required. Adopting a more interpretivist IS perspective seems to us to be the best vehicle for doing such. It provides a more fruitful basis for understanding IS and its evaluation.

REFERENCES

Ackoff, R., "The Future of Operations Research is Past," *Journal of the Operations Research Society*, Vol. 30, No. 2, February 1979.

Ackoff, R., "Resurrecting the Future of the Operational Research," *Journal of the Operations Research Society*, Vol. 30, No. 3, March 1979.

Argyris, C., and Schon, D., *Organizational Learning: A Theory of Action Perspective*, Addison-Wesley, Reading, Massachusetts, 1978.

Bailey, J., and Pearson, S., "Development of a Tool for Measuring and Analyzing Computer User Satisfaction," *Management Science*, Vol. 29, No. 5, May 1983.

Beer, S., "Questions of Metric," in Mason, R., and Swanson, B. (eds.), *Measurement for Management Decision*, Addison-Wesley, Reading, Massachusetts, 1981.

Bitran, G., and Chang, L., "Productivity Measurement at the Firm Level," *Interfaces*, Vol. 14, No. 3, May-June 1984.

Bjørn-Andersen, N., "Challenge to Certainty," in Bemelmans, Th. (ed.), *Beyond Productivity: Information Systems Development for Organizational Effectiveness*, North-Holland, Amsterdam, 1984.

Boland, R., and Day, W., "A Phenomenology of Systems Design," in Ginzberg, M., and Ross, C. (eds.), *Proceedings of the Third International Conference on Information Systems*, Ann Arbor, Michigan, 1982.

Boland, R., and Pondy, L., "Accounting in Organizations: A Union of Natural and Rational Perspectives," *Accounting Organizations and Society*, Vol. 8, 1983.

Boynton, A., and Zmud, R., "An Assessment of Critical Success Factors," *Sloan Management Review*, Vol. 25, No. 4, Summer 1984.

Brownstein, I., and Lerner, N., *Guidelines for Evaluating and Selecting Software Packages*, North-Holland, Amsterdam, 1982.

Bruwer, P., "A Descriptive Model of Success for Computer-Based Information Systems," *Information and Management*, Vol. 7, April 1984.

Bryan, W., and Siegal, S., "Product Assurance: Insurance Against a Software Disaster," *IEEE Computer*, Vol. 17, No. 4, April 1984.

Bulmer, M. (ed.), *Sociological Research Methods*, Macmillan, New York, 1977.

Burrell, G., and Morgan, C., *Sociological Paradigms and Organizational Analysis*, Heinemann, London, 1979.

Canning, R., "Making Office Systems Pay Off," *EDP Analyzer*, February 1985.

Carnall, C., *The Evaluation of Organizational Change*, Gower, Aldershot, 1982.

Conrath, D., and du Roure, G., "Organizational Implications of Comprehensive Communication-Information Systems: Some Conjectures," working paper, Institute d'Administration des Enterprises Centre d'Etude er de Recherche sur les Organizations et la Gestion, Aix-en-Provence, 1978.

Couger, J. D., "The Techniques for Estimating System Benefits," in Couger, J. D., Colter, M., and Knapp, R. (eds.), *Advanced System Development/Feasibility Techniques*, John Wiley and Sons, New York, 1982.

Curran, S., and Mitchell, H., *Office Automation: An Essential Management Strategy*, Macmillan, New York, 1982.

Dahl, O., Dijkstra, E., and Hoare, C., *Structured Programming*, Academic Press, New York, 1972.

Drucker, P., "Entrepreneurship in Business Enterprise," *Journal of Business Policy*, Vol. 1, 1971.

Earl, M., and Hopwood, A., "From Management Information to Information Management," in Lucas, H., Land, F., Lincoln, T., and Supper, K. (eds.), *The Information Systems Environment*, North-Holland, Amsterdam, 1980.

Ein-Dor, P., and Segev, E., "Organizational Context and the Success of Management Information Systems," *Management Science*, Vol. 24, No. 10, June 1978.

Ein-Dor, P., and Segev, E., *A Paradigm for Management Information Systems*, Praeger Publishers, New York, 1981.

Emery, J., *Cost/Benefit Analysis of Information Systems*, The Society for Management Information Systems, 1971.

Fay, B., *Social Theory and Political Practice*, George Allen & Unwin, London, 1975.

Ferrari, D., *Computer Systems Performance Evaluation*, Prentice-Hall, Englewood Cliffs, New Jersey, 1978.

Francis, I., *Statistical Software -- A Comparative Review*, North-Holland, Amsterdam, 1981.

Franz, C., and Robey, D., "An Investigation of User-Led System Design: Rational and Political Perspectives," *Communications of the ACM*, Vol. 27, No. 12, December 1984.

Gaines, B., and Shaw, M., "New Directions in the Analysis and Interactive Elicitation of Personal Construct Systems," *International Journal of Man-Machine Studies*, Vol. 13, No. 1, 1980.

Garfinkel, H., *Studies in Ethnomethodology*, Prentice-Hall, Englewood Cliffs, New Jersey, 1967.

Ginzberg, M., "Early Diagnosis of MIS Implementation Failure: Promising Results and Unanswered Questions," *Management Science*, Vol. 27, No. 4, April 1981.

Ginzberg, M., "Finding an Adequate Measure of OR/MS Effectiveness," *Interfaces*, Vol. 8, No. 4, August 1978.

Gowler, D., and Legge, K., "The Evaluation of Planned Organizational Change: The Necessary Act of the Possible?", *Journal of Enterprise Management*, Vol. 1, 1978.

Grudnitski, G., "Eliciting Decision-Makers' Information Requirements: Application of the REP Test Methodology," *Journal of Management Information Systems*, Vol. 1, No. 1, Summer 1984.

Gullo, K., "Too Many Choices," *Datamation*, June 15, 1985.

Halfpenny, P., "The Analysis of Qualitative Data," *Sociological Review*, Vol. 27, No. 4, 1979.

Hamilton, S., and Chervany, N., "Evaluating Information System Effectiveness," *MIS Quarterly*, Vol. 5, No. 4, December 1981.

Hirschheim, R., Land, F., and Smithson, S., "Implementing Computer-Based Information Systems in Organizations: Issues and Strategies," in Shackel, B. (ed.), *Human-Computer Interaction -- INTERACT '84*, North-Holland, Amsterdam, 1984.

Hogue, J., and Watson, H., "Management's Role in the Approval of Decision Support Systems," *MIS Quarterly*, Vol. 7, No. 2, June 1983.

Isenberg, D., "How Senior Managers Think," *Harvard Business Review*, November-December 1984.

Ives, B., Olson, M., and Baroudi, J., "The Measurement of User Information Satisfaction," *Communications of the ACM*, Vol. 26, No. 10, October 1983.

Keen, P., "Computer-Based Decision Aids: The Evaluation Problem," *Sloan Management Review*, Vol. 16, No. 3, Spring 1975.

Keen, P., "Information Systems and Organizational Change," *Communications of the ACM*, Vol. 24, No. 1, January 1981.

Keen, P., and Scott Morton, M., *Decision Support Systems: An Organizational Perspective*, Addison-Wesley, Reading, Massachusetts, 1978.

Kelly, G., *The Psychology of Personal Constructs*, Norton, 1955.

King, J., and Schrems, E., "Cost-Benefit Analysis in IS Development and Operation," *Computing Surveys*, Vol. 10, No. 1, March 1978.

Kleijnen, J., *Computers and Profits: Quantifying Financial Benefits of Information*, Addison-Wesley, Reading, Massachusetts, 1980.

Klein, H., and Hirschheim, R., "Fundamental Issues of Decision Support Systems: A Consequentialist Perspective," *Decision Support Systems*, Vol. 1, No. 1, January 1985.

Klein, H., and Hirschheim, R., "Issues and Approaches to Appraising Technological Change in the Office: A Consequentialist Perspective," *Office: Technology and People*, Vol. 2, 1983.

Klein, H., and Lyytinen, K., "The Poverty of Scientism in Information Systems," in Mumford, E., Hirschheim, R., Fitzgerald, T., and Wood-Harper, T. (eds.), *Research Methods in Information Systems*, North-Holland, Amsterdam, 1985.

Kling, R., "Computerization as an Ongoing Social and Political Process," paper given at the Conference on Development and Use of Computer-Based Systems and Tools, Aarhus, Denmark, 1985.

Kling, R., "Social Analyses of Computing: Theoretical Perspectives in Recent Empirical Research," *Computing Surveys*, Vol. 12, No. 1, March 1980.

Kling, R., and Iacono, S., "The Control of Information Systems Developments After Implementation," *Communications of the ACM*, Vol. 27, No. 12, December 1984.

Land, F., "Evaluation of Systems Goals in Determining a Design Strategy for a Computer-Based Information System," *Computer Journal*, Vol. 19, No. 4, November 1976.

Laudon, K., "Environmental and Institutional Models of System Development: A National Criminal History System," *Communications of the ACM*, Vol. 28, No. 7, July 1985.

Layard, R. (ed.), *Cost-Benefit Analysis*, Penguin Books, New York, 1980.

Legge, K., *Evaluating Planned Organizational Change*, Academic Press, New York, 1984.

Lessnoff, M., *The Structure of Social Science*, George Allen & Unwin, London, 1974.

Lucas, H., "Performance and Use of a Management Information System," *Management Science*, Vol. 21, No. 8, April 1975.

Markus, M., "Power, Politics and MIS Implementation," *Communications of the ACM*, Vol. 26, No. 6, June 1983.

Markus, M., *Systems in Organizations: Bugs and Features*, Pitman, Boston, 1984.

Mason, R., and Swanson, E., *Measurement for Management Decision*, Addison-Wesley, Reading, Massachusetts, 1981.

McCarthy, T., *The Critical Theory of Jurgen Habermas*, MIT Press, Cambridge, Massachusetts, 1982.

Mendelow, A., "Information Systems for Organizational Effectiveness: The Use of the Stakeholder Approach," in Bemelmans, Th. (ed.), *Beyond Productivity: Information Systems Development for Organizational Effectiveness*, North-Holland, Amsterdam, 1984.

Morgan, G. (ed.), *Beyond Method*, Sage Publications, Beverly Hills, 1983.

Morgan, G., and Smircich, L., "The Case for Qualitative Research," *Academy of Management Review*, Vol. 5, No. 4, 1980.

Mumford, E., Bancroft, N., and Sontag, B., "Participative Design -- Successes and Problems," *Systems Objectives Solutions*, Vol. 3, 1983.

Mumford, E., and Banks, O., *The Computer and the Clerk*, Routledge and Kegan Paul, Henley-on-Thames, 1967.

Mumford, E., Hirschheim, R., Fitzgerald, G., and Wood-Harper, T. (eds.), *Research Methods in Information Systems*, North-Holland, Amsterdam, 1985.

Myers, G., *The Art of Software Testing*, John Wiley and Sons, New York, 1979.

Orman, L., "Information Independent Evaluation of Information Systems," *Information and Management*, Vol. 6, No. 6, December 1983.

Reason, P., and Rowan, J. (eds.), *Human Inquiry: A Sourcebook of New Paradigm Research*, John Wiley and Sons, New York, 1981.

Reimann, B., and Waren, A., "User-Oriented Criteria for the Selection of DSS Software," *Communications of the ACM*, Vol. 28, No. 2, February 1985.

Robey, D., "User Attitudes and MIS Use," *Academy of Management Journal*, Vol. 22, No. 3, September 1979.

Rockart, J., "Chief Executives Define Their Own Data Needs," *Harvard Business Review*, March-April 1979.

Sanders, G., "MIS/DSS Success Measures," *Systems Objectives Solutions*, Vol. 4, No. 1, January 1984.

Schewe, C., "The Management Information Systems User: An Exploratory Behavioral Analysis," *Academy of Management Journal*, Vol. 22, No. 3, September 1976.

Smith, P., *Groups within Organizations*, John Wiley and Sons, New York, 1973.

Spencer, R., *Planning, Implementation, and Control in Product Test and Assurance*, Prentice-Hall, Englewood Cliffs, New Jersey, 1983.

Srinivasan, A., "Alternative Measures of System Effectiveness: Associations and Implications," *MIS Quarterly*, Vol. 9, No. 3, September 1985.

Strassmann, P., *Information Payoff: The Transformation of Work in the Electronic Age*, Free Press, New York, 1985.

Suchman, C., "Action for What? A Critique of Evaluative Research," in O'Toole, T. (ed.), *The Organization, Management and Tactics of Social Research*, Schenkman, Cambridge, Massachusetts, 1970.

Tapscott, D., *Office Automation: A User-Driven Method*, Plenum Press, New York, 1982.

Van Maanen, J., "Reclaiming Qualitative Methods for Organizational Research: A Preface," *Administrative Science Quarterly*, Vol. 24, No. 4, December 1979.

Van Tassel, D., *Program Style, Design, Efficiency, Debugging, and Testing*, Second Edition, Prentice-Hall, Englewood Cliffs, New Jersey, 1978.

Waters, S., *Introduction to Computer Systems Design*, NCC, Manchester, 1974.

Weiss, C., *Evaluation Research*, Prentice-Hall, Englewood Cliffs, New Jersey, 1972.

Wynne, B., and Otway, H., "Information Technology, Power and Managers," in Bjørn Andersen, N., Earl, M., Holst, O., and Mumford, E. (eds.), *Information Society: For Richer, For Poorer*, North-Holland, Amsterdam, 1982.

Zmud, R., "Individual Differences and MIS Success: A Review of the Empirical Literature," *Management Science*, Vol. 25, No. 10, October 1979.

Evolving Criteria for Information Systems Assessment
M.J. Ginzberg and R.W. Zmud

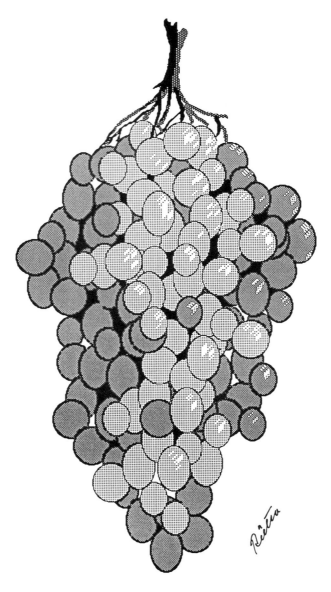

"Information systems integration efforts were, at
that time, just beginning to bear fruit."

INFORMATION SYSTEMS ASSESSMENT
N. Bjørn-Andersen, G.B. Davis (Editors)
Elsevier Science Publishers B.V. (North-Holland)
© IFIP, 1988

EVOLVING CRITERIA FOR INFORMATION SYSTEMS ASSESSMENT

Michael J. GINZBERG

Weatherhead School of Management
Case Western Reserve University
Cleveland, Ohio 44106 USA

Robert W. ZMUD

School of Business Administration
The University of North Carolina at Chapel Hill
Chapel Hill, North Carolina 27514   USA

Most information systems assessment (ISA) techniques in common use today were developed at a time
when the primary use of computers was limited to
automating isolated clerical processes within the
administrative core of the organization.   These
techniques were designed to enable reactive
evaluation, assessment for the purpose of controlling resource allocation and consumption.

Information systems are now playing a much larger
role in the management and operation of all types
of organizations. This growing range of roles and
functions has widened the group of relevant IS
stakeholders -- i.e., the individuals and groups
who are affected by the information system.   ISA
techniques which were adequate in an earlier period
are no longer adequate today.

This paper develops .a framework for information
system assessment which enables matching of the
characteristics of the assessment technique with
those of the assessment situation. Shortcomings of
existing ISA techniques are identified and suggestions for both research and practice are made.

1.   INTRODUCTION

Given the increasing importance of information technologies to
organizational success, the realization that relatively few
scholarly or practitioner articles address the topic of information systems assessment (ISA) is initially quite surprising. Most
of the articles that exist tend to take a very narrow perspective
of ISA; a perspective best characterized as having a direct cost
orientation, a short term horizon, an immediate user focus, and a
pro-computer bias.   Such a perspective, when applied to today's
most exciting information systems (IS) applications, is likely to
produce dysfunctional consequences such as (1) deciding not to
implement (or to discontinue) appropriate information systems, (2)
deciding to implement (or continue) inappropriate information

systems, and (3) adopting naive strategies for implementing an information system.

An examination of the issues, however, leads to a possible explanation for the current state of ISA approaches: most of the ISA techniques in common use today were developed over a decade ago. ISA techniques, basically, are management control tools used to insure that organizational resources being applied in information system implementations are allocated in an appropriate manner. As such, ISA techniques reflect the managerial needs, i.e., the managerial understanding and concerns, of the era during which they come into use.

The information systems being assessed at the time most of today's ISA approaches were developed tended to be single function applications targeted at transaction processing activities and their control. Information systems integration efforts were, at that time, just beginning to bear fruit. The information systems generally found in organizations a decade ago, and hence the information systems being evaluated, cover only a small portion of the range of information systems being developed and used in organizations today. As a result, most existing ISA techniques are not adequate to satisfy the wider range of evaluation situations and needs presented by the current generation of information systems (see Hamilton and Chervany, 1981).

This paper first reviews common ISA techniques. Here the paper limits itself to ISA techniques directed toward a single information system, rather than including ISA techniques examining the quality of a department's or an organization's overall utilization of information technologies. These latter techniques present a worthwhile area for future research, but are beyond the scope of the current paper. Next, frameworks for classifying ISA techniques and for identifying ISA needs are developed. Finally, current ISA techniques are compared against the identified ISA needs and some directions for alternative ISA approaches more likely to meet today's broader set of ISA objectives are presented.

2. CURRENT ISA TECHNIQUES

ISA most often occurs at three distinct points in the systems life cycle: the feasibility study, the post-implementation audit, and as a quality assurance check accompanying systems maintenance. The first two of these assessment efforts generally are *summative*, while the third tends to be *formative* (Hamilton and Chervany, 1981). A summative assessment addresses the evaluative question, "Will (Have) the objectives of the information system be (been) accomplished?" A formative assessment addresses the diagnostic question, "How well do the information system's design attributes contribute toward the accomplishment of its objectives?" Distinct ISA techniques tend to be applied toward each of these ISA activities.

A feasibility study is usually undertaken to decide whether or not a proposed information system should be implemented. Invariably, the primary concern revolves around the prudent use of generally scarce organizational resources. Three types of assessment should be performed to assess the viability of a proposed information system: technical, operational, and economic (see, for example, Zmud, 1983). Technical feasibility concerns the organization's ability to first muster and then apply appropriate information technologies in building the proposed information system. Operational feasibility asks whether the information system, if produced, will be used; i.e., will it fit into the organization and be accepted by organizational personnel. Economic feasibility concerns the advisability of investing the organization's resources in the proposed information system; i.e., is building the system a prudent use of resources given alternative uses for these resources? Cost/benefit analysis is universally recommended as the preferred ISA technique to use in a feasibility study. Most approaches for cost/benefit analysis, however, are limited to addressing economic issues. We know of no ISA techniques in common use at the feasibility stage that examine technical or operational issues. At best, a very limited set of the consequences of technical or operational problems are translated into economic terms and incorporated into the cost/benefit analysis.

The post-implementation audit, which tends to occur a short time after an information system has been installed, is generally confined to assessing the degree to which information system performance (input/output volumes, response times, job turnaround time, error rates) and economic (cost and benefit) objectives have been met. While the information system performance objectives do address certain technical and operational issues, these primarily occur at the *immediate system-user interface* and are limited to the specific information processing tasks being performed or supported by an information system. Several authors have identified broader and more robust post-implementation audit criteria (Carlson, 1974; Ginzberg, 1979); however, their use is seldom observed in practice.

At the other end of the systems life cycle, quality assurance evaluations involve periodic reviews of whether or not an implemented information system continues to meet the needs of its users. Here, the quality of an information system and of its delivery vehicle are assessed (Bailey and Pearson, 1983; Ives, et al., 1983; Swanson, 1974; Zmud, 1978). Normally, this formative assessment limits itself to a very limited number of system level measures (response time, turnaround times, and error rates) and immediate user perceptions of information system quality (obtained through interviews, questionnaires, or by monitoring complaints). Rarely does this assessment move beyond the immediate system-user interface. Thus, quality assurance checks tend to ignore economic issues and touch upon a very narrow range of technical and operational issues.

3. A FRAMEWORK FOR INFORMATION SYSTEMS ASSESSMENT

If an ISA technique is to adequately fit management's needs, a fit must exist between the characteristics of the ISA approach and managerial needs regarding the particular assessment situation. Before prescriptions can be offered regarding appropriate matches between ISA approaches and assessment situations, two central issues must be addressed:

> What are the characteristics of ISA techniques? and
> What are the characteristics of assessment situations?

Neither of these issues has been adequately developed in the research literature. This section develops a pair of frameworks that address these two issues.

3.1 Characteristics of IS Assessments

While there are no doubt many ways that one could characterize IS assessments, we contend that the three most important characteristics, given the aim of selecting an appropriate ISA technique, are:

1. the *domain* of the assessment,
2. the *time frame* of the assessment, and
3. the *nature* of the assessment.

Domain refers to the three assessment areas discussed earlier, i.e., the *technical, operational* or *economic* impacts of an information system. As was indicated in the previous section, assessments made at different points in the system life cycle tend to focus on different domains.

Time frame concerns the time horizon of the assessment, that is, does it look primarily to the *past*, the *present* or the *future*? Feasibility studies look to the future by incorporating prior and current experiences with related information systems into future projections. The other two assessments invariably focus on the present and the recent past.

The *nature* of an assessment refers to whether it is *summative* or *formative*. Summative assessments provide evaluative information only; they tell how well or how poorly an information system did in meeting its objectives. Formative assessments provide diagnostic information which helps to explain *why* the information system performed as it did. As mentioned earlier, feasibility studies and post-implementation audits tend to involve summative assessments, while quality assurance checks tend to be formative.

3.2 Dimensions of Assessment Situations

The characteristics of assessments discussed in the previous subsection will be useful only if we can identify dimensions of assessment situations which require different types of assessments. Here, we identify three major dimensions of assessment situations which indeed suggest the need for different types of assessments. These dimensions are *stakeholders* in the information system, the information system's *organizational role*, and the *evaluation purpose*.

3.2.1 Stakeholders

A number of parties possess vested interests in an implemented information system. Most ISA efforts have typically defined stakeholders in a very narrow manner, focussing on the immediate *producers, users,* and *auditors* of an information system. Such a view narrows the focus of an assessment to the *anticipated, desirable* and *direct* impacts of an information system. A complete examination of information system consequences, however, must also allow for *unanticipated, undesirable,* and *indirect* impacts (Rogers, 1983). Unanticipated consequences are those not contained in the project descriptions used in initiating or justifying an implementation effort. Undesirable consequences are those which, if considered in isolation of desirable consequences, would lead to a decision *not* to implement an information system. Indirect consequences are those that involve organizational activities or individuals not physically linked to an information system, i.e, a secondary or tertiary effect. ISA efforts that ignore unanticipated, undesirable, or indirect consequences are very likely to result in overly optimistic, incomplete, and invalid conclusions.

If an ISA technique is to identify *all* of the consequences of an information system, it must consider all of the system's stakeholders. The list of parties possessing vested interests in most information systems, i.e., all the parties affected by an information system's implementation, is extensive. Within an organization, the impacts of an information system often extend to operations and clerical workers, professionals, and managers throughout the entire organization. All of these people would, then, be stakeholders in the information system. Outside the organization, likely stakeholders include owners, labor unions, lenders, regulators, consumers/clients, suppliers, competitors, and the "public-at-large."

Stakeholder analysis can be performed at a number of aggregation levels. Attention may be focussed on the individual (e.g., a single user of an information system, a manager who receives a report produced by an information system, the chief designer of an information system), groups (e.g., work groups, development or maintenance teams, offices, senior management, plants, stockholder groups, consumer/client groups), organizations (e.g., business units, the enterprise, competing firms, suppliers, consumers/clients), or even larger aggregates (e.g., an industry, an economy, society at large). Most current ISA techniques are applied at an individual or group level of aggregation.

In summary, then, there are four important sub-dimensions for classifying, and hence identifying, stakeholders:

1. *Internal-External* -- An information system's stakeholders can be internal or external to the adopting organization.

2. *Relationship to the Information System* -- An information system's stakeholders include users, producers, auditors, sponsors and bystanders.

3. *Depth* -- An information system's stakeholders can be directly related to the information system (e.g., affected immediately by the information system's outputs) or indirectly related to it (e.g., affected only through the information system's effects on other stakeholders).

4. *Level of Aggregation* -- An information system's stakeholders can be examined as individuals, groups, organizations, or as societal segments.

The stakeholders normally considered in performing feasibility studies and post-implementation audits tend to be *internal users*, usually *individuals or groups* but not both, who *interact directly* with an information system. Stakeholders normally considered in performing quality assurance evaluations tend to be *internal users*, invariably *individuals*, who *interact directly* with an information system.

3.2.2   Organizational Role

Most current ISA techniques define (implicitly or explicitly) the information system's role as:

1. task or process automation;
2. task or process coordination; or
3. decision support.

This is a quite narrow view of an information system's role and is another major weakness of the ISA literature. Information systems consequences arise from the organizational roles served by information systems. If the role is viewed too narrowly, the ISA techniques applied to the information system are likely to inadequately represent all stakeholders and, hence, the true consequences of the information system (both desirable and undesirable) to the organization.

The information system role should be defined across three dimensions of organizational purpose:

1. target,
2. level, and
3. impact.

Targets, which represent the organizational actions being performed or supported by an information system, include *transactions* (resource exchanges), *communications* (information exchanges), and *decisions* (choice or uncertainty reduction activities that ultimately produce transactions or communications). These targets can exist at four organizational *levels* (Parsons, 1960): a *technology* level (the technological infrastructure for information processing), an *operations* level (the "work" of the organization), a *managerial* level (work coordination and resource allocation), and an *institutional* level (domain and strategic direction determination). Finally, the *impacts* at each target-level combination can be felt in terms of three types of organizational outcomes (Ginzberg, 1978; Kling, 1982; Mason, 1978; Sanders, 1984): *work quality* (including task performance, decision performance, and work performance), *quality of work-life* (relating to the satisfaction of human needs regarding security, social relations, self-esteem, and self-actualization), and *work related politics* (relating to the distribution of discretion and influence within a work context).

A complete understanding of the information system role must consider all 36 possible interactions among these targets, levels, and impacts. Too often, feasibility studies and post-implementation audits emphasize transaction targets at the technology or operations level expressed as work quality impacts. In a similar vein, it is rare to encounter quality assurance evaluations that focus on decision targets, that operate at the managerial or institutional levels, or that concern themselves with quality of work life or work-related political impacts.

3.2.3   Evaluation Purpose

There are at least three distinct intentions that underlie most IS assessments:

1. resource allocation;
2. system tuning; and
3. opportunity surfacing.

The first of these implies a very *reactive,* control-oriented assessment. System tuning is *preventative,* aimed at assuring that an information system continues to perform well. Opportunity surfacing represents an attempt to stimulate innovative use of information technology and, hence, is a quite *proactive* type of assessment. The required level of knowledge and understanding of information technology and its impacts differs significantly across these three types of assessments and they require substantially different tools and techniques. While all three of these evaluation purposes are desirable, many if not most ISA efforts project a very reactive orientation.

3.2.4 The ISA Situation Framework

The three dimensions of *stakeholder, organizational role,* and *evaluation purpose* define a cube of assessment situations. Considering their numerous sub-dimensions, several hundred possible assessment situations are implied. Fortunately, not all of these situations are likely to exist; some combinations of stakeholder, role and purpose either do not exist at all or occur only rarely. Still, the number of unique assessment situations is quite large, as is the diversity of assessment needs they imply. In the next section, we examine some selected situations in order to determine how well their needs are met by current ISA techniques.

4. MATCHING CURRENT ISA TECHNIQUES TO REPRESENTATIVE ASSESSMENT SITUATIONS

In order to assess how well current ISA techniques meet the range of needs for assessment tools, we must characterize these techniques along the three dimensions suggested earlier and identify situations for which those profiles are appropriate. Table 1 summarizes the key characteristics of the three common ISA techniques.

	Feasibility Study (Cost/Benefit)	Post Implementation Audit	Quality Assurance Check
Domain	Economic Some technical Some operational	Technical Economic	Technical Some operational
Time Frame	Future	Present Recent past	Present Recent past
Nature	Summative	Summative	Formative

Table 1

Feasibility studies employing cost/benefit analysis focus almost exclusively on future economic impacts of an information system.

Further, the assessment of these impacts is summative, boiling
them down to a single figure of merit which tells *what* will
happen, but not addressing *why*. This type of assessment is most
appropriate from the perspective of *internal* or *external sponsors*
or *auditors* at any aggregation level for making *resource allocation* decisions about information systems directed at *transaction*
targets at the *technology* or *operations* levels that impact *work
quality*.

Post implementation audits provide summative assessments of
current technical and economic performance of just implemented
information systems. This type of assessment is most appropriate
from the perspective of *internal sponsors, auditors, users,* and
producers at an *individual* or *group* aggregation level for making
resource allocation (and possibly *system tuning*) decisions about
information systems directed at *transaction* targets at the *technology* or *operation* levels that impact *work quality*.

Quality assurance checks provide a formative (or diagnostic) look
at the current technical, and to some extent operational, performance of an information system. This type of assessment is most
appropriate from the perspective of *internal users* and *producers*
at an *individual* or *group* aggregation level for making *system
tuning* decisions about information systems directed at *transaction, communication* and *decision* targets at the *technology,
operations* or *managerial* levels that impact *work quality* and, to
some extent, *quality of work life*.

That quality assurance assessments are more robust -- that is, are
appropriate to a wider range of situations -- than either feasibility studies or post-implementation audit assessments is not
surprising given the greater attention quality assurance assessments have received in the information systems literature. For
example, the measures of information systems usage and satisfaction often used as dependent variables in information systems
research are quite similar to measures used in quality assurance
assessments.

Each of these three approaches to IS assessment can be linked to
an assessment situation which fits it well. However, if we make
slight changes to the description of the assessment situation, we
may very well find that the technique no longer fills the need.
Take, for example, a situation appropriate for cost/benefit
analysis. A simple change in this situation can lead to a need
for a completely different type of ISA, as Table 2 illustrates.

While standard feasibility study techniques employing cost/benefit
analysis are appropriate for Situation 1, they are not at all
appropriate for Situation 2. The switch from *work quality* as the
target to *quality of work life* invalidates the use of economic
assessment and switches the focus to operational impacts.
Further, because these operational impacts tend to be diverse,
they cannot be easily summarized in a single figure of merit, as
can economic impacts; hence, a formative assessment which looks at
how the impacts will arise is needed. Such an assessment approach
enables the manager to "tune," or incrementally improve, the work
unit's quality of work life.

The standard IS assessment techniques used in performing a
feasibility study will not meet the needs of Situation 2. Equally
important, none of the three standard ISA approaches that have
been described will meet the assessment needs of this situation.

	Situation 1	Situation 2
Stakeholder	Internal manager (sponsor)	Internal manager (sponsor)
Organizational Role	Enhance work quality by improving transactional activities at both the technology and operations levels	Enhance quality of work life by improving transactional activities at an operations level
Evaluation Purpose	Resource allocation	Resource allocation System tuning
Evaluation Type	Economic Future Summative	Operational Future Formative

Table 2

5.   THE OVERRIDING IMPORTANCE OF STAKEHOLDER ANALYSIS

It is important to recognize the crucial role that stakeholder analysis plays in defining the characteristics of ISA techniques appropriate for today's expanded range of IS assessment situations. Stakeholder needs dictate both the desired characteristics of an ISA technique, e.g., its domain, time frame and nature, and the attributes of an assessment situation, e.g., an information system's organizational role and the evaluation purpose.

Recognizing indirect users as important stakeholders, for example, is likely to expand the range of relevant information system impacts. In comparison to direct users, indirect users are affected much more through an information system's impacts on quality of work life and work-related politics than through its impacts on work quality. Some other of the most apparent impacts of stakeholder on assessment requirements follow.

o   Economic assessment criteria are likely to be of most interest to internal sponsors and auditors and to certain external parties, notably stockholders and lenders. Within the organization, other personnel are more likely to be concerned with technical (users, information system producers, or operators) or operational (direct users, indirect users, and sponsors) impacts.

o   System developers and operators are primarily concerned with the impact of an IS on computing resources and computer systems operation, i.e., formative assessments of work quality impacts at the technology level (focusing primarily on transactions as the target). Sponsors and users are primarily concerned with the impact of an IS on work resources and operations, i.e., summative assessments of work quality impacts at operations, managerial, and institutional levels (focussing on all three types of targets).

o External stakeholders will primarily be concerned with operational effects that arise at an institutional level, such as
   the way the organization does business, interacts with other
   organizations, its success in the marketplace, etc. Specifically, unions may be interested in the change in labor demand
   (aggregate and specific mix) caused by the IS; competitors
   are interested in the competitive advantage being gained;
   government regulators are concerned with the extent to which
   the organization's activities infringe on the rights and
   interests of others; and, society at large is interested in
   the impacts of the organization's activities on the creation
   and distribution of wealth. Interestingly, each of these
   vested interests would require quite different IS assessment
   approaches.

6. IMPLICATIONS FOR PRACTICE AND RESEARCH

One important message from this analysis is directed toward
information systems practice: ISA efforts must utilize more
robust techniques, techniques that are applicable under a wider
range of situations and that address a more complete set of
assessment issues. As one moves beyond a very narrow and short-
sighted stakeholder perspective, assessment situations broaden
resulting in a wider collection of assessment needs. Who are the
stakeholders for a feasibility study? for a post-implementation
audit? for quality assurance? What are the concerns of these
stakeholders? What is their relation to the information system?
How influential are they?

While many practitioners may agree that such an orientation is
useful, they are also likely to raise the issue that few, if any,
techniques exist to be used in performing a more robust IS assessment. How exactly should one measure:

o communications targets,
o decision targets,
o targets at a managerial or institutional level,
o quality of work life impacts, or
o work-related politics impacts?

Practitioners in other disciplines, such as political analysts and
organizational development consultants, do measure these types of
factors. Can their techniques be transported to the IS context?
Researchers in other disciplines examine factors similar to these;
IS researchers are beginning to bring such factors into their
research programs. Can variants of these research instruments be
applied as ISA techniques?

A final set of issues relates to the three purposes of an IS
assessment: resource allocation, system tuning, and opportunity
surfacing. First, most ISA efforts would benefit by attending to
all three of these purposes. A feasibility study should address
(work) system tuning and (organizational or work group) opportunity surfacing in addition to (information system development)
resource allocation; a post-implementation audit should address
(organizational or work group) opportunity surfacing in addition
to monitoring the impact of resource allocation; quality assurance
efforts should address (information system alternatives) resource
allocation and (organizational or work group) opportunity surfacing in addition to (information) system tuning. Second, while
these three evaluation purposes are interrelated, little is known

of their interrelationships. Research aimed at uncovering these relationships is needed. Third, while IS assessment has given considerable attention to resource allocation and system tuning, very little attention as been given to opportunity surfacing. How can one identify with any accuracy the consequences of information systems that are not currently being exploited? Research directed at procedures and strategies for eliciting such appraisals is especially needed.

7. CONCLUSION

This paper has identified the mismatch between existing ISA techniques and the current (as well as expected future) range of ISA situations. The diverse range and varying needs of different stakeholders and the importance of a thorough stakeholder analysis have been illustrated. The paper, however, represents only the beginning of a solution to the ISA problem. Further theoretical work is needed to develop our understanding of organization role and evaluation purpose and the needs these place on the ISA process. Beyond this theoretical work, considerable empirical work is necessary to develop and test new ISA techniques. Finally, as mentioned in the introduction, we need to begin addressing the broader assessment questions concerning an organization's overall exploitation of information technologies.

REFERENCES

Bailey, J. E., and Pearson, S. W., "Development of a Tool for Measuring and Analyzing Computer User Satisfaction," *Management Science*, Vol. 29, No. 5, 1983, pp. 530-545.

Carlson, E. D., "Evaluating the Impact of Information Systems," *Management Informatics*, Vol. 3, No. 2, 1974, pp. 57-67.

Ginzberg, M. J., "Redesign of Managerial Tasks: A Requisite for Successful Decision Support Systems," *MIS Quarterly*, Vol. 2, No. 1, 1978, pp. 39-52.

Ginzberg, M. J., "Improving MIS Project Selection," *OMEGA*, Vol. 7, No. 6, 1979, pp. 527-537.

Hamilton, S., and Chervany, N. L., "Evaluating Information System Effectiveness -- Part I: Comparing Evaluation Approaches," *MIS Quarterly*, Vol. 5, No. 3, 1981, pp. 55-69.

Ives, B., Olson, M., and Baroudi, J., "The Measurement of User Information Satisfaction," *Communications of the ACM*, Vol. 26, No. 10, 1983, pp. 785-793.

Kling, R., "Social Analysis of Computing," *Information Age*, Vol. 4, No. 1, 1982, pp. 25-55.

Mason, R. O., "Measuring Information Output: A Communication Systems Approach," *Information and Management*, Vol. 1, 1978, pp. 219-234.

Parsons, T., *Structure and Process in Modern Societies*, Free Press, New York, 1960.

Rogers, E. M., *Diffusion of Innovation,* Free Press, New York, 1983.

Sanders, G. L., "MIS/DSS Success Measures," *Systems, Objectives, Solutions,* Vol. 4, No. 1, 1984, pp. 29-34.

Swanson, E. B., "Management Information Systems: Appreciation and Involvement," *Management Science,* Vol. 21, No. 2, 1974, pp. 178-188.

Zmud, R. W., "An Empirical Investigation of the Dimensionality of the Concept of Information," *Decision Sciences,* Vol. 9, No. 2, 1978, pp. 187-195.

Zmud, R. W., *Information Systems in Organizations,* Scott, Foresman, Glenview, Illinois, 1983.

DISCUSSANT NOTE

On: EVOLVING CRITERIA FOR INFORMATION SYSTEMS
      ASSESSMENT

By: Michael J. Ginzberg and Robert W. Zmud

Discussant's comments by: Jan ACHTERBERG

Free University
Amsterdam, The Netherlands

1.   INTRODUCTION

The comments on the paper will take place along the following
lines:

o   general appreciation of the paper
o   scope of the paper
o   comments within the scope
o   comments regarding the scope
o   new perspective

2.   GENERAL APPRECIATION OF THE PAPER

The paper gives a clear insight in the state of affairs for
current ISA techniques. It also offers an interesting approach to
more complete and richer assessments of *single* information
systems. Furthermore, I consider it a merit of the paper that it
hints at interesting fields of research for ISA approaches and ISA
objectives. However, I do have some critical comments on which I
will elaborate in the following sections of my note.

3.   SCOPE OF THE PAPER

The scope of the paper as stated by Ginzberg and Zmud is a review
of ISA techniques which are directed towards a single IS and the
development of a framework for classifying ISA techniques and
identifying ISA needs. The last part of this description of the
scope is my own addition to the scope stated by the authors and,
in my opinion, is one of the central issues concerning the paper.

4.   COMMENTS WITHIN THE SCOPE

Accepting the scope as stated by the authors, I have the following
comments on the paper:

a.   The ISA situation framework is not complete. There are some
     missing dimensions as, for instance:
          o   phase of evolution of automation
          o   culture of an organization
          o   organizational level of analysis

b. There are also some missing characteristics, for instance,
    the type of data (subjective versus objective data). These
    omissions in the framework prevent an overall assessment of
    the utilization of information technologies. In paragraph
    3.2.3, it is stated that opportunity surfacing "attempt[s] to
    stimulate innovative use of information technology" as one of
    the distinct intentions of most ISAs. My question regarding
    this exclusion is in which way this exclusion does affect the
    ISA situational framework.

5. COMMENTS REGARDING THE SCOPE

Before commenting on the scope, I want to express clearly that
these comments cannot be considered as a critique on the paper as
such. Limiting the scope is a legitimate and useful thing to do.
It does, however, have some drawbacks of which the most important
is that by limiting the scope to single information systems, all
issues which go beyond that level are missed.

Some of these issues are mentioned in the paper by Dickson, Wells
and Wilkes:

o overhead activities, e.g., hardware and software conversions
   and planning

o acquisition of generalized software

Other issues are:

o organizational aspects of IS activities; for instance,
   functional authorities, planning procedures and structuring
   of the IS function

o assessment of the choices made in drawing system boundaries,
   in using decomposition criteria, etc.

New developments in our field tend to support the idea of integrated conceptual and technical architectures and infrastructures
for information processing. ISA techniques will have to keep at
close quarters with these developments in order to be able to
deliver an adequate assessment.

ISA techniques which are only focused on a single IS will give an
incomplete or (even worse) wrong image of the efficiency and
effectiveness of the IS activities.

6. NEW PERSPECTIVE

Underlying (most) current ISA techniques is a Cartesian/Newtonian
view of the world. Characteristics of this view are:

o quantitative
o mechanical
o atomistic -----> single IS
o reductionistic -----> breaking up into elements

These characteristics are reflected in ISA techniques such as
cost-benefit analysis, system performance, and response time. In
applying these techniques, we run the risk of missing important

issues of "soft" origins; the social, political, and infological
issues.

To overcome the disadvantages of the Cartesian/Newtonian paradigm,
we need to shift to a new paradigm. Fritjof Capra (1982) strongly
recommends a shift to the systems approach which I would like to
support here. Characteristics of this paradigm are:

o a holistic/ecological view on the world and consequently a
   multi-objective decision making process

o a recognition of the fact that systems have a conscience and
   have an ability for self-organization and self-renewal

This paradigm shift will have some implications for ISA techniques:

o acceptance of "subjective" human criteria in addition to
   "objective" systems requirements

o paying attention to the relationships between systems in the
   assessment of these systems

o looking at ISA techniques in a structured manner

Assessment can be organized as an architecture which is hierarchical or relational.

REFERENCES

Capra, Fritjof, *The Turning Point: Science, Society, and the
    Rising Culture,* Simon and Schuster, New York, 1982.

Assessing IS Design Methodologies as Methods of IS Assessment
J. Iivari

"The levels of detail, on the other hand, enable the
decomposition or refinement of the information
systems in smaller and smaller subsystems
which in principle could be realized separately."

INFORMATION SYSTEMS ASSESSMENT
N. Bjørn-Andersen, G.B. Davis (Editors)
Elsevier Science Publishers B.V. (North-Holland)
© IFIP, 1988

ASSESSING IS DESIGN METHODOLOGIES AS METHODS OF
IS ASSESSMENT*

Juhani IIVARI

University of Oulu, Institute of Information
Processing Science Linnanmaa, SF-90570 OULU,
Finland

Most IS design methodologies do not treat IS
assessment at all or consider it a subsidiary
activity to specifying, designing and implementing
information systems. In view of the broad spectrum
of problems dealt with in IS assessment, this paper
suggests that the whole IS design process should be
seen as an inquiry supporting IS assessment and
that IS design methodologies should be developed
and assessed from this perspective as methods of IS
assessment. A set of desirable features of IS
design methodologies as methods of IS assessment is
derived, and these are employed as criteria for the
assessment of the ISAC, ETHICS and PIOCO methodologies as methods of IS assessment.

1. INTRODUCTION

It is clear that IS development always includes the explicit or
implicit consideration and selection of alternative information
systems. Without this opportunity for choice, the development of
information systems would be subject to a technological determinism which would not leave any room for meaningful participation
by the various groups involved (King, 1982). The consideration
and "rational" choice of alternative information systems requires
a certain IS assessment, i.e., evaluation of the consequences and
characteristics of information systems relevant to the interest
groups involved and affected by IS development. Conversely, it is
clear that IS assessment, without any subsequent opportunity to
change the system on the basis of the assessment reached, is a
quite futile exercise. We thus see IS assessment and decisions
concerning the information system as being intimately connected.

It is obvious, however, that IS assessment includes many problem-
atical features, which will be discussed in the next section. The
main message of this problem analysis is that the assessment of IS
design methodologies as means of IS assessment should not be
restricted to IS assessment "in the small," but the whole IS
design process should be regarded as an IS assessment process "in
the large." In section 3 we derive some requirements for IS design
methodologies as methods of IS assessment on the basis of the
problem analysis, and these in turn form a basis for the development and assessment of IS design methodologies as methods of IS

_____
* This work was supported financially by the Academy of
Finland.

assessment.   Section 4 applies these requirements to the assessment of the ISAC, ETHICS and PIOCO methodologies as means of IS
assessment.   Finally, the results of the paper are summarized in
section 5.

2.   PROBLEMS OF IS ASSESSMENT

This section consists of two parts.   In section 2.1, we analyze
the problems of IS assessment leading to six major categories.   We
suggest that IS assessment "in the small," being only a subsidiary
activity in the IS design process, cannot treat effectively the
problems identified, but that the whole IS design process should
be regarded as an IS assessment "in the large."

2.1 Problem Analysis

The problems of IS assessment can be classified in six major categories.

1.   First of all, we should recognize that ultimately the quality
     of information systems is like "beauty in the eyes of the be-
     holder":   it is a subjective feeling.   Furthermore, many
     "beholders" are not very well aware of what that feeling is,
     and insofar as they are, it is hard for them to express that
     feeling in words due to its tacit nature.

2.   The selection of information systems usually forms a social
     choice in which the preferences of different groups affected
     by the IS development are or should be taken into account.
     Recognizing the subjective and tacit knowledge of IS quality
     pointed out above and the different preferences of the
     interest groups, it is extremely difficult or impossible to
     explicate a common "social welfare function" expressing the
     combined preferences of the interest groups.   Irrespective of
     this, we could insist that the development of information
     systems should always express some more or less implicit
     social welfare function.

3.   The object of assessment, the information system, is problem-
     atic from the viewpoint of IS assessment.   Information
     systems are multi-faceted and tend to be relatively complex,
     and many people are not very accustomed to dealing with them.

4.   The information system representations (abstract descriptions
     or prototypes) may be felt to be deficient and hard to
     evaluate in ex ante assessment.

5.   The consequences of information systems are usually produced
     by a variety of exogenous, uncontrollable future factors, the
     understanding and prediction of which is far from complete as
     is that of their related cause-effect relationships.   Largely
     due to this fact, it is impossible to foresee all the
     relevant consequences of an information system.

6.   Many relevant consequences of information systems are
     qualitative and intangible and consequently hard to measure,
     quantify or render commensurate.

Referring to the problems listed above, it is easy to see that
some include quite general matters of planning, evaluation and

decision-making treated in planning theory, system analysis, OR, utility theory, cost-benefit analysis, economics, etc. Although these discipline have provided general ideas and insights relevant to IS assessment, their more concrete, practical contribution has been quite limited. This is partly due to the special character-istics of IS assessment as such and in relation to its various applications and the different interest groups.

The main message of the problem analysis above is that the prob-lems of IS assessment concern practically all features of IS design. This leads us to the dominant idea of this paper, that the whole IS design process should support IS assessment and that IS design methodologies should be developed and assessed from this perspective as a means of IS assessment. We shall return to these points in the next section.

2.2 IS Assessment "In the Large" and "In the Small"

By the phrase "IS assessment in the small," we refer to the eval-uation of the consequences of information systems as a subsidiary activity of specifying, designing and implementing information systems. IS assessment as a subsidiary activity of this kind is without doubt an important part of IS design, but taking into account the fact that the problems identified are general problems of IS design rather than specific ones of IS assessment "in the small," the whole IS design process should be regarded as an "IS assessment in the large."

Taking this viewpoint IS, design methodologies should be developed to support the IS assessment process "in the large" and should be evaluated on this basis. We shall put forward some requirements imposed upon IS design methodologies by their role as means of IS assessment "in the large." These requirements form a basis for the evaluation of IS design methodologies as methods of IS assess-ment.

Before proceeding to these requirements, however, we wish to illustrate the difference and relationship between IS assessment "in the large" and "in the small" by identifying two potential roles of IS design methodologies. Applying Faludi's characteriza-tion of "rational planning" (Faludi, 1973), we can state the first role of IS design methodologies, corresponding to the role of "IS assessment in the small," as follows:

1. IS design methodologies should be methods for reconstructing the argumentation to be used in the justification of the choice of information system to be developed.

In this case it is by no means assumed that the actual IS design process takes place according to the method of recon-structing (cf., Faludi, 1973). This leads to the second role of IS design methodologies.

2. IS design methodologies should be operational methods (cf., Iivari, 1983a) for the actual IS design process.

We prefer this latter interpretation of IS design methodologies, and the main tenet of this paper is that the actual IS design process should be interpreted as a process of IS assessment "in the large." IS assessment "in the large" and "in the small" are not yet mutually exclusive concepts, but we regard it as important to have the latter embedded in the former. IS assessment "in the small" is a process of presenting the results of the actual IS design process in a form which "facilitates criticism and establishes an unambiguous basis for agreement or conflict" (Faludi, 1973, p. 38).

3. REQUIREMENTS FOR IS DESIGN METHODOLOGIES AS METHODS OF IS ASSESSMENT

For reasons of clarity, we shall discuss the requirements in the order of the six categories of problem identified in previously. They are summarized in section 3.7.

3.1 Subjectivity of IS Design and Assessment

When discussing the subjectivity of IS design and assessment, we should specify the subjects we are talking about. They include as a subset various interest groups associated with and affected by the IS development (Hawgood, 1975). Classifications of interest groups are quite fixed structures, however, which do not clearly take into account the special role of some individuals or groups which may have a highly dominant role in the specific IS development situation. In order take this into account more clearly, we supplement the interest group approach with a special actor perspective emphasizing the role of individual actors in IS design and implementation.

Our main point is that the quality of information systems as a subjective feeling implies a subjectivistic approach not only to the evaluation of quality, but also to the whole IS design process. In order to crystallize this idea, let us apply a simple formalism. If we use the subscript I for the interest groups and actors involved, we can express the quality of an information system as a function

$$Q_I = g_I(E_I, P_I, G_I, O_I)$$

where E_I denotes the existing state, P_I the problems experienced, G_I goals imposed upon the IS development and O_I the consequences (and more immediate characteristics) of the system relevant to the interest group or actor I.[1]

We shall return to the goals (G) and consequences (O) of the information system later on in sections 3.2 and 3.5, respectively. In the present context we shall discuss in more detail the subjectivity entailed in the analysis of the existing situation (E) and in the problem analysis (P). We use the term problem in the spirit of Zaltman, Duncan and Holbek (1977, p. 55; see also Hage, 1980, p. 211) to refer to the perception that the present or future state is not as good as it might be. A problem is always a subjective assessment which may be more or less intersubjective and is always related to a feeling of dissatisfaction (Zaltman, et al., 1977) or a mere feeling of uneasiness (Checkland, 1981). Consequently, different interest groups and actors may experience different factors as being problematic, and even in the case of

---

[1]In the case of O we shall concentrate on the consequences on the following rather than the immediate characteristics.

common problems they may have different explanations for the causes (cf., function f in section 3.5).

In the case of the existing situation (E), we wish to point out that the consequences are always evaluated in the context of the current situation, comparing with it the changes implied by the consequences of the IS development. It is obvious that different interest groups and actors regard different consequences and aspects of the existing situation as relevant to IS assessment. Consequently, we find the subjectivity in the analysis of the existing situation very important for IS design. This subjectivity is naturally more compatible with a subjective approach within an organization theory that recognizes that organizations are socially created, contractual entities based on goals, beliefs, expectations, rules, norms, language, etc., shared to a greater or lesser degree by the interest groups and actors involved (Burrell and Morgan, 1979; Pfeffer, 1981).

It will be emphasized in section 3.5 that an evaluation of the consequences of information systems should recognize the importance of subjective views as determinants of the consequences. In the context of the present section, it is significant that many problems may arise from differing views concerning the organization. Consequently, special attention should be paid to the analysis of the relationships between these different views. Even though this may lead to the removal of some discrepancies, it should be observed that different views are unavoidable and by no means generally dysfunctional.

3.2 Information Systems as Negotiated Social Choices

Referring to the discussion above, we can conclude that the problems of social choice attached to information systems concern not only different preferences, but, more generally, different views inherent in the whole IS design process. Furthermore, there is considerable uncertainty about the consequences of IS development (see section 3.5). In this situation of subjectivity and uncertainty, it is obvious that the selection of an information system is a social negotiation and bargaining process rather than a choice based on indisputable rational argumentation.

Consequently, we consider it very important that IS design methodologies should be able to support this negotiation process at least by "structuring debate" (Checkland, 1981, p. 150). The negotiation and bargaining can take place at two levels: at the level of goals (G above) and/or at the level of alternative information systems, or more strictly of their models (M). In the former case the aim is to agree upon common goals to be imposed upon the information system. In this case the design of alternative information systems can be conceived as a problem solving activity of finding an alternative which satisfies the goals imposed. There is some evidence that this goal-oriented approach is a good strategy from the implementation viewpoint (cf., Iivari, 1985a), but in common with Checkland (1981), for example, we cannot assume it to be feasible in all situations. In the latter case, the negotiation can take place directly in terms of alternative information systems. This alternative-oriented approach does not necessarily require that there are any clear goals preceding the generation of alternatives and the final choice, but the goals may be imposed afterwards in order to rationalize and legitimize the choice made (cf., Brunson, 1982). In this sense, the goals follow rather than precede the choice, causing the approach to resemble the "garbage can" model (March and Olson, 1976).

3.3   Abstraction Mechanisms in IS Assessment

Information systems are usually complex systems. Their complexity is both extensional, as a result of their size and scope, and intensional in the sense that information systems are not only technical systems, but also linguistic communication and organizational systems. Since most interest groups and actors are not interested in all the features of information systems, there is a need for effective mechanisms of abstraction. With reference to the discussion in the previous section, we suggest levels of abstraction, levels of detail, partial views and local views as important mechanisms for structuring the debate concerning IS assessment and selection.

In the case of levels of abstraction, there is growing agreement about the fruitfulness of distinguishing three hierarchical levels in the modelling of information systems (Falkenberg, et al., 1983):

1. The organizational level, defining the organizational context of the future information system

2. The infological or conceptual level, defining a "technical implementation" independent specification for the system

3. The datalogical or technical level, which defines the technical solution for the system.[2]

In the case of levels of abstraction, we have a predefined number of levels which describe the different features of the whole, real information system. There are genuine alternatives at each level (Kerola, 1981), the assessment and selection of which can take place in the above hierarchical order. It is important, however, to observe that each level has its own specific evaluation or quality criteria which are meaningful at the level in question (cf., section 3.6).

The levels of detail, on the other hand, enable the decomposition or refinement of the information system into smaller and smaller subsystems which in principle could be realized separately. The number of hierarchical levels, e.g., the whole system, subsystems, subsubsystems, etc., is not defined in advance. The principle of levels of detail can be applied at each level of abstraction mentioned above. This makes it possible to discuss and assess the information system in crude terms at each level of abstraction. We consider this capability particularly important in the case of complex and fuzzy information systems, the delimitation of which is far from clear at the beginning of IS design.

---

[2]A clarifying terminological remark is needed here. Reflecting on our perspective of IS design methodologies, we use the level 1 introduced above as an abstraction level for information systems, even though models at that level usually describe the organizational context of an information system rather than the information system itself (change analysis and organizational options in section 4).

We use the term "partial view" to refer to the selection of a certain specified aspect of an information system for consideration (e.g., user-IS interaction, databases, etc.). Partial views can be applied at each level of abstraction and the levels of detail can usually be used in the modelling of these partial views.

Our term "local view" refers to the modelling of an information system from the viewpoint of an individual actor in the spirit of external views and schemas in database management systems. These local views also can be applied at different levels of abstraction and may include different partial views and be modelled at various levels of detail.

3.4 Abstract Descriptions and Prototypes as IS Representations

The ex ante assessment of information systems is always based on models (M) rather than on real use of actual information systems. This is true in the case of "abstract" representations, such as diagrams describing the information system, and also in the case of prototypes, which are always prototypes of some model of the information system (Iivari, 1984). The model can be a separate description or it may be the specification of the prototype using some high-level language of the application generator to be used in the implementation of the prototype.

Prototyping offers an important opportunity for facilitating the assessment of certain relatively direct, situation-independent quality characteristics of information systems (e.g., the quality of user-IS interaction), while its contribution is much more limited in the case of indirect situation-dependent quality characteristics (e.g., indirect consequences of information systems, [Iivari, 1984]). Referring to the discussion above, we do not yet consider prototyping an alternative to more traditional modelling of information systems (as in Naumann and Jenkins, 1982), but rather a complementary process (cf., also Goldkuhl, 1980). Consequently, we find the description languages of information systems still highly relevant from the viewpoint of IS assessment.

There also exists the well-known problem of understandability and formality in IS description languages. The fact that highly formal languages tend to be quite difficult to understand has led to the idea that there should be several languages for different purposes, some less formal and more understandable and some more formal and unfortunately less understandable. This need is evident when we are discussing description languages at different levels of abstraction,[3] but also to some extent within each level of abstraction. In the latter case we propose that there should be a language, or an integrated system of languages, to allow a gradual, well-defined transition from relatively informal and easily comprehensible descriptions to highly formal ones. This is important since IS assessment and the consequent decisions made on the level of informal descriptions should nevertheless be operational, i.e., it should be possible to verify that the refined and more formal descriptions are consistent with the choice made.

---

[3]The different languages may nevertheless use a uniform notation. In this case the "same" symbols have different meanings at different levels of abstraction.

3.5 IS Design and Assessment as a Future Oriented Action

IS development is clearly future-oriented action, its real consequences emerging more or less immediately after the implementation
and institutionalization of the system. In ex ante assessment the
consequences (O) can only be predicted by considering the model of
the system to be assessed (M), the existing situation to which the
system is to be embedded (E), future factors (F) and potential
special constraints (R) and finally the co-production relationship, the function f

$$O = f(E,M,F,R),$$

which expresses the relationship between the consequences O and
the arguments E, M, F and R.

With reference to the function f, it is clear that there is much
uncertainty involved in the prediction of the consequences O.
First of all, our understanding of the co-production relationship
is very limited. Second, referring to the discussion in section
3.1, we should observe that the existing situation is not one and
only one objective state, but an interrelated collection of different subjective views of the interest groups and actors participating in the organization. Third, due to our limited understanding of the function f, we are not clearly aware of which
future factors are relevant in the assessment, and finally our
capability to predict the factors F in the case of highly dynamic
circumstances is very limited.

In view of these uncertainties, we suggest three adaptation (or F)
strategies to be considered in IS design and assessment (Iivari,
1985b): 1) freezing strategy, in which the information system is
frozen for a preplanned period, so that all the change requirements are damped, 2) forecasting strategy, in which one aims at
predicting the change requirements and the information system is
designed to be flexible to such changes, and 3) flexibility
strategy, in which case the information system is designed to be
flexible in general terms. These strategies suggest that IS
development should not be modelled as the metaphor of one life
cycle, but rather as an evolutionary process in which the life
cycles of the information system succeed each other (Iivari,
1983a; see also Lehman, 1984, and Rzevski, et al., 1982). In the
light of the uncertainties and problems associated with IS assessment, it is also obvious that the importance of an evolutionary
approach cannot be overestimated.

3.6 Quality Criteria for IS Assessment

There is an obvious need for evaluation or quality criteria for
facilitating the understanding, communication and measurement of
the different consequences of information systems and their
development. It is clear that many consequences of information
systems are qualitative and intangible, and consequently hard to
measure, qualify and render commensurate. Considering our discussion above concerning the subjectivity and uncertainty of IS
assessment and the social choice of information systems, we do not
regard these problems as very critical. They should be accepted
as facts of life and models for the quality criteria should primarily be developed as means of increasing understanding about the
quality of information systems by putting forward meaningful questions rather than as means for providing exact answers, since

over-quantification and formalization of the criteria can easily lead to a superficial feeling of objective and nonproblematic measurement of the quality of information systems.

Referring to the discussion on the levels of abstraction in the modelling of information systems (section 3.3), we wish to point out that different criteria are meaningful at different levels of abstraction. This means that there are certain value assumptions rooted in those hierarchical levels, and consequently we find it very important that IS design methodologies, if based on levels of abstraction, should also make explicit the value assumptions underlying those levels by specifying the quality criteria presumed to be relevant at each level.

3.7 Summary of the Requirements

Referring to the discussion above, we can conclude that there is considerable uncertainty involved in IS assessment. Consequently, decisions concerning information systems cannot be taken on the basis of indisputable rational arguments, but rather are based on a social negotiation process in which the different interest groups and actors involved try to assess the alternatives from their perspective.

IS design methodologies should support this assessment by providing information about the different constituents of the assessment process identified above, I, E, P, F, G, R, M, f and g. On the basis of this classification the requirements placed upon IS design methodologies can be organized into ten categories

1. Interest group and actor analysis (I)
    - the actor perspective

2. Analysis of the existing situation (E)
    - subjective views

3. Problem analysis (P)

4. Future analysis (F)
    - adaptation strategies

5. Goal analysis (G)
    - social negotiation

6. Constraint analysis (R)

    Design of IS alternatives (M)

7. Generation and refinement
    - problem solving activity/social negotiation

8. Modelling and representation
    - abstraction mechanisms (levels of abstraction and detail, partial and local views)
    - description languages
    - prototyping

9. Evolution
    - life-cycle metaphor/evolution metaphor

10.   Evaluation of the quality of information systems (f, g)
      - quality criteria at different levels of abstraction

4.   THE ISAC, ETHICS AND PIOCO METHODOLOGIES AS METHODS OF IS
     ASSESSMENT

4.1 Introduction

Most IS design methodologies do not treat IS assessment at all
(e.g., most CRIS1 methodologies, [Olle, 1982]), or else they
regard it as a subsidiary activity to the specifying, designing
and implementing of information systems (e.g., ISAC and D2S2 in
CRIS1 methodologies. See also Lundeberg (1982) and Macdonald and
Palmer (1982). Referring to the requirements summarized above in
section 3.7, we can also recognize that most of these methodologies (ISAC and D2S2 are again the most notable exceptions among
the CRIS1 methodologies) scarcely treat categories 1-6 at all, due
to their non-diagnostic nature. Their contribution from the viewpoint of IS assessment lies in categories 7-9 in providing
abstraction mechanisms, corresponding description languages and
potential prototyping environments to support IS assessment.

There are some exceptions, however. The ISAC methodology (Lundeberg, 1981), in spite of our remark that it regards IS assessment
as a subsidiary activity of IS design, includes features which
support IS assessment in most respects in the sense of categories
1-10 above, even though it does not reflect all the qualifications
related to these categories. We shall return to the evaluation of
ISAC as a methodology of IS assessment in section 4.2. ETHICS
(Mumford, 1983, Mumford and Weir, 1979) forms a second well-known
example of an IS design methodology which pays considerable
attention to IS assessment and related activities. We shall
return to this in section 4.3. Finally, in section 4.4, we shall
discuss the PIOCO model or methodology, which is explicitly based
on the idea that IS design is an inquiry process supporting the
assessment and choice of information systems by those responsible
for deciding about the principal alternatives.

Since there are obvious differences in scope between the three
methodologies, we shall compare them primarily as methodologies of
IS design at the organizational level (cf., section 3.3). The
infological/conceptual and datalogical/technical levels are only
taken into account in the context of requirements 8-10 (see
previous section). The organizational level corresponds to change
analysis and activity studies in ISAC, while ETHICS, according to
our interpretation, is primarily intended for this level, even
though this is not clearly stated (e.g., in Mumford, 1983). In
the PIOCO model the organizational level corresponds to the P
(pragmatic) level.

4.2 ISAC as a Method of IS Assessment

Since ISAC is internationally well-known and well-documented
(Lundeberg, et al., 1981; Lundeberg, 1982), we shall proceed
directly to discuss it as a method of IS assessment. ISAC
includes interest group analysis as an explicit activity which is
assumed to take place in terms of interest groups rather than
specific actors.

In the description of current activities, ISAC recognizes different views, but at the same time suggests that the final description of current activities should be formulated as some kind of
synthesis which is acceptable for all involved.   This is, in fact,
in contrast to the purpose of describing the current activities.
The synthesis, insofar as it can be achieved and accepted, may be
a compromise which does not describe the current situation and has
not been used by any actor as a reference model in the sense of an
"espoused theory" or "theory-in-use" (Argyris and Schon, 1978).
It is itself the result of IS development and may not form a fair
contrast for assessing the consequences of this IS development.

Problem analysis is well-recognized in ISAC, even though treated
quite briefly.   Problems are clearly conceived of as subjective
perceptions of the interest groups.

Future analysis is not explicitly treated and, overall, the ISAC
methodology can be regarded as a quite reactive approach (Iivari
and Kerola, 1983).

Goal analysis is introduced very briefly, even though the methodology is very clearly based on a goal-oriented approach.   The fact
that different interest groups may have different desires is
recognized, but the methodology does not make any special provision for social negotiation of the goals.   ISAC does not include
any clear constraint analysis.

ISAC views the generation and refinement of information systems as
a problem-solving activity based on stated goals and needs for
change rather than as a process of social negotiation.   It is
significant, however, that the evaluation of alternative information systems (or alternative changes or ambition levels) in the
change analysis and activity studies does not take place in terms
of the goals or objectives imposed.   This means that ISAC is not
based in any extreme sense on the metaphor of problem-solving in
these earliest phases.

ISAC provides quite an elaborate system of levels of abstraction
and corresponding description languages for the modelling and
description of information systems.   The description languages
support the principle of levels of detail and also provide various
partial views, but the strict precedence relationship requirements
in the A and I graphs make it difficult to extract local views
(Iivari and Kerola, 1983).   The comprehensibility of the graphs is
relatively high, even though reduced somewhat by the complexity of
the whole system of description languages (Iivari and Kerola,
1983).   The languages allow quite precise descriptions, even
though they do not have a formal basis.

Prototypes are mentioned as IS representations, but are not
integral parts of the methodology.   Information systems are also
conceived of in metaphorical terms as consisting of one life cycle
rather than as evolutionary systems and the whole idea of IS
evolution is taken into account only implicitly (Iivari and
Kerola, 1983).

Finally, ISAC includes the evaluation of information systems
(evaluation of alternative changes, cost-benefit analysis in
activity studies and evaluation of the processing philosophy) and
also suggests some quality criteria, but it does not provide any
systematic model for quality evaluation at the different levels of
abstraction proposed by the methodology.

4.3 ETHICS as a Method of IS Assessment

ETHICS is also internationally well-known and well-documented
(Mumford and Weir, 1979; Mumford, 1983) and, therefore, we shall
not introduce the methodology but shall proceed directly to its
assessment.

Interest group analysis in ETHICS is embedded in the design of the
project organization and in the definition of system boundaries.
Even though the actor perspective is not clearly emphasized, we
find that the interest groups and participants are discussed in
more actor-oriented terms than in ISAC.

The analysis of the existing situation in ETHICS explicitly recognizes partial views (Mumford, 1983, p. 69), or local views in our
terminology, but does not discuss the implications of these
different views. One gets the impression, however, that these
partial views are assumed to be compatible with each other rather
than fundamentally contradictory.

Problem analysis in ETHICS takes place in two parts: diagnosis of
efficiency needs and diagnosis of job satisfaction needs, both of
which are discussed in detail.

Future analysis is an explicit activity, and even though the
adaptation strategies are not explicitly discussed, one can conclude that ETHICS reflects the forecasting and flexibility strategies mentioned in section 3.5.

Considerable attention is paid to goal analysis in ETHICS and it
is also very clearly conceived of as a social negotiation process
(Mumford, 1983, pp. 88-89) in which the efficiency and job satisfaction objectives and objectives related to future change are
weighed, reconciled, assigned priorities, and made operational.

Constraint analysis in ETHICS is embedded in the definition of
system boundaries and in the evaluation of the merged organiza-
tional/technical options (Mumford, 1983, p. 97).

ETHICS views the generation and refinement of alternatives as a
problem-solving activity rather than a social negotiation process
(Mumford, 1983, p. 90), but it is significant that the generation
of organizational options is not based on the results of the goal
analysis described above but on the definition of key objectives
and key tasks in the organizational system to be developed. The
efficiency, job satisfaction and future change objectives and
related priorities are used to evaluate the organizational and
technical alternatives.

ETHICS pays relatively little attention to the modelling of
information systems since its main contribution lies in the
modelling of organizational changes related to IS development
(cf., section 4.1). Due to this orientation, ETHICS does not
provide any clear abstraction mechanisms for modelling information
systems. The description languages used by Mumford (1983), for
example, are quite fragmented and should obviously be interpreted
as exemplary rather than essential ingredients of the methodology.

ETHICS similarly does not pay any special attention to prototyping. This may be partly explained by its scope, since the
applicability of prototyping is most limited at the organizational

level (Iivari, 1984); however, the evolutionary nature of information systems is well-recognized.

The evaluation of alternative information systems (organizational
and technical and their merged options) is an integral part of the
ETHICS methodology. As discussed above, this evaluation takes
place mainly in terms of the efficiency, job satisfaction and
future change objectives defined in the goal analysis.   ETHICS
also provides a set of criteria for the assessment of job satisfaction.

4.4   The PIOCO Model as a Method of IS Assessment

The PIOCO model consists of four major parts: 1) a metamodel for
an information system (Iivari and Koskela, 1980, 1983; Iivari,
1983b), defining explicitly the product of IS design and the
object of IS assessment, 2) the description languages (Iivari and
Koskela, 1982, 1983), forming a set of compatible graphical
languages for the description of information systems, 3) a model
for the IS design process (Kerola, 1975; Iivari, 1978, 1982,
1983b, 1985b; Iivari and Koskela, 1984), and 4) a model for choice
and quality criteria (Iivari, 1978, 1983b; Iivari and Koskela,
1979), which expresses and explicates the values underlying the
PIOCO model. The whole methodology is based on the socio-cyberne-
tic metamodel for IS design, in which the latter is explained as
an inquiry process supporting decisions regarding principal
alternatives for the information system and controlling the IS
design process (Iivari, 1983a, 1983b). In more concrete terms,
this metamodel views IS design primarily as an interaction between
the design group and the steering committee, and the specification
and design of the information system is assumed to take place in
this context of interaction.

Due to this background, the PIOCO model pays particular attention
to IS assessment. The basic ideas of the whole methodology can be
summarized as follows: 1) Taking into account the multi-faceted
nature and complexity of information systems, their selection and
assessment should be decomposed into simpler problems.   In the
PIOCO model the selection problem is decomposed into three parts:
selection of the pragmatic (P), input-output (I/O) and construc-
tive-operative (C/O) models for information systems corresponding
to the three levels of abstraction mentioned in section 3.3. The
selection is furthermore assumed to take place in a linear order
in the sense that the P model is selected first, the I/O model
next and the C/O last.   2) There are special choice and quality
criteria at each level of abstraction and consequently in each
selection problem. The choice of the P model is assumed to take
place in terms of the cost/effectiveness criterion, the choice of
the I/O model in terms of the total user (information) satisfac-
tion/cost criterion and the C/O model in terms of the total
efficiency criterion.   3) The IS design process can be divided
into three design phases on the basis of the linear order of the
selection of an information system: the P main phase supporting
the choice of the P model, the I/O main phase supporting the
choice of the I/O model and the C/O main phase supporting the C/O
model for an information system.

Principal attention will be paid to the P level, defining the
information system in the context of an organizational change.
The presentation is mainly based on Iivari (1985b).

In its interest group and actor analysis, the PIOCO model emphasizes the importance of a comprehensive approach for ethical and
practical reasons. It recognizes, however, the different forms
and degrees of participation or involvement and emphasizes that
the degree of participation should be balanced against the
relevance of the design situation to the potential participants.
The actor perspective is highly explicit in the analysis.

In its analysis of the existing situation, the methodology points
out that different interest groups and actors may have different
views about the current situation.   Since these differences may
underlie many organizational problems, it is important to reveal
rather than conceal them.   Consequently, the methodology aims
first at identifying the views of different interest groups and
actors as genuinely as possible. After that the views are tenta-
tively reconciled in order to discover the commonalities and
differences and the differences are explained as far as possible.
Potential explanations suggested by the methodology include
terminology and conceptual differences and different assumptions,
expectations, goals and ideologies.

The problem analysis also recognizes the importance of different
views and starts out from the problem perceptions and explanations
of different interest groups and actors.   In order to achieve a
more holistic image of the problem situation, these individual
views are combined and decomposed into problem areas, which form
the basis for problem restriction.   Some problem areas may also be
selected for thorough analysis using structured diagnostic tools
(e.g., job satisfaction using Mumford's job satisfaction questionnaire [Mumford, 1983], IS function using Pearson's questionnaire
[Bailey and Pearson, 1983]). At this stage it is usually possible
to evaluate whether IS development is relevant in the given
problem situation.   Problem analysis has a very important role in
the methodology, since its results are assumed to cause the P
design to proceed in essentially different ways.   In the case of
"well-defined" problems the P design proceeds according to a
"goal-oriented strategy" resembling the traditional decision-
making strategy, while in the case of a highly problematic
analysis the P design takes place according to the "alternative-oriented" strategy (cf., section 3.2).

The two approaches also influence the comprehensiveness and depth
of the future and constraint analyses, the goal-oriented strategy
justifying a more comprehensive and deeper analysis.   In view on
the well-known problems of future analysis, one of its main ideas
is to relate the analysis to alternative adaptation strategies,
e.g., the freezing strategy, forecasting strategy or flexibility
strategy (cf., section 3.5).

In the case of constraint analysis, the methodology reminds us
that the controllability of the relevant factors is not generally
obvious, but constitutes a restriction specific to the P design
situation in question.

The goal analysis is divided into two essentially different procedures on the basis of the strategies -- goal-oriented versus
alternative-oriented.   In the former the goal analysis aims at as
concrete change goals as possible, and recognizes that the
imposition of goals is primarily an organizational negotiation
process.   The purpose of the goal analysis is to support this
process by operationalizing the relevant goal factors, which may
be nominal, ordinal or quantitative, and by analyzing the impor-

tance of the goal factors from the viewpoint of different interest groups and actors. In the analysis of importance, it is significant to observe that the interest groups are not expected to express their opinions about the importance of all the goal factors (for example, ETHICS [Mumford, 1983]), but can define their own goal areas, including their intrinsic and instrumental goals in the P design situation in question. Importance is evaluated using mainly qualitative ordinal scale expressions such as "very important," "important," "rather important," and "rather insignificant," which are used in the identification of insignificant goal factors (all expressions "rather important" or "rather insignificant"), conflicting goal factors (not insignificant, different opinions about the desirable direction of development), crucial goal factors (not conflicting, all expressions "very important" or "important," relatively wide consensus), potential complementary goal factors (the remainder). In the alternative-oriented strategy the depth of the goal analysis is based on the mutual agreement of the project group and the steering committee about the sufficiency of the analysis.

In the case of the goal-oriented strategy the concrete change goals may directly suggest certain change ideas, making the process resemble a problem-solving activity. We should take into account the fact that the change alternatives identified may require some precondition changes producing necessary or desirable preconditions for the successful institutionalization of the changes implied by the P model, as well as complementary changes compensating for some undesirable impacts of the changes with respect to some interest groups and actors involved. This suggests that even in the case of the goal-oriented approach the generation and refinement of alternative P models is also a social negotiation process, an aspect which is still more important in the case of the alternative-oriented strategy.

In the context of the modelling and representation of information systems we refer to the PIOCO metamodel for an information system, which is based on the three levels of abstraction, P, I/O and C/O. The corresponding metamodels for an information system support the principle of levels of detail, have in-built partial views (e.g., the I/O metamodel is defined at the highest level as a quadruple of INFORMATION MODEL, INFORMATION PROCESS MODEL, INTERACTION MODEL and OBJECT SYSTEM MODEL for the UoD), and also allow the easy extraction of local views. The PIOCO description languages form a system of integrated graphical languages which make it possible to proceed gradually from simple block diagrams to relatively precise, even though not completely formal, descriptions.

In the case of prototyping and the evolutionary approach, we refer to Iivari (1982, 1983c), in which the PIOCO model for IS design process was extended to cover the experimental (prototype) and the evolutionary approaches at each level of abstraction.

Finally, the PIOCO model for the IS design process includes the evaluation of the information system at each level of abstraction using the corresponding choice and quality criteria. The criteria are explicitly defined in the PIOCO model for choice and quality criteria. Referring to the discussion on IS assessment "in the small" (section 2.2), we can conclude that the evaluation of information systems at each level of abstraction constitutes a summarizing activity in which the results of the corresponding main phases and the argumentation about the quality of the information system are presented. Even though we are well aware

Methodology / Requirements	ISAC	ETHICS	PIOCO
Interest group and actor analysis	yes	yes	yes
- actor perspective	no	to some extent	yes
Analysis of the existing situation	yes	yes	yes
- subjective views	to some extent	to some extent	yes
Problem analysis	yes	yes	yes
Future analysis	no	yes	yes
- adaptation strategies	no	to some extent	yes
Goal analysis	yes	yes	yes
- social negotiation	to some extent	yes	yes
Constraint analysis	no	yes	yes
Design of IS alternatives			
Generation and refinement	yes	yes	yes
- problem-solving/social negotiation	problem solving	problem solving	problem solving & social negotiation
Modelling and representation	yes	not systematically	yes
- abstraction mechanisms	levels of abstraction, levels of detail, partial views	concentrates on IS design at the organizational level (*)	levels of abstraction, levels of detail, partial views, local views
- description languages	an integrated system of graphical languages	some fragments (see * above)	an integrated system of graphical languages
- prototyping	mentioned	(see * above)	optional approach at each level of abstraction
Evolution	no	yes	yes
- life-cycle/evolution as a metaphor	life-cycle	life-cycle	evolution as successive life-cycles at each level of abstraction
Evaluation	yes	yes	yes
- quality criteria	fragmented suggestions	job satisfaction (see * above)	effectiveness criteria, user information satisfaction criteria, total efficiency criteria

Table 1

of the difficulty of this assessment, it is our firm conviction that the rich understanding of the whole IS design situation, based on previous interest group and actor analysis, the analysis of the existing situation, the problem, future and goal analyses, and the identification and refinement of IS alternatives gives the best opportunity for a reasonable assessment and understanding of the quality of the system.

5. SUMMARY

The content of the paper is summarized in Table 1, which identifies the requirements imposed upon IS design methodologies as methods of IS assessment and summarizes the results of the assessment of ISAC, ETHICS and PIOCO as methods of "IS assessment in the large."

ACKNOWLEDGEMENTS

The author wishes to express his gratitude to Erkki Koskela for his cooperation in developing the PIOCO model and to the two anonymous referees for their valuable suggestions for improving this paper.

REFERENCES

Argyris, C., and Schon, D., *Organizational Learning: A Theory of Action Perspective,* Addison-Wesley, Reading, Massachusetts, 1978.

Bailey, J. L., and Pearson, S. W., "Development of a Tool for Measuring and Analyzing Computer User Satisfaction," *Management Science,* Vol. 29, No. 5, 1983.

Brunson, N., "The Irrationality of Action and Action Rationality: Decisions, Ideologies and Organizational Actions," *Journal of Management Studies,* Vol. 19, No. 1, 1982.

Burrell G., and Morgan, G., *Sociological Paradigms and Organizational Analysis,* Heinemann, London, 1979

Checkland, P., *Systems Thinking, Systems Practice,* John Wiley and Sons, Chichester, England, 1981.

Goldkuhl, G., "Framställningar och Änvandning Av Informationsmodeller," TRITA-IBA DB-4099, Stockholm, 1980.

Falkenberg, E., Nijssen, G. M., Adams, A., Bradley, L., Bugeia, P., Campbell, A. L., Carkeet, M., Lehmann, G., and Shoesmith, A., "Feature Analysis of ACM/PCM, CIAM, ISAC and NIAM," in Olle, T. W., Sol, H. G., and Tully, C. J. (eds.), *Information Systems Design Methodologies: A Feature Analysis,* North-Holland, Amsterdam 1983.

Faludi, A., *Planning Theory,* Pergamon Press, Oxford, 1973.

Hage, J., *Theories of Organizations,* John Wiley and Sons, New York, 1980.

Hawgood, J., "Quinquevalent Quantification of Computer Benefits," in Frielink, A. B. (ed.), *Economics of Informatics*, North-Holland, Amsterdam, 1975.

Iivari J., "A Planning Theory Perspective on Information Systems Implementation," in Gallegos, L., Welke, R., and Wetherbe, J. (eds.), *Proceedings of the Sixth Annual International Conference on Information Systems*, Indianapolis, 1985a.

Iivari, J., "A Sociocybernetic Metamodel for Systemeering as a Framework for the Contingency Research into Information Systems Development," in Bemelmans, Th. M. A. (ed.), *Beyond Productivity: Information Systems Development for Organizational Effectiveness*, North-Holland, Amsterdam, 1983a.

Iivari, J., "Contributions to the Theoretical Foundations of Systemeering Research and the PIOCO Model," Acta Universitatis Ouluensis, A150, Oulu, 1983b.

Iivari, J., "Pragmaattinen ohjaus tietojenkäsittelyn kehittämisessä", Report A8, Institute of Data Processing Science, University of Oulu, Oulu, 1978.

Iivari, J., "Pragmaattinen systemointi: Ongelma ja tilanneanalyysi," Institute of Data Processing Science, University of Oulu, Oulu, 1985b.

Iivari, J., "Prototyping in the Context of Information Systems Design," in Budde, R., Kuhlenkamp, K., Mathiassen, L., and Züllighoven, H. (eds.), *Approaches to Prototyping: Proceedings of the Working Conference on Prototyping*, Springer-Verlag, 1984.

Iivari, J.,"Taxonomy of the Experimental and Evolutionary Approaches to Systemeering," in Hawgood, J. (ed.), *Evolutionary Information Systems*, North-Holland, Amsterdam, 1982.

Iivari, J., and Kerola, P., "A Sociocybernetic Framework for the Feature Analysis of Information Systems Design Methodologies," in Olle, T. W., Sol, H. G., and Tully, C. J. (eds.), *Information Systems Design Methodologies: A Feature Analysis*, North-Holland, Amsterdam, 1983c.

Iivari, J., and Koskela, E., "An Extended EAR Approach for Information System Specification," in Davis, C. G., Jajodia, S., Ng, P. A., and Yeh, R. T. (eds.), *Entity-relationship Approach to Software Engineering*, North-Holland, Amsterdam, 1983d.

Iivari, J., and Koskela, E., "Choice and Quality Criteria for Data System Selection," in Samet, P. A. (ed.), *Proceedings of EuroIFIP 79*, European Conference on Applied Information Technology, London 25-28 September 1979, North-Holland, Amsterdam, 1979.

Iivari, J., and Koskela, E., "HSL: A Host System Language for Pragmatic Specification and Host System Descriptions in Data System Development," in Nurminen, M., and Gaupholm, H. T. (eds.), *Report of the Sixth Scandinavian Research Seminar on Systemeering*, Bergen, 1983.

Iivari, J., and Koskela, E., "On the Modelling of Human-Computer Interaction as the Interface Between the User's Work Activity and the Information System," in *Proceedings of INTERACT'84, First IFIP Conference on Human-Computer Interaction*, London, 1984.

Iivari, J., and Koskela, E., "PIOCO Model for a Data System," in Lyytinen, K., and Peltola, E. (eds.), *Report of the Third Scandinavian Research Seminar on Systemeering Models*, Jyväskylä, 1980.

Iivari, J., Koskela, E., Similä, J., and Viippola, R., "IOSL: An Infologically Oriented Input-Output Specification Language for Data Systems," in Goldkuhl, G., and Kall, C-O. (eds.), *The Report of the Fifth Scandinavian Research Seminar on Systemeering*, Stockholm, 1982.

Kerola, P., "On Hierarchical Information and Data Systems in Data System Life Cycle," in Lundeberg, M., and Bubenko, J., Jr (eds.), *Systemeering 75*, Studentlitteratur, Lund, 1975.

Kerola, P., "On the Comparison of the Highest Level Problem Solving Approach in Information Systems Development," in Kerola, P., and Koskela, E. (eds.), *Report of the Fourth Scandinavian Research Seminar on Systemeering*, Institute of Data Processing Science, University of Oulu, Oulu, 1981.

King, W. R., "Alternative Designs in Information System Development," *MIS Quarterly*, December, 1982.

Lehman, M. M., "Program Evolution," *Information Processing and Management*, Vol. 20, No. 1, 1984.

Lundeberg, M., Goldkuhl, G., and Nilsson, A., *Information Systems Development: A Systematic Approach*, Prentice-Hall, Englewood Cliffs, New Jersey, 1981.

Lundeberg, M., "The ISAC Approach to Specification of Information Systems and Its Application to the Organization of an IFIP Working Conference," in Olle, T. W., Sol, H. G., and Verrijn-Stuart, A. A. (eds.), *Information Design Methodologies: A Comparative Review*, North-Holland, Amsterdam, 1982.

Macdonald, I. G., and Palmer, I. R., "Systems Development in Shared Data Environment: The D2S2 Methodology," Universitets Forlaget, Bergen, 1976.

March, J. G., and Olsen, J. P., "Ambiguity and Choice in Organizations", Universitets Forlaget, Bergen, 1976.

Mumford, E., "Designing Human Systems for New Technology: The ETHICS Method", Manchester Business School, 1983.

Mumford, E., and Weir, M., *Computers System in Work Design - The ETHICS Method*, Associated Business Press, 1979.

Naumann, J. D., and Jenkins, A. M., "Prototyping: The New Paradigm for Systems Development," *MIS Quarterly*, September, 1982.

Olle, T. W., Sol, H. G., and Verrijn-Stuart, A. A. (eds.),
     Information Design Methodologies: A Comparative Review,
     North-Holland, Amsterdam, 1982.

Pfeffer, J., "Management as Symbolic Action: The Creation and
     Maintenance of Organizational Paradigms," in Cummings, L. L.,
     and Staw, B. M. (eds.), *Research in Organizational Behavior*,
     Vol. 3, JAI Press, 1981.

Rzevski, G., Trafford, D. B., and Wells, M. (eds.), "The Evolutio-
     nary Design Methodology Applied to Information Systems," in
     Olle, T. W., Sol, H. G., and Verrijn-Stuart, A. A. (eds.),
     Information Design Methodologies: A Comparative Review,
     North-Holland, Amsterdam, 1982.

Zaltman, G., Duncan, R., and Holbek, J., *Innovations and Organiza-
     tions*, John Wiley and Sons, New York, 1977.

DISCUSSANT NOTE

On: ASSESSING IS DESIGN METHODOLOGIES AS METHODS
     OF IS ASSESSMENT

By: Juhani Iivari

Discussant's comments by: Paul A. van der POEL

Technical University of Eindhoven
The Netherlands

1. INTRODUCTION

This paper puts forward the interesting idea that IS design
methodologies should be developed and assessed as methods of IS
assessment. Taking this viewpoint, an analysis of the problems of
IS assessment is taken as a starting point to arrive at requirements to be imposed upon IS design methodologies.

2. REQUIREMENTS

The first part of the paper gives a very complete, in-depth treatment of those requirements dealing with the effectiveness of the
IS design process. This makes this paper especially valuable for
those people dealing with IS design methodologies.

3. METHODOLOGY EVALUATION

The second part of the paper evaluates the ISAC, ETHICS and PIOCO
methodologies as methods of IS assessment. The PIOCO methodology,
being explicitly based on the idea that the IS design process
should support the assessment and choice of information systems,
meets the stated requirements much better than the well established methods ISAC and ETHICS. This leads us to the following
question:

           In which respect can the PIOCO methodology deal
           more effectively with IS development efforts than
           the ISAC and ETHICS methodologies?

The answer to this question, which was not considered in this
paper, could have made more clear how important it is for IS
design methodologies to meet the stated requirements.

4. CONCLUSION

There are a few more points regarding IS design methodologies
which are relevant in the given context, but were not taken into
account in the paper:

o Requirements concerning the efficient management of the IS
   development process should be met as well by IS design
   methodologies.

o Improvements to IS design methodologies come not only from IS
   assessment but also from other fields such as database
   management, software engineering, and artificial intelligence.

Finally, I would like to state that the paper very clearly makes
the point that IS assessment is not given the attention it
deserves in present IS design methodologies.

Incorporating User Diversity into Information Systems Assessment
J.G. Davis and A. Srinivasan

"In the indirect mode, users, typically in higher
managerial echelons, interact with computer systems
through non–IS department intermediaries who are staff
analysts or assistants."

INFORMATION SYSTEMS ASSESSMENT
N. Bjørn-Andersen, G.B. Davis (Editors)
Elsevier Science Publishers B.V. (North-Holland)
© IFIP, 1988

INCORPORATING USER DIVERSITY INTO
INFORMATION SYSTEMS ASSESSMENT

Joseph G. DAVIS
Ananth SRINIVASAN

Department of Operations and Systems Management
Graduate School of Business
Indiana University
Bloomington, Indiana 47405 USA

The Management Information Systems (MIS) literature
has generally tended to treat the Information
Systems (IS) user in relatively monolithic terms.
When diversity among users is acknowledged, it is
typically confined to their cognitive/psychological
differences or to the degree of usage (regular
versus casual users). The rapidly changing
information technology has contributed to a
spectrum of system usage modes or patterns that are
functionally distinct from one another. These
developments have significant implications for
measurement of IS effectiveness.

Based on a review of the literature, we identify
three dominant usage modes: direct, autonomous, and
indirect. The relevance and validity of this
classification scheme is explored through a case
study of a "sophisticated" IS environment in a
high-technology division of a diversified Fortune
500 company in the United States. A framework for
Information Systems Assessment (ISA) that examines
four ISA approaches in the light of the above
classification scheme is proposed.

1. INTRODUCTION

The role dichotomy between Information Systems (IS) users and
analysts is deeply entrenched in the traditional MIS literature.
The critical assumption underlying the System Development Life
Cycle (SDLC) model which dominated research in the field was a
division of labor between the two groups according to which the
role of users was restricted to specifying information needs,
involvement and participation in the design process, and ongoing
system use for decision making purposes while the analysts
actually "built" the system. However, with the rapid evolution of
information technology and the introduction of powerful workstations, microcomputers and their networks on the one hand, and
user-friendly, general-purpose software packages and Decision
Support Systems (DSS) generators on the other, the SDLC model can
account only for a segment of the IS-related activities in
organizations. The upshot of these developments has been greater
user access to IS resources and the consequent diversity and
heterogenity in terms of what IS users actually do in the capacity

of IS users. Thus the functionally homogeneous view of users that underlies a significant proportion of the MIS research needs to be revised in favor of a more comprehensive model of IS usage.

Such a revised model has direct implications for Information Systems Assessment (ISA). The different ISA approaches proposed in the literature make certain implicit or explicit assumptions regarding the type of systems and the manner in which users relate to the systems. To the extent that these assumptions are based exclusively on the SDLC model and the resulting passive view of users, the results of the assessment process are likely to be biased, incomplete, or inaccurate. The existing ISA techniques may require some fine-tuning in some situations or radically new approaches may have to be devised in order to account for the variety of systems and usage modes in contemporary IS environments. Consequently, ISA approaches have to exhibit the same kind of variety observable in what they are attempting to measure. We focus on one aspect of this variety, the existence of diverse modes of systems usage, and develop a framework for examining its implications for four different ISA approaches.

The remainder of this paper is divided into six sections. In the following section, we review the literature on users. This provides the basis for the development of the classification scheme of usage modes in the third section. The fourth section presents details of a case study that seek to establish the validity and relevance of the classification followed by a section devoted to delineation of four IS assessment approaches and explication of their underlying user models. The sixth section develops a framework for examining the implications of the classification scheme for the four ISA approaches. The final section presents the concluding remarks.

2. THE USER IN MIS LITERATURE

The predominant user model that emerges from the literature is that of the organizational participant who accesses systems to obtain information or receives reports (routine or ad hoc) through IS departments for decision making. The users were expected to provide a detailed description of their information requirements to be derived from analysis of users' decisions in order to identify the information needed to make the decisions (Langefors, 1966) or through a variety of techniques discussed under the rubric of Information Requirements Analysis (Bariff, 1978). They were further required to be involved in the various stages of the systems development process (Edström, 1977; Olson and Ives, 1981) and to be active participants in the design of systems they will eventually use (Mumford, et al., 1983).

The user, as a psychologically heterogeneous and complex entity, has been the focus of considerable amount of research in MIS. Users were argued to belong to different Jungian psychological types (Witkin, 1964; Mason and Mitroff, 1973) or different cognitive styles (Schroeder, 1971; Doktor and Hamilton, 1973; McKenney and Keen, 1974). A number of studies have addressed the impact of such user diversity on decision making behavior and system implementation effectiveness. Zmud (1979) and Taylor and Benbasat (1980) have drawn attention to the inconsistent findings and general inconclusiveness in cognitive styles research. In his critique and review of this stream of research, Huber (1983) lamented the lack of operational guidelines emerging from it.

Huber's allusion to a functionally different user or at least mode of usage has been echoed by several papers in recent years. References to such a user can be found from the early days of the DSS era. The main feature of these users is that they can exercise direct, personal control over all aspects of the information technology which includes equipment selection, software selection, software development, customization of applications, and data management. As Hackathorn (1978) observes, "emphasis is on the end user of the technology acting as programmer, analyst, etc., without role differentiation." At least for certain classes of applications, the user-analyst divide begins to dissolve.

Martin (1982) traces the trend toward increasing end user computing in a wide spectrum of organizations and stresses the need for MIS departments to learn to acquire necessary applications without programmers. The drastic reduction in computer costs vis-a-vis systems-related personnel costs, the rising demand for new applications and the consequent huge backlog of applications, both visible and invisible, are cited as reasons for this trend (Martin, 1982). Carlson, Grace, and Sutton (1977) developed case studies of end user requirements in interactive problem solving situations. Canning (1981) attests to the validity of the preponderance of end user programming that "enable end users to perform some of their own programming-handling query and report requests and even complete some applications." Rivard and Huff (1984) provide a good background on the "User Developed Applications (UDA) phenomenon" in their study of ten of the largest 100 Canadian business firms and propose a framework for the assessment of UDA success.

The end user role has been studied by McLean (1979), who identified four distinct subgroups within it. Johnson (1984) reported on the sixteen information centers established at various locations in Exxon which provide consulting, training, and technical assistance in the application of end user computing. In a more comprehensive study on end user computing (EUC), Rockart and Flannery (1983) attempted to learn more about end users by interviewing 200 end users and 50 members of information systems staffs responsible for EUC support in seven major organizations. They recorded the phenomenal growth in EUC, identified the scope and types of applications of end user systems, made recommendations for effective management of EUC, and proposed strategies for deriving maximum benefits from it.

The evolving role of the end user in organizations has been facilitated by the developments in information technology. The advances in software design enabling these developments have been taking place since the early to mid-seventies (e.g., Haney, 1973). Extensive availability of user-friendly software packages has given further impetus to end user computing. Development of easy-to-learn-and-use languages such as SMALLTALK, which is really a complete, user-oriented programming environment, are drastically altering the personal computing world. Hardware developments have also played their part. The impact of time-sharing systems and powerful mini- and micro-computers on the MIS function is significant. Networking of these computers with the traditional systems and office automation technology add yet another dimension to the bewildering complexity of MIS in contemporary settings.

One distinction that is often made in the computing literature, especially in the context of database query systems, is that of casual as opposed to regular or committed users. The former type

are users who may wish to extract data occasionally from databases, but do not possess a detailed knowledge of data, organization, and procedure or programming skills (Date, 1977). This
group of users has been studied in the context of design of
appropriate user interfaces. Cuff (1980) provides a detailed
profile of casual users in terms of frequency of use, level of
programming background, complexity of queries, and job motivation.

Yet another type of user or usage mode that is increasingly
receiving attention from MIS researchers is the typical top management person who has little to do directly with the computer-
based IS. Their mode of usage is indirect in that they make use
of reports prepared by staff analysts or assistants. These
intermediaries interface with decision support-type systems or
databases and develop applications based on the decision models
and information requirements of the real user. Such "chaufferred"
users (Bennett, 1975; Keen and Scott Morton, 1978) are acquiring
importance with the emerging emphasis on provision of informa-
tional support for these higher level functionaries. Welsch
(1980) reported that the facilitation functions of the intermediary were significantly related to the user manager's overall
measure of perceived implementation success.

3.   A CLASSIFICATION SCHEME OF USAGE MODES

The foregoing discussion has identified three distinct modes of IS
usage. While individual users may operate in one or more of these
modes, it is to be expected that they are likely to exhibit one
dominant mode. The three functionally distinct modes of usage
that constitute the classification scheme are termed *direct,
autonomous,* and *indirect.*

3.1 Direct Mode

Users in the direct mode interact directly with the IS. They
either engage in terminal access in a casual sense to obtain
elements of information or receive periodic or ad hoc reports from
the IS department. The systems in question are designed, developed, implemented, and maintained by the IS department analysts
either in concert with the user or independently. This usage mode
is typically characterized by a low level of computing skills.
Most samples in empirical MIS research contain a large proportion
of users operating in this mode.

3.2 Autonomous Mode

The autonomous mode is very similar to the end user mode discussed
earlier. The expression "end user" simply means the ultimate user
of computing applications such as accountants, purchasing executives, production schedulers, etc. (Martin, 1982), though "end
user" was initially coined to describe the usage mode of users who
by virtue of their command over higher level languages were able
to exploit the facilities offered by time-sharing systems to
develop and use their own application programs (McLean, 1979).
Rockart and Flannery (1983) and Hackathorn and Keen (1981) have
extended the meaning to include usage of workstations and personal
decision support systems, but the shadow cast by the earlier definition still lingers. In order to overcome the semantic difficulty, a more expressive label, "autonomous use," is adopted. It

should, however, be noted that this term is used in a relative
sense.

This mode of IS usage is characterized by development, design,
implementation, and use of application programs by the users
themselves in either interactive or personal computing environments to support personal or small group information requirements
for decision making. Users operating in this mode make use of a
variety of software tools such as general purpose software, user-
friendly operating systems, fourth generation and higher level
programming languages. Interaction with IS personnel may be
confined to limited support from the information center or analyst
assistance on a piece-meal basis.

3.3 Indirect Mode

In the indirect mode, users, typically in higher managerial
echelons, interact with computer systems through non-IS department
intermediaries who are staff analysts or assistants. The relationship with the computer-based IS results from the fact that
they process and act upon reports they receive from the intermediaries. It is the latter who interface (either in direct or
autonomous mode) with the systems to generate information which is
further analyzed and interpreted by them to produce reports for
the ultimate user manager.

4. A SHORT CASE STUDY[1]

The relevance and validity of the classification was empirically
examined through a case study of the computing environment of a
high-technology division of a large, diversified company in the
United States. The choice of the particular division (Delta) that
dealt in large-scale transportation systems was guided by the
following considerations:.

o Delta's commitment to keeping abreast of information techno-
  logy-related innovations.

o A well-articulated strategic thrust to develop a distributed
  IS that impacted the entire organization.

o An extensive network of readily accessible personal computers
  (PCs) and workstations.

o Delta's willingness to extend co-operation for data collection.

The choice of field research method in an exploratory fashion was
guided by the fact that prior research on the issues of interest
are limited and fragmented. In such situations, it is a useful
research strategy to identify an appropriate setting in which the
relevance of the major dimensions of the problem can be established through direct observation and to ensure that "the researcher's account of the studied scene (should) be provided by
the most knowledgeable members of that scene" (Van Maanen, 1979).

---

[1]A richer description of the environment is contained in a
longer version of the paper that is available from the authors.

Data on Delta's background, history, the evolution of its IS
department, hardware configuration, and the variety of systems
were gathered through interviews with six IS department personnel
including the department head and three managers who reported to
him.   The department head and Office Automation Manager were
interviewed a second time for the purpose of obtaining a list of
users to be interviewed.   They were provided with a detailed
description of the three modes of usage and asked to classify the
users based on the predominance of the mode in which each listed
user operated.   While the existense of the three distinct functional usage modes was clearly established, classification of the
users as operating predominantly in one mode or the other proved
to be difficult in some cases.   As we shall see later, there were
some Delta users who operated in both direct and autonomous modes
simultaneously.   Table 1 presents a breakdown of 24 users by
predominant usage mode (as determined by the IS and Office Systems
managers) and by functional area within the two business segments
in Delta.   Semi-structured interviews with these users were then
conducted to obtain a thorough understanding of the environment.

	ORIGINAL CLASSIFICATION		
	Direct Mode	Autonomous Mode	Indirect Mode
TRANSPORTATION SYSTEMS			
Manufacturing	2	3	1
Design & Engineering		2	
Marketing		1	1
Personnel & Training		1	
Finance & Accounting	2	1	
INTEGRATED LOGISTICS SUPPORT			
Marketing	1		
Finance & Accounting	1		
Administration & Planning		1	1
Program Support		2	
Program Administration		4	1
TOTAL	6	14	4

Table 1.   Breakdown of Respondents by Divisional Segment and by
           Functional Area

Though the sample of users was by no means random, the larger
number of users identified as operating primarily in the autonomous mode (14 out of 24) is consistent with Delta's IS strategy of
putting in place all the necessary hardware and software tools so
that users can operate relatively autonomously.   While autonomous
mode users were distributed across all functional areas, direct
users tended to be clustered in the Finance, Accounting, and Manufacturing areas.   The sample contains few indirect mode users.

Two of the fourteen autonomous mode users actually served primarily as intermediaries for their superiors who were indirect mode
users and were part of our sample.

A brief summary of the findings is:

o Thirteen (three direct and ten autonomous) out of the 24 user
   respondents received periodic computer-based report(s) either
   from the divisional or corporate IS department. Though the
   frequency of such report receipts by autonomous mode users
   was low (on the average one or two per month), it is clear
   that users cannot be understood as belonging to a particular
   mode exclusively. Also, two of the direct mode users did
   make use of micro-computers to work in an autonomous mode,
   though to a limited extent.

o Despite the similarities among autonomous mode users, they
   tended to exhibit differences along dimensions such as prior
   background in the use of computers, degree of sophistication
   in the use of tools, amount of time spent on information
   system-related work, and attitudes toward MIS.

o Indirect mode users relied heavily on the intermediaries who
   were exclusively subordinates drawn from their own departments. While the intermediaries operated in the autonomous
   mode and provided reports (typically interpreted) in response
   to the users' vaguely specified problems, the users themselves confined their access to use of electronic mail and
   calendaring (activity-scheduling) functions.

o Training provided for autonomous mode of usage was described
   as inadequate; probably as a consequence, there was under-
   utilization of computing tools (in relation to potential).
   Other forms of support for such users were also sporadic and
   unsystematic, resulting in these users having to fend for
   themselves. They tended to gravitate toward more experienced
   and knowledgeable users for assistance.

o The indirect mode users expressed satisfaction with the
   developments in computing which enabled them to describe
   their problems in their own terms and rely on non-IS intermediaries to provide the necessary information. The work
   done by the intermediaries varied considerably; it included
   graphical and statistical analysis, generation of ad hoc
   reports using the database, and development of decision
   support-type systems. The IS-related factors causing
   satisfaction for autonomous mode of users were easy access to
   hardware and software tools and not having to bear with the
   long delays in processing of requests by the IS department.
   They also commented on the productivity gains (time saving)
   as a result of having the tools at their disposal.

The computing environment at Delta can best be described as being
in a state of transition at the time of the study. The strategy
of distributed computing by providing access to computing resources to (most of) the users had been undertaken for about two
years, but the expectation was that much of the information needed
at lower and middle management levels could be generated by the
users themselves once all the tools were in place.

5. MIS ASSESSMENT APPROACHES

Traditional MIS approaches may be broadly categorized as

o System Use
o System Performance
o User Satisfaction
o Decision Performance

Each of the approaches is described in some detail in this section.

5.1 System Use

Traditionally, system use has been the most widely adopted measure of system effectiveness. This approach to the measurement of system quality is primarily derived from early attempts to evaluate the utility of operations research models. The argument proposed in favor of the degree-of-use measure was that if the user exhibited increased incidence of system use in situations where use was not mandatory then the system must be useful. A number of early studies where extent of system use was utilized as a measure of quality are reported in Schultz and Slevin (1975) and in Lucas' extensive work on MIS implementation (1975, 1976). Ein-Dor and Segev (1977) argue strongly in favor of using this approach by saying that it is strongly correlated with most widely held notions of MIS success. It is clear from the foregoing discussion that several factors are responsible for the use of this approach toward measuring system effectiveness. First, it has been argued that the degree of use is highly correlated with the extent to which the system has been found to be useful. Second, measuring extent of use (number of minutes of connect time, number of times the user logged on to the system, etc.) is easily facilitated by system monitors. Third, it provides an objective measure of the utility of a system, provided the use of the system itself was not mandated by organizational policy.

5.2 System Performance

The system performance approach is hinged on the ability to accurately measure costs and benefits associated with utilizing information systems. Typically, the nature of the benefits that were considered were cost reduction or avoidance, error reduction, increased speed of activity, etc. (see King and Schrems [1978] for a detailed discussion of this approach). In computer applications that were production oriented, such efficiency related measures were obtained with relative ease. It was fairly clear as to what the costs of obtaining a particular system were (hardware and software procurement costs, manpower costs for development, and maintenance cost). On the benefits side, the financial benefits of having implemented the system were again easily measurable either in dollar amounts or in terms of increased throughput of work.

The pressure to justify systems based on tangible costs and benefits was great, given the trend of increasing data processing budgets coupled with several backlogged projects (Keen, 1981). The nature of the criteria to measure performance now included items such as increased flexibility to carry out management activities and improved management planning and control. With the variety of systems rapidly increasing by utilizing vastly improved technology, it was becoming obvious that although the cost of developing a system was estimable with reasonable accuracy, it was virtually impossible to accurately account for the benefits accrued from a system or a collection of system applications. In response to this complexity, several multiple criteria scoring approaches were proposed that presumably took into account a whole range of benefits due to a system (Lucas and Moore, 1976).

5.3 User Satisfaction

Several authors have argued against approaches such as those cited above for a variety of reasons. For example, Ginzberg (1978) argues that in some decision environments, the extent to which the system is used may have nothing to do with how the user estimates that he/she has benefitted from using the system. Concepts such as the timely production of data, data that is relevant to a given problem, and appropriate presentation formats of information become key in determining a high quality system.

Early attempts to operationalize user satisfaction have been overly simplistic and have since been widely criticized. More recently, we have witnessed several attempts to produce more valid and comprehensive instruments to measure user satisfaction (Ives, et al., 1983; Pearson, 1977). The approach hinges on the following assumptions. First, the perception of the user with regard to the system being used is an accurate indicator of system effectiveness. Second, perceptions of several users of a system can be aggregated to arrive at an overall assessment of the system under study. Third, user satisfaction with a system can be accurately measured. It is this third assumption that has generated most of the literature regarding system effectiveness measurement using this approach.

5.4 Decision Performance

Ideally, we would like to get a measure of the incremental decision performance that has resulted as a consequence of using the system. As is obvious, the measurement problems associated with obtaining such data are enormous. The approach has been successfully used in the laboratory (King and Rodriguez, 1978) where it is possible to exercise significant control over one or more variables involved in a research study.

However, when one attempts to use this approach in the field, several problems arise. When one considers using an appropriate measure of decision performance, the most widely accepted measure is financial in nature. Using a financial measure also has the benefit of being easily available and accurately measurable. The problem is that the introduction of a new system could just be one of several existing and rapidly changing variables that impact financial performance.

If we consider non-financial measures of decision performance, such measures have to be obtained from sources other than the user. Here we begin to encounter many of the issues that have been raised in the context of user satisfaction.

6. THE IMPACT OF USER DIVERSITY

As pointed out in the previous section, several assumptions are made about system environments and usage modes in each of the assessment approaches. The appropriateness of these assumptions tends to make one approach more appropriate than another, depending on the environment under study. Perhaps the most crucial of these underlying assumptions pertains to the mode of usage applicable for the system(s). In this section, we argue that the relevance of assessment approaches is predicated on the predominant system usage mode. Along with an identification of the nature of the user are a number of auxilliary assumptions that make one assessment approach more or less suitable than another.

A *direct* mode of usage is characterized by users engaged in well-defined system interaction situations. These users are predominantly concerned with characteristics such as timely system response, and, if use of the system is not mandatory, will tend to use it frequently, if in fact its use provides some distinct advantage. A good example of such a usage mode is found in Robey's (1979) description of salesmen using an online system to access current product data. In such a situation, it is entirely appropriate to consider system use measures to assess the effectiveness of the system. Measures such as number of times a user logged in and the amount of connect time provide a good indication of whether the system is providing effective support for the user. Further, given the concern with timely system response, system performance measures would complement system use measures to provide a more comprehensive measure of system effectiveness. In the travelling salesmen example, one could conceivably use a measure such as the increased number of successful sales calls that a salesperson is able to make as a result of using the system.

However, if one considers the user satisfaction approach, in the direct mode of system usage, it is certainly a less objective measure than either of the two discussed above. It is possible that satisfaction is correlated with system usage because of the increase in potential benefits and associated user satisfaction to be derived from the use of the system. Decision performance is again an obtuse measure of effectiveness, considering that the decisions engaged in by these users are typically routine and do not involve extensive interpretation or analysis of the information received from the system. With this particular mode of usage, the more objective measures, namely system use and system performance, are accurate indicators of system effectiveness. In fact, if one persists in obtaining effectiveness measures using either the information satisfaction or the decision performance approaches,the opportunity of obtaining more reliable and easily measurable indicators of system effectiveness may be overlooked.

The *autonomous* mode of usage is essentially characterized by system building/application development using tools that are readily available and easily learned. As explained earlier, the emphasis in this mode of usage is on circumventing long delays involved in having IS departments in charge of the system development process for problems in which simple system solutions can be developed and implemented rapidly with the aid of hardware and software tools that are increasingly available. Given the limited extent of design and development skills possessed by users who operate in this mode, coupled with the capabilities of the tools that enable this kind of developmental activity, a large part of the system interaction is characterized by lack of efficiency concerns. The user is predominantly concerned with developing a system, albeit in preliminary form (for example, a prototype [Carey and Mason, 1983]), in a time-effective fashion. This may be followed up by a series of revision activities before arriving at the final form of the system.

Clearly, system use is an inappropriate indicator of effectiveness here, considering that a large part of the user activity might involve exploring and testing, especially in the initial learning stages. The results of such activity might never be embodied in a system. However, this process is extremely beneficial to the user in that it enables him/her to become familiar with the potential benefits of developing applications and/or systems in this mode. After a certain amount of learning has occurred on the part of the user, the extent of use of the system may actually reduce with no impact on how useful this mode of usage is to the users' operations. This suggests the need for a longitudinal assessment approach to cover the stages of learning that a user undergoes in this mode of usage. User-perceived measures of system effectiveness are perhaps most appropriate with this mode of usage. With the impact of learning that takes place over time due to continued use by the user, the ability of the user to adequately define problems and attempt solutions will directly contribute to the positive evaluation of the system by the user. Notice, however, that we are talking about the process aspects of the system environment (what is the user able to achieve by way of system design and development) that impact the perceptions of the user about the system. Perhaps what we need are new and more relevant dimensions that are different from those found in traditional instruments geared to the direct usage mode. Although the decision performance approach is relatively difficult to implement (as has been discussed earlier), at least conceptually, the approach makes sense for autonomous users. The real question here is how should the user's decision performance be evaluated? Perhaps the most appropriate approach in the field is to have the evaluation performed by the user's superiors or peers.

The *indirect* usage mode presents a situation that is unique in today's computing environment. On the one hand, this mode of usage implies that there is an intermediary who actually executes, requests or prepares reports on behalf of the user (Culnan, 1983; Welsch, 1980). This intermediary is typically not part of the IS department and, hence, his or her use does not involve all of the delays usually associated with dealing with an IS department. On the other hand, the nature of use of the system is very unstructured and often tends to be ad hoc. The emphasis for the user manager is more on the attributes of the information that is retrieved and the relevance of those attributes and reports on decision making.

While at first sight the more traditional measures of system use may be inappropriate to examine effectiveness, it may be possible to carefully choose relevant system use measures. Examples of these would be the number of reports generated through the intermediary, the number of ad hoc queries addressed to the system, and the intensity of the *intermediary's* use of the system. System performance measures appear to be totally inappropriate for this mode of usage where relevance of information is of central concern as opposed to efficiency features of the system itself.

ISA Approach / Mode of Usage	SYSTEM USE	SYSTEM PERFORMANCE	USER SATISFACTION	DECISION PERFORMANCE
DIRECT	Terminal connect time; number of inquiries, appropriate when system use is voluntary.	Primarily reduction in cost of operations	Variety of instruments available that identify multiple dimensions primarily applicable for this mode of usage.	Primarily employment in laboratory experiments. Very difficult to measure in organizational situations since the link between systems and specific decision is weak.
AUTONOMOUS	Needs to be viewed longitudinally. More appropriate once the user is adept in the use of relevant tools. Impractical to measure for stand-alone workstation use.	Cost-benefit analysis (post hoc) in which costs include training, time spent by users in learning the features of tools and benefits include time saving and other efficiency measures.	Entirely appropriate provided dimensions relevant for this mode such as quality of tools and support, degree of control over computing activities, and level of training are incorporated into measuring instruments.	Problematic. Measures of incremental performance on the job. Evaluation of decision performance attributable to system interaction by peers, superiors, etc.
INDIRECT	Number of reports generated. Number of ad hoc queries. Intensity of inter-mediaries' use.	Not particularly relevant. In cost-benefit analysis, benefits highly difficult to quantify.	Primarily pertaining to characteristics of information attributes and quality of reports (output oriented).	Difficult except for highly specific decision support-type systems used through intermediaries when some quantitative measure of decision quality can be obtained.

Table 2:   Possible Measures and Implications of Usage Modes for Different ISA Approaches

The perception of the system is really dependent on how the information has impacted the quality of decision making as perceived by the user. This in turn is a function of the attributes of the information that the system generates and the nature of the interaction between the user, the intermediary, and the system. User satisfaction with the system appears to be an appropriate approach to use; however, the specific dimensions of a measuring instrument should account for the issues raised above.

As is true with autonomous users, decision performance is a desirable approach but it is difficult to measure. If it is possible to obtain superior or peer evaluation of a user's decision performance, that may be a viable alternative to user satisfaction which is really a self appraisal. If the decision performance of a user is evaluated by some external party, it is imperative that the person have close knowledge of the nature of the user's interaction with the system and the resulting decision performance over an extended period of time. Although the feasibility of obtaining such a measure may be low, the value of such data should not be underemphasized.

The foregoing discussion is best captured in the form of a matrix, as shown in Table 2. The entries in the matrix highlight the issues that are important at the intersection of a particular usage mode and a particular approach to IS assessment.

7. CONCLUSIONS

In this paper we have attempted to establish the existence of diverse system usage modes in the context of rapidly changing information technologies. We proceed to make a strong case for assessing system effectiveness in a manner contingent on the modes of system usage. The major implications of the paper are that a multiplicity of measurement approaches need to be adopted within the same organizational unit and that they should be matched with the characteristics of users in terms of what they actually do and the systems they use. While some of the existing assessment procedures may be adequate in some situations, newer and more innovative approaches and measures may have to be devised in order to ensure that information system assessment taps into all relevant aspects of the phenomenon being assessed.

REFERENCES

Bariff, M. L., "Information Requirements Analysis: A Methodological Review," unpublished Working Paper WP-76-08-02, University of Pennsylvania, November 1978.

Bennett, J., "Integrating User and Decision Support Systems," in White, J. D. (ed.), *Proceedings of the Sixth and Seventh Annual Conferences of the Society for Management Information Systems*, University of Michigan, Ann Arbor, 1976, pp. 77-86.

Canning, R. G., "Programming by End Users," *EDP Analyzer*, Vol. 19, No. 6, May 1981, pp. 1-15.

Carey, T. T., and Mason, R. E. A., "Information System Prototyping: Techniques, Tools, and Methodologies," *INFOR*, Vol. 21, No. 3, 1983, pp. 177-191.

Carlson, E. D., Grace, B. F., and Sutton, J. A., "Case Studies of End User Requirements for Interactive Problem Solving Systems," *MIS Quarterly*, Vol. 1, No. 1, March 1977, pp. 51-63.

Cuff, R. N., "On Casual Users," *International Journal of Man-Machine Studies*, 12, 1980, pp. 163-187.

Culnan, M. J., "Chauffeured Versus End User Access to Commercial Databases: The Effects of Task and Individual Differences," *MIS Quarterly*, Vol. 7, No. 1, March 1983, pp. 55-67.

Date, C. J., *Introduction to Database Systems*, Second Edition, Addison Wesley, Reading, Massachusetts, 1977.

Doktor, R. H., and Hamilton, W. F., "Cognitive Styles and the Acceptance of Management Science," *Management Science*, Vol. 19, 1973, pp. 884-894.

Edström, A., "User Influence and the Success of MIS Projects: A Contingency Approach," *Human Relations*, Vol. 30, No. 7, 1977, pp. 589-607.

Ein-Dor, P., and Segev, E., "Organizational Context and the Success of Management Information Systems," *Management Science*, Vol. 24, No. 10, June 1978, pp. 1065-1077.

Ginzberg, M. J., "Finding an Adequate Measure of OR/MS Effectiveness," *Interfaces*, Vol. 8, No. 4, August 1978, pp. 59-62.

Hackathorn, R. D., "Research Issues in Personal Computing," *Proceedings of the National ACM Conference*, December 1978, pp. 547-551.

Hackathorn, R. D., and Keen, P. G. W., "Organizational Strategies for Personal Computing in Decision Support Systems," *MIS Quarterly*, Vol. 5, No. 3, September 1981, pp. 21-27.

Haney, F. M., "The Architecture of Software," *Data Base*, Vol. 5, No. 1, Fall 1973, pp. 5-10.

Huber, G. P., "Cognitive Styles as a Basis for MIS and DSS," *Management Science*, Vol. 29, No. 5, May 1983, pp. 567-579.

Ives, B., Olson, M. H., and Baroudi, J. J., "The Measurement of User Information Satisfaction," *Communciations of the ACM*, Vol. 26, No. 10, October 1983, pp. 785-793.

Johnson, R. T., "The Infocenter Experience," *Datamation*, January 1984, pp. 137-142.

Keen, P. G. W., "Value Analysis: Justifying Decision Support Systems," *MIS Quarterly*, Vol. 5, No. 1, March 1981, pp. 1-15.

Keen, P. G. W., and Scott Morton, M. S., *Decision Support Systems: An Organizational Perspective*, Addison Wesley, Reading, Massachusetts, 1978.

King, J. L., and Schrems, E. L., "Cost-Benefit Analysis in IS Development and Operation," *Computing Surveys*, Vol. 10, No. 1, March 1978, pp. 19-34.

King, W. R., and Rodriguez, J. I., "Evaluating Management Informa-
     tion Systems," *MIS Quarterly*, Vol. 2, No. 3, September 1978,
     pp. 43-51.

Langefors, B., "Theoretical Analysis of Information Systems,"
     Studentlitteratur, Lund, Sweden, 1966.

Lucas, H. C., "Performance and Use of a Management Information
     System," *Management Science*, Vol. 23, No. 4, April 1975, pp.
     908-919.

Lucas, H. C., *The Implementing of Computer Based Models*, National
     Association of Accountants, New York, 1976.

Lucas, H. C., and Moore, J. R., "A Multiple Criterion Scoring
     Approach to Information Systems Project Selection," *INFOR*,
     Vol. 14, No. 1, February 1976, pp. 1-12.

Martin, J., *Application Development Without Programmers*, Prentice-
     Hall, Englewood Cliffs, New Jersey, 1982.

Mason, R. O., and Mitroff, I. I., "A Program for Research on
     Mangaement Information Systems," *Management Science*, Vol. 19,
     No. 5, January 1973, pp. 475-487.

McKenney, J. L., and Keen, P. G. W., "How Managers' Minds Work,"
     Harvard Business Review, Vol. 52, No. 3, May-June 1974, pp.
     79-90.

McLean, E. R., "End Users as Application Developments," *MIS
     Quarterly*, Vol. 3, No. 4, December 1979, pp. 34-46.

Mumford, E., Bancroft, N., and Sontag, B., "Participative Design:
     Successes and Problems," *Systems, Objectives, Solutions*, 3,
     1983, pp. 133-141.

Olson, M. H., and Ives, B., "User Involvement in System Design:
     An Empirical Test of Alternative Approaches," *Information and
     Management*, Vol. 4, No. 4, 1981, pp. 183-196.

Pearson, S. W., *Measurement of Computer User Satisfaction*,
     unpublished Doctoral Dissertation, Arizona State University,
     1977.

Rivard, S., and Huff, S. L., "User Developed Applications:
     Evaluation of Success from the DP Department Perspective,"
     MIS Quarterly, Vol. 8, No. 1, March 1984, pp. 39-49.

Robey, D., "User Attitudes and MIS Use," *Academy of Management
     Journal*, Vol. 22, No. 3, September 1979, pp. 527-538.

Rockart, J. F., and Flannery, L. S., "The Management of End User
     Computing," *Communications of the ACM*, Vol. 26, No. 10,
     October 1983, pp. 776-784.

Schroeder, H., "Conceptual Complexity and Personality Organiza-
     tion," in Schroeder, H., and Seudfeld, P. (eds.), *Personality
     Theory and Information Processing*, 1971, pp. 240-273.

Schultz, R. L., and Slevin, D. P. (eds.), *Implementing Operations
     Research/Management Science*, American Elsevier Publishing
     Company, New York, 1975.

Taylor, R. N., and Benbasat, I., "Cognitive Styles Research and Managerial Information Use: Problems and Prospects," paper presented at the Joint National Meeting of TIMS/ORSA, Colorado Springs, Colorado, 1980.

Van Maanen, J., "Reclaiming Qualitative Methods for Organizational Research: A Preface," *Administrative Science Quarterly*, Vol. 24, No. 4, December 1979, pp. 520-526.

Witkin, H. A., "Origins of Cognitive Style," in Scheere (ed.), *Cognition: Theory, Research, Promise*, Harper and Row, New York, 1964, pp. 172-205.

Zmud, R. W., "Individual Differences and MIS Success: A Review of the Empirical Literature," *Management Science*, Vol. 25, No. 10, October 1979, pp. 966-997.

DISCUSSANT NOTE

On: INCORPORATING USER DIVERSITY INTO INFORMATION
    SYSTEMS ASSESSMENT

By: Joseph G. Davis and Ananth Srinivasan

Discussant's comments by: Philip SELIGMANN

The Hague Business School
The Netherlands

1. INTRODUCTION

In its introduction, the paper touches, in a summary way, on some
implicit assumptions in the traditional Systems Development Life
Cycle (SDLC), the user-designer dichotomy, and the view of users
as a homogeneous group. After discussion of the literature on the
last subject, the authors propose a classification scheme of three
usage *modes* and present a short case. Finally, they look at MIS
assessment approaches and the possible consequences of their
findings on usage modes. The work presented in this paper is part
of a more extensive research project.

2. CRITIQUE

I find the questioning of more or less implicit assumptions in
(M)IS literature an important subject; it is important to support
this by empirical work. My critical questions are directed at
unclear points of argumentation, presentation, or domain of
validity of the conclusion.

It is not clear whether the study is restricted to MIS or more
general IS -- the words are seemingly used as synonyms (I hold it
on MIS).

The discussion on the user in the literature remains somewhat
inconclusive and the interesting switch from *user* to *usage* modes
comes somewhat suddenly. Further (perhaps as a result of the
foregoing), the meaning of the usage modes remains unclear. I do
not ask for sharper definitions (which possibly would require an
IS and application taxonomy) but a clarification (perhaps by
description). In the present context, it would be a question of
whether the mailing address of an IS report (the manager himself
or his secretary) would make the manager a direct or indirect
user.

The case gives some interesting exploratory data, especially on
the conjectured phenomenon of "main usage mode," but more data are
needed on this as well as possible contingency factors.

3. ASSUMPTIONS

In their considerations on MIS assessment approaches, the authors take the assessment goals and criteria too much for granted with the real risk of pooling incommensurable data.

4. CONCLUSION

Although it formally falls outside the scope of the paper, an interesting question is "to what extent are the four assessment approaches correlated?" I could imagine that specifically there would be notable correlations between the system usage, user appreciation, and decision performance approaches. Empirical research on this would be interesting and could have an impact on the conclusion of the paper.

A Multivalent Approach to Information System Assessment
J. Hawgood and F. Land

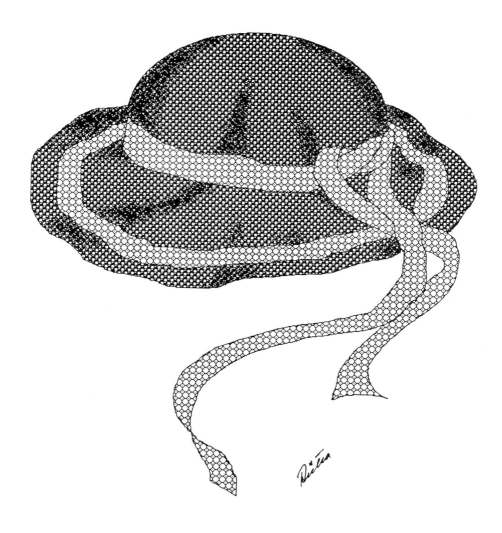

"Remember that the same person may be a manager,
an employee, a customer and an owner: his assessment
of the systems and subsystems will change as he
changes hats."

INFORMATION SYSTEMS ASSESSMENT
N. Bjørn-Andersen, G.B. Davis (Editors)
Elsevier Science Publishers B.V. (North-Holland)
© IFIP, 1988

A MULTIVALENT APPROACH TO INFORMATION SYSTEM ASSESSMENT

John HAWGOOD

PA Computers and Telecommunications
Rochester House
33 Greycoat Street
London SW1P 2QF   England

Frank LAND

London Business School
Sussex Place
Regent's Park
London NW1 4SA   England

This paper defines an approach to information system assessment based on careful distinction between systems in the business value chain and those with support functions. For both types, the approach starts by defining system effectiveness separately for each main stakeholder group, in terms of their different goals and the different factors they consider important. For an IS in the value chain, the primary assessment is from the viewpoint of the business as a whole, whereas for the support function it is from the viewpoint of the departmental manager directly responsible for the IS. Both should make their assessments in the light of information about the secondary assessments by the other significant stakeholders.

1.   INTRODUCTION

We normally use the phrase "information system" to denote a part of the organization with an information function. Such an IS can be regarded as a human activity system (Checkland, 1981; Wilson, 1984), comprising people, organizational procedures and physical subsystems all working together to provide and/or improve information for the system's clients.

However, many people use "information system" just for the mechanical subsystem of computers, peripherals and communications which acquires input, processes and stores the information, presents it to the client and/or passes it to another system.

Information systems assessment takes place from a number of different viewpoints. Each viewpoint can legitimately define the boundaries within which the object of assessment lies. Thus the focus of attention for the DP department treated as a business in its own right is very different from that of the chief executive attempting to assess the change of effectiveness of marketing management after the introduction of a marketing decision support system. A framework for IS assessment should be capable of catering for a wide range of assessment viewpoints.

It is clear both from practice and from the study of the relevant literature (see Hirschheim and Smithson, this volume) that information system assessment -- the evaluation of the effectiveness of an IS -- raises many problems. Underlying these are three fundamental difficulties:

1. Effectiveness is itself difficult to measure because it is a subjective concept, seen differently by different people.

2. The phrase "information system" covers a wide range of different systems designed to serve very different needs, and hence achieving very different goals.

3. An IS should be evaluated by comparing the effectiveness of operations with and without its aid; no such comparison is possible in real life.

In this paper, we analyze different types and views of assessment and go on to examine the first two of these difficulties and suggest an approach which may help to provide a framework for IS assessment.

2. TYPES AND VIEWS OF ASSESSMENT

In their paper, Hirschheim and Smithson point out that we have to distinguish between formal assessment procedures, which may or may not be part of the apparatus of management in an organization, and informal assessment which always takes place, and which plays an important role in determining the response of individuals or groups to changes in systems. Informal assessment is often tacit, subjective, and frequently based on incomplete or wrong information. As such, it is not subject to verification. Nevertheless it plays a crucial role in determining behavior. Formal assessment, on the other hand, is at least in principle capable of checking by third parties. Any formal assessment procedure must be capable of incorporating, articulating, and validating the informal assessments which always take place.

Formal assessment is a valid process only if it is carried out for a specified purpose leading to specific actions or decisions. The process of assessment must be capable of adding value by permitting more "profitable" actions to take place or by improving the quality of decisions.

Typical assessment functions can be described as follows:

o   *The assessment is part of a control system* and takes the form of a feedback mechanism. Control systems can exist at all levels in the organization. The papers by Davis and Hamann (this volume) and by Dickson, et al. (this volume) are concerned with controlling the overall performance of an organization's DP function. The purpose of the assessment is to find weaknesses in the existing organization, and to propose measures which will improve performance.

o   At another level, the purpose of the assessment is to measure the progress of an MIS development project so that requisite

action can be taken if the assessment suggests that the
project is in trouble.

o At yet another level, the assessment may concern itself with
   the performance of an individual -- perhaps a programmer in
   the project team -- in order to determine additional training
   the programmer may need or whether the programmer is worthy
   of promotion.

o *The assessment is a necessary part of a planning process.*
   All planning activities include forms of formal assessment.
   They may range from such questions as "what will the enterprise be like in five years?" or "do we have the skills
   available to make the proposed changes?" to assessments of
   the form of "what risks are attached to the proposed
   changes?"

o *The assessment is part of a diagnostic process* aimed at
   identifying the reasons why there has been a loss of performance, why worker morale has fallen, or why customers are
   deserting the organization and buying from a competitor.

o This kind of diagnosis can take place at all levels within
   the enterprise. It may be concerned with an evaluation, on
   behalf of the chief executive, of the reasons for the
   apparent unpopularity of the DP department or with the
   identification of reasons for an unexpected fall in accuracy
   by data entry staff carried out on behalf of the computer
   operations manager.

o Whereas the control type of assessment is mainly concerned
   with the measurement or assessment of past activities--
   requiring the establishment of operation measurement systems
   based on some kind of feedback by means of reports or
   instrumentation -- the kind of assessment needed for planning
   tends to be predictive and may be based on formal methods,
   such as statistical forecasting, or less algorithmic methods,
   such as brainstorming or Delphi techniques. Diagnostic
   assessment, on the other hand, is often not based on an
   established feedback system providing assessment information,
   but relies on the introduction of ad hoc measurement methods
   by the diagnostician at the time the need for assessment is
   realized. These may be qualitative and based on judgment--
   the measurement of job satisfaction, for example -- or
   quantitative and precise -- the measurement of response time
   in a real-time quotation system by an insurance company, for
   example.

o *The purpose of assessment is to reduce uncertainty.* Uncertainty inhibits action. A reduction of uncertainty can
   stimulate action. The introduction of formal prediction
   methods may reduce the uncertainty of the planner. The
   introduction of a formal control system helps in the assessment of the impact of past events and enables follow up
   action to be taken with confidence. The purpose of this kind
   of assessment is often to give reassurance and confidence
   that planned action is likely to have predictable and
   positive outcomes.

The above list is not intended to be a comprehensive list of
assessment functions, but merely to illustrate that assessment is

concerned with a wide range of different functions and that each function may require specific assessment tools.

In the Information Systems field, assessment normally has six major functions:

1. *To establish the feasibility of a new project.* The emphasis in feasibility studies will be on methods which are diagnostic and predictive. They must be capable of assessing economic feasibility, technical feasibility, organizational feasibility and social feasibility.

2. *To provide input to the enterprise's investment decision process.* Most organizations have a standard method for evaluating projects involving substantial capital resources. These methods are normally based on some form of assessment of return on capital investment. In principle, all information systems projects requiring substantial capital investments should be judged by whatever formal method is used by the enterprise in competition with any other project requiring capital investment. The assessment methods to provide the input for the investment decision process tend to emphasize tangible financial costs and benefits of a kind compatible with the existing accounting system of the enterprise. Unfortunately, these methods may be incapable of making due allowance for costs and benefits which do not fit the accounting model. And in information systems assessment, non-tangible probabilistic benefits are frequently those which could make the most contribution to the future operation of the enterprise.

3. *To review the progress of an information system development project* in order to ensure that the project is executed in an efficient manner, both with respect to time and cost. Project control involves, in the first instance, an assessment of the resources required and the preparation of a project plan and, secondly, the assessment of progress (and estimate of work still to be done) on the project compared to the project plan. The emphasis in project control is on the use of techniques such as critical path planning and cost control.

4. *To review the achievements of the project during its operational life.* The achievements should be compared to those originally envisaged in the feasibility study (modified by subsequent changes in plan) and consider economic, technical, organizational, and social factors. However, there are no formal assessment methods which can relate observed effects to prime causes with any degree of certainty. An organization exists in a complex changing world. The planned changes in information systems are only one of a range of changes, planned and unplanned, which will have an impact on the organization. The main emphasis in post-implementation assessments is on establishing cause and effect relationships.

5. *To assess the proportion of total IS costs which any application incurs* in order to levy a charge on the user of the IS service. The problem of providing an equitable costing system is that of allocating the typically high proportion of fixed and joint costs. The emphasis in assessment is on cost

accounting methods which satisfy both the provider of the service and its users.

6. *To assess the value added by the IS function* as a service providing department. Because the value added is a consequence not only of the way the service is delivered but also of the skill with which it is used, assessment of the IS department has tended to be couched in technical terms and with a strong emphasis on efficiency rather than effectiveness criteria.

3. DIFFICULTY 1: SUBJECTIVITY

> Effectiveness is itself difficult to measure because it is a subjective concept, seen differently by different people.

The extent to which any system can be effective is at least in part determined by the attitude towards that system of those who are, in one way or another, affected by it. However, different groups and different individuals may have widely varying expectations of what the system is expected to deliver. Negative attitudes to the system arising from a failure of the system to deliver what is required of it can lead to the total rejection of the system or a low level of performance.

The assessment problem can be illustrated by examining the sort of qualities which each of a number of stakeholder groups might be expected to demand of an IS. Some of these can be expressed in terms of qualities which can be improved, others in terms of existing qualities which should be preserved.

The system's sponsors or owners are often senior management on whose behalf the system is created and who set out the main mission for the system. The kind of qualities they demand from the system include:

o   The system should give the organization a competitive advantage -- perhaps through better customer service, better products, lower, more stable prices, or more wide ranging and more varied products or customer services.

o   The system should enable the organization to respond more quickly and more predictably either to changes in its environment or to internal changes.

o   The system should be flexible and capable of rapid adjustment.

o   The system should enable the sponsor to have some control over the performance of the system's users and operators, and should enable him to evaluate the users' and operators' performance.

The sponsors are likely to regard the IS as a human activity system, including people as well as computers and other devices.

The system's users may be located anywhere in the organization's structure, but are often found in the ranks of middle management. The user may use the system actively, perhaps by interacting via a keyboard, or passively, perhaps via printed reports put on his desk. A system's user may also be the system's sponsor as when a system is created for the use of senior (board-room) executives. The kind of qualities users seek to obtain from an IS include:

o   The system should meet the user's personal objectives. These objectives might include enhancement of the user's career prospects, or power and standing in the organization. At the same time, the system should not reduce the user's autonomy or range of discretion.

o   The system should assist the user in achieving departmental objectives. The user may perceive organizational objectives (the sponsor's objectives) in terms of achieving local objectives.

o   The system should not permit the sponsor to obtain information about the user's performance without the information first being seen by the affected user.

o   The system should be easy to learn, easy to use, reliable, accurate, and flexible. The system should not be so complex that it defeats the learning process or leaves the user with uncertainty as to what is happening.

o   The system should remain usable and friendly under unexpected or adverse conditions.

o   The system should enable the user to exercise some control over the system's operators and enable him to assess the operators' performance.

The users probably tend to think of the IS purely in terms of its mechanical parts.

The system's operator is responsible for operating the system. Operational tasks range from data preparation and data entry tasks to the operation of computer controlled machine tools or the stock taking task in a supermarket using a hand-held data recording device. The system's operator may be also be the system's user or even the system's sponsor. The qualities the operator expects the system to deliver include:

o   The system should enhance rather than reduce the "quality" of working life. This may be taken to include such factors as health risks, stress, job enhancement and enrichment, the amount of discretion left to the operator, the use of special skills, the esteem in which the operator is held, and remuneration and career prospects.

o   The system should not be used for reducing the work force.

o   The system should be easy to learn and to operate and should be understandable by its operators.

The operators also tend to concentrate on the computer-based subsystem when thinking about the IS, though they themselves are components of the IS when it is seen as a human activity system.

The system's builder may be the professional IT expert responsible for the analysis, design, construction and implementation of the system. Builders include programmers, systems analysts, database administrators and their managers. On the other hand, the system's users may have designed and built their own system. The qualities they may demand from the system include:

o   The system should be designed as a state-of-the-art system using the most up-to-date technology. Its design should be technically advanced and technically elegant.

o   The system should gain the esteem of its builder's professional peers.

o   The system should be appreciated by the users and gain its designers and builders the esteem of the management of the organization in which they are working.

o   The system should help to gain its builders more power in the organization in which they are working.

The builder may well, but should not, see the IS purely in mechanical terms.

Stakeholders outside the organization are those whc may benefit or be affected by the introduction of a new system. They may be the target of the IS design, as in a bank's automatic teller system. They include customers, clients, suppliers, benefit claimants, hospital patients, and many others. The qualities they expect from the introduction of a system which affects them include:

o   The system should deliver an improved service. This may be expressed in the form of better quality products, speedier service, more reliable service, more accurate service, a cheaper product or service, a more personalized service, or a simpler to use, more easily learned service.

o   The system should provide a wider range of facilities, products and services.

Outside stakeholders will usually not differentiate between the human activity IS and the computer-based subsystem.

To each stakeholder group, the qualities which are perceived as important have a vital role in determining how the members of the stakeholder group respond to the introduction of the new IS. The effectiveness of the system is crucially dependent on that response. Some of the assessments of quality may be objective and capable of measurement. For example, the sponsor's requirement for improvement in quality of service, in the situation where the relevant factor is time taken between a customer's order being received and the delivery being made, can be objectively assessed and actually measured. However, the impact of the improved service, depending as it does on customer and competitor responses, is much more difficult to assess with any precision. Other assessments are subjective and their measurement must be based on judgment, perhaps expressed through numerical scales. For example, the user's requirement in terms of personal objectives such as improved career prospects is based on a subjective assessment and is not capable of objective measurement.

4.   DIFFICULTY 2:   VARIETY

The phrase "information system" covers a wide range of different systems designed to serve very

different needs, and hence achieving very different
goals.

There are two dimensions of variety to be considered -- in the
nature of the systems to be discussed and in their place in the
organization.   The first has been mentioned already -- "information systems" may be taken to be either human activity systems or
mechanical systems.

The other dimension of variety is concerned with the place of the
IS in the business or organization it serves: is it part of the
primary value chain of the business, or is it in a support
function not forming part of the value chain? The assessment will
have a different emphasis according to the answer.

Figures 1, 2, and 3 show system structures for three different
types of business (manufacturing, personal service, and information service), and the places that information systems might
occupy in them.   Before describing the diagrams, we need to
distinguish between several types of system and subsystem involved:

o *A human activity system* is part of an organization with an
   identifiable purpose; it usually includes all three types of
   subsystem distinguished below.

o *A personal subsystem* essentially consists of people performing activities not within the competence of machines; it
   may include some mechanical devices as sub-subsystems, also
   people performing routine activities.

o *A physical subsystem* mainly consists of machines, buildings,
   cables, etc.; it may include the machines' operators and
   other people in personal sub-subsystems.

o *An information subsystem* is mainly devoted to providing
   and/or improving information; it may have both personal and
   physical sub-sub-systems.

These will be distinguished symbolically as rectangles, circles,
triangles, and hexagons, respectively, in three diagrams which
show a very crude system structure analysis for three types of
business:

o *A manufacturing business* (Figure 1) has as its primary functional subsystem the value chain receiving raw materials or
   components from the suppliers, performing physical operations
   successively increasing the product value as the links in the
   chain are traversed, and finally delivering end products to
   the customers. The manager of this primary subsystem will
   have some direct supporting activities under his/her own
   control but not themselves forming part of the value chain.
   These might include information subsystems for production
   scheduling and inventory control, and personal subsystems for
   supervision, progress chasing, quality control, etc.   The
   value chain itself might include information sub-subsystems
   which control robots or other machines. Support subsystems
   of the business, not controlled by the manager of the primary
   subsystem, might include accounting, welfare, building
   maintenance, legal, data processing, and marketing departments.

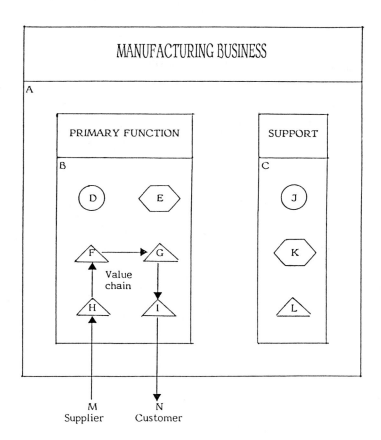

M
Supplier

N
Customer

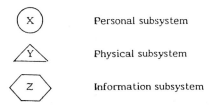

Personal subsystem

Physical subsystem

Information subsystem

Figure 1: Business System Structure Diagram

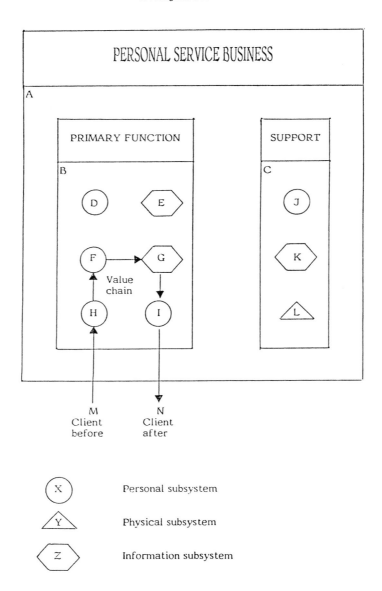

Figure 2: Business System Structure Diagram

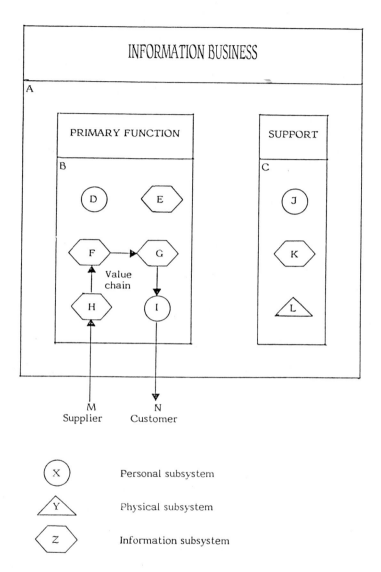

Figure 3: Business System Structure Diagram

o   *A personal service business* (Figure 2), such as a hospital,
    has a primary subsystem mainly comprising personal subsys-
    tems.   The "value added" is represented by improvements in
    the patients' health.   Probably the information subsystem
    used by the doctors to process and present results of
    pathological tests should be regarded as part of the value
    chain, whereas the medical record system would be outside the
    value chain itself but within the primary subsystem.   The
    support functions would be similar to those in a manufac-
    turing business.

o   *An information business* (Figure 3), such as a bank or travel
    agency, would have a value chain mainly composed of informa-
    tion subsystems, probably with a personal subsystem dealing
    with the client.   Again support functions would be similar to
    those in manufacturing or personal service businesses.

As outlined in the previous section, assessment of information
systems will vary according to the point of view of the assessor.
In the next section, we compare the attitudes towards assessment
likely to be held by people at different points in the diagrams
(indicated by letters A to N).

5.   ASSESSMENT FROM DIFFERENT VIEWPOINTS

We will deal first with assessments by top management (A) and
primary subsystem management (B), then by other managers, employees, and outsiders (owners, suppliers, customers, clients).
Remember that the same person may be a manager, an employee, a
customer and an owner: his assessment of the systems and subsystems will change as he changes hats.

o   *The assessment by A and B* of an information subsystem
    actually in the value chain (G in Figure 2; F, G, and H in
    Figure 3) should be on exactly the same basis as for any
    other subsystem in the value chain: namely, according to the
    net value added to the product by that link in the chain.
    Note, however, that A and B may have different ideas about
    what "value" actually means: A is likely to take more
    account of owners' or other stakeholders' opinions when
    forming his/her value estimates.

o   The assessment by A and B of any subsystem within the primary
    subsystem, but not actually forming a link in the value chain
    (D and E), is less direct but will still be according to its
    contribution to the total value added in the chain, as they
    see it, and the cost of the subsystem being assessed.

o   A and B may be expected to assess the subsystems so far men-
    tioned in similar ways, because they are both responsible, at
    different levels, for the primary function of the business.
    However, when we consider the support subsystem managed by C,
    containing subsystems J, K, and L, we may expect different
    attitudes from A and B because A is responsible for C's acti-
    vities, but B is not.   B should not care at all about how C
    provides support, but only about the value to the primary
    subsystem of the total support provided (he will not need to
    know that J, K, and L exist).   B will tend to suspect that C
    (an overhead) is draining the business of the resources
    provided by and for the primary value chain, and will look
    critically at the total cost of the support system.   On the

other hand, A will be concerned with proposed changes to subsystems for which C is responsible, but not with their routine operation when things are going well. Thus, A will wish to be able to assess such subsystems with regard to the contribution they make to the business as a whole, in comparison to the likely contribution of changed subsystems.

o *Assessment by support subsystem managers* (C, D, E, J, K, L) of the effectiveness of their own systems will be in terms of critical success or failure factors and performance measures defined in terms of each system separately, in consultation with direct bosses. They will each see the systems for which they are responsible as businesses, with value chains of their own. For example, manager K will consult with manager C about assessment of subsystem K. That does not necessarily mean that C and K will assess K identically, because C will be consulting with A about his assessments. These managers will tend to assess each other's systems, or those in the main value chain, only in terms of impact on their own systems.

o *Assessment by value-chain managers* (F, G, H, I) of their own systems will tend to be in terms of the value added to the main product, but they will assess each others' systems or the support systems in terms of impact on their own systems.

o *Assessment by employees* at any position in the organization will be in terms of their own concerns for job satisfaction, security of employment, remuneration and status. They will probably assess the business as a whole in terms of job security and status in the community, and the departments in which they work in terms of personal remuneration and job satisfaction. Other departments will only be assessed in terms of interaction with their own.

o *Assessment by suppliers and customers* (M and N in Figures 1 and 3) will concentrate entirely on their interactions with the business, so that M will tend to see only H, while N will see only I. They will not know or care about the other systems behind the scenes, judging the whole system A by the part they see.

o *Assessment by clients* (M and N in Figure 2) will again be confined to the subsystems they see, but here they may see more. In the hospital, for example, since the patient is also the product, "value added" must ultimately be judged by everyone else in terms of its perception by the client.

o *Owners of the business* will assess it in terms of its overall performance according to their own concerns, not necessarily solely financial. Though looking at the same system as the top manager A, they will see it differently.

6. A FRAMEWORK FOR ASSESSMENT

We propose a dual approach to information system assessment:

o *Information systems in the main value chain* should be assessed, like all links in the value chain, in terms of their contribution to the product's net value. The viewpoint taken as dominant should be that of the top manager (A in the

diagrams). However, this emphatically does not mean that
other viewpoints should be neglected, because A should take
into account all the other stakeholders' assessments when
forming his/her own estimates of the value added. The
concept of effectiveness, that is to say, is itself to be
seen as "multivalent" -- containing all the attributes felt
to be important by all the interest groups. The weighting to
be put on each group's opinion, though, should be decided by
the top manager, A.

o *Information systems not in the main value chain* should be
   assessed as businesses in their own right, primarily by the
   manager directly responsible for the IS being assessed (such
   as K in the diagrams). As above, this primary assessment
   should take into account the secondary assessments by all the
   other stakeholders thought to be significant by the person
   making the primary assessment, weighted by the primary
   assessor.

The resulting assessment process for the analyst is the same: he
or she is to produce assessments from every relevant point of
view, separately. For the value-chain systems, the top manager
should take all these into account in forming his own judgment of
the value of each system or subsystem. For non-value chain
systems, the manager of the IS being assessed performs the same
function.

We must distinguish between pre-assessment of a possible future
change and post-assessment of an actual past change:

o *An information system is pre-assessed* by comparing the
   expected effectiveness of a proposed policy with that of a
   reference policy, where the two policies differ only in
   respect of the IS. The reference policy is (normally) to
   continue using the existing IS; the proposed policy is
   hypothetical.

o *An information system is post-assessed* by comparing the
   actual effectiveness of a policy that has already been
   adopted with that of a reference policy, where the two
   policies differ only in respect of the IS. The reference
   situation in this case is hypothetical -- we have to estimate
   what might have been the result of continuing the previous
   policy, now abandoned.

Even when the only policy change proposed or adopted is a change
of IS (which is unusual), the pre-assessment and post-assessments
are not strictly comparable. The former compares a possible
future using the proposed IS (call it "A") with a possible future
continuing the existing IS (call it "O"), whereas the latter
compares an actual present with IS "A" against what it might have
been had IS "O" been continued, other things being equal. More
often, other things are not equal and we have to compare policies
which differ in respect of more than the IS. Strictly, such a
comparison should not be called an IS assessment.

The effectiveness of a policy can be presented as a vector in S-
dimensional space, where S is the number of significant stakeholder groups being considered (so S itself is a subjective
quantity). Each component of the effectiveness vector is the
subjective relative utility of the policy as seen by one stakeholder group, when compared with the reference policy. The

relative subjective utility of two policies is estimated by a stakeholder by comparing the desirability to him/her of their complete set of attributes.

The subjective relative utility for each stakeholder group depends on all the factors or attributes that group uses to measure or describe the achievement of the different goals which are important to its members. These goals can often be represented as the leaves of a semantic goal tree. The method we propose for obtaining the measures is due to Efstathiou, et al. (1985); their method is applicable also to more general networks -- it does not depend on the applicability of a simple tree structure. They suggest that each "significant" stakeholder should specify all attributes of the policy or system being considered which are important to him/her as the nodes or extremities of a semantic network. A simple example for a word-processing system is shown as Figure 4. Each attribute must be provided, by the stakeholder, with a reference scale with which to measure the attainment of his/her goal in relation to that attribute. The scale may be verbal or numerical, whichever feels more natural to that stakeholder.

The effectiveness of a policy (as seen by that particular stakeholder) is the relative utility to him/her of the combination of attribute measures which represent the policy in question, and that combination which represents the reference policy. The estimation is done in two ways -- by precalibration before particular policies are defined, and by recalibration after they are defined. Stakeholders' preliminary calibrations tend to change when concrete examples are given, and when they know about other stakeholders' assessments.

Figure 5 gives two-dimensional effectiveness vectors for the word-processing examples for three different proposed policies, A, B, and C, compared with the reference no-change policy O. It is immediately obvious that only Policy B is desirable both for owners and for workers: A and C would each be worse than the reference policy for one group or the other.

7.   THE STEPS IN AN INFORMATION SYSTEM ASSESSMENT

To summarize, we recommend the following steps:

1.   Define policy to be assessed and a reference policy differing only in respect of the information system.

2.   For each significant stakeholder group, obtain the utility calibration by identifying their most important objectives and finding ways of measuring how far these have been (or would be) achieved in terms of the attributes. Every combination of attributes of any IS policy then corresponds to a value of relative utility as seen by each stakeholder group.

3.   Define future scenario (in pre-assessment case) or likely past scenario if the old IS had been continued (in post-assessment case).

4.   Determine the relative utilities of the two policies for each stakeholder group by estimating all the attribute measures corresponding to the policies, hence obtaining preliminary

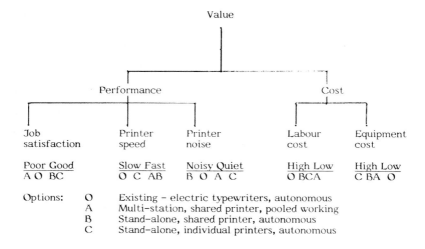

Options: O   Existing – electric typewriters, autonomous
            A   Multi-station, shared printer, pooled working
            B   Stand–alone, shared printer, autonomous
            C   Stand–alone, individual printers, autonomous

Figure 4: Semantic Goal Tree for Choice of WP System

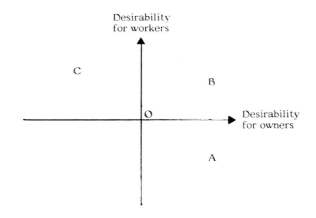

Figure 5: Effectiveness Vectors for Choice of WP System

estimates of the components of the effectiveness vector. This process requires conceptual modelling or even computer simulation of the part of the organization (the human activity system) which might be, or has been, changed.

5. Validate/recalibrate by describing/demonstrating the changed IS to stakeholders, and by informing them of each others' opinions.

6. If the IS is in the main value chain, assess primarily from the "chief executive" viewpoint, and secondarily from the other viewpoints. The chief executive must know the secondary viewpoints before making his primary assessment.

   If the IS is not in the main value chain, assess primarily from the viewpoint of the manager of the information system being assessed (treating it as a small business in its own right), secondarily from other viewpoints. Again the manager doing the primary assessment should be informed about the secondary assessments.

8. CONCLUSIONS

We have suggested ways of coping with two of the three difficulties mentioned at the beginning of the paper, by treating information system effectiveness as a multi-valued function of IS attributes and stakeholder viewpoints, and by taking careful note of the position of the information system in the organization's system structure with relation to the main value chain leading from "raw materials' to "final products." We have not made any suggestion about the third difficulty -- the lack of control comparisons. The only way of surmounting this difficulty, it seems to us, is to develop really good business simulations which can be run with and without proposed changes to information systems.

ACKNOWLEDGEMENT

We would like to thank Dr. Agneta Olerup for her useful comments at the Information Systems Assessment Conference, most of which have been used in improving the paper for publication in these *Proceedings*.

REFERENCES

Checkland, P., *Systems Thinking, Systems Practice*, Wiley, New York, 1981.

Davis, G. B., and Hamann, J. R., "In-Context Information Systems Assessment: A Proposal and an Evaluation," this volume.

Dickson, G. W., Wells, C. E., and Wilkes, R. B., "Toward a Derived Set of Measures for Assessing IS Organizations," this volume.

Efstathiou, J., Rajkovic, V., and Bohanec, M., "Expert Systems and Rule Based Decision Support Systems," in Mitra, G. (ed), *Computer Assisted Decision Making*, North Holland, Amsterdam, 1985.

Hirschheim, R., and Smithson, S., "A Critical Analysis of Information Systems Evaluation," this volume.

Wilson, B., *Systems Concepts, Methodologies, and Applications, Wiley,* New York, 1984.

DISCUSSANT NOTE

On: A MULTIVALENT APPROACH TO INFORMATION SYSTEM
      ASSESSMENT

By: John Hawgood and Frank Land

Discussant's comments by: Agneta OLERUP

Department of Information
  and Computer Sciences
University of Lund
Lund, Sweden

1.   INTRODUCTION

In this discussant note, I shall first mention several brief
points before elaborating on two issues which were not adequately
covered at the conference.

2.   COMMENTS

Hawgood and Land attempt to develop an approach for assessing
information systems taking into account goals and qualities sought
by different individuals. The paper suggests several stakeholders. However, unions are not found in the list in spite of
the fact that they are important stakeholders who will seek goals
and qualities different from those sought by users and operators.
Furthermore, the major problem with a stakeholder approach is that
it ignores power and influence, including who takes the initia-
tive. This is important with regard to the goals and qualities
sought and finally achieved by each stakeholder.

The paper introduces a distinction between information systems as
human activity systems and as mechanical systems, which could have
been used with benefit when discussing stakeholders as well as
when discussing the variety of information systems.

Effectiveness and efficiency are mentioned as subjective components, but they are also relative because an effective decision at
one level of a system or an organization will be an efficient
decision at some higher level. Thus, applying the notions of
effectiveness and efficiency depends on both the context and the
actual groups involved (cf. Moore and Chang, 1983). The relationships between the two concepts are even more complex when actions
and decisions are distinguished (Brunsson, 1982).

It is also stated that the goals form the leaves of a semantic
tree, when the method used in order to obtain the goal-measures is
based on fuzzy logic. A tree is a very special kind of di-graph
(i.e., a directed graph using arrows to show connections between
nodes or elements). In a more realistic case, the goals will form
a proper di-graph. Which adjustments would then be necessary?

3. QUALITIES OF INFORMATION SYSTEMS AND
    SEMI-AUTONOMOUS GROUPS

An approach for assessing information systems needs a theory or
model of *how* to assess. Equally important is a theory or model of
the object to be assessed (for example, a measuring theory). In
particular, it is necessary to clarify the characteristics of
information systems in order to satisfy the goals or qualities
sought by different stakeholders. This requires a model of the
organization of work and the context of work to be supported by an
information system.

There is considerable unanimity that the design of work needs to
meet certain qualities of work (such as variety, possibilities for
planning and deciding, support for learning) when new information
technology is introduced. Such qualities of work can be realized
in several ways, for example through job enrichment or semi-
autonomous groups.

Traditional approaches for designing computerized information
systems are directed towards information systems where requirements can be clearly and unambiguously specified before any
detailed design. It is presumed that a selection of information
requirements can be made in advance and, further, that the
selection will remain valid and unchanged for some period of time.
A fundamental assumption is, therefore, that it is possible to
describe the real world objectively in an unambiguous way.

Traditional design approaches result in information systems which
are unchanging and constant. The information system determines
which factors are important in evaluating and thus in performing a
task or a job; therefore, there is no need for the worker to judge
and assess which information is required. The workers acquire
sophisticated knowledge on the information system at the expense
of understanding the actual work situation, as many studies have
shown (e.g., Hotvedt, 1974). They become increasingly adept at
handling and understanding the information systems. The effects
are that:

o   opportunities for learning disappear (or are concentrated
    exclusively on the computerized information system)

o   there is no need to form and revise conceptualization of the
    world

o   there is access to only one standardized type of information
    which has been determined based on one model of the task and
    its context

Thus, the information system provides workers with predefined
information for performing a production task while higher managerial levels receive information for long-term assessment of
production tasks or for assessing the cooperation of several
departments.

A semi-autonomous group performing some productive tasks, forming
an integrated and self-contained unit, may use a computerized
information system for planning and reporting their activities.
An information system designed according to traditional principles
will not be appropriate, since there is a considerable risk of
undermining the capabilities and possibilities of a semi-autonomous group to continue working efficiently and effectively. This

is in accordance with the principle of requisite variety (Ashby, 1964). Semi-autonomy requires sufficient competence and means to be able to handle varying contingencies and changes, that the means need to be powerful enough, and that genuine uncertainty needs to be limited (Nylehn, 1974).

The distinguishing feature of semi-autonomous groups in general is the capacity for coping with contingencies. This means that such a group must have possibilities and capabilities for learning about the work situation, coordinating activities internally, and accessing information about objectives and variations. This means that it must be possible to judge and assess what information is required -- both short-term and long-term -- and to retrieve such information based on changing conceptualizations of the task and the work situation. In order to learn, to increase the understanding of the tasks, and to plan activities to be performed, feedback on results achieved is necessary. Further, it must be possible to allocate and distribute information within the group. Finally, access to information about the current position and operation is necessary (Nylehn, 1974). Thus, an information system for a semi-autonomous group should not be limited to one single standardized type of information; instead, several types of information should be available from different perspectives. Similarly, information should not be selected and prespecified and then presented to the group once and forever.

4. LEVELS OF ASSESSMENT

Hawgood and Land propose a practical approach for assessing information systems. It is useful to distinguish three levels of study in information systems assessment: a theoretical, a methodological, and a practical level.

The *theoretical* level of information system assessment includes theoretical, philosophical, ideological, and aesthetical issues. It penetrates assumptions, preconceptions, and concepts in assessment. It is concerned with analytical versus interpretivist perspectives on assessment. It involves formulating theories of assessment and theories about assessment.

On the *practical* level of information system assessment, the actual work of assessing an information system is performed. The practical process of assessment is also the object of study for the theoretical level and the methodological level.

Between the previous two levels, a *methodological* level can be included. On this level, methods, techniques, and practical guidelines are developed and formulated for use in practical assessment. The lode-stars are the usefulness of methods, techniques, and guidelines for actual information system assessment as well as prospects for improving the practice of information system assessment.

The levels are distinct and should not be confused. Still, work on one level can make contributions to the work on other levels; for example, the practical level will benefit from work on the theoretical level. The practice of assessment can be greatly improved by using scientific methods, utilizing scientific findings or knowledge, but this does not mean that the practice of design should be confused with the theoretical level and treated as a scientific discipline, since this would only result in pseudo-science or scientism.

5. CONCLUDING WORDS

In this discussant note, I have elaborated on the two issues which could not be properly penetrated at the conference. First, I have argued that it is not sufficient merely to assess information systems with regard to lists of goals or qualities sought; the organization of work needs to be considered. Second, it is necessary to distinguish more clearly between three levels of information system assessment.

REFERENCES

Ashby, W. R., *An Introduction to Cybernetics*, Methuen University Paperbacks, London, 1964.

Bennett, J. L. (ed.), *Building Decision Support Systems*, Addison-Wesley, Reading, Massachusetts, 1983.

Brunsson, N., "The Irrationality of Action and Action Rationality: Decisions, Ideologies, and Organizational Actions," *Journal of Management Studies*, Vol. 19, 1982.

Hotvedt, E., "Nye systemer, nyttig for hvem?", in Høyer, R. (ed.), *...over til EDB*, Tanum, Oslo, 1974.

Høyer, R. (ed.), *...over til EDB*, Tanum, Oslo, 1974.

Moore, J. H., and Chang, M. G., "Meta-Design Considerations in Building DSS," in Bennett, J. L. (ed.), *Building Decision Support Systems*, Addison-Wesley, Reading, Massachusetts, 1983.

Nylehn, B., "Selvstyre og Formella Informasjonssystemer," in Høyer, R. (ed.), *...over til EDB*, Tanum, Oslo, 1974.

PART II
THEORETICAL FRAMEWORKS FOR INFORMATION SYSTEMS ASSESSMENT

Toward a Derived Set of Measures for Assessing IS Organizations
G.W. Dickson, C.E. Wells and R.B. Wilkes

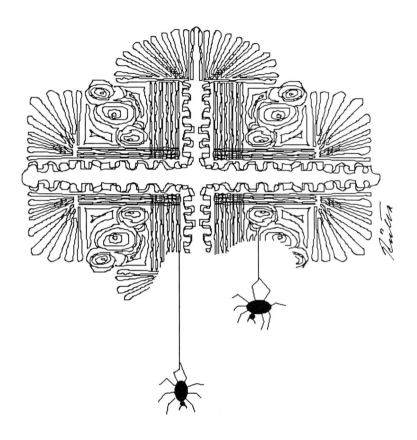

"Thus, answering the questions 'Where are we now?',
and 'Are our present and planned resources consistent
with our plans?' are major objectives of an IS assesment."

INFORMATION SYSTEMS ASSESSMENT
N. Bjørn-Andersen, G.B. Davis (Editors)
Elsevier Science Publishers B.V. (North-Holland)
© IFIP, 1988

TOWARD A DERIVED SET OF MEASURES
FOR ASSESSING IS ORGANIZATIONS

Gary W. DICKSON

Management Information Systems
Carlson School of Management
University of Minnesota
Minneapolis, Minnesota 55455 USA

Connie E. WELLS
Ronald B. WILKES

Computer Information Systems
Georgia State University
University Plaza
Atlanta, Georgia 30303 USA

Assessing the information systems (IS) function
within organizations has been identified as one of
the most critical issues of information systems
management. Despite the importance of the subject
to both executive management and IS professionals,
not much progress has been made toward assessing
the contribution of the IS function to the enterprise. One reason for this state of affairs is the
fact that pure IS evaluation is an illusive concept. This paper addresses the problem of assessing the IS function and provides a foundation for
development of specific measures for IS assessment.
The issues involved in an assessment are discussed
along with the need and demand for such assessment.
Traditional approaches to IS assessment are
presented and a comprehensive approach which
considers several perspectives is recommended.

1. INTRODUCTION

Assessing the information systems (IS) function within organizations has been identified as one of the most critical issues of
information systems management. A 1982 survey (Ball and Harris,
1982) found "gauging MIS effectiveness" to be the second most
important issue reported in a poll of the membership of the
Society for Information Management (SIM). A more recent Delphi
study of leading IS professionals (Dickson, et al., 1984) determined that "measuring and improving IS effectiveness and productivity" is one of the ten most critical information systems managerial issues of the coming decade. The problem of IS assessment
is not new. In fact, a series of interviews with senior executives in leading U.S. organizations, published in the *MIS Quarterly* during 1977 and 1978, indicated that evaluating the contribution of the IS function to the organization was both a very
important and a difficult problem to solve.

Despite the importance of the subject to both executive management and IS professionals, not much progress has been made toward assessing the contribution of the IS function to the enterprise. One reason for this state of affairs is the fact that pure IS evaluation is an illusive concept. In the interviews with senior executives cited above, there was little agreement on how to determine the specific contribution of the IS function to the organization and no suggestions on how to operationalize measures of IS performance. In very practical terms, Dickson and Wetherbe (1985, p. 162) have observed that assessment of the IS function "is so difficult that hard-nosed executives simply throw up their hands in desperation when confronted with this problem" and listen to "screams in the hallways" to tell them how the IS function is performing.

This paper addresses the problem of assessing the IS function and provides a foundation for development of specific measures of IS assessment. In the following sections, the issues involved in an IS assessment are discussed along with the need and demand for such assessment. Traditional approaches to IS assessment are presented and a comprehensive approach which considers several perspectives is recommended.

2.   ISSUES IN IS ASSESSMENT

2.1   Definition of Assessment

Although the terms "evaluation" and "assessment" are often used synonymously in regard to IS, slightly different connotations are associated with each word. *Evaluation,* as we define the term, is the act of placing a value on the object. In the context of the IS function, the theoretical ideal evaluation would be to determine the impact of the IS on the profit of the firm; that is, to be able to know what return the firm is receiving on its investment in IS. Another, less ideal evaluation, would be to arrive at some numerical value on a relative scale. For several reasons, which will be discussed later, the ideal evaluation is not possible.

Rather than evaluating the IS function, we aim, in this paper, to derive a set of measures for *assessing* the IS function (see Matlin, 1977, for a description of the assessment process). Assessing, in this sense, is qualitatively answering the question, "How good is the IS function?" In other words, we wish to be able to assure executive management that the IS function of the enterprise is effective and efficient. Alternatively, if the IS function is not providing the support as effectively or efficiently as it should, we would like to be able to describe specific areas that are deficient and should be improved.

Cameron (1980) suggests that, when assessing organizational effectiveness, the evaluator must address six critical questions. These questions and examples of how to address them are shown in Exhibit 1. In developing the approach to IS assessment presented in this paper we consider these critical questions.

Critical Questions	Examples
1. What domain of activity is being focused on?	Internal activities versus external activities.
2. Whose perspective, or which constituency's point of view, is being considered?	Internal constituencies versus external constituencies; satisfying one constituency maximally.
3. What level of analysis is being used?	Individual effectiveness, subunit effectiveness, or organizational effectiveness.
4. What time frame is being employed?	Short-time perspective versus long-time perspective
5. What type of data are to be used?	Perceptual (from individuals) versus objective (from organizational records).
6. What referent is being employed?	*Comparative* -- relative to a competitor; *normative* -- relative to a theoretical idea; *goal-centered* -- relative to a stated goal; *improvement* -- relative to past performance; *trait* -- relative to effective traits.

(From K. Cameron, "Critical Questions in Assessing Organizational Effectiveness," *Organizational Dynamics*, Autumn, 1980.)

Exhibit 1. Six Critical Questions in Assessing Organizational Effectiveness

2.2 Single System versus the IS Function

Cameron's third question, in the IS context, asks that the scope of the assessment be carefully defined. Is the subject of the assessment a single information system (application) or the entire IS function? Our interest in assessment is focused on the total IS function, not individual application systems. These two levels of analysis are related in that the sum of the evaluations of all the individual information systems is a part of the assessment of the total IS function. But the IS function is more than just the sum of the individual information systems it contains. For example, the ongoing support and interaction between the IS function and other functions within the organization are not fully addressed by an approach which looks only at individual information systems. Additional areas critical to the IS function that would be missed by evaluations or assessments of individual systems include:

o overhead activities, including hardware and software conversions and planning

o   acquisition of generalized software, including:
     -    fourth generation languages
     -    database management systems
     -    other special purpose software packages; e.g., software
          for statistical analysis or for graphics.

2.3 Efficiency and Effectiveness

A major consideration in conducting an IS assessment is whether
the focus is on efficiency or effectiveness. This consideration
relates to Cameron's first question. He defines the "domain of
activity" as being either internal or external. The internal
activity is primarily concerned with the efficiency of the IS
function and the external activity focuses on the effectiveness.

Efficiency is often defined as "doing the thing right" while
effectiveness is defined as "doing the right thing." In the IS
context, efficiency generally is associated with cost, accuracy,
and timeliness of information delivery while effectiveness is
associated with the degree to which organizational objectives are
supported by the IS function. Many IS organizations have an
efficiency orientation in that consideration focuses on cost,
hardware utilization, and/or budget performance. There has been
little formal consideration of or concern for assessing the
effectiveness of the IS function.

The emphasis on efficiency and the lack of concern for the
effectiveness of IS is changing. As Edelman (1981, p. 21) said:

               A useful concept of system efficiency must take
               into account *all* of the systems components. This
               must certainly include the most important and most
               expensive component, which happens to be the end
               user. When that is done...then this distinction
               [between efficiency and effectiveness] disappears
               and the *effective system is also efficient*. This
               broader perspective of system efficiency, on the
               part of the information professional, is totally
               essential to survival.

There are many different approaches to, or definitions of,
effectiveness. Two views predominate. Hamilton and Chervany
(1981) describe these as the "goal-centered view" and the "systems
resource view." The first and most widely accepted approach
defines effectiveness in terms of how well an organization
achieves its goals (the goal-centered view). This definition of
effectiveness involves identifying the task objectives of the IS
function, identifying measures of task attainment, and determining
the extent to which task objectives are satisfied. The comparison
of task objectives to actual performance yields a measure of
effectiveness. Goal-centered effectiveness is the perspective assumed by those taking a rational view of decision making, including Simon (1964), Cyert and March (1963), Mintzberg (1973),
and others.

The second predominant view, the systems resource view, is used by
Katz and Kahn (1966). This perspective defines a system as effective if it acquires the resources needed to function well and
satisfy the members of the organization. The systems resource
view is most commonly used as a measure of the effectiveness of

service organizations. Hamilton and Chervany (1981, p. 56) apply
the systems resource view to the IS function in the following way:

> The MIS function is to develop and operate/maintain
> information systems that will enhance the organization's
> ability to accomplish its objectives. Accomplishment of
> this objective can be evaluated from two perspectives:
>
> o The efficiency with which the MIS development and
>   operations process utilize assigned resources
>   (staff, material, machines, money) to provide the
>   information system to the user.
>
> o The effectiveness to the users, or the users'
>   organizational unit, using the information system
>   in accomplishing their organizational mission.

The second part of the systems resource view defines the IS as
effective if it is able to receive increased funding and attract
high quality personnel. In this view, the outputs (the decisions
made regarding distribution of the funds received) are not judged
directly. The quality of the decisions are considered by the
various constituents and will have an impact on the resources that
will be made available to the IS function in the future.

2.4 What is Assessed?

Cameron's fifth question asks what type of data are to be used.
In assessing the IS function there are several sources and types
of data that can be used. The data may be classified as objective
or subjective. The objective data is collected from organizational records and represents economic and non-economic elements.
Subjective data is often perceptual in nature and consists of the
opinions of IS professionals as well as the users of the IS. The
various types and sources of data used in IS assessment are discussed in more detail later in the paper as the various approaches
to IS assessment that are currently in use are considered.

3. WHY ASSESS?

A formal assessment of the IS function is sometimes performed as a
result of problems that are known or suspected to exist. This is
certainly one major reason for assessment, but there are a number
of other, sometimes less obvious, reasons for conducting an assessment.

3.1 A Basis for Planning

A very important reason for a complete examination of the IS
function is as a basis for planning (perhaps in conjunction with a
Business Systems Planning exercise). The relationship of assessment to planning is made clear by Dickson and Wetherbe (1985, p.
164) when they say, "Before embarking on new systems or a major
systems planning activity, it is very useful to know the current
state of affairs or the starting point." In elaborating on this
point, these authors stress the importance of plans being consistent with one's capabilities, e.g., not planning some very sophisticated advanced applications when the enterprise's personnel
resources are in short supply and, perhaps, not of the level of

experience to embark on an ambitious undertaking. Thus, answering the questions "Where are we now?" and "Are our present and planned resources consistent with our plans?" are major objectives of an IS assessment.

3.2 A Basis for Comparison

Frequently information passes by executive management that causes them to ask for a comparison of the IS organization with the competition. In particular, they want to compare levels of spending, distribution of IS expenses, e.g., salaries versus hardware, and/ or levels of sophistication in technology or managerial practice. These comparisons, of course, are often surrogates for what they would really like to know: "What rate of return are we getting for our significant expenses on information processing?" As we have pointed out, the inability to establish the economic return for the entire IS function can lead to a fallback position of comparative analysis.

3.3 A Basis for Problem Identification and Treatment

It is appropriate to draw an analogy between assessing an IS function and visiting a clinic for an annual health checkup. In the latter case, various measures are taken to see if any problems are present requiring treatment. If they are, the treatment is applied and the patient is remeasured to assure that the problem is controlled. Similarly, an assessment of an IS organization takes formal measures and makes subjective observations to identify problems. The baseline data resulting from an assessment allows later reassessment after some corrective action has been taken to see that matters are improved.

As part of the assessment process, quantitative measures may be taken (e.g., measures of on-line response time) and judgments may be made about the conformance to what is known to be "good practice." Additionally, "business risk" vis-a-vis IS must be investigated. A survey of senior executives (Merton and Severance, 1981) found that the exposure of the IS function to risk from computer failure, computer crime, and the misuse of computer resources was the number one concern of executives regarding risk to the corporation. This point is also brought out by Buss (1981), who argues that there may be significant business risk from improper management of the IS resource, and by McFarlan, McKenney, and Pyburn (1983), who suggest major, even fatal, flaws that many businesses would face should their main computer center be shut down for even a short period of time. The dependencies that many firms, indeed entire industries, have on the computer emphasize the importance of including business risk in an IS assessment.

4.   CURRENT APPROACHES TO IS ASSESSMENT

Several approaches to IS assessment have been proposed. These approaches are based on a variety of views or perspectives of the IS function and its role in the organization. The approaches to IS assessment may be characterized as: (1) pure economic evaluation, (2) comparison to standards, (3) financial risk assessment, (4) managerial risk assessment, (5) IS managerial assessment, and (6) organizational IS assessment.

4.1 Pure Economic Evaluation

Ideally, an assessment of the IS function would result in a
determination of the total economic impact of the IS function on
the organization, but this is rarely, if ever, possible. While
determination of the costs of an enterprise's IS function is
relatively straightforward, determination of the benefits is
difficult and sometimes impossible. This difficulty stems from
the fact that many changes are taking place in an organization and
sorting out the effects of IS expenditures from the effects of all
the other changes is an imposing task. Also, the time lags
between investment and the resulting benefits further complicate
the process of determining the contribution of the IS function to
the enterprise.

Matlin (1979) has suggested an approach to determination of the
economic benefits of the IS function which involves aggregating
the economic benefits of all the individual information systems.
But the contribution of the IS function to the enterprise is more
than just the sum of the economic benefits of all the systems
which are developed. Opportunities for the development of systems
which would have positive benefits may not be exercised. Systems
which are developed may expose the enterprise to one or more types
of risk. Because of the difficulty of determining the economic
return on investment of the IS expenditures, surrogate measures,
such as are identified in the remaining approaches, are often
employed.

4.2 Comparison to Standards

One alternative to a pure economic approach to assessment of the
IS function is to compare the IS expenditures of an organization
with standards. These standards may be based on overall industry
averages, spending of competitors, or allocation of costs into
specific IS expenditure categories.

Industry average investments in IS are available from a variety of
sources such as *Infosystems* and *Datamation* as well as trade
publications. These industry averages are frequently given as a
percentage of revenue spent on the IS function. Lusa and Winkler
(1982) report industry average DP budgets as a percent of revenue
ranging from .38 percent in food/drugs manufacturing to 1.62
percent in banking.

There are several problems in using reported industry averages as
a basis for assessment of IS expenditures. Sample sizes are
frequently small and the industry groupings may not be meaningful.
Also, some organizations may categorize expenses differently than
others. For example, information center or voice communications
costs may be included as a part of total IS expenditures in one
organization and not included for another. Finally, there may be
errors in reporting or processing the data.

An organization's IS expenditures may be compared to the IS
expenditures of individual competitors. While these competitor
expenditure figures may be more difficult to obtain than industry
averages, expenditures of a direct competitor may appear more
relevant than the average expenditures of a total industry. This
type of comparison can be dangerous. There is an implicit assumption that the competition knows what they are doing. This obviously may not be the case. Also, the role of IS may differ

significantly in the organizations being compared. In one organization IS may be performing a "strategic" function while in another it may have only a "support" role (see McFarlan, McKenney, and Pyburn [1983] for a discussion of the roles of IS in an organization).

An organization may compare the percentages of its total budget allocated to specific categories of expenses to some standard. Examples of specific budget categories are personnel, hardware, maintenance, and communications. Figures to serve as standards for allocation of budgets are available from generally the same sources as industry average IS investments. Many of the same problems of using industry average or competitor expenditures apply to cost breakdown standards. In addition, IS is very dynamic and the relative expenditures for the different categories will change over time and will vary based on the role of IS in the organization.

In summation, although the comparison with standards approach may be used, there are a variety of reasons for organizations spending more or less on the IS resource than competitors or some standard. Less money should be spent if a good rate of return is not being achieved. Likewise competitors' levels of spending or standards should not prevent increased spending in IS if there is the potential of a good rate of return. IS expenditures greater than standards are sometimes warranted to overcome competitive disadvantages or to implement new organizational strategies. Also every organization has characteristics and situations different from all other organizations. These unique factors may indicate that greater or lesser levels of IS expenditures are desirable.

4.3   Financial Risk Assessment

One approach to IS assessment is the type of assessment generally performed by internal or external auditors. This approach may be referred to as a financial risk or financial control assessment. This type of assessment seeks to identify and control or minimize risk to the organization from failure or inferior performance by the IS function. The Institute of Internal Auditors (1978) has identified the following areas in which auditors typically make judgments:

1. Reliability and integrity of information:

    o   Financial and operating systems and their reports should contain accurate, reliable, timely, complete, and useful information.

    o   Controls over the system record keeping and reporting should be accurate and effective.

2. Compliance with policies, plans, procedures, laws, and regulations:

    o   Management systems should be in place to set policies and procedures regarding the use of information and information systems development. Planning systems should also be in place. These policies, procedures, and planning systems should be complied with. Finally, systems should not violate local, state, or federal laws or regulations.

3. Safeguarding of assets:

   o Systems should be evaluated to insure that they are safe from various types of losses, such as those resulting from theft, fire, and improper or illegal activities.

4. Economical and efficient use of resources:

   o Standards should exist for economical and efficient use of the system's resources (equipment and personnel). An evaluation should establish that standards have been developed; that they are understood by systems personnel; that deviations from operating standards are identified, analyzed, and communicated to those responsible for corrective action; and that corrective action is taken when standards are not complied with.

5. Accomplishment of established objectives and goals for operations or programs:

   o Management should have established operating or program goals and objectives, developed and implemented control procedures, and accomplished desired results. A determination should be made to ascertain whether such goals and objectives conform with those of the organization and whether they are being met.

This type of assessment looks at the objectives, policies, procedures, and planning of the IS area and seeks to determine the extent to which these adhere to organizational guidelines and normative standards. The financial risk assessment is a largely qualitative process and is conducted primarily through interviews and examination of documents. Typically, financial risk assessments of the IS function (EDP audits) are communicated to top management personnel. (An extensive questionnaire to assess IS controls is given by Thierauf and Reynolds [1982] along with suggestions for its use. Also, many accounting and management consulting firms have checklists for identifying appropriate IS controls.)

4.4 Managerial Risk Assessment

There are other aspects of risk in development and use of information systems not generally considered in the financial risk assessment process described above. This risk, here called managerial risk, might be dichotomized as the risk from systems development described by McFarlan and McKenney (1983a) and the risk from systems in use described by Buss (1981).

4.4.1 Risk in Systems Development

Assessing the risk from systems development involves determining the likelihood that a proposed system cannot be developed to perform as required and the impact that the inability to properly develop this system might have on the organization. In this context, risk is the probability and consequences of failure to achieve the desired objectives from a system. McFarlan and McKenney (1983a) have identified several factors which affect the riskiness of system development projects. These factors may be characterized as: uncertainty of output, also described as problem structuredness or project flexibility; level of technology to be employed in the system; and project size in terms of staff assigned and the duration of their effort. Balancing risk of project development through the use of a portfolio approach is recommended. A balanced portfolio could include projects of high, moderate, and low risk. A key point here is that the degree of risk inherent in a given systems development project should be recognized and the management approach appropriate for that type of risk applied. Honeywell (1982) has developed a project risk assessment package which addresses these factors of project risk and provides guidelines for managing projects in each of the different risk categories.

Another risk in the development of systems is that adequate controls of the type described in the Financial Risk Assessment section above will not be a part of the developed system. Purdy (1978) and Coopers & Lybrand (1984) recommend that auditors participate in the process of designing new systems to reduce this risk. This participation or lack of it is another element in evaluating both financial and managerial risk.

4.4.2 Risk in Operational Systems

Buss (1981) observes that an organization may experience risk from existing operational systems. These operational systems may become unmaintainable due to being "patched" and maintained long beyond the time when they should be replaced with newer and better systems. Failure to replace these systems could result in the lack of flexibility needed to accommodate changing business or competitive situations or complete failure of systems to handle increasing volumes of input. This risk can be addressed by careful attention to overall IS expenditures and the portion of these expenditures over time devoted to maintenance as compared to new development activities.

4.5 IS Managerial Assessment

One approach to assessment of the IS function is to evaluate the extent to which the management of IS subscribes to "good management practices." There are numerous sources of areas of managerial responsibility and descriptions of what constitutes good managerial practices. Management textbooks describe the scope of managerial responsibilities in the areas of planning, organizing, staffing, directing, and controlling the activities of an organization (Leontiades, 1982; Trewatha and Newport, 1976).

Categories and associated measures of IS managerial performance have been suggested (Dickson and Wetherbe, 1985) and are presented in Exhibit 2. Formal objective measurement can generally be made of the financial performance and organizational efficiency categories while subjective measures, such as questionnaires, may have to be used to assess managerial performance and the ability to properly anticipate and provide for future IS needs.

Coopers & Lybrand (1984) have identified and discussed the significance of the 26 "Executive Issues in Information Management" listed in Exhibit 3. The extent to which IS management takes the lead in addressing the issues presented in this list is another measure of the performance of the IS function.

Financial Performance

    Budget performance (for the overall organization)
    Cost Recovery (if on cost recovery chargeout)
    Distribution of costs by industry standards

Organizational Efficiency

    Developmental performance
    Meeting project time and cost goals
    Staff turnover
    Size of system request backlog
    System maintenance cost (as percent of total cost)
    Operational performance
    System availability/downtime
    Late jobs
    On-line response time
    System utilization
    Throughput (job steps performed per standard time period)
    Job reruns (percent)

Managerial Performance

    Attitudes of senior management
    Attitudes of user managers
    Performance on evaluation by external assessors (consultants,
        external auditors, et al.)

Other

    Availability of capacity in systems resources (hardware and
        personnel) to meet future operational and developmental
        requirements

(From G. Dickson and J. Wetherbe, *The Management of Information Systems*, McGraw-Hill Book Company, New York, 1985.)

Exhibit 2. Measures of IS Performance

Another factor to consider in evaluating "good practice" is the extent and quality of communication between the IS function and the rest of the organization. Van de Ven and Ferry (1980), as part of their Organization Assessment Instruments, have constructed questions to determine the "perceived effectiveness of relationship" and "quality of communications" between individuals and organizational units. These questions can be valuable in identifying problems between the IS function and the rest of the organization.

4.6 Organizational IS Assessment

There has been much discussion in the last few years on the need to use IS strategically or as a competitive weapon (McFarlan, 1984; McFarlan and McKenney, 1983a; Parsons, 1983). Organizational IS assessment focuses on determining and satisfying organizational information needs, and seeks to determine the extent to which the competitive business needs of the organization are anticipated and satisfied by the IS function.

o   Is the organization providing for compatibility of systems across corporate entities?

o   Is the organization addressing the growing shortage of experienced programmers?

o   Is the organization coping with its portfolio of obsolete, unmaintainable, and inefficient software?

o   Are priorities assigned within the application backlog to reflect corporate strategic requirements?

o   Is appropriate use being made of new system development productivity tools?

o   Does the organization have an effective program to manage the creation of its software assets?

o   Is the organization properly prepared for disasters and other contingencies?

o   Does the organization have an effective balance between centralization and decentralization of its information systems to support corporate objectives?

o   Are long-range implications of system decisions fully understood and periodically re-evaluated?

o   Are internal and external auditors functioning effectively in advanced systems environments?

o   Are the implications of integrating information systems being adequately considered in planning for acquisitions, mergers, and divestitures?

o   Is the organization preparing for integrated computer-based executive support capabilities?

o   Is the organization using appropriate tools and techniques to ensure the accuracy and consistency of its information resources?

o   Has the organization protected its data asset against adverse impacts of computer proliferation?

o   Is there an effective strategy for taking advantage of new telecommunications service alternatives when appropriate?

o   Does the organization have a strategy for addressing the shortfall of skilled *technical* and *managerial* resources for telecommunications?

o   Does the organization have an effective strategy to capitalize on new technologies by relocating professional employees and information processing?

o   As accessible information becomes a more critical asset of the business, have adequate precautions been taken to ensure security?

o With dramatically increased dependence of organizations on
   communication networks, has DP taken adequate measures to
   guarantee availability?

o Does the organization have an effective plan to capitalize on
   network savings through integration?

o What are the objectives for office automation, and whose
   responsibility is it to determine them?

o Since the productivity of white collar "knowledge workers" is
   inherently hard to measure, how will office automation
   approaches be evaluated and financially justified?

o Is the organization prepared for the impact of office automation on its white collar work force?

o Does the strategic plan of the organization capitalize on new
   computer based information technologies?

o Has the organizational structure been adapted to direct the
   use of information technologies?

o Does the organization have a comprehensive, effective process
   for strategic information systems planning?

(From Coopers & Lybrand Corporation, *Executive Issues in Information Management*, 1984.)

Exhibit 3.   Checklist of Executive Issues in Information
             Management

Following up on these ideas, Ives and Learmonth (1984) have constructed a framework, drawing on work by IBM (1981) and Burnstine
(1980), to guide the process of determining what opportunities for
strategic or competitive use of the IS resource exist for an
organization. This framework, shown in Exhibit 4, can be used to
assess what potential strategic opportunities in the use of IS
have and have not been pursued.

5.   CONDUCTING AN OVERALL ASSESSMENT OF
     THE IS ORGANIZATION

The discussion above of the reasons for and scope of an IS assessment shows the complexity and multifaceted nature of such an evaluation. None of the approaches described above appears capable of
capturing all the factors that should be considered in a total
assessment of the IS function within organizations.

We offer a comprehensive evaluative framework, shown in Exhibit 5,
consisting of a package of approaches to deal with the variety of
views and differing concerns of the assessment problem. This
package borrows from and expands on the existing approaches of
comparison to standards, a financial risk assessment, a managerial
assessment, an IS managerial assessment, and an organizational IS
assessment described above.

IBM Stage	Extended Model	Description
1. Requirements	1. Set Requirements	How much of the resource is required?
	2. Specify	What are the resources' attributes?
2. Acquisition	3. Select Source	Where will we buy it from?
	4. Order	Order a quantity from the supplier.
	5. Authorize*	Authorize monies to be spent.
	6. Acquire*	Take possession of the resource.
	7. Test and Accept	Ensure it meets specifications.
3. Stewardship	8. Integrate	Add to existing inventory.
	9. Monitor	Control access and use of the resource.
	10. Upgrade	Upgrade resource if necessary.
	11. Maintain	Repair resource if necessary.
4. Retirement	12. Transfer or Dispose	Move, return, or dispose of the inventory as necessary.
	13. Account For and Pay For	Monitor where and how much money is spent on the resource.

*Not included in Burnstine's (1980) original list but subsumed instead under *Order* and *Test and Accept.*

(From B. Ives and G. Learmonth, "The Information System as a Competitive Weapon," *Communications of the ACM,* December, 1984, p. 25.)

Exhibit 4.   The Customer's Resource Life Cycle Model

6.   PROCEDURES FOR AN IS ASSESSMENT

Ideally, in a world where resources are free, the total assessment consisting of all measures of all parts of the package would be performed continuously.   Practically, however, this cannot and should not be done.   The first assessment within our suggested framework should be as comprehensive as possible.   Thereafter, management should look at the set of measures and determine which to apply depending on specific concerns, desired completeness of assessment, and anticipated costs of and benefits from the assessment of specific factors.   Complete evaluations should, however, be performed at intervals to reduce the subjectivity of the assessment process and ensure that unseen problems are not developing.

Attitudes of Senior Management

o Overall attitude toward IS, its contribution to the organization and its efficiency
o Perception toward the head of IS as a manager and as a technician
o Attitude toward and role in information related policy determination
o Perception of IS "problems"

Attitudes of User Management and Users

o Overall attitude toward IS, its contribution to the organization and its efficiency
o Perception toward IS staff regarding business ability and orientation, communications and problem solving skills, responsiveness, and technical capability
o Perception toward IS systems regarding accuracy, timeliness, usefulness
o Perception toward IS systems development process regarding timeliness, responsiveness, cost, procedures
o Perception of IS "problems"

IS Planning and Priority Setting

o Role of senior management in planning process
o Degree to which organizational planning process includes IS
o Presence of IS plan (including applications, technology, and personnel)
o Quality of IS planning process and IS plan (including relationship between organizational strategic plan and IS plan)
o Balance of risk in development portfolio
o Formal forecast of future technology and its meaning
o Formal forecast of IS capabilities (hardware, software, and personnel)
o Methods employed for information requirements analysis
o Process by which projects are selected for inclusion in IS plan (including resource allocation mechanisms such as cost/benefit analysis and/or zero-based budgeting)
o User management role in IS planning and priority setting

System Development Practice and Project Control

o Availability, quality, and use of formal system development methodology
o Availability, quality, and use of structured design methods
o Availability, quality, and use of project control system
o System development productivity aids (hardware/software, prototyping/heuristic design, information center concept, and technologies)
o Role of user in design and implementation process
o Role of internal auditor in design and implementation process
o Responsiveness to user requests, especially in the case of systems problems or the need for quick but minor systems evolution
o Quality of user documentation
o System development chargeout system
o Quality of systems documentation

Applications Portfolio

o   How computing resources are being employed (including systems
    currently operational, under development, and planned)
        Transactions-oriented systems
        Monitor systems
        Exception systems
        Inquiry systems
        Analysis (DSS) systems
o   Quality of the applications (including the appropriateness of
    the content of the systems, their timeliness, and their
    accuracy)
o   Age of major systems

Operational Efficiency

o   Appropriateness of hardware and software (including systems
    software)
o   Evolvability of hardware and software
o   Efficiency of hardware utilization
o   Chargeout system for system operation
o   Hardware and systems downtime
o   Systems for data security and privacy
o   Backup, recovery, and disaster systems

Personnel Evaluation

o   Technical quality of DP analysts and programmers
o   Staff professionalism
o   Business knowledge of DP personnel
o   User IS knowledge
o   Appropriateness of training -- user and systems
o   Projection of future personnel needs and plans
o   IS job satisfaction
o   Compensation and career planning system

IS Measurement Systems

o   Meeting project time and cost goals
o   Staff turnover
o   Maintenance cost
o   Systems responsiveness
o   EDP audit reports
o   Industry standard comparison

IS Organization

o   Reporting relationship and fit with overall organization
o   Internal organization structure and functions
o   Extent and quality of communications with the rest of the
    organization

Exhibit 5.   Areas and Factors in an IS Assessment

A variety of techniques are necessary to gather the data required
to assess the IS function along all the dimensions presented here.
Reports, documents, surveys, questionnaires, and observations are
all needed as sources of information.   The data ranges from very
quantitative and objective to very qualitative and subjective.
Some data deals with only factual information while other data

focuses only on attitudes. Although data is provided in many ways by many members of the organization, it is critical that each type of data required for each aspect of assessment is gathered with great care to ensure its accuracy and reliability.

To improve objectivity, and probably accuracy, the assessment should be conducted by evaluators from outside the organization. These external auditors should be assisted by internal audit personnel, IS management and personnel, and others in the organization using or affected by information systems. It is essential that the assessor(s) have access to any and all information which is pertinent to the assessment. The results of the assessment should be provided to senior management, IS management, and the audit function in forms appropriate for their specific uses and responsibilities.

7. CONCLUSION

A comprehensive evaluative framework consisting of a package of approaches is recommended as a foundation for an overall assessment of the IS function. The approaches which comprise this package are: comparison to standards, a financial risk assessment, a managerial risk assessment, an IS managerial assessment, and an organizational IS assessment. Although the time and cost of an assessment of the scope recommended here may appear great, the potential benefits of an assessment of a function so vital to the functioning of many modern organizations appears to warrant the effort.

The purpose of the IS assessment is to identify both strengths and weaknesses of the IS function. By giving management both the good news and the bad news, the assessment process enables them to correct problems and to exploit the strengths of the IS function.

REFERENCES

Ball, L., and Harris, R., "SMIS Members: A Membership Analysis," *MIS Quarterly*, March, 1982.

Burnstine, D., "BIAIT: An Emerging Management Engineering Discipline," working paper, BIAIT International, Inc., 1980.

Buss, M., "Penny-wise Approach to Data Processing," *Harvard Business Review*, July-August, 1981.

Cameron, K., "Critical Questions in Assessing Organizational Effectiveness," *Organizational Dynamics*, Autumn, 1980.

Coopers & Lybrand Corporation, *Executive Issues In Information Management*, 1984.

Cyert, R., and March, J., *A Behavioral Theory of the Firm*, Prentice-Hall, Inc., Englewood Cliffs, New Jersey, 1963.

Dickson, G., Leitheiser, R., Wetherbe, J., and Nechis, M., "Key Information Systems Issues for the 1980's," *MIS Quarterly*, September, 1984.

Dickson, G., and Wetherbe, J., *The Management of Information Systems*, McGraw-Hill Book Company, New York, 1985.

Edelman, F., "The Management of Information Resources -- A Challenge for American Business," *MIS Quarterly*, March, 1981.

Goodman, P., Pennings, J., and Associates, *New Perspectives on Organizational Effectiveness*, Jossey-Bass Publishers, San Francisco, 1977.

Hamilton, S., and Chervany, N., "Evaluating Information Systems Effectiveness -- Part I: Comparing Evaluation Approaches," *MIS Quarterly*, September, 1981.

Hamilton, S., and Chervany, N., "Evaluating Information Systems Effectiveness -- Part II: Comparing Evaluator Viewpoints," *MIS Quarterly*, December, 1981.

Honeywell Information Systems, Inc., *Project Management Risk Assessment Method*, Order number GA09-00, 1982.

IBM Corporation, *Business Systems Planning: Information Systems Planning Guide*, 1981.

Institute of Internal Auditors, *Standards for the Professional Practice of Internal Auditing*, Altamonte Springs, Florida, 1978.

Ives, B., and Learmonth, G., "The Information System as a Competitive Weapon," *Communications of the ACM*, December, 1984.

Katz, D., and Kahn, R., *The Social Psychology of Organizations*, John Wiley and Sons, Inc., New York, 1966.

King, W., and Rodriguez, J., "Evaluating Management Information Systems," *MIS Quarterly*, September, 1978.

Leontiades, M., *Management Policy, Strategy, and Plans*, Little, Brown and Company, Boston, 1982.

Lusa, J., and Winkler, R., "The Real Truth about DP Salaries," *Infosystems*, June, 1982.

Matlin, G., "How to Survive a Management Assessment," *MIS Quarterly*, March, 1977.

Matlin, G., "What is the Value of Investment in Information Systems?", *MIS Quarterly*, September, 1977.

March, J., and Simon, H., *Organizations*, John Wiley and Sons, Inc., New York, 1958.

Merton, A., and Severance, D., "Data Processing: A State-of-the-Art Survey of Attitudes and Concerns of DP Managers," *MIS Quarterly*, June, 1981.

McFarlan, F., "Information Technology Changes the Way You Compete," *Harvard Business Review*, May-June, 1984.

McFarlan, F., and McKenney, J., *Corporate Information Systems Management: The Issues Facing Senior Executives*, Richard D. Irwin, Inc., Homewood, Illinois, 1983a.

McFarlan, F., and McKenney, J., "The Information Archipelago--Governing the New World," *Harvard Business Review*, July-August, 1983b.

McFarlan, F., McKenney, J., and Pyburn, P., "The Information Archipelago -- Plotting a Course," *Harvard Business Review*, January-February, 1983.

McKenney, J., and McFarlan, F., "The Information Archipelago--Maps and Bridges," *Harvard Business Review*, September-October, 1983.

Mintzberg, H., *The Nature of Managerial Work*, Prentice-Hall, Inc., Englewood Cliffs, New Jersey, 1973.

Nolan, R., "Managing the Crisis in Data Processing," *Harvard Business Review*, March-April, 1979.

Parsons, G., "Information Technology: A New Competitive Weapon," *Sloan Management Review*, Fall, 1983.

Purdy, C., "The Internal Auditor's Role in MIS Developments," *MIS Quarterly*, December, 1978.

Rockart, J., "Managers Define Their Own Data Needs," *Harvard Business Review*, March-April, 1979.

Simon, H., "On the Concept of Organizational Goal," *Administrative Science Quarterly*, June, 1964.

Thierauf, R., and Reynolds, G., *Effective Information Systems Management*, Charles E. Merrill Publishing Co., Columbus, Ohio, 1982, pp. 293-347.

Trewatha, R., and Newport, M., *Management -- Functions and Behavior*, Business Publications, Inc., Dallas, Texas, 1976.

Van de Ven, A., and Ferry, D., *Measuring and Assessing Organizations*, John Wiley and Sons, Inc., New York, 1980.

DISCUSSANT NOTE

On: TOWARDS A DERIVED SET OF MEASURES FOR
     ASSESSING IS ORGANIZATIONS

By: Gary W. Dickson, Connie E. Wells,
     and Ronald B. Wilkes

Discussant's comments by: Frank LAND

The London Business School
Great Britain

1. INTRODUCTION

The paper provides a comprehensive overview of the problems met in
attempting to assess the "value" to the organization of the IS
function.   The authors consider a number of alternative approaches, discuss their shortcomings, and go on to provide their
own more comprehensive framework for assessment.   They argue that
the full assessment of the IS function should be carried out at
intervals, and that, to ensure objectivity and improve accuracy,
the assessment should be carried out from outside the organization.

2. FRAMEWORK

The framework for assessment lists over 50 factors classified
under nine headings to be considered.   The factors range from
attitudes to the IS manager by top management "perception towards
the head of IS as a manager and as a technician" to factors under
the heading of "applications portfolio," including "age of major
systems."

3. BIAS?

Since the authors provide the lists as a framework, they do not
consider or comment on the actual measures to be used. Suppose an
organization has a "successful" system which has been working
operationally for a number of years. Is its age a plus or a minus
factor in terms of the goodness of the IS function?   In other
words, listing relevant factors begs the important question of the
values to be assigned to the outcomes. In some ways, it may even
bias the perception of the evaluator.   Merely listing "age of
major system" as a factor in assessment suggests that having old
applications in the portfolio is a minus factor.   Further, the
lists do not attempt to pick key factors.   Each evaluator must
determine the weight to apply to the factors in arriving at any
general conclusions about the efficiency and effectiveness of the
IS function.

On the other hand, properly used, the framework can provide the
evaluator with a list of factors which may be relevant and which

should form part of an exploratory procedure yielding the kind of
"rich picture" for which a methodology such as that of Checkland
(1981) calls. In such a process, the factor "age of major system"
becomes the subject for a debate, and perhaps new insights into
what is meant by obsolescence of IS.

In calling for outside evaluators, the authors assume that a kind
of objectivity is possible. However, relying only on outside
evaluators may deny the organization the value of using the
factors as a means for exploring the perceptions of value as seen
from different viewpoints and stakeholders. In "A Multivariate
Approach to IS Assessment," Hawgood and Land (this volume) point
out that the qualities different stakeholders look for are
diverse, even with respect to a single factor. Thus, the factor
"methods employed for information requirements analysis" (Exhibit
5) may be viewed very differently by the system's sponsors, the
system's users, and the system's builders. Thus, each stakeholder
may have a different view of the effectiveness of the IS function.
It could be argued that only the evaluation which most closely
mirrors the preferences of top management is relevant. In
practice, however, the view of the other stakeholders governs
their response to the IS function, and hence is crucial to the
ultimate effectiveness of IS.

5. CONCLUSION

By providing a comprehensive framework, the authors have attempted
to take some of the complexity out of IS assessment. I suggest
that the framework, in identifying relevant factors, serves a
useful purpose for further exploration, but leaves the complexity
(and subjectivity) of IS assessment intact. Assessment should
only be carried out if it is clear it will yield a result acceptable to its sponsors, and one which can lead to action which is
acceptable to a range of stakeholders.

REFERENCES

Checkland, P., *Systems Thinking, Systems Practice*, John Wiley and
        Sons, New York, 1981.

Hawgood, J., and Land, F., "A Multivariate Approach to IS Assess-
        ment," this volume.

Benefit Analysis of Office Systems:
Concepts for a Method
G. Schäfer

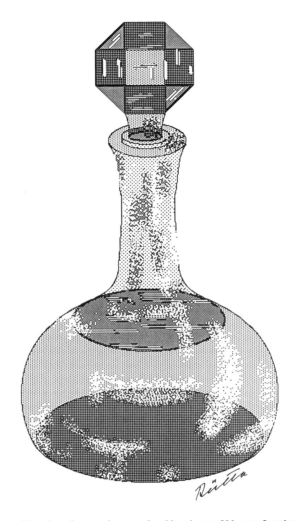

"Of particular importance to the benefit analysis are
those changes which concern factors such as the
content of the work process, division of labor,
sequence of the work process, ... bottlenecks, either
newly generated or recently overcome, etc."

INFORMATION SYSTEMS ASSESSMENT
N. Bjørn-Andersen, G.B. Davis (Editors)
Elsevier Science Publishers B.V. (North-Holland)
© IFIP, 1988

BENEFIT ANALYSIS OF OFFICE SYSTEMS:
CONCEPTS FOR A METHOD*

Gunter SCHÄFER

Betriebswirtschaftliches Institut für Organisation
und Automation (BIFOA)
University of Köln

The benefit analysis approach taken by the Functional Analysis of Office Requirements (FAOR)
project is introduced. Within the broader framework of FAOR, the benefit analysis serves as an
instrument which in practical applications is
combined with other instruments and tailored to the
specific conditions of a client organization. The
approach takes a functional view of office work and
provides criteria for identifying and evaluating
efficiency and effectiveness benefits which are
specific to the organization analyzed. Based on a
three level concept of benefits, a stepwise
approach is suggested which should help the analyst
to investigate the extent to which technological
capabilities materialize into actual benefits.

1. THE NEED FOR A BENEFIT ANALYSIS OF OFFICE SYSTEMS

Early investigations into the impact of office systems pointed out
their considerable potential for productivity increases in the
performance of office work. Such studies were valuable as
explorations of the magnitude of benefits achievable through the
application of office systems and of the question "where is the
real pay-off of office systems" (Bair, 1978). They often assumed
office systems to consist of a relatively fixed set of tools
which, with a few adjustments, were applicable to a wide range of
situations. However, many researchers (Driscoll, 1980; Hammer,
1983; Sirbu, 1982) and practitioners (Topfer, et al., 1985) have
doubts about the predictability of the impact of office systems
without considering the individual characteristics of different
offices.

In addition to the generality of survey studies, their assumption
of a stagnating productivity rate in office work can be seriously
challenged. Studies by Panko (1984) suggest that office productivity is not the lame duck it is tacitly taken for, nor does
there exist anything like a common level of office productivity
which office systems would improve by a similar margin for all
office situations.

---

*This research is part of the FAOR project (Functional Analysis of
Office Requirements) which is supported by the Commission of the
European Community under ESPRIT contract No. 56.

Moreover, the assessment of benefits must be based on considerations of the specific nature of office systems. Office systems
tend to support rather than to automate work processes carried out
by an office worker, with the result that the main benefits cannot
be identified using cost-avoidance or cost-displacement factors,
e.g., by directly replacing manpower, but have to cover qualitative effects on work results. Furthermore, many functions of
office systems focus on supporting communications between office
workers so that an assessment of benefits has to take into account
the interdependencies between work processes where benefits cannot
be directly allocated to certain tasks or individual office
workers.

A comprehensive analysis of the costs and benefits of an applied
or planned office system must rely on concepts which, although
independent from the various conditions of the organizational
setting, pay sufficient respect to the particular benefit categories of office systems (Szyperski, 1961). In this context the
issue of identifying and pointing out benefits and arguing their
respective importance is as important or even more important than
a necessarily inaccurate assessment in money terms.

For reasons of space, the benefit analysis as outlined in this
paper only deals with "benefits to the organization," although
"benefits to the office worker" are perceived as an essential
supplement and are thus extremely important for a comprehensive
analysis.

2. A FUNCTIONAL VIEW OF OFFICE SYSTEM BENEFITS

The problem of developing an approach for evaluating benefits of
office systems immediately leads to the issue of what should be
understood under office systems and office work. Kunin (1982),
for example, states:

>   The term "office automation"is perhaps the most
>   visible buzz-phrase in the contemporary computer
>   environment. It has been applied to such disparate
>   products and ideas (ranging, for example, from word
>   processors to PABXs, to decision support systems,
>   to personal computers, to distributed computing)
>   that it has been rendered meaningless.

For the benefit analysis, however, a more specific understanding
would be very advantageous. In this respect, experience from the
area of systems analysis and design methods also holds for the
benefit analysis; "like any other tool a method must be adapted to
the structure of the task it is to perform. The more universal a
method, the less effective. And conversely, the more specialized
it is, the more effective" (Malouin and Landry, 1983).

It is hardly applicable to characterize office systems mainly by
means of technical factors. "The great potential of these systems
lies not simply in the power of their individual applications, but
in the synergy resulting from increasingly profound integration of
various system components" (Tapscott, 1982).

A more suitable approach to obtaining a specific understanding of
the subject area aims at analyzing the nature of the office work
the office systems are designed to support and the kind of support
they provide. Szyperski describes office work as physical activities on mental objects for the purpose of fulfilling business

objectives (Szyperski, 1961; Höring, 1985). The objects in this case are conceptual in nature; however, they still have to be given a physical existence in order to be manageable, i.e., to form the basis for decisions, communication, etc. Thus the domain of office work can be described as centering on those activities which are concerned with expressing mental constructs by means of symbols and manipulating these symbols. In the following, the term "information object" will be used to denote these objects. Activities of office work are concerned with generating, communicating, and processing as well as storing and retrieving information objects. In this understanding, office work takes place independent of the location "office" and should not be confused with administrative work, since in some circumstances the primary business function of an organization requires office work (e.g., a solicitor's claim, an engineer's technical design) which is not administrative (Nordsieck, 1956).

At first, a concept of office work which concentrates on the generation (resulting in a certain form) and handling of information objects seems like a simplification because it excludes the conceptual work, such as making decisions. However, office work is not independent but strongly intertwined with aspects of the "content" of an information object and its usage in performing business functions. The form of a message, for example, has to reflect its information content while the requirements for its transmission depend on the business function for which the message is exchanged. It is the content of an information object and the functions it has to serve which give the office activities their meaning. The information objects have to be generated and manipulated in such a way that they provide effective support for the performance of business functions and the achievement of business objectives (Figure 1).

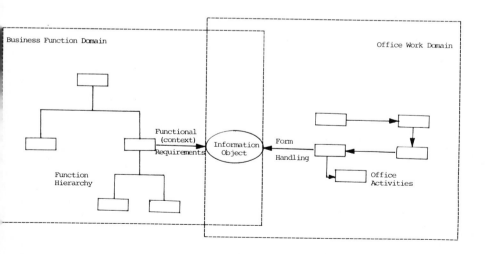

Figure 1. Role of Information Objects in Office Work

This view of the office fulfills Hammer and Zisman's (1979) characterization of a functional approach:

> The difficulty with both the standard view of offices (activity view) and the conventional approach to office automation is that they are too general and do not relate to the purpose for which the office exists. They focus on the form rather than on the content of office work. There are many different kinds of offices, performing many different kinds of activities. We are suspicious of any perspective which glosses over these differences. An office does not exist to enable its inhabitants to engage in paper-pushing. An office exists in order to meet the specific business needs of an organization.

Office work is relevant not only to the functional view; it relates directly to office systems and the kind of support they are able to give.

> The objective of OA (office automation) is simply to improve the performance of business functions through the use of whatever applications are appropriate. The emphasis is on the specific applications that the particular organization requires. There is no such thing as automation in the office; there is only building a system to serve the applications in a particular office. [Hammer, 1983]

The FAOR Benefit Analysis applies a functional view of office work in the form of "measurement units." A measurement unit is a selected sequence of work processes carried out in the organization. In order to be considered as a basis for identifying and evaluating benefits, it must:

1. be important for the achievement of major business functions;
2. consume resources in terms of the activities of office work;
3. have clearly identifiable information objects which are generated or handled;
4. be meaningful in terms of the possible benefits accruing from the technology investigated.

The choice of suitable measurement units is crucial for the success of a benefit analysis. Office system evaluations often take a very narrow view on isolated activities, like typing or the transmission of messages. This approach does not take into account the major changes which an office system causes in the structure and content of the work, e.g., the division of labor in the correction cycle of a typed text or the secondary influence of changes on related work processes.

Only the broader context in which the directly affected work processes occur and their role within the framework of the more comprehensive measurement unit provide the criteria for a meaningful evaluation. At the center of attention are not factors like typing speed or the transmission time of messages, but effects on the preparation time of urgent reports, the contribution of a fast message exchange to the ability of the organization to react, and the avoidance of negative developments.

This argument does not, however, imply that an evaluation should be based on the broadest scope possible. The choice of the "right" sequence of work processes is essential. The office technology under investigation may affect only the last stage of preparing a larger document. In this case, it would not be adequate to include the time-consuming activities of collecting information and preparing concepts in the measurement unit.

It should be emphasized that the measurement units of the benefit analysis represent only a small fraction of all the processes occurring in the organization. Their selection determines which areas of work are actually scanned by the benefit analysis for possible benefits (and detriments). Experience shows that a few major sequences of work processes already provide a good basis for investigating the main areas where benefits of a particular office system are likely to occur.

3. FAOR CONCEPT OF OFFICE SYSTEM BENEFITS

One of the most valuable contributions to the benefit analysis has been the clear distinction between different levels of benefit assessment. Bair (1978) as well as Picot and Reichwald (1984) identified the following levels:

1. equipment performance
2. throughput performance
3. organizational performance
4. institutional performance

The structuring of benefit assessment into levels is based on the differing "scope of variables that must be taken into account for meaningful productivity measurement" (Bair, 1978). On the first level, for example, a faster retrieval access is already perceived as a kind of benefit. The functional view, however, takes a more restrictive approach of that which may be termed a "benefit." A benefit can not be generated in the equipment performance or even in the operator-machine interaction but only through the effects of office technology on performance that and result in criteria attributable to organizational functions.

The introduction of the effects of office technology on work processes is an intermediate step in the assessment of benefits which takes the form of a pyramid (Figure 2). The office system itself merely provides technical functions and features meant to be used by an office worker as a type of tool to support work. Thus, the office system has a "technology potential" which is available to the office worker. Usage of the system, i.e., the terms of the office system application, determines whether the office system has implications on how work is performed. In FAOR terminology, the kind of application(s) and the prevailing organizational conditions strongly influence the "effects" an office system is able to generate. In turn, benefits only result from such changes if they are desirable from the organizational point of view. Such effects may easily be benefit-neutral, i.e., they change the way the office work is carried out without affecting the achievement of quality criteria and at the same time do not cause perceivable cost savings. Such effects have to be filtered out in the evaluation process.

G. Schäfer

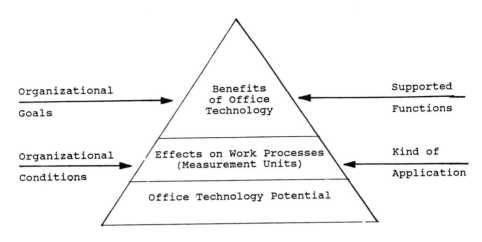

Figure 2. FAOR Concept of Office System Benefits

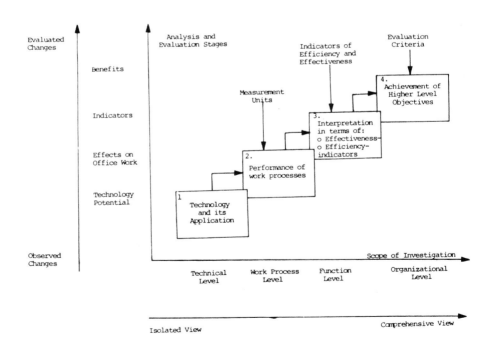

Figure 3. Basic Steps of the FAOR Benefit Analysis

4. STEPS OF THE BENEFIT ANALYSIS

The FAOR Benefit Analysis has been designed to utilize this three level concept in its approach to evaluating benefits. Figure 3 shows the fundamental steps to be carried out.

Starting from a thorough analysis of the actual changes brought about by the introduction of office technology, the perspective of the benefit analysis is continuously enlarged to cover the wider implications on the organization. It follows a bottom-up approach which may be viewed as a reversal of the design process. By reviewing the considerations that have gone into the design process, an investigation of their benefit implications is possible. The analysis of one level is based on the results of the previous level. Beside the correspondence with the pyramid concept of benefits, there are two reasons for proceeding bottom-up:

1. This facilitates a realistic assessment of how far-reaching the effects and benefits of an office system are. Only in exceptional cases are high-level functions of the organization likely to be significantly affected by an office system. Therefore, an analysis of effects on higher-level functions has to be based on well-founded reasons for assuming influences on lower-level functions.

2. The economy of analysis can be well-supported by following up only promising paths of effects and benefits. In contrast to a top-down approach, the tedious task of investigating business functions, their underlying objectives, quality and achievement criteria can be significantly reduced. At each step, the FAOR Benefit Analysis contains means for reducing complexity.

Undertaking these steps does not constitute a comprehensive study since important activities, such as the analysis of costs, are omitted for reasons of space. Furthermore, this description does not address the issue of adjusting the benefit analysis to the application situation, e.g., the question of how the time of analysis regarding the planning and implementation stages of an office system influences the way the analysis is carried out.

4.1 Technology Potential Analysis

The FAOR Benefit Analysis is based on a comparison between the situations before and after the introduction of an investigated office system. Thus, the analyst has to obtain detailed knowledge of the actual change undergone by introducing the office system. The important aspects of this change are not restricted to the technology itself, but also concern the question of where and how the technology is applied (its application condition). Both aspects are important for accumulating information on what should be evaluated in the benefit analysis.

For example, the same technology can be applied in different ways which would then result in different effects and benefits being created. A word processor may be used in a central typing pool but could also be applied decentrally to assist secretarial work. In the first case, mainly lengthy, pressing documents, requiring frequent alteration are typed using the office system, whereas, in the other, it may be employed by the secretary to accelerate the typing of smaller documents or assist in the organization of work.

The circumstances of office system application raises three major questions:

- who uses the system, under which circumstances, and with what limitations, for instance, time and access restrictions, is the system used?

- which business functions are earmarked for office technology support?

- where is the office system located?

In the FAOR understanding of benefits, the office technology in the context of application creates the capability for causing effects, termed the "office technology potential." This potential can be expressed by specifying how the information objects dealt with could be affected by the usage of the office system. It may affect aspects of the form of the information object, e.g., by allowing a type of graphical representation not available before, or of its handling, such as creation time, response time or access reliability to stored data.

It should be emphasized that it is not the task of the technology potential analysis to identify some type of "absolute" potential but rather the technology potential implied by the change which is subject to investigation by the benefit analysis. In general, an analysis of benefits is only meaningful if two situations can be clearly defined and their differences are open to inspection. This implies, for example, that in the case of an already existing office system about to be replaced by a superior one, only the aspects of improvement against the already existing system should be included in the technology potential.

The concept of technology potential in terms of potential implications on the form and handling of information objects is an abstraction tool which helps to identify those aspects of a technological change which are essential, i.e., which may concern results of the work, and to suppress the manifold other features. For example, the technology potential closely examines whether a sophisticated user interface constitutes only an ergonomic improvement and in so doing excludes itself from benefits attributable to the organization (though not from human factor considerations) or whether it also has implications on the information objects, e.g., a more appealing graphical design. Only the latter aspects are being included in investigations into the technology potential.

4.2 Analysis of Office Technology Effects

An office technology potential is not yet meant to indicate an effect on the way an office worker is doing his job or on the output he produces. The concept of technology potential is too restrictive in that it only considers individual office activities on the information objects. It is the measurement units which provide the basis for considering work processes in a larger context and understanding their purpose. It is only in the light of these more comprehensive units of work that implications on the work and on the output produced can be realized. For example, the availability of a new communication medium with the potential for fast graphics transmissions can only generate new patterns of communication if this mode of communication fits the way a person works.

The identification of effects of office technology on measurement units is of central importance for analyzing benefits. The analyst conceptually applies the technology potential to the real situation and tries to foresee which changes in the work processes or their interconnections are likely to occur. In other words, he has to come to a conclusion on what he expects to be different in the work performed, the resources required, and the output generated. Of particular importance to the benefit analysis are those changes which concern factors such as the content of the work process, division of labor, sequence of work processes, bottlenecks, either newly generated or recently overcome, etc.

While the technology potential analysis requires a considerable degree of judgment on the part of the analyst, the task of the second step, the identification of effects as consequences of a proposed change (the application of an office system) is essentially an "exercise in prediction" (Klein and Hirschheim, 1983). Klein and Hirschheim point out the difficulty of such predictions which can only to a minor extent be based on "the cause-effect mode of analysis" and which must therefore involve extensively the judgment of an "indeterminate human will, i.e., the result of conscious and free choices for which the agent (and not some law of nature) is responsible" (Klein and Hirschheim, 1983). Despite the high degree of uncertainty involved in any prediction of how the work will be performed after the introduction of an office system, there is no way to assess the impact of an office system in a specific organizational context prior to implementation without such a prediction.

The FAOR Benefit Analysis assists the analyst in his prediction by indicating to him aspects likely to either support or inhibit a change. For example, the way people work is, to a considerable degree, determined by factors like historical development, "organizational culture"and working style. As long as the predicted changes affect only the work of one office worker, discretion may be used in deciding whether or not to actually implement the changes. If, however, the work of others is even marginally concerned these factors have found their manifestations in rules and regulations which, although in most cases not even documented, may nevertheless be a strong impediment to the realization of changes.

4.3 Application of Benefit Indicators

The functional view of FAOR based on a sequence of work processes called measurement units corresponds well with the distinction between efficiency and effectiveness (Hettich, 1981; Drucker, 1967), on the one hand, and the goal approach (Price, 1968) to the measurement of organizational performance on the other. Following these approaches, the measurement unit is interpreted as a large aggregated process. Evaluation takes place by constructing two major ratios (Figure 4) (Höring, 1985):

1. Efficiency expresses the input required to produce a specified unit of output.

2. Effectiveness assesses how well the output corresponds to specified goals.

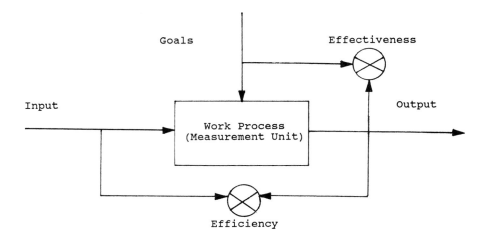

Figure 4. Application of Benefit Concepts to Measurement Units

Although the concepts of efficiency and effectiveness constitute a framework for thinking in terms of benefits, they are not sufficient for evaluation because they fail to tell the analyst what he should actually measure and how these benefits should be expressed. Any analysis of benefits must include the development of indicators which express the benefit factors in the same specific terms and objects with which the analysis deals. In one area, the number of units produced per time period may be the appropriate indicator of efficiency while in another, because of scarce raw material, its consumption is the main indicator for efficiency. In most cases, however, it is a question of selecting the proper indicator mix.

The choice of indicators clearly depends on the characteristics of the system evaluated. This also applies to office systems:

- the efficiency of the office system, and thus its contribution to reducing the resource consumption, is determined by the supporting character of office systems. Aspects of automation and the consumption of raw material are of lesser importance. Moreover, the output units of office work, i.e., information objects, are for the most part not as easily "countable" as manufacturing output. The degree of support can be assessed on the basis of:

    1. Manpower requirements, since the working time for carrying out the work processes of the measurement unit is subject to change.

    2. Utilization of services or facilities. These may be rendered obsolete by the office system, e.g., telex facilities which are no longer needed.

- the effectiveness of the office system, and thus its contribution to the goal achievement, is determined mainly by the power and integration of the tools it is directly and permanently offering to the office worker and by its concentration on information. Areas where office systems primarily enhance the capabilities of the office worker are:

1. Increased ability to react to unforeseen events because the office worker has the necessary information and tools at hand.

2. Reduced elapsed time for carrying out a measurement unit due to communication support and tool integration which also often allows a lower degree of division of labor.

3. Improved information basis by making information readily available.

A further indicator refers to the so called value-added benefit, often seen as an office system's major benefit. It occurs when the office system allows the office worker to do new things or additional work he could not do without the support of the office system (Lodahl, 1980).

With the set of indicators mentioned above, FAOR attempts to align the most important categories of benefits to the organization. However, the analyst must be aware that the indicators themselves are the result of selection and structuring. They are intended as a guide for the analyst but cannot claim to be comprehensive in all possible evaluation situations.

A further feature of these indicators which determines their practical usage should also be mentioned: in investigating office work, it is difficult to get absolute figures which, for example, pertain to the manpower requirements for carrying out a specific work process or the degree of goal achievement. For most studies, however, it is sufficient to clarify aspects which are likely to change in terms of indicators used or to derive rough estimates of the degree of change. To know these aspects and the determining factors of their occurrence is more important in an evaluation than a forced quantification which introduces a high error rate.

This can even apply to the indicators of efficiency. Although the concept of efficiency aims at evaluating the resource utilization and thus concentrates on costs, it is often based on factors which cannot be reliably quantified. The approach applied in the benefit analysis will be illustrated using the example of manpower requirements. The usage of facilities and services as the other indicator employs similar principles.

An investigation of the work processes belonging to the measurement unit may well show that some work processes are likely to require significantly less working time if supported by an office system. However, a thorough analysis has to look at the interdependencies between the work processes as well. Some work processes might merely be replaced by shadow functions relating to the handling of the office system such as learning, configuring and updating. If a fairly accurate estimate of changes in the manpower requirements for carrying out the work processes can really be derived, the analyst faces the difficulty of evaluation in terms of costs. This is, at the same time, an aggregation with an extended scope of investigation. Its problems are illustrated by the well known example of the half hour time saving prediction for each office worker which invariably cannot be converted into personnel reductions, even if a large number of office workers are

involved.   This issue of evaluation and aggregation requires an
additional step.

4.4 Evaluation and Aggregation

A benefit analysis method cannot solve this dilemma nor can it
provide the analyst with reliable data in indeterminate and
complex situations. However, it can point out the aspects crucial
for consideration and the criteria to be applied, e.g., under
which circumstances conclusions relating to aggregations can be
drawn. Experience with the practical evaluation of office systems
has shown that expectations of substantial cost avoidance or
improved economic results are usually too optimistic because the
office work load cannot be freely allocated to the available
office workers as it does not render itself easily divided into
small, fairly independent parts and office workers tend to
substitute the available time for other tasks, such as efforts to
improve the quality of the output they produce. Since the
application of work processes and support geared towards achieving
higher-quality output belong to the strongest of arguments in
favor of office systems, these impediments against the realization
of economic benefits should not be viewed as generally negative.
However, the analyst must remain well aware of the fact that there
is a kind of trade-off between economic and non-economic benefits.

The FAOR Benefit Analysis has developed some concepts to assist
the analyst to derive realistic cost-saving assumptions. They are
orientated towards existing "cost paradigms" and thus form a
framework of thinking rather than providing concrete criteria.
For example, the evaluation of working-time savings towards a
reduction in manpower costs is based on the concept of "opportunity costs." Working-time savings can only be counted as cost
reductions according to the best alternative usage of this manpower. It does not make sense to count as benefits time savings
which only occur seasonally when the manpower concerned is not
fully utilized or in cases when the work load cannot be reallo-
cated and there is no alternative usage of spare time generated as
an effect of the office system.

The analyst facing the issue of aggregating efficiency benefits
must also be aware, more than in the case of individual benefits,
that these can only be achieved if the introduction of the office
system is accompanied by a thorough organizational design or
redesign of the office work and the chosen organizational measures
are stable and exceptions adequately considered, otherwise short-
term effects can be easily misinterpreted as benefits.

Unfortunately, the evaluation and aggregation of effectiveness
benefits cannot be based on such well established criteria as
"opportunity costs." The approach chosen for the FAOR Benefit
Analysis rests on the evaluation of changes in the degree of goal
achievement. Although, theoretically, goals can be attributed to
the measurement unit, in practice, goals are fuzzy and difficult
to identify and specify. To state the set of goals, possibly
together with achievement criteria, almost always involves significant subjective interpretation on the part of the analyst as
well as a strong bias simply by selecting particular office
workers for interviews.

Despite these shortcomings, the concept of effectiveness in terms
of goal achievement is useful as it gives a fairly clear idea of

the purpose the investigated office system is intended to serve. By deliberately trying to identify measurement unit goals and through an attempt to evaluate the contribution that the office system makes to the achievement of these or even higher-level goals, the analyst has a means by which he may closely investigate the impact of the office system on work results. In particular, the question of secondary or propagated benefits has to be given extensive thought. An example of such secondary benefits would occur if a generally faster reaction to customer inquiries produced more customer orders.

The goals attributable to the measurement units and their relationship to higher-level objectives are highly situational. The criteria for this evaluation can only have the effect of inducing the office worker to carry out a careful analysis, e.g., to argue convincingly that the office system plays an important role in removing an existing bottleneck or that the technology factor is apparent in the output change assumed to be the cause of the improvement.

It is also important for the analyst to recognize the strong interdependencies between the different benefit categories, e.g., that efficiency benefits are often a prerequisite for achieving effectiveness benefits. Particularly in the fourth step of the FAOR Benefit Analysis, which discusses evaluation and aggregation, the office system must be perceived in the wider context of the organization in which it functions.

5. CONCLUSIONS

A benefit analysis study should be done on a basis specifically related to the organization if it aims at achieving a comprehensive evaluation. Investigations into the general productivity potential of office systems can only give a very rough impression of the types of benefits that can be expected. In particular, they do not take into account:

- differences in the occurrences of office work;
- evaluation and aggregation problems associated with analyzing efficiency benefits;
- that reliable criteria for effectiveness evaluation can only be derived from the objectives of the individual organization.

The functional view selected as the basis of the FAOR Benefit Analysis provides an effective filter for distinguishing mere effects from countable benefits and, at the same time, it provides a framework for a stepwise approach.

An important aspect not dealt with in this paper is the application condition of a benefit analysis method. Three main categories exist which require specific attention:

1. Determining on an aggregate level a rough estimate of the benefits office technology in general might generate in the investigated organization.

2. Comparison of the benefits of various alternatives on a detailed level in order to find the best one and to derive insight into where improvements can be made.

3. Post-implementation, in order to compare the real benefits with the forecasted ones. The results should indicate the reasons for any deviations from the predicted results and hence necessary further actions, i.e., in terms of additional organizational measures.

The FAOR Benefit Analysis has been deliberately constructed so that it has sufficient flexibility to cope with all three situations.

REFERENCES

Bair, J. H., "Productivity Assessment of Office Information Systems Technology," in *Trends and Applications 1978: Distributed Processing*, National Bureau of Standards, Gaithersburg, Maryland, May 18, 1978.

Bair, J. H., "Communication in the Office of the Future: Where the Real Pay-off May Be," in Inose, H. (ed.), *Evolutions in Computer Communications: Proceedings of the Fourth International Conference on Computer Communication*, Kyoto, Japan, September 26-29, 1978, pp. 733-740.

Booz, Allen and Hamilton, *Multi-Client Study of Managerial/Professional Productivity*, 1980.

Driscoll, J. W., "Office Automation: The Dynamics of a Technological Boondoggle," in Landau, R. M., Bair, J. H., and Siegman, J. H. (eds.), *Office Systems*, Norwood, New Jersey, 1980, pp. 259-277.

Drucker, P. F., *The Effective Executive*, Harper and Row, New York, 1967.

Hammer, M., and Zisman, M., *Design and Implementation of Office Information Systems*, Exxon Enterprises Incorporated, May 1979, pp. 1-43.

Hammer, M., "The OA Mirage," *Datamation*, Vol. 30, No. 2, 1983, pp. 36-46.

Hettich, G., *Struktur, Funktion und Effizienz betrieblicher Informations-systeme*, unpublished dissertation, Eberhard-Karls-Universitat zu Tubingen, 1981.

Höring, K., "Büroarbeit als Schlüssel für das Verständnis des Bürosystems," in Seibt, D., Szyperski, N., and Hasenkamp, U. (eds.), *Ange wandte Informatik*, Wiesbaden-Braunschweig, 1985, pp. 99-106.

Höring, K., "Die MAPIT-Analyse: Produktivität des Management und Verwaltungsbereiches und der Informationstechnik," presentation at the BIFOA Seminar, Instrumente der Burosystemplanung, Walberberg, November 28-29, 1985.

Klein, H. K., and Hirschheim, R., "Issues and Approaches to Appraising Technological Change in the Office: A Consequentialist Perspective," *Office Technology and People*, Vol. 2, No. 1, August 1983, pp. 15-42.

Kunin, J. S., *Analysis and Specification of Office Procedures*, Massachusetts Institute of Technology, Cambridge, Massachusetts, 1982.

Lodahl, T. M., "Cost-Benefit Concepts and Application for Office Automation," *AFIPS Office Automation Conference*, Atlanta, Georgia, 1980.

Malouin, J. L., and Landry, M., "The Mirage of Universal Methods in Systems Design," *Journal of Applied Systems Analysis*, Vol. 10, April 1983, pp. 47-62.

Nordsieck, F., *Die schaubildliche Erfassung und Untersuchung der Betriebsorganisation*, 5. Aufl., Stuttgart, 1956.

Panko, R. R., "Office Work," *Office Technology and People*, Vol. 2, 1984, pp. 205-238.

Picot, A., and Reichwald, R., *Bürokommunikation, Leitsätze für den Anwender*, C. W. Publikationen, Munchen, 1984.

Price, J. L., *Organizational Effectiveness*, Richard D. Irwin, Inc., Homewood, Illinois, 1968.

Rauch, W. D., *Büro-Informations-Systeme*, Wein-Köln-Graz, 1982.

Sirbu, M. A., "Understanding the Social and Economic Impacts of Office Automation," Massachusetts Institute of Technology, Report CPA-82-19, November 1982.

Strassman, P. A., "Xerox Case Studies with High-Performance Work Stations," *Convention Informatique ISICOB*, Paris, September 1981.

Szyperski, N., "Analyse der Merkmale und Formen der Büroarbeit," in Kosiol, E. (ed.), *Bürowirtschaftliche Forschung*, Berlin, 1961, pp. 75-132.

Tapscott, D., *Office Automation: A User-Driven Method*, Plenum Press, New York, 1982.

Töpfer, A., Bromann, P., Odemer, W., Möller, R., and Herold, A., "Neue Techniken der Bürokommunikation," *Kienbaum Unternehmensgruppe*, October 1985.

Uhlig, R. P., Faber, D. J., and Bair, J. H., *The Office of the Future*, North-Holland, Amsterdam, 1979.

DISCUSSANT NOTE

On: BENEFIT ANALYSIS OF OFFICE SYSTEMS:
      CONCEPTS FOR A METHOD

By: Gunther Schäfer

Discussant's comments by: F. J. HEEMSTRA

Technical University Eindhoven
The Netherlands

1.   INTRODUCTION

In my daily work, I focus my attention primarily on the research
of cost estimation for the development of software (not only
coding, but starting from the requirements analysis until maintenance). From this point of view, I want to give my opinion on this
paper. I think there is much correspondence in the problems for
identifying/estimating the costs and benefits for an office system
to realize or a software product to develop. Also, in the
approach to handling these problems there are (in my opinion) many
parallels.

2.   IDENTIFICATION PROCESS

The process of identifying the effects of a proposed change (i.e.,
the application of an office system or the realization of a specific software product) has to contain the following three elements:

1)   *Historical data.*   In identifying/estimating the costs and
     benefits of a software product/office system, there must be a
     comparison of the data of old projects and the specific new
     project. The more comprehensive the data, the better such a
     comparison or estimation can be.

2)   *A model.* A model uses formulas, derived from the empirical/
     historical data, to predict the factors that influence the
     costs and benefits of a system and also to predict the degree
     of these influences (often in a subjective and qualitative
     way, as you can read in the paper).

3)   *Data about the specific system.* It is necessary to charac-
     terize the system that must be realized; "the proposal
     change," mentioned in this paper. These characteristics are
     the input for the model. This is the task of the analyst, an
     expert in my opinion.

3.   DISCUSSION POINTS

When I am looking at the subject of identifying/estimating the
costs and benefits of office systems in this way, there are some
questions that may be a starting point for the discussion.

a) Identifying the characteristics of a specific office system
    will be the task of an expert; the analyst in the paper. Is
    it possible to objectivize this task? Another expert with a
    different background might look for other characteristics and
    this, of course, means different benefits.

b) The FAOR-analyst uses, I suppose, a certain implicit model.
    A model for identifying and estimating costs and benefits
    should exhibit certain characteristics;for example:

    o the results of the estimation have to meet certain
       quality requirements, such as accuracy, stability,
       objectivity, etc.

    o the model should include possibilities for sensitivity
       analysis

    o it should be easy to use

    Does the analyst indeed use such a model and, if so, does
    this model meet these kinds of requirements?

c) The analyst shall (certainly) make use of historical data
    (experience); in this paper, "exercise in predictions." I
    think there are many arguments to build a database for these
    historical data.

Assessing Conflict in System Design
D. Robey, D.L. Farrow and C.R. Franz

"Conflict is an important organizational process
because of its close relation to
innovation and change."

INFORMATION SYSTEMS ASSESSMENT
N. Bjørn-Andersen, G.B. Davis (Editors)
Elsevier Science Publishers B.V. (North-Holland)
© IFIP, 1988

ASSESSING CONFLICT IN SYSTEM DESIGN

Daniel ROBEY

Department of Management
Florida International University
Miami, Florida 33199 USA

Dana L. FARROW

Department of Management
Florida International University
Miami, Florida 33199 USA

Charles R. FRANZ

Department of Management
University of Missouri
Columbia Missouri 65211 USA

The design and implementation of information
systems typically engages a number of participants
in a process of social and technical change. So
far, information systems assessment has focused on
the outcome of this process and paid less attention
to the process itself. This paper describes a
study undertaken to assess the process of user-led
system development, with particular attention to
conflict during system design. By assessing
conflict with a variety of methods -- including
interviews, questionnaires, and structured observations of group meetings -- a change agent or
project manager can make adjustments where necessary to use conflict more constructively.

1. INTRODUCTION

1.1 Assessing Process

In recent years the process of information system (IS) development
has received considerable attention in the management science and
IS literature. Expensive system failures have led many writers to
recommend more structured methodologies for systems design.
Failures have also been attributed to behavioral and organizational factors, and prescriptions for user involvement in system
development (Bjørn-Andersen and Hedberg, 1977; Lucas, 1976)
frequently accompany such diagnoses. User involvement promises
not only improvements in the technical performance of information
systems, but also greater understanding and acceptance by users.

The assessment of IS success has been conceived as a broad problem
of evaluating both process and outcomes. As Keen has stated,
"Evaluation is part of the wider process of implementation and

begins before the system is designed" (Keen, 1975, p. 19).
Hamilton and Chervany (1981) include user participation in their
objectives for IS effectiveness and recommend that the amount and
type of involvement be measured along with more concrete measures
such as budget variances, schedule compliance, training expenditures, and productivity. Few studies, however, have addressed
this need for longitudinal assessment of the development process.
Edelman (1981) performed a natural experiment at RCA Corporation
to assess the economic impact of a large IS for industrial
relations, but he did not assess the development process directly.
Ginzberg (1981) successfully predicted post-implementation
attitudes and behavior from users' pre-implementation expectations
of a large bank's portfolio management system. However, the
involvement of users during the four years between system definition and completion was not assessed directly.

Our purpose is to describe a method for assessing user involvement
and conflict during system development. Our approach views
conflict as a potentially constructive process that can lead to
creative solutions for difficult problems. However, conflict can
also produce destructive outcomes. It thus becomes necessary to
assess the process of conflict during system development projects,
in which users are directly involved, in order to keep them on a
productive course. The use of this assessment methodology is
illustrated by tracking an IS development project over one-and-a-
half years.

1.2   Conflict and System Development

Conflict is an important organizational process because of its
close relation to innovation and change. Performance problems may
stimulate a search for innovative solutions, which in turn provide
opportunities for different interest groups in an organization to
engage in conflict. Conflict unfolds as a series of episodes
(Pondy, 1967) and may be traced to structural causes such as
differentiation of goals, interdependence, and resource scarcity
(Watson and Dutton, 1969). In attempting to achieve its own goals
as completely as possible, each group may inadvertently or
intentionally interfere with the efforts of other groups to
achieve their goals (Schmidt and Kochan, 1972). The result is
conflict.

Conflict can be either a destructive or constructive force in
organizations. Deutsch (1969) used the term "productive conflict"
to describe cases where conflict helps to prevent domination and
stagnation, raise problems and encourage their solution, stimulate
interest and curiosity, and foster creativity and innovation.
Managing conflict to get these productive results requires high
levels of participation and influence among all parties faced with
a common problem. By confronting differences and resolving them,
the possibilities for higher quality solutions that have group
acceptance are increased (Lawrence and Lorsch, 1967; Leavitt,
1965; Lewin, 1952; Maier, 1967).

In system development, the potential for conflict is great.
System development brings different groups such as users and
designers together in intense interactions, where the goals of the
different parties may be incompatible (Markus and Robey, 1983;
Robey and Markus, 1984). Pressures to meet specific deadlines,
incorporate state-of-the-art technology, and be "user-friendly"
may be difficult to satisfy with a single set of guides for system

design. Accordingly, strong disagreements may surface as users try to assert their needs for control over technological choices that affect them. These assertions may be countered aggressively by systems professionals who believe that they understand the best way to design information systems.

While user involvement is frequently recommended for such situations, and can lead to successful outcomes under some circumstances, its general usefulness has been questioned. Ives and Olson (1984) reviewed the empirical studies on user involvement and found very mixed support for the general hypothesis that user involvement leads to system success. They criticized most of the studies on user involvement for a number of methodological weaknesses and for their lack of theoretical grounding.

To this criticism we add the failure of these studies to describe the way conflicts between users and developers were managed during the development process. Theories of conflict represent a relatively strong conceptual basis for research on user involvement, but one which has been neglected. Yet, conflict can be thought of as a general process through which disagreements on design issues are confronted, addressed, and resolved. Because conflict can result in either productive or destructive outcomes, depending on how it is managed, an understanding of conflict can potentially explain the mixed results found currently in the literature.

Robey (1984) has described a model which spells out the assumptions behind the constructive use of conflict for joint problem solving in system development. Assumptions include: (1) the recognition of superordinate goals in addition to group subgoals; (2) the importance of a third party consultant or group leader with behavioral skills; (3) information sharing; (4) the belief that consensus can be achieved; and (5) the belief that greater influence for each party produces more effective solutions and more satisfied participants. Robey contrasts these assumptions to those of a "negotiation" model that can also be used in system development.

One of the most important assumptions of the model of constructive conflict is the sharing of information through open communication. This aspect of constructive conflict has direct implications for group meetings involving users and designers. If communication is one-way, or is not balanced between the parties, open communication has not occurred. The ideal is for all members at a meeting to participate fully, to respond to questions in an honest fashion, and to volunteer information that one thinks will be helpful to solve a problem. An imbalance among participants can be a sign of problems if it indicates that views are being held privately but not expressed, or if more powerful members are controlling a meeting by not allowing others to speak.

The role of conflict in system development has been the focus of few studies. Robey and Farrow (1982) developed a descriptive model showing the relationships among user participation, influence, conflict, and conflict resolution during the various stages of system development. The model was supported in their study of 62 users involved to some degree in system development. Kaiser and Bostrom (1982) and White (1984) explored the role of personality differences and similarities in project groups. Where project teams were composed of different psychological types, as measured by the Myers Briggs Type Indicator, project performance was more successful than in a more homogeneous group. Group diversity creates communication problems within a group, and more potential conflict, but addressing these differences constructively can lead to design of a system that meets diverse user needs. Finally, Salaway (1987) developed and tested a model of system development based on the Argyris and Schon (1978) theory of organizational learning. She demonstrated that ordinary transactions between users and designers are typified by defensive and error-prone communication. Salaway engaged subjects in a training program where they learned more authentic, error-free communication for system development.

These studies, while few in number, support the notion that conflict is an important process in system development. Those interested in successful project outcomes would be well served by an assessment of the conflict process during system development. In the remainder of this paper we describe a case in which such an assessment was conducted. While the authors were not process consultants to the organization in question, our data and analyses could have been used to modify the events described below. This assessment and intervention might have altered the outcome from one that showed signs of failure to more positive outcomes for both users and designers.

2.   METHOD

This research took place in a medium-sized insurance company called Northeast in this paper. Details of the case are reported in Franz and Robey (1984) and only a brief summary is given here. In March 1982, authorization was given by management to design a new IS for processing automobile insurance policies. From the beginning the new Auto INsurance System (AINS) was to be developed according to the principles of user-led design. Accordingly, the head of the processing department was given authority to direct the entire project. Over the next two years, the researchers studied Northeast's attempts to design AINS. The development activities included an initial attempt to enhance the old auto policy system so that AINS could be built over it, development of functional specifications for AINS, and the design of program modules, system logic, and database. In January 1984, the researchers ended their relationship with Northeast, with the AINS project seriously behind schedule and suffering from turnover of key personnel and other unresolved problems.

Past research on the process of system development has been limited by static research methods which provide little insight into a dynamic process (Franz and Robey, 1987). It was our objective to describe in a complete fashion what went on during the process of IS development, and to relate this description to the concept of constructive conflict developed previously (Robey and Farrow, 1982). Elsewhere (Franz and Robey, 1984), we have described, in narrative form, the events of the case and provided rational and political interpretations of these events. In this paper we draw upon the quantitative data that were collected and provide corroborating evidence for the narrative description. This use of multiple sources of data improves the chance that our assessment of conflict is not biased toward one data collection method. Jick (1979) has called this data collection strategy "triangulation," and we view it as a necessary part of process assessment.

Two types of quantitative data were collected at various time intervals throughout AINS's design history. First, participants' perceptions of participation, influence, conflict, and conflict resolution were collected by questionnaire. Data collection usually followed a project meeting involving the participants. The scales used were based on the single-item measures used by Robey and Farrow (1982), but the number of items was increased to three or four to improve reliability. The reliabilities of the four scales were estimated by coefficient alphas. Since the number of respondents was rather small at each time of data collection, and since some of the individual respondents changed from meeting to meeting, coefficient alpha reliabilities were calculated for each of the scales for each meeting and then averaged using the Fisher Z transformation. (Reliability estimates from the May 3 meeting were excluded because there were only three participants in that meeting, causing the reliability estimates to be extremely unstable). Our estimates of internal consistency reliabilities were based on seven data collection periods, with six to 14 respondents at each period. Mean alpha reliabilities for each scale were (with the range for each scale in parentheses): .79 for participation (.68 to .86), .94 for influence (.88 to .97), .78 for conflict (.43 to .91), and .87 for conflict resolution (.65 to .93).

Second, the researchers attended seven group meetings during which interactions were recorded and coded as either questions or statements. This provided a sociometric analysis of communications in each meeting. Because our primary interest was balance of communication between users and developers, participants were classified as designer-users (DU), data processing experts (EX), and non-designer-users (ND), and the data aggregated for each type of participant. Non-designer-users were members of top management or members from departments that were affected by AINS but who were not on the design team. Interactions involving non-designer-users generally took place only in steering committee meetings. Data were collected on meetings held between April 5, 1982 and March 21, 1983. In addition, questionnaire data only were collected on January 11, 1984.

3. RESULTS AND DISCUSSION

3.1 Perceived Participation, Influence, Conflict, and Resolution

Figure 1 plots the means for perceived participation, influence, conflict, and conflict resolution for each of the eight data collection periods. The vertical scale of the graph indicates the average response on a 5-item scale. The horizontal scale indicates the dates for data collection. The number of respondents at each point in time and the purpose of each meeting is also indicated on Figure 1.

Figure 1 shows considerable change in conflict and influence during the first four meetings, followed by relatively little change in all four variables through January 1984. Most notably, the overall perception of conflict increased dramatically after initial meetings in April 1982 to a high level during a design team meeting in May 1982. The amount of influence began at a high level, dropped during the second steering committee meeting, and remained about the same throughout the remaining observation periods.

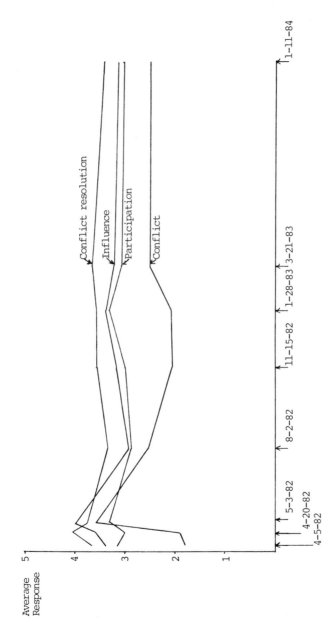

Figure 1:   Means for Participation, Influence, Conflict and Conflict
            Resolution for All Time Periods

This pattern suggests that the participants were dealing with some major issues early in the project. In fact, it was during May and June of 1982 that disagreements over the direction of the project were aired, especially on the issue of who would control the development of AINS. The designer-users wanted to begin system design by specifying formats for data collection screens, whereas data processing wanted to enhance the old system first and begin new system design with a complete review of existing procedures and problems. In the meeting on August 2, 1982, the steering committee decided to abandon the approach favored by data processing and authorized the head of the user department to proceed with new system specifications.

The aggregated responses in Figure 1 do not reveal how the members of different subgroups perceived their own involvement. The disaggregated perceptions for each of the three subgroups (designer-user, non-designer-user and data processing expert) were also analyzed, although space does not allow the inclusion of the plotted data. The general pattern for each participant group is discussed individually below.

3.1.1 Designer-Users' Perceptions

The designer-users rated their participation during the first two steering committee meetings as high. In these meetings they played a major role in sponsoring and defining the direction of the new system. The perceived influence of the designer-users was also very high during the first steering committee meeting. They perceived low conflict, due mostly to shared enthusiasm by other departmental managers who anticipated the benefits of the system for their own departments. The designer-users' perceptions of satisfactory conflict resolution probably result from the support given by upper management and other departments for a long overdue redesign of the current automobile system.

The second steering committee meeting was led by the designer-users to propose that the company proceed with planning and designing new system specifications. The designer-users had become impatient with enhancing the old system and wanted to proceed as quickly as possible. Their thorough presentation to Northeast management during the meeting won management's approval for their planned control over the development of detailed user specifications for the new system. This appears to account for the high participation perceived by the designer-users. Yet they rate their influence during the second meeting as diminishing from the initial proposal to enhance and redesign AINS. The decrease in designer-user influence could be due to the role the data processing analyst played in presenting two critical issues to the company (payment plan method and new policy holder identification numbers). Considerable discussion took place to air differences and understand major design plans and decisions about AINS. The designer-users rated conflict as increasing and seemed to perceive that attempts at resolving differences were much less effective than in the first steering committee meeting.

Participation decreased during subsequent meetings when the logical design specifications became finalized and subject to user signoff. Non-designer-users participated more actively in the third steering committee meeting. The reduction in designer-user participation and influence during this meeting probably resulted from the Underwriting Vice President's concern about adding comprehensive auto coverage to AINS. This issue produced other questions from upper management that were answered by the Vice President of Underwriting. Although the designer-users' influence decreased, sharing presentation time with non-designer-users appeared to reduce the perceptions of conflict and increase perceptions of conflict resolution.

The fourth steering committee meeting was held to approve the functional specifications of AINS developed by the designer-users. The data reveal that the designer-users perceived increased conflict during this meeting as upper management and other non-designer-users addressed some critical problems in AINS's functional design. Omissions and errors in handling liability coverage were pointed out but not resolved in the meeting, resulting in the perceptions of low conflict resolution. The head designer-user later sent a written request to executive management for clarification on the many decisions about issues raised during this meeting.

Overall, the data on the designer-users show participation and influence beginning at high levels during meetings emphasizing planning and design decisions, followed by lower levels when meeting time was shared with others to clarify problems and issues. Conflict was low and conflict resolution high during discussions of AINS's design objectives. During the later meetings, discussion focused more on problems, which heightened the perceptions of conflict. Since the conflicts were not resolved in the meetings, designer-users' perceptions of conflict resolution were low.

3.1.2 Non-designer-users' Perceptions

The non-designer-users were excluded from most of the preliminary planning between April and August 1982. Hence, they rated their participation much lower than the designer-users. Although they perceived themselves as moderately involved during the first steering committee meeting, they participated much more during the third and fourth meetings when problems with AINS became apparent to them. During the fourth steering committee meeting (March 1983), non-designer-users from Claims and Underwriting detected some major omissions in the proposed design of AINS. Discussions on these problems account for the high amount of conflict for both the designer-users and the non-designer-users. However, both groups perceived that considerable conflict resolution took place. The exchange of viewpoints during the fourth steering committee meeting was an attempt to resolve the problems and communicate to the designer-users the remaining changes that needed to be included in the AINS design.

It is interesting to compare the designer-users' and non-designer-users' perceptions. The designer-users initially wanted to gain control over the AINS project. They rated their participation and influence much higher than did the non-designer-users. Our field notes support the interpretation that the non-designer-users regarded AINS as belonging to the designer-users and that the Processing Department stood to benefit the most from a new system. Yet as the system design progressed, non-designer-users became aware of errors and omissions. This explains why they perceive themselves as participating more and exerting higher influence to effect necessary changes. Although their perceptions of conflict tend to parallel those of the designer-users, their perceptions of conflict resolution during the later meetings are quite different. The data indicate non-designer-users expressing much more satis-factory resolution of conflict than that expressed by the de-signer-users.

3.1.3 Data Processing Experts' Perceptions

The high degree of control by the designer-users over the design of AINS's functional specifications relegated the data processing experts to the role of observers, responding only when asked ques-tions about the technical feasibility of certain design features. Initially the experts tried to be influential by initiating their own research on existing system problems and recommending various enhancements to the existing system. They also attempted to impose traditional methods of project management on the develop-ment of AINS, but the designer-users contested these efforts. The designer-user manager agreed on enhancements proposed by the experts, but objected when they began to take too long. Both the experts and the designer-users perceived moderately high conflict during meetings in May 1982, but both groups perceived conflict resolution to be high. Since the experts and the designer-users interacted very little with each other during this time, each might have believed that both were contributing positively to the objectives of the new system.

The second steering committee meeting was dominated by presen-tations from designer-users and one presentation by the system analyst. According to the data, the experts perceived themselves as having little participation and influence. Most of the discus-sion occurred between designer-users and non-designer-users on company-wide policy issues, which the experts did not regard as conflict.

Data processing personnel were consulted more often during the third and fourth steering committee meetings about the technical feasibility of some proposed design features. Much of this participation was response to questions asked of them by the non-designer-users. Expert influence was not as high during the third and fourth steering committee meetings as it was during their earlier attempt to influence the direction of system development. In contrast to the other participants, the experts perceived much less conflict during the third and fourth meetings, but they also perceived lower amounts of conflict resolution. Data processing perceived the lowest conflict and conflict resolution in January 1983. At this time, the system analyst was the primary technical participant in design and all participants acknowledged upper management's desire for cooperation to develop the "best possible system for the company."

In summary, data processing experts played a background role to both groups of users during the planning and design of AINS. However, their perceptions changed dramatically over the course of the project. The designer-users' successful pressure on top management for user-led design forced the experts into a less active role once the contest for control was decided. However, when the experts regained control of AINS after signing off on the system's functional specifications, their influence and conflict with the designer-users increased sharply. The experts at this point excluded the designer-users from remaining technical design considerations.

3.2 Observational Data

The interpretation of the perceptual data is corroborated by a focus on the interactions observed between participants at the seven meetings. Figure 2 displays the interactions in pie chart form. The total number of interactions is recorded for each meeting and is proportional to the area of each chart. The percentage of statements is represented by the area beginning at the "12 o'clock" position and moving clockwise. The remainder of the circle represents "questions."

The general picture from the first three meetings -- April 5, April 20 and May 3 -- suggests balanced communication, where each party took the opportunity to express viewpoints about the course of the AINS project. Meeting transcripts, interview data, and the questionnaire results support the interpretation that the designer-users and experts were in conflict over the proper course that AINS development should take. The meetings were apparently used as forums for the debate to occur.

The first meeting consists mainly of questions by designer-users to experts, and experts explaining their plans in response to those questions. The pie chart is dominated by statements made by experts to designer-users.

The second meeting involved a large steering committee with five non-designer-users present. The function of the data processing experts was again primarily technical consultation, answering questions from users and management. Although the enhancements were still being proposed, the pattern of interactions indicates more balance of discussion among the designer-users and non-designer-users. This would be expected in a meeting where the objective was to plan the objectives and critical features of the AINS system.

A smaller design team meeting was held on May 3, 1982 to discuss the data processing analyst's research on the old system. The designer-users had questions about the technical difficulty of making certain enhancements. Additionally, the manager asked many questions of his supervisor about procedures for processing new business applications. These data suggest that both parties exerted considerable influence, which is consistent with the questionnaire data.

By summer, the designer-user manager had become impatient with the lack of progress on enhancements, which were estimated to take another six or eight months to complete. He used his influence to solicit management's approval to convene a steering committee meeting in August for the purpose of declaring the formal beginning of AINS design, ending any further work on enhancements. The designer-user manager proposed a plan of implementation that included some presentations by data processing experts and designer-user presentations on plans for installment billing. Much of the agenda at the August meeting stemmed from earlier enhancement objectives and is confirmed by written memos from the designer-user manager to the data processing manager. The designer-user manager appeared to have employed a tactic of minimally involving the experts and including some of their enhancement objectives as a means to resolve conflict over the enhancement issue. At this meeting, the non-designer-users agreed with this strategy.

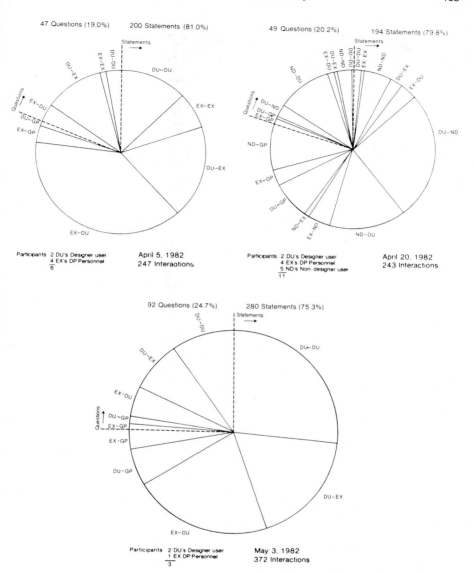

Figure 2: Interaction Percentages for Meetings

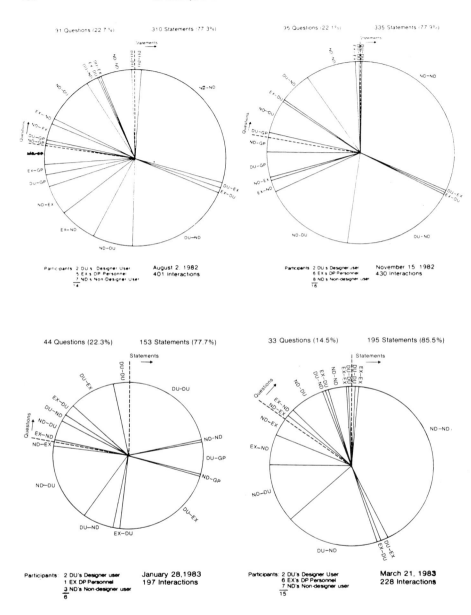

Figure 2: Interaction Percentages for Meetings (Continued)

The interaction pattern in the fourth meeting, on August 2 1982, indicates a shrinking role for the data processing experts. Discussion was monopolized by the seven non-designer-users present and the two designer-users. The non-designer-users posed many questions to the designer-users about their plans for designing the new system. Tape recordings from this meeting revealed that the non-designer-users were attempting to clarify among themselves some of the AINS features and functions. Most of the statements made by experts seem to be explanations to non-designer-users. However, the largest proportion of statements were made by non-designer-users to other non-designer-users and by the designer-user manager to explain and clarify his plan for AINS.

Interactions among users and experts remained minimal from this point until the seventh meeting on March 21, 1983, even though experts continued to be present at all meetings. The steering committee meeting on November 15, 1982 was dominated by communications between designer-users and non-designer-users with minimal contributions by experts. A major issue arising at this meeting was the proposed inclusion of a new comprehensive insurance coverage in AINS, a feature that would delay completion of the project by two or three more months. Part of the discussion was on whether to acquire this feature or develop it in-house, and part of it dealt with problems that new comprehensive coverage presented, such as new processing procedures and new liabilities. Claims had many questions and much expertise to offer regarding these problem areas. The experts had virtually no questions for anyone and offered just a few statements, most likely to clarify or confirm that something was technically feasible.

The smaller meeting on January 28, 1983 continues this pattern of communication among users and the exclusion of experts. Particularly significant is the relatively large proportion of questions from the designer-users to the experts and the paucity of statements by the experts in response to these questions.

The last meeting for which we have interaction data took place on March 21, 1983. This was to be a structured "walk through" of AINS's functional specifications conducted by the designer-users in preparation for the hand off of the project to data processing for physical construction of the system. Again, designer-users and non-designer-users dominated the discussion and virtually excluded the experts. Almost half of the interactions consisted of non-designer-users making statements to other non-designer-users. Discussion centered on two key concerns: the ability of AINS to reflect impending changes in insurance law and the compatibility of AINS' with the needs of users in other departments, such as Claims and Underwriting. Sixty percent of the questions were posed by the non-designer-users to the designer-users, while most of the remaining questions were for non-designer-users to clarify issues and concerns among themselves. The field notes from this meeting indicate that the designer-user manager was embarrassed by many of the questions and felt forced to make promises that would delay the project schedule. After six additional weeks of work, the functional specifications were formally handed off to the experts on May 1, 1983.

While our analysis of meeting data ends at this point, the field notes indicate that the designer-users drastically reduced their involvement with AINS after the hand off in May. AINS was now data processing's project, and any more problems with it would be blamed on the experts. By January 11, 1984, the date of our last questionnaire administration, the project had slipped even further behind schedule. Three separate changes in project leadership had occurred and several data processing personnel left the company. Designer-users remained uninvolved, and the data processing experts were coming under increasing pressure from top management to finish the project.

4. CONCLUSIONS

4.1 Implications for Management

Comprehensive assessment of a system design project can reveal problems and point to courses of corrective action and to prevention of further problems. By analyzing perceptions of participation, influence, conflict, and conflict resolution over time, we have seen where the problems with AINS arose. By charting interactions at group meetings, we have also seen when one important subgroup dropped out of the discussions almost entirely. These warning signs would be evident to a process consultant conducting an assessment such as the one described here. A skilled project leader could also use the data and directly encourage more balanced participation at group meetings.

Our experience in this research yields two suggestions for process consultants, project managers, or others responsible for project success. First, the most critical points in this project were early, during the planning phase. The data show that group members engaged in conflict and tested their influence up until the time when the direction for the project was decided. The conflict over control can potentially be a source of energy for creative problem solving. In these early stages, the process consultant should recognize group perceptions of their own influence and be ready to confront the conflict that will most likely coincide with influence. Later in the project, conflict potential is likely to be less. So the prime time for using conflict constructively should be early in the project.

Second, the consultant needs a method for confronting differences constructively to avoid situations that lead to destructive conflict. A questionnaire may be one tool used to detect and substantiate a process consultant's awareness of conflict. Observations and interviews could also be used. In the case of AINS, the researchers were able to monitor changes in conflict with questionnaires and to interpret the meaning of these changes by observing the group and interviewing individuals. The data collected can be shared with the participants to raise the group's consciousness of their own interpersonal dynamics.

4.2 Limitations of the Research

Our research objective was to capture the social dynamics of a systems development project. To accomplish this objective, we used a variety of methods to collect data longitudinally while the events of interest were actually occurring. The primary strength of this approach is the ability to discover and analyze in detail the process used to develop a single system.

The limitations of this strategy are also important to recognize. The internal validity of our findings may be questioned because no control group was used for comparison. We do not know what "caused" the events we described to occur, nor can we test any hypotheses regarding the effectiveness of systems development processes. External validity is also absent. Using a single organization makes it impossible to generalize to other systems and/or organizations. But the objective of the research was thorough description, not hypothesis testing. By demonstrating the usefulness of techniques used in one case, we believe we have served the interests of practitioners in other organizations where similar issues arise.

In conclusion, satisfaction of an information system's technical demands is a challenging task made even more difficult by the demands of managing the social dynamics that accompany technical change. However, if parties are made aware of the need for monitoring their own behavior, and consciously try to use the data they generate about themselves, it is possible to change the course of events like those observed at Northeast. Ideally, constructively managed conflict can produce feelings of teamwork and superior designs for information systems. The methodology described in this paper can allow participants to use conflict more constructively in the system development process.

REFERENCES

Argyris, C., and Schon, D., *Organizational Learning: A Theory of Action Perspective*, Addison-Wesley, Reading, Massachusetts, 1978.

Bjørn-Andersen, N., and Hedberg, B. L. T., "Designing Information Systems in an Organizational Perspective," *TIMS Studies in the Management Sciences*, 5, 1977, 125-142.

Deutsch, M., "Productive and Destructive Conflict," *Journal of Social Issues*, 25, 1969, 7-42.

Edelman, F., "Managers, Computer Systems, and Productivity," *MIS Quarterly*, 5, 1981, 1-19.

Franz, C.R., and Robey, D., "Investigation of User-Led System Design: Rational and Political Perspectives," *Communications of the ACM*, 27, 1984, 1202-1209.

Franz, C. R., and Robey, D., "Strategies for Research on Information Systems in Organizations: A Critical Analysis of Research Purpose and Time Frame," in Boland, R., and Hirschheim, R. (Eds.), *Critical Issues in Information Systems Research*, Wiley, New York, 1987, 205-225.

Ginzberg, M. J., "Early Diagnosis of MIS Implementation Failure: Promising Results and Unanswered Questions," *Management Science*, 27, 1981, 459-478.

Hamilton, S., and Chervany, N. L., "Evaluating Information System Effectiveness -- Part I: Comparing Evaluation Approaches," *MIS Quarterly*, 5, 1981, 55-69.

Ives, B., and Olson, M. H., "User Involvement and MIS Success: A Review of Research," *Management Science*, 30, 1984, 586-603.

Jick, T. D., "Mixing Qualitative and Quantitative Methods: Triangulation in Action," *Administrative Science Quarterly*, 24, 1979, 602-611.

Kaiser, K. M., and Bostrom, R. P., "Personality Characteristics of MIS Project Teams: An Empirical Study and Action-Research Design," *MIS Quarterly*, 6, 1982, 43-60.

Keen, P. G. W., "Computer Decision Aids: The Evaluation Problem," *Sloan Management Review*, Spring, 1975, 17-29.

Lawrence, P. R., and Lorsch, J. W., *Organization and Environment*, Harvard, Boston, 1967.

Leavitt, H. J., "Applied Organizational Change in Industry: Structural, Technological, and Humanistic Approaches," in March, J. G., (ed.), *Handbook of Organizations*, Rand-McNally, Chicago, 1965.

Lewin, K., "Group Decision and Social Change," in Newcomb and Hartley (Eds.), *Readings in Social Psychology*, Holt, New York, 1952.

Lucas, H.C., Jr., *The Analysis, Design, and Implementation of Information Systems*, McGraw-Hill, New York, 1976.

Maier, N. R. F., "Assets and Liabilities in Group Problem Solving: The Need for an Integrative Function," *Psychological Review*, 74, 1967, 239-249.

Markus, M. L., and Robey, D., "The Organizational Validity of Management Information Systems," *Human Relations*, 36, 1983, 203-226.

Pondy, L. R., "Organizational Conflict: Concepts and Models," *Administrative Science Quarterly*, 12, 1967, 296-320.

Robey, D., "Conflict Models for Implementation Research," in Schultz, R. L., and Ginzberg, M. J. (Eds.), *Applications of Management Science: Management Science Implementation*, JAI Press, Greenwich, Connecticut, 1984.

Robey, D., and Farrow, D. L., "User Involvement in Information System Development: A Conflict Model and Empirical Test," *Management Science*, 28, 1982, 73-85.

Robey, D., and Markus, M. L., "Rituals in Information System Design," *MIS Quarterly*, 8, 1984, 5-15.

Salaway, G., "An Organizational Learning Approach to Information Systems Development," *MIS Quarterly*, Vol. 11, 1987, 245-264.

Schmidt, S. M., and Kochan, T. A., "Conflict: Toward Conceptual Clarity," *Administrative Science Quarterly*, 17, 1972, 359-370.

Walton, R. E., and Dutton, J. M., "The Management of Interdepartmental Conflict: A Model and Review," *Administrative Science Quarterly*, 14, 1969, 73-82.

White, K. B., "MIS Project Teams: An Investigation of Cognitive Style Implications," *MIS Quarterly*, 8, 1984, 95-101.

DISCUSSANT NOTE

On: MEASURING THE PRAGMATIC QUALITY OF
      INFORMATION SYSTEMS

By: Gunhild Sandström

Discussant's comments by: Juhani IIVARI

University of Oulu
Finland

1.   INTRODUCTION

Sandström suggests the semantic differential technique as a method
for measuring the "pragmatic quality" of information systems.
"Pragmatic quality" should to depend on five areas: the computer
display language, the computer-based decision bases, the computer,
the user's professional language after computerization, and the
user's work after computerization.

2.   THE TERM "PRAGMATIC"

Sandström's choice of the term "pragmatic" is, to some extent,
unfortunate.   Although it is quite obvious that the use of the
word is based on semiotics rather than on the ordinary dictionary
meaning of the term ("practical"), it is by no means clear that it
is applied in the semiotic sense.   Pragmatics in semiotics refers
to "the effect of information vehicles on interpreters and the use
made of it by interpreters" (Nauta, 1972).   This semiotic meaning
includes, at least implicitly, a change aspect, the existence or
non-existence of the information vehicles or messages, a change
aspect which is not included in "pragmatic quality" as such (see
below).

3.   EARLIER RESEARCH

In assessing the importance of Sandström's work, it should be
observed that the first three areas of "pragmatic quality" seem to
correspond closely with or overlap the concept "User Information
Satisfaction" (UIS) or its variants (cf. Bailey and Pearson, 1983;
Ives, et al., 1983).   There has been substantial earlier research
in this area and the semantic differential technique is also
widely used (cf. Swanson, 1981).   In Sandström's paper, the
earlier research is referred to as an afterthought rather than as
a starting point.   This is unfortunate, since the use of existing
measurement instruments should be preferred in order to increase
the possibilities of cumulative research, or else the development
of a new measurement instrument should be carefully justified.

The last area of "pragmatic quality" in Sandström's framework is
closely related to the quality of work.   There has also been

significant earlier research on this topic and there are several frameworks available for its analysis.

The professional knowledge of users seem to be the least explored area of "pragmatic quality" and, in that sense, the most promising for further research. Sandstrom pays principal attention, however, to the UIS part of her framework and in particular to the computer-based decision bases, for which the measurement instrument is illustrated and its use briefly described in two case studies.

4.   "PRAGMATIC QUALITY" AND USER INFORMATION SATISFACTION

Sandström regards the measurement of "pragmatic quality" as quite non-problematic and seems to be unaware of the problems of UIS, to which increasing attention has been paid recently (e.g., Treacy, 1985; Swanson, 1986). One problem or paradox in UIS is the relative ease of "measurement," which has led to overuse of the concept and has overloaded it with various connotations. For instance, in accordance with much existing research into UIS, Sandstrom suggests that "pragmatic quality" reflects an effectiveness approach and can be used to measure the "success" of a system.

In our view, IS effectiveness is always related to an IS change (cf. Hawgood and Land, 1986). It is obvious that "pragmatic quality" describes a user-related state rather than the effects of an IS change and does not describe directly IS effectiveness. But used longitudinally, it may provide useful information on IS effectiveness from the user's point of view.

In the case of IS "success" it should be observed that many information systems are good, if they make themselves obsolete reasonably soon by supporting learning and stimulating IS evolution (cf. Hedberg and Jönsson, 1978). This means that the UIS aspect of "pragmatic quality" should be assessed longitudinally and that UIS may be inversely related to IS success. On the other hand, recognizing that learning on the part of the user can be interpreted as growth in his/her professional knowledge, it seems that the framework of "pragmatic quality," when used longitudinally, could take this aspect into account as well.

5.   CONCLUSION

In conclusion, the framework for "pragmatic quality" suggested by Sandstrom looks interesting and promising for the analysis of information systems. In particular, the user's professional knowledge forms an interesting extension to existing research. It is obvious, however, that the theoretical analysis of the framework is still deficient. As far as empirical research is concerned, the analysis should be extended longitudinally to capture the dynamics and effects of IS change.

REFERENCES

Bailey, J. E., and Pearson, S. W., "Development of a Tool for Measuring and Analyzing Computer User Satisfaction," *Management Science*, Vol. 29, No. 5, 1983.

Hawgood, J., and Land, F., "A Multivalent Approach to Information System Assessment," this volume.

Hedberg, B., and Jönsson, S., "Designing Semi-Confusing Information Systems for Organizations in Changing Environments," *Accounting, Organizations and Society*, Vol. 3, No. 1, 1978.

Ives, B., Olson, M. H., and Baroudi, J. J., "The Measurement of User Information Satisfaction," *Communications of the ACM*, Vol. 26, No. 10, 1983.

Nauta, D., *The Meaning of Information*, Mouton, 1972.

Swanson, E. B., "Measuring User Attitudes in MIS Research: A Review," *Omega*, Vol. 10, No. 2, 1982.

Swanson, E. B., "Channel Disposition Assessment: Toward the Diagnosis of Information System Utility," this volume.

Treacy, M. E., "An Empirical Examination of a Causal Model of User Information Satisfaction," Center for Information Systems Research, Sloan School of Management, Massachusetts Institute of Technology, 1985.

**Measuring the Pragmatic Quality
of Information Systems
G. Sandström**

" He/she can also see the sender's gestures
and facial expressions."

INFORMATION SYSTEMS ASSESSMENT
N. Bjørn-Andersen, G.B. Davis (Editors)
Elsevier Science Publishers B.V. (North-Holland)
© IFIP, 1988

MEASURING THE PRAGMATIC QUALITY OF
INFORMATION SYSTEMS*

Gunhild SANDSTRÖM

Information and Computer Science
University of Lund
Sölvegatan 14 a
S-223 62 Lund, Sweden

With the help of a semantic differential method
(Osgood, et al., 1957), empirical studies have been
made in a manufacturing company and a hospital in
Sweden.   One group of people in each of the two
organizations, using the same computerized information system in their daily work, have given their
opinions on work, language and the system.   The
opinion data were collected from questionnaires and
follow-up discussions.   With this material as a
basis, improvements to the measurement method for
possible further uses within the field of information sciences are discussed.

1. INTRODUCTION

This research is empirical and part of a research program named
"User Oriented Information Systems -- Their Use and Development"
(Nissen, et al., 1982).   The aim of this work in its entirety is
to develop ideas that will make it possible for people to become
more aware of what a computerized system can offer and how such a
system can restrict.   The realm of this work concerns the use of
information systems and this report deals with the need for
measuring the quality of such systems with respect to interpretations and actions by people.

Evaluations in a manufacturing company and in a hospital in Sweden
have been made and examples are shown from one group in each
organization.   System use is not voluntary for either of the two
groups, so the criterion "usage" to measure "success" of the
systems is not used.   The workers used their systems both to
process transactions and to be supported in decision making.
These evaluation phases were about 25 percent of the total
research work conducted in the organizations.

The hypothesis is that methods with both quality and quantity
features such as "semantic differential" could serve as instruments to elicit new knowledge from the computerization of administrative work.   It may aid somewhat in exploring the inner nature
of this phenomenon.

*This report has been developed with financial support from the
Swedish Work Environment Fund.

2. INFORMATION SYSTEMS AND PRAGMATIC QUALITY

When the sender and the receiver of a message can speak to each other face to face, they have fair possibilities to really understand the message, as the receiver can ask for further explanations in order to get a correct interpretation. He/she can also see the sender's gestures and facial expressions. The sender can also get an opinion of how his/her message has been perceived. But if they communicate via a computer, they cannot get a clear idea of the whole message because non-verbal informative parts are not interpreted. In fact, they are not even transmitted. Today, we may not even know who sends us a message. Even if we know the name of the sender, we might never meet him/her. There are fundamental differences between different communication situations: face to face, voice to voice, letter mailing, face to display. Different kinds of interfaces -- telephone, paper, television, computer -- have different kinds of constraints according to the signals transmitted. All of the following factors decide the interpretation of and the action on the message, i.e., the "pragmatic quality" of information (cf. Sandström, 1985):

- o the knowledge of the people involved
- o the historical and intentional contexts of a message
- o the interface used
- o the contents of the message itself

This environmental knowledge cannot be completely described without abstraction. Therefore, every trial to make such a description is an approximation. Hence, absolute correctness of the message contents as a whole is not a real issue. It is the useability of the message and the relevance of the pursuing action(s) that must be the main concern. Useability as a main issue is also supported in computer science regarding programs, which are seen as parts of the world they model (cf. Lehman, 1980).

As computerized information systems are becoming a more common linkage between people, it is very important to measure the quality of such systems from the user's point of view.

The *information system* in an organization can be looked upon differently depending on who is looking at it. A person who just acts on another person's order may not see a system at all. They see a person, a paper, or a terminal/computer and perceive a problem. They see real things and they do not speak of systems. The decision maker may imagine an information system as something designed to support him even if he cannot explicitly describe it. He may describe a computerized system or a database better as it is more concrete than the invisible information system. For these reasons, it is hard to discuss and define an information system with a user and even harder to do it with respect to the quality of such a system.

An information system is a *designed tool*, the purpose of which is to serve people in active work with information and in an organization. It is an *organized construction* with subsystems for collecting, processing, storing, retrieving, and distributing information together, influenced by people. It becomes an *abstraction of a service function* when studied.

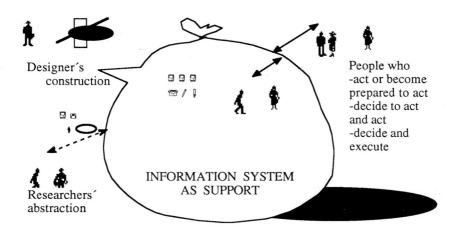

Figure 1. Different Views on an Information System

The concept of an information system is difficult to define for all participants. Those who are concerned with an information system (see Figure 1) are either part of it or possess it; either design it, use it, or study it. It seems abstract even though it is very concrete. The quality of such a system could be measured in many ways. When doing this measuring, information systems can be seen as purposeful tools.

In previous empirical work (Sandström, 1985), it was discovered that, in order to assist users of the information system on an equal basis, it is necessary to meet them as professionals in their own respective professions. They are not data feeders, data needers, or program operators. They are professional workers -- laboratory assistants, doctors, and clerks -- who use the system as a supporting tool to better manage their work. When investigating the use or quality of an information system, it must be kept in mind that these workers use the system as a supporting tool to better manage their work.

When measuring the *pragmatic quality* of an information system, this author adheres to an effectiveness approach, using the measures of effectiveness perceived by the users of the information system. Arguments for such an approach are given by Ginzberg (1981), who views the system as a service instead of a product. The effectiveness approach uses measures such as user satisfaction and system quality. This latter measure has been broadened in this research to contain both opinions from and actions by the users of the information system studied.

To measure pragmatic quality of information in a system or to get ideas of what pragmatic quality is, studies must be focussed on the mediated expressions and their relation to the individuals and their actions. The pragmatic aspect is how information is used, if and for what it is used, about the intention of a sender and the opinion and action of a receiver. Within pragmatics, the

interpretation of messages also plays a part, as do the message
performance and the appearance of a sign.

3.   NEED FOR INTEGRATED QUALITATIVE AND
     QUANTITATIVE VALUES

For evaluation of effectiveness, there is a need for both qualitative and quantitative methods. The quantitative values are needed
as preliminaries for qualititative values and vice versa.   A
reason for this could be to see if the effects are great enough to
merit extra attention.   The effect itself is often of a nondeterministic character. Both qualitative insight into the users'
real problems and quantitative overviews of general conditions are
needed.   Qualitative insight and quantitative overviews may be
achieved in parallel or interleaved.   These kinds of integrated
perspectives are shared by other researchers and good arguments
for their use come from Gronmo (1982) and Tschudi (1982), who have
had a great deal of experience and found it necessary to alter or
mix the two perspectives.

Qualitative methods take care of "relevance," "critique," etc.
Quantitative methods take into account "precision," "categorizing," etc.   Some strategies for combining the two perspectives
could be:

    o   a quality base of effects on which we count/weigh and get the
        importance in numbers

    o   a quantity of apparently the same effects on which we give
        quality aspects

    o   a method with built-in qualitative and quantitative features

It is important to take both into account as logical reasoning
based on quantities only often misses the point.

4.   A MIXED MEASURING METHOD

4.1 Description

In these investigations, the semantic differential has been used
to measure part of the pragmatic quality of information systems.
The method was developed in the 1950s by C. E. Osgood at the
University of Illinois.

The author wished to try an ordered quantitative method that was
combined with measuring qualitative values to see how it worked.
It is a mixed method because of its two-fold features. There is a
need for both qualitative and quantitative values in practice as
well as in research, and the semantic differential is an instrument which can be used to get both kinds of values.   Another
reason for using the method was to discover the users' opinions
through anonymous investigations within the work groups.

"The semantic differential is a method of observing and measuring
the psychological meaning of concepts" (Kerlinger, 1964, p. 566).
In all concepts, there is some common core of meaning.   The
semantic differential is meant to measure the connotative meanings
of concepts as points in what is called a semantic space (Osgood,
et al., 1957).

Within such a space, we are looking for the dimensions of messages, which are sent between people without or by means of a
computer in the following context:

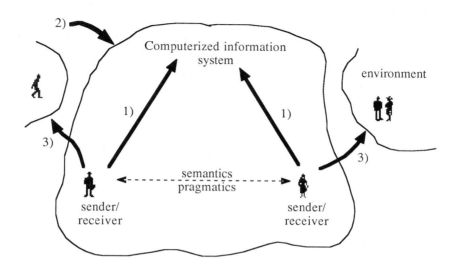

1) speech acts in real situations
2) a system of logical rules of language normally used
3) other acts (which also include speech acts) as effects of
   speech acts

Figure 2: Context for Studying Semantics and Pragmatics of Using
          Today's Computerized Information Systems

Some dimensions of a message could be:

o *relational* -- what a message and the very fact of sending
   that message now implies about the relation between a sender
   and a receiver. This in itself may call for several dimen-
   sions/levels, e.g., what the sender feels about the receiver,
   what the sender believes the receiver feels about him/her,
   etc.

o *intentional* -- intentions of the sender, his/her apprehension
   of and belief in the intention of the receiver within the
   network situation, etc.

o *factual* -- some facts contained in the message (cf. Sandström, 1985).

A semantic differential consists of a number of scales, each of
which is a bipolar adjective pair. The bipolar adjectives are
usually seven point rating scales, where *the underlying nature has
to be determined empirically*. In these investigations, the
bipolar pairs of adjectives for the conclusions after the fill-in

phase were clustered. Pairs of adjectives for the measurement
were chosen based upon an intuitive and experienced knowledge of
the users and their data systems.

4.2 An Example

To illustrate the method, the following example is given.   In
working groups, teams, or a whole small department, the members
were asked to fill in five forms about different concepts regarding their own work.   One of these forms concerned the "computerized decision bases."   People were asked to associate spontaneously with computerized decision bases, something between the
pairs of evaluating and action-related adjectives presented in
Figure 3 (the adjectives presented are English equivalents of
Swedish terms used in the study).

trivial	*	*	*	*	*	*	* interesting
up to date	*	*	*	*	*	*	* out of date
useless	*	*	*	*	*	*	* usable
correct	*	*	*	*	*	*	* wrong
fuzzy	*	*	*	*	*	*	* clear
unimportant	*	*	*	*	*	*	* important
naive	*	*	*	*	*	*	* sophisticated
subjective	*	*	*	*	*	*	* objective
boring	*	*	*	*	*	*	* fascinating
reliable	*	*	*	*	*	*	* unreliable
old	*	*	*	*	*	*	* new
imperative	*	*	*	*	*	*	* unconstraining

Figure 3. Form for Measuring Opinions on "Computerized Decision
          Bases"

Instead of having the "good" adjectives to the left and the "bad"
to the right on the scale, they were mixed stochastically.   Also,
adjectives that were very close and sometimes overlapping were
used in the same form.

Five similar studies in total have been made about the concepts
within each of the two groups:

   o   computer display language
   o   computer-based decision bases
   o   computer
   o   user's professional knowledge after computerization
   o   user's work after computerization

The evaluation for a whole group was made in two hours. The participants received a set of six pages consisting of an introduction (see Appendix) and five forms, one for each concept.

The results obtained were then grouped according to kinds of professionals and also according to closely related adjectives for presentation and discussion purposes among the participants (Sandström, 1985). The clustering of the adjectives was made according to similarities between the adjectives. Typical values were used when showing the results in the scales (see Appendix).

4.3 "Intended" and "Unexpected" Nature of Results

Looking upon the results as a whole for the people within these two groups, the following was noted:

o *The first group*, the department with 28 people in the manufacturing company, would not be happy to lose their computerized system. Even if they do not love their data system, they trust it and feel secure using it. They may have become so used to it that they do not want to lose it or exchange it because that would disturb the routines. This group is an export team that handles all papers concerning import and export at a manufacturing company. The workers at the department are informed, for example, of available means of transport, kinds of customers, kinds of agents available, rules and sales conditions for different countries. The people were used to working with structures, rules and forms before computerization. The computerized decision bases became very "useful, interesting and important" (1).[1] Material from their computerized information system was said to be "up to date, correct, clear, reliable, and new" (2). An interpretation of their apparent thinking is "Good things in and good things out -- but more efficient." They trusted the material mediated by the computer system and the ordinary users found it objective. The computer was placed on the premises where they worked. They could both see and hear it. The computer was a machine of their own, and they had to pay for it out of their own budget (cf. Sandström, 1985).

o *The second group*, the team of 34 people in the hospital, looked upon the computerized part of their work as something necessary because somebody else needed it. The "data system" was not built for them even if it was intended to be so in a specification made before the system was built. They dared not use the computerized decision bases. Three of the 29 answers to this form said "I do not know" and another three forms were not filled in. They did not rely on it. They also found it "fuzzy and often wrong" (4). The computer decision bases were, moreover, "unimportant, trivial, and useless" (3). On the whole, the hospital team found the computer-based material less valuable than did the administration department. This user group worked in quite a different field ("to cure sick people") and under very different circumstances. They worked with people and with very severe issues, sometimes dealing with "life and death." They would not take responsibility for decisions on material

---

[1]Figures within parentheses refer to the examples of results presented in the appendix.

passing through a machine, or they would not have these matters registered. Their tacit knowledge could not be taken into account as input to a decision base or as output for a decision. Therefore, it could not be logically approved afterwards and hence no doctor/professor/laboratory assistant wanted it registered. They used the machine to put in and pick out formal facts about people and references in a rather sophisticated retrieval system, which was founded on an international convention. They did not know anything about the machine and they did not pay for it from their own budget. No one in the group appeared to be responsible for the information system and its use.

"The more severe the problem, the less use of computerized material" for various reasons seems to be one result from these cases.

In these studies, the people involved belonged to a specific work situation, a small department, or a work team, and all of the people in a group were asked to participate. They were given an opportunity to have their discussions noticed, discussions of what they had done in the study and the meaning of it. They might themselves (as representatives for "user" groups) have improved the method of the study and their own work situations with respect to their information system. The research was, in both cases, directly connected to the reality.

After the formal and voiceless investigation, the participants of the first group started to discuss the investigation, the data collection form, the pairs of adjectives, their work, their language, and their computer system. At first they did this very aggressively in critical terms, but later on in a rather constructive way. Permission was given for the researcher to listen to the discussions and to take notes. In the second group, the participants were more passive and seemed to be more relaxed in the discussion after. The secretary, all the doctors but one, and three of the nurses had to return to work, but even among these people, there was a willingness to describe changes for the system and the investigation.

There were possibilities to intervene and discuss conflicts and, at the same time, to obtain valuable quantitative information. The forms in the studies functioned as initiating factors to a very important process for the users, who then had a "legal" reason to "criticize" and "create" their own work. This is an extremely good opportunity to see what is wrong in a department. In addition to the formal measurement, there will be informal data from the involved persons. They disputed words, forms, and methods -- the researcher received feedback. They discussed the work, display, decision bases, routines, computerization, their wages, and so on -- the workers involved at the working place and the enterprise both got feedback.

Studies with the help of semantic differential are worth repeating in other work groups. They are soft and well organized. They are sufficiently anonymous and not too time consuming. They also serve as triggers for learning about other issues.

5. SIMILAR RESEARCH WITHIN INFORMATION SCIENCE

In order to access attitudes towards information systems with the help of semantic differential, there have been some interesting investigations. They are mentioned here in order to get support for the efforts in this research and in order to present sources of further ideas on the topics of evaluation. These research studies are also good sources for similar methods within information science.

Katzer (1972) measured attitudes toward one specific system, an on-line interactive retrieval system, among library science students with the help of the semantic differential. He may have been the first researcher to use the semantic differential method for measuring purposes within the field of information science. His main contribution was that he broke up the traditional groupings -- evaluative, potency, and activity (Osgood, et al., 1957) -- of the adjectives and put them into three other groups-- evaluative, desirability and enormity -- which seem more useful within the area of information research.

Gallagher (1974) made an empirical study about perceptions of the value of a management information system concerning expenses and budget. The study was about determining the monetary value of a report from such a system. The method measured user perception with the semantic differential technique. Out of the 103 questionnaires mailed, 74 usable replies were received. The study "showed that information value was (a) enhanced by participation in report design, (b) related to organizational position" (p. 46). He found that the semantic differential performed well basically but was weak in certain areas in his application and, therefore, that better scales need to be found.

Allen and Matheson (1977) tried to develop a semantic differential in order to access users' attitudes toward a batch mode information retrieval system. They did their evaluation on the Educational Resources Information Center (ERIC) tape database, with the help of Katzer's grouping, which they found very useful. They tested ten concepts representing input and output of the system together with some general opinions on it. Thirty five faculty members and graduate student users participated, which meant a 37 percent return on the questionnaires.

To concentrate the measuring on effectiveness, instead of on efficiency, was an important task for Pearson and Bailey, who say "there is a need for quantitative measures of effectiveness to counterbalance the influence of efficiency only measures" (Pearson and Bailey, 1980, p. 59). They also see "user satisfaction" as a multi-dimensional attitude and define it as "the sum of feelings or affective responses to distinguishable factors of the computer-based information products and services that are provided within the organization" (Pearson and Bailey, 1980, p. 59). The base for their study is the semantic differential. They developed and evaluated a questionnaire. The evaluation took place among 32 middle managers and indicated the questionnaire was both reliable and valid. It was also objective and economical to administer.

Studies on different types of communications, such as comparisons between various media, with and without differences in time and space, have been made in related fields. For example, Short, Williams and Christie did such a study in the mid-1970s to measure

the relative degree of social presence among some media, from
face-to-face and business letter (Christie, 1981).

The semantic differential has also been successfully utilized by
Gingras and McLean (1982) to measure profiles of the designer, the
user, and the "ideal" user of an operational information system.
They made some interesting comparisons from 17 (of 17) designers'
and 52 (of 111) users' opinions about their self-image, their
image of each other, and their image of the "ideal" user through
17 quite different pairs of adjectives and a seven point scale.

Ives , Olson and Baroudi (1983) have made measurements with the
help of the semantic differential with other purposes. They used
user information satisfaction as an evaluation mechanism to
determine whether an information system is needed or if an
implemented system functions properly. Their user has been the
manager. User information satisfaction measures how managers
regard their information system. Others involved are not
encountered in this study.

An instrument to measure MIS/DSS success has been designed by
Sanders (1984) based on Likert scales with reasonably interpretable and clear dimensions reflected in a set of questions
concerning assistance in decision making and contribution to
overall job performance. He concentrates on measuring the ability
of tailored information systems to support decision making and to
contribute to the users' overall satisfaction. Here again, it is
not just about efficiency; it is about organizational effectiveness.

6. KERNEL FOR MEASURING PRAGMATIC QUALITY-DISCUSSION

Following are some themes which may be of interest for further
discussions regarding the measurement of people's opinion of and
the effectiveness of "their" information system, containing both
people and computerized parts.

o   The need for these kinds of measurements within information
    and software science

o   Improvements of similar studies for future uses

o   Research ethics and intervention in connection with such
    studies

o   Different lay-outs of forms for measuring opinions about
    information systems and computerization

The development of a kernel of "quality-quantity-method," similar
to the semantic differential method, for information science is
also suggested. Such a method should be performed for various
uses with necessary adaptations depending on whether it is going
to be used for

o   practice or in research

o   developing an information system or for information systems
    use and education

o   measurement or also for intervention purposes

o getting quantitative results or for improving the quality of data

ACKNOWLEDGEMENTS

I thank my research fellows, Professors Niels Bjorn-Andersen, Gordon B. Davis and Hans-Erik Nissen, for their constructive advice.

REFERENCES

Allen, S., and Matheson, J., "Development of a Semantic Differential to Access Users' Attitudes Towards a Batch Mode Information Retrieval System (ERIC)," *Journal of the American Society for Information Science,* September 1977, pp. 268-272.

Christie, B., *Face to File Communication -- A Psychological Approach to Information Systems,* John Wiley and Sons, Ltd., New York, 1981.

Gallagher, C. A., "Perceptions of the Value of a Management Information System," *Academy of Management Journal,* Vol. 17, No. 1, 1974, pp. 46-55.

Gingras, L., and McLean, E. R., "Designers and Users of Information Systems: A Study in Differing Profiles," *Proceedings of the Third International Conference on Information Systems,* 1982.

Ginzberg, M. J., "Early Diagnosis of MIS Implementation Failure: Promising Results and Unanswered Questions," *Management Science,* Vol. 27, No. 4, April 1981, pp. 459-478.

Gronmo, S., "Forholdet mellon kvalitative og kvantitative metoder i samfunnsforskningen," *Kvalitative metoder i samfunnsforskning,* red av Holter, H., & Kalleberg, R., Universitetsforlaget, Drammen, Norway, 1982.

Ives, B., Olson, M. H., and Baroudi, J. J., "The Measurement of User Information Satisfaction," *Communications of the ACM,* Vol. 26, No. 10, October 1983.

Katzer, J., "The Development of a Semantic Differential to Assess Users' Attitudes Towards an On-Line Interactive Reference Retrieval System," *Journal of the American Society for Information Science,* March-April 1972, pp. 122-127.

Kerlinger, F. N., *Foundations of Behavioral Research,* Holt, Rinehart and Winston, New York, 1964; 1973 (reprint).

Lehman, M. M., "Programs, Programming and the Software Life Cycle," Department of Computing and Control, Imperial Colleges of Science and Technology, 180 Queen's Gate, London, SW7, 2BZ, 1980.

Nissen, H-E., Carlsson, S., Flensburg, P., Holmberg, K-A., Sandström, S., and Wormell, I., "User Oriented Information Systems -- A Research Program," Department of Information and Computer Sciences, University of Lund, Sweden, 1982.

Osgood, C. E., Suci, G. J., and Tannenbaum, P. H., *The Measurement of Meaning*, University of Illinois Press, Urbana, 1957; 1967 (reprint).

Pearson, S. W., and Bailey, J. E., "Measurement of Computer User Satisfaction," *Performance Evaluation Review*, Vol. 9, No. 1, ACM SIGMETRICS, Spring 1980.

Sanders, G. L., "MISS/DSS Success Measure," *Systems, Objectives, Solutions*, Vol. 4, No. 1, 1984, pp. 29-34.

Sandström, G., *Towards Transparent Data Bases -- How to Interpret and Act on Expressions Mediated by Computerized Information Systems*, Dissertation, Studentlitteratur-Chartwell Bratt, Lund, Sweden, 1985.

Tschudi, F., "Om nodvandigheten av syntese mellom kvantitative og kvalitative metoder," *Kvalitative metoder i samfunnsforskning*, red av Holter, H., & Kalleberg, R., Universitetsforlaget, Drammen, Norway, 1982.

APPENDIX: INTRODUCTION LETTER

Gunhild Sandström   October 1984
Information and Computer Sciences
University of Lund

INVESTIGATION OF WORK, LANGUAGE AND COMPUTER SYSTEM

PLEASE, DO NOT TURN THE PAGE UNTIL YOU ARE CONVINCED THAT YOU
UNDERSTAND WHAT IS ON THIS PAGE!

I am a researcher in information and computer sciences and am paid
by The Swedish Work Environment Fund and The National Swedish
Board for Technical Development and Lund University. I have got
permission to make an investigation at some departments in "XXX"
company concerning the use of computer system and langauge. I am
going to question some people who work directly or indirectly with
the system "aaa". On the following pages you will see some
diagrams looking like this:

                         WRITING TABLE

full   *   *   *   *   *   *   * empty

orderly   *   *   *   *   *   *   * messy

and so on with 10-12 such lines.

In these diagrams you shall mark what you associate with WRITING
TABLE. If you primarily think of WRITING TABLE as tremendously
"full," put a mark at the sign nearest "full" or as completely
"empty," put a mark at the sign nearest "empty." Almost "empty"
could be shown next furthest to the right. An example of a mark
is given at the line "orderly...messy." This is about values that
you give and you decide yourself the meaning of "empty" and "full"
and the five possible spaces between on the line. There are about
ten lines for each CONCEPT and five in total concepts. On each
line you may show where you want to associate between the two
extremes. Answer spontaneously -- do not think too long! It does
not matter if it looks constraining. Do not bother if you see the
same things appear again.

When answering have your own work in mind, and it is the computer
system "aaa" which is referred to where appropriate.

Thank you for your help.

Before you turn the page write down your position, function or
title at the department:

_____

In other respects this investigation is anonymous.

APPENDIX: EXAMPLE OF RESULTS FROM GROUP 1

(adjectives are English equivalents of Swedish terms used)

SUMMARIZED TYPICAL VALUES from the shipping department in the manufacturing company

from the groups:
```
     4    sales personnel (SP)       of  4   among  6
     5    order personnel (OP)       of  6   among  8
     4    forwarding agents (FA)     of  4   among  6
     5    shipping assistants (SA)   of  7   among  6
     2    data experts (DE)          of  2   among  2
    20    answers                    of 23   among 28  (5 were absent)
```

COMPUTERIZED DECISION BASES[a]

```
                                                   FA              (1)[b]
useless       *     *     *     * / SP*SA  DE*OP \   *  useful
trivial       *     *    *FA ( *SA    *OP  SP*DE  * ) interesting
                                       OP
unimportant   *     *     *     *      *SP SA*FA DE* ) important
                                   FA OP
naive         *     *     *     *SA SP*DE    *      *  sophisticated
                                       DE              (2)
out of date   *     *     *     * /   *SA SP*FA OP* \ up to date
wrong         *   *SA     *   ( *FA   *SP  OP*DE  *  ) correct
fuzzy         *     *     *   ( *SA SP*FA DE*    OP* ) clear
unreliable    *     *     *    *|  SP*SA    *DE OP* | reliable[c]
old           *     *     *     * \ SA*   FA*OP DE*/ new[d]
objective     *  OP*SA SP*      *     *     *DE      *  subjective[c]
                     SA
imperative    *     *  FA*DE SP*OP    *     *        *  unconstraining
boring        *     *   SA*  SP*   OP*FA   *DE       *  fascinating
```

---

[a]Two people from the SA-group have not answered at all (left empty forms).

[b]These encircled fields are commented on in the main text.

[c]In the FA-group, the same amount of people answered both-and.

[d]In the SP-group, they answered both-and to the same extent.

APPENDIX: EXAMPLE OF RESULTS FROM GROUP 2

(adjectives are English equivalents of Swedish terms used)

SUMMARIZED TYPICAL VALUES from the team in the hospital

from the groups:

0	archivists	of	2	among	2
4	clerks (c)	of	4	among	4
6	nurses (n)	of	7	among	8
12	laboratory assistants (l)	of	12	among	14
6	doctors (d)	of	6	among	9
1	secretary (s)	of	3	among	3
29	answers	of	34	among	40	(6 were absent)

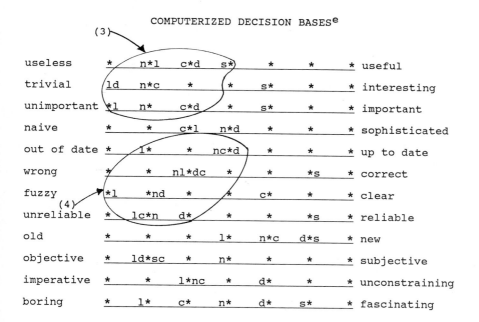

COMPUTERIZED DECISION BASES[e]

(3)

useless	*	n*l	c*d	s*	*	*	* useful
trivial	ld	n*c	*	*	s*	*	* interesting
unimportant	*l	n*	c*d	*	s*	*	* important
naive	*	*	c*l	n*d	*	*	* sophisticated
out of date *		l*	*	nc*d	*	*	* up to date
wrong	*	*	nl*dc	*	*	*s	* correct
fuzzy	*l	*nd	*	*	c*	*	* clear
(4) unreliable	*	lc*n	d*	*	*	*s	* reliable
old	*	*	*	l*	n*c	d*s	* new
objective	*	ld*sc	*	n*	*	*	* subjective
imperative	*	*	l*nc	*	d*	*	* unconstraining
boring	*	l*	c*	n*	d*	s*	* fascinating

[e]Two nurses and one laboratory assistant wrote on the form "I do not know" and three of the laboratory assistants gave back an empty form without explanation.

A Taxonomy of Computerization Expenditure in Organizations
G. Motta

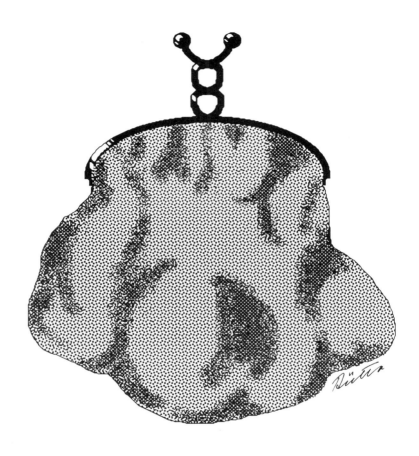

"Cost items are the easiest way to break down
expenditure."

INFORMATION SYSTEMS ASSESSMENT
N. Bjørn-Andersen, G.B. Davis (Editors)
Elsevier Science Publishers B.V. (North-Holland)
© IFIP, 1988

A TAXONOMY OF COMPUTERIZATION EXPENDITURE IN
ORGANIZATIONS

Gianmario MOTTA

Telos Management
Via Moscova 12
20121, Milano, Italy

Dipartimento di Elettronica
Politecnico di Milano
Milano, Italy

Most approaches to the assessment of information
systems consider variables such as quality, efficiency, and performance. Much of this evaluation
may be subjective if not supported by quantitative
data on expenditures. This paper presents a taxonomy of the expenditure that organizations sustain
in computerizing their information systems. Expenditure is analyzed at two levels: level one considers the total expenditure and level two considers
structure. Structural analysis involves several
criteria of expenditure segmentation, such as
application families, user organization areas,
resources used for computerization, and computerization functions. Expenditure analysis is viewed
as a tool both for the assessment of individual
organizations and general research on computerization.

1. INTRODUCTION

The purpose of this paper is to identify a taxonomy of the
expenditures for computerization. "Expenditures" means the amount
of dollars or resources that an organization spends for its
computerization. "Computerization" refers to the process through
which an organization automates its information handling systems
by means of computer technology.

The computerization process in organizations and its economics
have been investigated by (i) research studies, which have the
purpose of interpreting or making predictions about the computerization phenomenon, and include theories, surveys and case-studies,
and (ii) assessment methodologies, which have the purpose of
examining the quality of computerization of an individual organization.

A central question in the research domain is: are there expenditure-based indicators that can depict the pattern and trend of an
organization's computerization? What are these general trends and
patterns? A classic example of theory is Nolan's Stage Hypothesis,
which perceives organization's computerization as an organizational learning process that evolves by stages (Nolan, 1973). The
S-shaped curve of total computer expenditure reflects the learning

process, and each technology wave (batch processing, database, personal computers, networking) engenders its own learning and expenditure curve (Nolan, 1979; 1982). There is an ongoing discussion about Stage Hypothesis theoretical foundations and empirical evidence. For example, it is argued that the mere computer budget and the expenditure growth rate are too crude as variables to describe a complex process such as the computerization of organizations (Benbasat, et al., 1984; King and Kraemer, 1984). Based on the idea that computer systems are primarily a technology of information handling, and information handling chiefly involves white-collar workers, Strassmann (1976) proposes the unit of computer expenditure per white-collar worker as a fundamental indicator of computerization. In his case study about the 1990 Xerox computerization scenario, Benjamin (1982) assumes that computerization is driven by a decreasing employee/workstation replacement ratio, which is proposed as a physical measure of computerization. The economic impact of computerization is also discussed in Kleijnen (1980), Chismar and Kriebel (1985), and Cron and Sobol (1983).

Ideally, surveys should provide evidence on expenditure trends and computerization patterns. Unfortunately, most commercial surveys, such as *Datamation's* annual review of computer budgets (Crane, 1981; Marion, 1984; Verity, 1985), report on expenditure items (personnel costs, rentals, etc.) rather than its segmentation by application area. Only a few surveys by industry associations consider multiple computerization variables, such as organizations' employees, computer workstations, computer specialists, etc. (ISRIL, 1979; AICA, 1984; Lusa and Winkler, 1982). In an assessment perspective, expenditure analysis can address certain user management issues, such as "What is (or can be) the bottom line contribution of information technology?" or "How much should we spend?" To answer "How much should we spend," a wide set of indicators is needed that analyzes expenditures from different and complementary view points. For example, Norton develops an expenditure-based assessment of the organization's portfolio of applications (which is conceived as a portfolio of investment opportunities) (Norton, 1982). Norton's indicators focus on maturity, obsolescence, allocation, etc., of expenditure. The assessment provides the diagnosis for a multi-variable action plan. In going through the literature, one gets the impression that only a few particular aspects of expenditure are examined. For instance, Dickson and Wetherbe (1984) consider only two aggregate indicators, namely the DP budget as a percentage of revenues and its mix by cost item, and, therefore, they conclude that expenditure analysis can give only limited support to an assessment of information systems.

On the other hand, the relationship between information investment and the bottom line of organizational profit is challenging, but difficult to demonstrate. As Hamilton and Chervany (1981) point out, information systems provide information which affects the use process and user performance, which in turn influences the overall organizational performance. Hence, a lot of cause-effect chains are between information technology and organizational performance and the evidence may be contradictory. For instance, Strassmann reports a case in which non-computerized organizations perform better (Strassmann, 1985) while Edelman (1981), in comparing the costs of infoworkers of two divisions of the same organization, one with manual systems and one with computerized systems, finds that the automated division improved productivity of by 24 percent. It is noticeable that a more humble approach -- the relation between costs (instead of the bottom line) of a specific, well-defined functional area (instead of the whole organization) -- has seldom been addressed. Yet, in this case, cause-actions chains are shorter and a dependable correlation appears likely. In short, the review of literature raises a number of questions: a) What is the potential domain of expenditure analysis? What is its logic and structure? b) Are there expenditure-based indicators that can depict the general pattern and trend of organizational computerization? c) To what extent can expenditure-based indicators be used in assessing information systems of an individual organization? Our purpose is to answer these questions through:

(a)   a taxonomy, that identifies indicators and potential levels of expenditure analysis

(b)   a discussion of a subset of expenditure indicators in terms of
      (i)   conceptual soundness (can they lead to paradox?)
     (ii)   potential scope (degree of intrinsic generality)
    (iii)   potential contribution to general research and/or assessment of information systems.

2.   OVERVIEW OF THE EXPENDITURE TAXONOMY

2.1   Levels of Analysis

In examining the computerization expenditure of an organization, one can focus on its total amount (aggregate analysis) or go through its structure (structural analysis). In doing the analysis at these different levels, one will use indicators that basically consist of expenditure ratios. Each level groups a set of indicators and is characterized by the expenditure segmentation on which it is based. So, levels and indicators are the basic ingredients of the taxonomy. Indicators specify what one is measuring, while levels specify the segment of expenditure one is dealing with.

Expenditure indicators include a certain set of variables. The first group examines the absolute amount of expenditure and contains variables; it is called "absolute indicators." A typical example is the expenditure growth rate. A second group considers the ratio of expenditure to certain size parameters of an organization; it is called "cross-indicators." Since parameters can concern the organization's outputs (e.g., sales, revenues, value-added) or resources (e.g., employees) and they can be based on money values (e.g., dollar sales, wages and salaries) or physical quantities (e.g., number of units sold, number of employees), the potential indicators are almost innumerable. Each analysis level may include both absolute and cross-indicators.

The levels of analysis require more discussion. Aggregate analysis reflects a "non-segmentation" of expenditure and shows overall trends and patterns. Of course, even aggregate comparisons require a certain investigation on the underlying data. Total expenditure may or may not include important items such as the costs for office automation, industrial automation or telecommunications. Furthermore, different depreciation rates and acquisition policies (purchasing, leasing, renting) may raise or reduce the total expenditure.

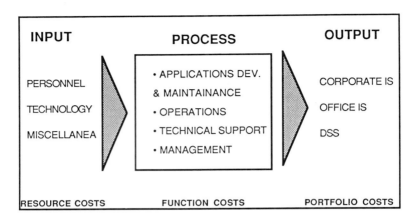

Figure 1: A Conceptual Model of Structural Analysis of Expenditure

On the other hand, structural analysis uses different perspectives which break down expenditure according to alternative approaches to segmentation. Figure 1 shows the conceptual model of structural analysis which develops a concept by Nolan and Wetherbe (1980). Computerization is conceived as an input-output process. The input consists of the resources that fuel the computerization process (technology, personnel, miscellanea). Computer applications (corporate information systems, office systems, decision support systems) represent the output. Finally, the process consists of the activities that make the computerization process work and includes development and maintenance of applications, operation of computer centers, and management and technical support to the whole process. Input, output and process identify the three branches of structural analysis, namely the analysis of (i) resources, (ii) application portfolio, and (iii) functions. In resource analysis, expenditure is subdivided in conformity with the natural classification of costs and shows the resource mix used for computerization (e.g., personnel, technology, miscellanea). Function analysis considers the costs associated with the typical missions of a systems department (development of applications, operations, management). Finally, portfolio analysis examines the allocation of expenditure to the application lines (e.g., corporate information systems) and/or user areas (e.g., sales). Each branch of structural analysis requires (i) a conceptual model of segmentation and (ii) an appropriate accounting of computer costs, as shown below:

o Resource analysis
     (i) Natural classification of costs
     (ii) General accounting (general ledger)

o Function analysis
     (i) General functions of computerization
     (ii) Mission-oriented accounting (responsibility accounting)

o Portfolio analysis
     (i) Conceptual models of portfolio
     (ii) Application/project and/or user-oriented accounting

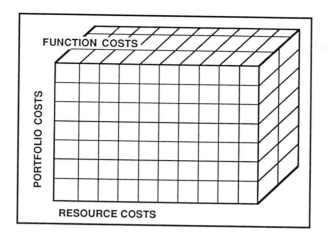

Figure 2. Dimensions of Structural Expenditure Analysis

The three dimensions of structural analysis can intersect. Of course, the more sophisticated the segmentation, the more complex the investigation will be. (See Figure 2.)

2.2 Expenditure Measures

Expenditure indicators can reflect alternative data with respect to: (i) time span (annual cost data versus time series); (ii) pricing (current versus deflated dollars); and (iii) evaluation (annualized costs versus investment levels).

Within the time span alternative, time series are powerful tools because they highlight expenditure trends. However, it is difficult to get reliable series and meaningful panels of organizations.

In the pricing alternative, deflated values are useful in order to focus on specific aspects, such as the so-called replacement ratio, e.g., how many salaries a standard computer costs, say in 1960 versus 1970 and 1980. However, current dollars are more intuitive and useful in general analysis.

Within the evaluation alternative, annualized costs represent the sum of current costs and depreciation rates that form a typical computer budget, while investment levels result from the expenditure capitalized into the portfolio of existing applications. Although annualized costs are the usual measure of expenditure, investment could give a more precise view of the effort required to build an application. Generally, we assume that the investment reflects the cost of application programs.

2.3 Expenditure-Based Versus Physical Measures

Often, organizations do not have (or do not disclose) cost data. Physical measures can be a surrogate for costs. A preliminary investigation on a sample of large Italian corporations belonging

to different industries (Motta, 1986) used two physical indicators
to measure aggregate computerization: (i) white-collars/(terminals + personal computers), and (ii) white-collars/ information-
professionals. Both indicators seem highly interrelated and
candidates as potential surrogates for expenditures as a percentage of salaries. On the other hand, Batiste (1986) pro-poses a
quantitative spreadsheet to measure the performance of individual
applications that can be used as a physical surrogate of function
costs to measure the efficiency of computerization. Of course,
these preliminary findings should be further tested and validated.
Many cost-based measures can be complemented or replaced by physical benchmarks.

2.4 Expenditure Analysis, Assessment and Research

Our taxonomy can be regarded as a generator of indicators. Of
course, research and assessment will typically use different
indicators and rely on different analysis levels.

Aggregate analysis can show trends at various levels of generality: industry, national, inter-industry, etc. In a research
perspective, aggregate analysis is a key ingredient, since it can
be used to test general predictions such as the relationship
between organization size and expenditures. Underlying indicators
will be meaningful as far as they are unambiguous, comparable and
able to be validated. In an assessment, aggregate analysis can be
useful in answering very general "background" questions, such as
"how high is our expenditure, how intensive is our overall
computerization, and how fast is it growing?"

Structural analysis can support various aspects of assessment.
Specifically, function analysis can focus on productivity parameters of the information systems department and, more generally,
its performance. Thus, it can respond to the question "how efficient are our computerization activities?" In turn, portfolio
analysis will assess the economics of a given portfolio segment.
Typically, portfolio analysis will address issues such as "does
our expenditure allocation reflect business priorities and/or
opportunities?" Resource analysis can only provide background
information, since it points out where expenditures come from, not
what they are for. In a research perspective, structural analysis
could give a segmented comparison, provided that both conceptual
segmentation criteria and accounting approaches are homogeneous
within the sample investigated. However, these are tough constraints. In portfolio analysis, the taxonomy of systems and user
areas can be defined through alternative approaches; a certain
degree of interpretation is involved even within the same taxonomy. The same is true with function analysis, which, moreover,
requires qualitative integrations, so findings are very hard to
generalize. Finally, data resource analyses are moderately easy
and comparable, but they can offer only ancillary indicators.

2.5 Summary

Figure 3 gives a general overview of the taxonomy. Rows indicate
the analysis levels and columns summarize some key features of
each level:

(a) Potential relevance to research and assessment

ANALYSIS LEVEL	POTENTIAL RELEVANCE		COST ACCOUNTING REQUIRED	COST MEASURE (INVESTMENT VS ANNUALIZED)	CONCEPTUAL MODELS FOR SEGMENTATION
	RESEARCH	ASSESSMENT			
AGGREGATE	▓	⋯	NATURAL	ANNUALIZED	NONE
· RESOURCE	⋯	⋯	NATURAL	ANNUALIZED	(COST CLUSTERING)
· FUNCTION	⋯	▓	RESPONSABILITY	ANNUALIZED	CLASSIFICATION OF IS DPTS ACTIVITIES
· PORTFOLIO	▓	▓	USER	ANNUALIZED + INVESTMENT	FRAMEWORKS FOR PORTFOLIO ANALYSIS

▓ RELEVANT

⋯ PROVIDES BACKGROUND OR ANCIILLARY DATA

Figure 3. Analysis Levels and Perspectives

(b) Underlying cost accounting (natural, responsibility, user, multiple)

(c) Cost measures -- are investment-oriented or annualized costs applicable?

(d) Underlying conceptual model for expenditure segmentation

The following sections discuss a subset of indicators for each analysis level.

3. AGGREGATE ANALYSIS

Figure 4 shows a classification of the potential indicators for aggregate analysis. Our discussion will concentrate on a subset.

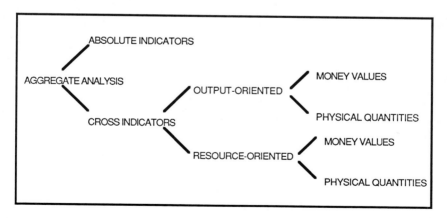

Figure 4. Breakdown of Aggregate Analysis

EXPENDITURE RANK	PROFILE OF SYSTEMS DEPARTMENT	PROFILE OF APPLICATIONS	TYPICAL USER ORGANIZATIONS
<0.5 M $	Rare as a separate function	Usually purchased turnkey systems	Small industrial firms
0.5 to 2 M $	Development separated from computer ops (10 to 20 professionals)	Some small in-house applications; customization of purchased packages	Medium industrial firms Regional banks Regional public agencies
2 to 10 M $	Development divided into user areas Significant technical support staff (20 to 100 professionals)	Several in-house systems Sophisticated software development tools Formal project management	Large industrial corporations National banks
> 10 M $	Often multiple systems departments (divisional) (Hundreds of professionals)	The same as above	Very large corporations International banks National public agencies

Figure 5. Ranks of Absolute Expenditure

3.1   The "Scale Indicator"

The absolute amount of expenditure could be a very straightforward indicator if we assume that the degree of specialization and the ability to build in-house applications are proportional to the computer budget, ceteris paribus.   Some elements support this hypothesis. First, the cost of a given application depends on the functions it provides and not on the number of potential end users it serves; large corporations will be inherently more efficient. Second, there are economies of scale.   For example, a survey conducted on the largest 100 Italian banks shows that the ratio of computer professionals to bank employees is inversely proportional to the bank size, measured on the amount of deposits.   The ratio is 4.42 percent in smaller banks; it drops to 1.92 percent in the larger ones, thus showing a "scale effect" near 100 percent (AICA, 1984).

If computer expenditure is sensitive to economies of scale, large organizations will draw a twofold advantage: not only do they have the critical mass to make (or fund) innovative applications, but they also pay comparatively less.   This advantage is significant when computerization is crucial to operations (e.g., airlines, iron and steel industry) or to pursue competitive business opportunities (e.g., banking).   Figure 5 develops the idea of a "scale indicator," where the level of total expenditure measures the potential innovation through computer technology (e.g., banking).   Computer expenditure is ranked in four classes which identify a certain expenditure scale.   At the lowest rank, the organization is almost totally dependent on outside application software. Intermediate ranks allow a significant application development in selected areas, but only the highest rank permits large innovative projects.

3.2 Percentage of Revenues and Output-Based Indicators

The percentage of revenues is a popular indicator of the extent (weight) of expenditures and is expressed as follows:

(1) $RP = EXP/S * 100$

where:

> RP = Revenue percentage
> EXP = Expenditure (annualized costs)
> S = Annual revenues (or equivalent output measure)

As can be seen in several surveys, the percentage (a) is specific to each industry and (b) varies in different industries. For instance, it is quite low in conventional manufacturing (often less than 1 percent), a little higher in automotive (usually 1.5 to 2.5 percent), and much higher in technology-intensive businesses. For example, IBM is said to spend some 6 to 7 percent for its internal computerization. On the other hand, banks show very low percentages because of their specific structure of costs.

If we regard the revenue percentage not only as a weight indicator but also as a benchmark of computerization, (a) it should grow over time, reflecting the increasing use of computer technology, and (b) it should mirror the "reality of expenditure." Let us consider the two questions.

Given the continual innovation of information technologies, one would expect a parallel increase in the percentage. The percentage rises, but at a slow pace. Let us take the years 1971 to 1980, which witnessed the advent of database and interactive applications in most organizations. A survey based on computer budgets reports an average of 1.33 percent in 1980, which is only a slight increase over the 1971 figure of 1.19 percent (Crane, 1981). Although the subsequent wave of personal computers, end-user computing applications, and computer networks is probably raising the percentage, there is no ultimate evidence of its extent. This apparent paradox is probably due to the following:

(a) Computer related costs have been decreasing while revenues of user organizations have been raised by inflation. Hence, a 1 percent expenditure in 1985 weighs much more than in 1975.

COMPANY	SALES	PURCHASES	VALUE-ADDED	EXPENDITURES	SALES %	VA %
SMITH	100	30	70	2	2%	3%
JONES	100	65	35	1	1%	3%

Figure 6. Expenditures as Percentage of Revenues and Value-Added (Example)

(b) Decreasing computer costs have extended the user market
     rather than raised the expenditure percentage of large
     corporations; futhermore, a growing expenditure share is
     escaping formal budgets.

(c) After an initial growth, expenditure levels off and reflects
     general budget policies and business cycles (Benbasat, et
     al., 1984).

Finally, let us comment on the "reality" of the percentage of
sales. Even in the same industry and in organizations of comparable size, a lower percentage does not always imply a lower expenditure. Figure 6 describes the case of two manufacturing corporations, Smith and Jones. Smith makes all the parts for his end
products in-house, with $100 of sales, $30 of purchased raw
materials, and a $2 computer expenditure. Jones gets the same
sales, spends only $1 on computers, but buys all the parts, so he
purchases $65 of raw materials. As a percentage of sales, Smith
spends twice as much as Jones, but the ratio on value-added is the
same (value-added is defined as the difference between revenues
and purchases). Hence, the mere ratio on revenues may be misleading.

To overcome "Smith's paradox," one could use the percent ratio of
value-added:

(2) VAP = EXP/VA *100

where:

        VAP = Value-added percentage
        EXP = Expenditure (annualized costs)
        VA   = Value-added

VAP is a very attractive indicator, since it can also be used in
portfolio analysis, as we will see later on. A third output-
oriented indicator is the cost per output unit:

(3) OC = EXP/OU

where:

        OC   = Cost per output unit
        EXP = Expenditure (annualized costs)
        OU   = Number of output units

This indicator will identify how many dollars an automotive company spends on each car made, thus allowing a number of industry-
wide analyses about the correlation between a given level of computerization and a given level of performance. Of course, it
requires some sophistication and it is not suitable for a first-
glance examination. Figure 7 summarizes the profile of the above
discussed output-oriented aggregate indicators in some industries.

3.3 Percentage of Salaries and Resource-Based Indicators

To a large extent, computer related costs can be viewed as
replacement or transferred costs, i.e., costs of automated processes replacing manual activities chiefly performed by white-
collar workers. In this hypothesis, white-collars are a primary
target of computerization (Strassmann, 1976) and the total expen-

INDUSTRY	% OF REVENUES	% OF VALUE-ADDED	COST PER OUTPUT UNIT
Manufacturing	Sometimes misleading	More sound but not always available	Permits correlation of product costs and computerization degree
Insurance	Equivalent: % of collected or retained premiums		Cost per policy handled
Banking	Equivalent: % of deposits and/ or operative costs		Cost per customer account and/ or counter transaction
Public Administration	Equivalent: % on total operative budget		Requires ad hoc definitions

Figure 7. Output-Oriented Indicators

diture divided by the number of white-collars is the most straightforward benchmark of the related computerization. However, a percent ratio is more homogeneous with other aggregate indicators:

(4)   TC = EXP/SAL * 100

where:

    TC = Transferred costs (percentage)
    EXP = Expenditure (annualized costs)
    SAL = Salaries

Figure 8 shows data from a survey on a sample of different industries conducted in 1979 (ISRIL, 1979). It can be seen that the range of salary percentages is narrow while the percentage of employee costs is very variable. Furthermore, personal observations show that the percentage is growing: the 10.5 percent ratio of industrial organizations reported in Figure 8 rose to 13 to 16 percent in 1985 (Bracchi and Motta, 1985). Therefore, the percentage of salaries also reflects the growth of overall computerization (while the percentage of revenues does not). Hence, the percentage of salaries is a candidate for a general indicator of aggregate computerization.

INDUSTRY	PERCENT OF COLLAR COST	PERCENT OF TOTAL EMPLOYEE COST
Industrial Organizations	10.5	3.5
Banking and Insurance	11.0	11.0
Trade	10.5	3.5
Services	9.0	3.0

Figure 8. Expenditure as Percentage of Internal Costs

4. RESOURCE ANALYSIS

Cost items are the easiest way to break down expenditure. Each
item identifies a certain family of resources, as shown below:

Technology: Hardware
               System software
               Application software
               Communications

Personnel: Wages and salaries

Miscellaneous: Outside services
               Consulting
               Education

This natural classification of costs shows the amount and mix of
resources that an organization should have in order to fuel application development and computer operations and, therefore, it is
widely used in budgeting.   It is interesting that expenditure
patterns do not change substantially as time passes nor in different industries and countries.   Surveys report a relative growth
of communications and personal computers in large organizations
against a slight decline of personnel costs.   The growth of
communications is consistent with the increasing number of
terminals and networked personal computers (Crane, 1981; Marion,
1984; Verity, 1985).   Although very important to practitioners,
the natural classification provides little information to computerization research since it tells where resources come from and
not what are they for.

5. ANALYSIS OF FUNCTION COSTS

This analysis considers the resources (personnel, technology,
miscellanea) associated with the general functions on which the
computerization process is based:

(a) Applications development and maintenance that encompass both
     personnel (analysts, programmers) and technology costs (hard-
     ware and software tools used for development)

(b) Operations that include costs of personnel (e.g., operators,
     data entry services) and computer/communications equipment
     allocated to run systems

(c) Technical support that typically includes personnel costs of
     the professional groups such as database, systems software,
     and network specialists who plan, design, and maintain the
     technological infrastructure on which applications are
     developed, maintained, and operated

(d) Management and management support staffs such as general
     planning and internal control

Information systems departments widely use function-oriented accounting (responsibility accounting) in order to control their own
costs.   For diagnostic and research purposes, this analysis allows
an assessment of the degree of efficiency and rigidity of expenditure.

5.1 Efficiency Assessment

In order to assess efficiency, appropriate output measures should be defined for each function (e.g., applications development and maintenance) or subfunction (e.g., applications development). Generally:

(5) EFF (i) = RES (i) / OM (i)

where:

> EFF = Efficiency indicator of the ith function
> OM = Output measure of the ith function
> RES = Cost of resources allocated to the ith function

For instance, the lines of codes released per year can be assumed as an output measure of an applications development function. The related efficiency indicator will be the unit cost of released lines of code. In this perspective, the analyst will proceed with an approach similar to a Zero Base Budgeting project (Phyrr, 1970). However, the quantitative efficiency reflects an inter-action among many variables, such as organizational structure, procedures, quality of manpower, and technology, as well as contingent factors (history of the organization, punishment and reward system, etc.). For example, technology may reduce the labor cost in software development. As long as technology is cheaper than the replaced labor, overall efficiency will be improved. On the other hand, a bureaucratic procedure of software acceptance (procedure) or unexperienced staff (manpower quality) may slow down productivity. Therefore, a quantitative analysis is just the starting point of an efficiency assessment. The analyst should evaluate (i) the effect of influencing variables on the recorded quantitative performance and (ii) to what extent variables can be altered in order to improve productivity with a better or equal service level.

5.2 Assessment of Expenditure Rigidity

Growth in computerization increases the amount of "software capital" that has to be kept updated and adapted to the changing environment and technology. The associated maintenance burden is growing over time and, in mature environments, it eventually attains 80 percent of the expenditure for applications, thus reducing the resources that an organization can allocate to new projects. On the other hand, the amount of resources allocated to the maintenance of applications represents a "viability cost," i.e., the resources needed to keep systems viable. Hence, the maintenance rate indicates the rigidity of expenditure (Nolan, 1973):

(6) MR = MAIN/APP * 100

where:

> MR = Maintenance rate (percentage)
> APP = Amount of human resources allocated to the development
>
> and maintenance of computer applications
> MAIN = Number of human resources allocated to maintenance

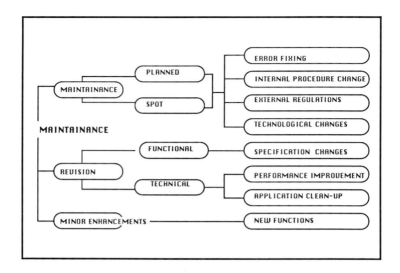

Figure 9. A Classification of Applications Maintenance Activities

Maintenance rate is a diagnostic indicator of expenditure that is applicable not only to an individual organization but also to industry-wide and cross-industry panels, provided that a standard classification of maintenance is defined.

Unfortunately, the borderline between development and maintenance is rather subtle. Converting an application to a new computer technology can be regarded as development because new user functions are provided or as maintenance because an existing application is merely replaced. A possible rationale of differentiation is illustrated in Figure 9. The maintenance concept encompasses spot and planned maintenance as well as revisions. Therefore, all projects that do not extend the application portfolio or automate new functions will fall into the maintenance concept regardless of their size; a development project will also fall into maintenance when involving a minor effort, say less than six man-months, and no equipment acquisition.

6. PORTFOLIO ANALYSIS

The "applications portfolio" is the set of computer applications of a given organization or industry. Portfolio analysis segments expenditure according to its destination areas (i.e., a portfolio segment). Since each portfolio segment represents a subset of the organization (or of information systems), one can meaningfully assess both efficiency and effectiveness of each expenditure segment. Furthermore, since the same portfolio segments (e.g., transaction oriented accounting systems) can be found in several organizations, portfolio analysis could be a challenging field for research on functional computerization patterns. Hence, portfolio is the most complex and potentially powerful branch of expenditure analysis. The following discussion considers the conceptual models by which expenditures can be segmented, identifies the typical branches of portfolio analysis, and illustrates a subset of portfolio indicators.

6.1 Conceptual Models of Applications Portfolio

Portfolio can be segmented according to two criteria: (i) the applications and (ii) the users served. "Users" represent the demand side, i.e., the potential or actual consumers of applications. Users can be organizational departments (e.g., the sales department), organizational processes involving several organizational departments (e.g., the distribution process of finished products), or a meaningful combination of both. In turn, "applications" represent the supply side and can be application lines (e.g., information systems), computer technologies (e.g., personal computers), or a meaningful combination of both. The analysis can be further sophisticated by using multiple grids that merge both application and user dimension. Figure 10 lists a selection of segmentation criteria which will be discussed.

SEGMENTATION	MAJOR SEGMENTS	DATA REQUIRED	COMMENTS
Application Line	o Corporate IS o Office Systems o DSS	Usually easy to get	Suitable for general research and management assessments
User Area	o Sales o Manufacturing o Accounting o Etc.	Needs some form of user-oriented cost accounting	
Management Processes (Anthony, 1966)	o Strategic planning o Management control o Operations control	Requires subjective integrations	In its original form is suitable only to corporate IS
Application Portfolio (Nolan, 1979)	Combines User Area and Management Processes	User-oriented cost accounting plus subjective integrations	Typical of management oriented strategy assessment
General Families (Motta, 1986)	o Product systems o Administrative systems o Control systems	User-oriented cost accounting plus subjective integrations	Three detail levels: o general o industry o organization

Figure 10. Conceptual Models for Portfolio Analysis

The segmentation into application lines involves a simple breakdown of expenditure, since corporate information systems, office
systems, and decision support systems often use dedicated hardware, software, and personnel resources. It indicates the mix of
technology and applications underlying a given aggregate expenditure. Therefore, it allows sharper aggregate comparisons but can
convey only limited information about the quality of computerization.

The segmentation into user areas requires a user-oriented accounting of computer costs, since a given user area may use multiple
application lines. A variety of indicators apply to this segmentation, thus allowing a powerful analysis of an individual organization. However, industry-wide comparisons require a standard
taxonomy of user areas in order to avoid the pitfall of homonyms
(areas with the same name but performing different functions) and
synonyms (areas with different names but performing the same function). Expenditure can also be segmented according to the organization processes. A simple model is the well-known Anthony's
triangle (Anthony, 1966), which requires segmentation of expenditure according to the management processes supported by computer
applications (strategic planning, management control, operations
control). This segmentation potentially enables the analyst to
understand the degree of support that each management process
receives from computerization, but it should be enhanced in order
to be comprehensive. The original Anthony's triangle does not
include transaction processing, which accounts for a substantial
share of applications. The allocation of applications to the
appropriate management process implies some subjective judgments,
thus limiting comparability.

Anthony's triangle can be further sliced into user areas, thus
obtaining a grid where each cell identifies a given level (e.g.,
operations control or transaction processing) and a given area
(e.g., customer accounting). Nolan's application portfolio is
based on this model (Nolan, 1979); of course, its greater sophistication requires ad hoc data.

Recently, a methodology (Motta, 1986) which segments the portfolio
into families has been proposed. Each family of information
systems serves a given family of business processes. The families
are identified through a stepwise approach. Step one breaks down
information systems into three general families: administrative
systems, product systems, and control systems. Step two identifies the sub-families that are specific to each industry. Step
three tailors the sub-families to individual organizations. The
methodology has the objective of standardizing segmentation and
limiting subjective integration.

6.2 Portfolio Indicators

The segments of applications portfolio can be regarded as investment opportunities of a generic financial portfolio (Norton,
1982). The analyst can compare the overall consistency of the
actual expenditure allocation with an ideal or standard computerization strategy. Figure 11 shows typical portfolio indicators:
(i) distribution indicators, (ii) cross-indicators, and (iii)
compound indicators.

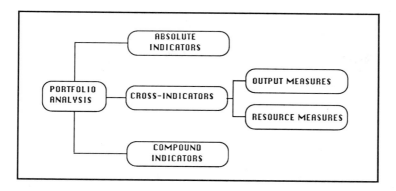

Figure 11.   Indicators of Portfolio Analysis

6.2.1   Distribution Indicators

A first distribution indicator is the break down of expenditure by
application line.   The percent distribution shows the relative
weight of application lines (corporate information systems, office
systems, decision support systems) and points out the application
mix underlying a given aggregate level of computerization.   Hence,
it is highly desirable when comparing the computerization profiles
of different industries or of different organizations.   Furthermore, if historical data are available, one can plot the curves of
absolute expenditures associated with each application line and
measure how technologies are growing, declining or replacing each
other (e.g., on-line applications are replacing batch applications).   This gives a further insight to the dynamics underlying a
given expenditure mix, which is too general in the equivalent
aggregate indicator (i.e., the aggregate growth rate).   Both percent distribution and absolute growth of application line are used
in Nolan's Stage Hypothesis as stage benchmarks (Nolan, 1973,
1979).

A second distribution indicator is the breakdown of expenditures
by user area (or process).   It provides understanding of what the
computer technology is used for and (if historical data are available) it helps in pointing out which area or process is driving
computerization.   In management-oriented assessments, the resulting distribution will be compared with an ideal allocation, which
can be developed from a variety of approaches (interviews of top
management, "normative allocation," resource allocation based on
the organization's critical success factors, etc.).

6.2.2   Cross-Indicators

As in the case of aggregate analysis, portfolio cross-indicators
allow us to assess the weight and intensity of computerization
within a given portfolio segment.   Of course, portfolio cross-
indicators are slightly different from aggregate ones, as shown in
Figure 12.   For instance, the output-oriented indicators will
focus on value added (if based on money values) instead of sales
and output quantities typical of the process or functional area
examined (if based on physical quantities).

INDICATOR	AGGREGATE ANALYSIS	PORTFOLIO ANALYSIS
Output-Oriented Indicators		
o Money Values	Sales percentage Value added	Not applicable Applicable in most cases
o Physical Quantities	Unit cost per output unit	Requires ad hoc output definition for each area or process analyzed
Resource-Oriented Indicators		
o Money Values	Percentage of salaries	Applicable
o Physical Quantities	Unit cost per employee	Applicable

Figure 12. Application of Cross-Indicators in Portfolio Analysis

6.2.3 Compound Indicators

Segmented expenditures potentially provide an excellent database to support a diagnosis of application portfolios. Based on segmented expenditure data, the analyst can monetize a number of quality parameters as (i) obsolescence, (ii) coverage, and (iii) user productivity improvement.

User requirements change as organizations evolve and technology innovation offers less expensive solutions so an application portfolio becomes obsolete. The related obsolescence ratio measures the percentage of expenditure allocated to obsolete applications:

(7) OR = EXP (OSW)/EXP * 100

where:

$$OR = \text{Obsolescence ratio (percentage)}$$
$$EXP = \text{Expenditure (annualized costs or investment levels)}$$
$$OSW = \text{Obsolete applications}$$

The higher the percentage, the larger the expenditure share that is potentially required to rebuild the application portfolio. Computer applications are designed to support users' activities. The amount of support given is called "coverage" and it is defined as the percentage of computer-supported activities in a given user area or process (e.g., accounts payable). The related indicator weighs the percent coverage versus the associated expenditure as shown below:

(8) CO = (AA/TA*100)/(EXP/SAL*100)

where:

```
CO  = Coverage (weighted .coverage)
EXP = Associated expenditure (annualized costs or investment
      levels)
SAL = Salaries of white-collar workers
AA  = Automated (or computer-assisted) activities
TA  = Total activities
```

The higher the weighted coverage, the better the efficiency of the expenditure. Of course, the coverage indicator is appropriate to highly structured activities where standardization makes industry-wide comparisons meaningful. Computers are widely used for volume processing of transactions, such as general ledger entries or banking operations. The resulting productivity improvement can be calculated by comparing the costs of an almost manual organization versus a highly computerized one. Costs are computed as follows:

(9) $UC = (SAL + EXP)/O$

where:

```
UC  = Unit costs of the area or process
SAL = Salaries
EXP = Associated expenditure (annualized costs)
O   = Output measure of the area or process
```

7. CONCLUSION

Our goal is a very preliminary contribution to what we think will be a challenging field of research: the economics of information technology in organizations. This contribution consists of identifying the potential levels of analysis (expenditure segmentation), discussing a subset of indicators, and reviewing some evidence. It appears that the analysis of expenditure can potentially support both the assessment of information systems and research about an organization's computerization. Of course, expenditure indicators, when used in assessments, should be integrated: indicators are a starting, not an ending, point. In turn, predictions associated with research studies and theories should be validated by appropriate sampling. Figure 13 lists the subset of indicators discussed and summarizes their characteristics:

(a)   Focus -- what the indicator potentially aids us to understand, i.e., expenditure/computerization weight and/or intensity, allocation, efficiency (productivity of computer-related resources), constraints, and effectiveness (i.e., productivity gain in user process)

(b)   Conceptual soundness -- may the indicator be misleading? should it be tested?

(c)   Degree of generality -- can the indicator be used only in assessing individual organizations or also in comparing organizations of the same or different industries?

(d)   Integrations needed in assessment or research perspectives for a meaningful interpretation -- regression analysis on a meaningful sample, other expenditure indicators, references for comparison, analysis of influencing variables, functional evaluation of the quality of applications underlying a given portfolio segment.

ANALYSIS LEVEL	INDICATOR DESCRIPTION	FOCUS	CONCEPTUAL SOUNDNESS	DEGREE OF GENERALITY	INTEGRATIONS NEEDED
AGGREGATE	• SCALE INDICATOR	ECONOMIES OF SCALE	TO BE TESTED	INDUSTRY	REGRESSION ANALYSIS
	• EXPEND. AS % OF REVENUES	WEIGHT	MAY MISLEAD	INDUSTRY	OTHER INDICATORS
	• EXPEND AS % OF VALUE ADDED	WEIGHT & INTENSITY	HIGH	INDUSTRY	REFERENCE STANDARDS
	• EXPEND. AS % OF SALARIES	WEIGHT & INTENSITY	HIGH	CROSS-IND.	REFERENCE STANDARDS
RESOURCE	ALL INDICATORS	ALLOCATION, MIX	HIGH	CROSS-IND.	NON MEANINGFUL PER SE
FUNCTION	• FUNCTION EFFICIENCY	EFFICIENCY	IF CRUDE MISLEADS	CROSS-IND.	ANALYSIS OF INFLUENCING VARIABLES
	• EXPENDITURE RIGIDITY	ALLOCATION, CONSTRAINTS	GENERALLY HIGH	CROSS-IND.	REFERENCE STANDARDS
PORTFOLIO	• DISTRIBUTION INDICATORS	ALLOCATION	HIGH	CROSS-IND.	REFERENCE STANDARDS
	• EXPEND. AS % OF VALUE-ADDED	WEIGHT & INTENSITY	HIGH	CROSS-IND.	FUNCTIONAL ASSESSMENT
	• EXPEND. AS % OF SALARIES	WEIGHT & INTENSITY	HIGH	CROSS-IND.	FUNCTIONAL ASSESSMENT
	• OBSOLESCENCE RATIO	ALLOCATION, CONSTRAINTS	HIGH	CROSS-IND.	FUNCTIONAL ASSESSMENT
	• WEIGTHED COVERAGE	WEIGHT, INTENSITY, EFFICIENCY	TO BE TESTED	CROSS-IND.	FUNCTIONAL ASSESSMENT
	• PRODUCTIVITY IMPROVEMENT	(EFFECTIVINESS)	TO BE TESTED	CROSS-IND.	FUNCTIONAL ASSESSMENT

Figure 13.   Indicators and Their Characteristics

ACKNOWLEDGEMENTS

The discussion of efficiency indicators reflects many informal talks with Giorgio Fardin (Telos).   The revision of this paper would not have been possible without the dedication of Graziella Gloria Schwendimann.

REFERENCES

AICA, "Problematiche del Personale EAD Negli Istituti di Credito, a Cura del Gruppo di Lavoro Informatica Negli Istituti di Credito in Collaborazione con ABI e Banca d'Italia (A Survey on EDP Professionals in Banks, Edited by the Working Group on Computer Systems in Banks of the Italian Society for Computer Science, in Cooperation with the Italian National Bank Association and Bank of Italy)," Roma, 1984.

Anthony, "Planning and Control Systems: A Framework for Analysis," Division of Research, Harvard Business School, 1966.

Batiste, J. L., "The Application Profile," *MIS Quarterly,* Vol. 10, No. 3, 1986.

Benbasat, I., Dexter, A. S., Drury, D. H., and Goldstein, R. C., "A Critique of the Stage Hypothesis: Theory and Empirical Evidence," *Communications of ACM,* Vol. 27, No. 5, 1984

Benjamin, R. I. "Information Technology in 1990's: A Long Range Planning Scenario," *MIS Quarterly,* Vol. 6, No. 2, 1982.

Bracchi, G., and Motta, G., "Spesa e Investimenti Informatici Nelle Imprese (Computer-Related Investments and Expenditure in Organizations)," Atti del Congresso AICA, 1984; "La Spesa Informatica Nelle Aziende (The Computer Expenditure in Large Organizations)," *Sviluppo and Organizzazione,* No. 88, 1985.

Chismar, W. G., and Kriebel, C. H., "A Method for Assessing the Economic Impact of Information Systems Technology on Organizations," *Proceedings of the Sixth International Conference on Information Systems*, December 16-18, Indianapolis, 1985.

Crane, J., "Trends in DP Budgets," *Datamation*, 1981.

Cron, L. W., and Sobol, M. G., "The Relationship between Computerization and Performance: A Strategy for Maximizing the Economic Benefits of Computerization," *Information and Management*, No. 6, 1983.

Dickson, G. W., and Wetherbe, J. C., *The Management of Information Systems*, McGraw-Hill, 1984, (see Chapter 6, "Management Assessment and Evaluation of MIS").

Edelman, F., "Managers, Computer Systems and Productivity," *MIS Quarterly*, Vol. 5, No. 3, 1981.

Hamilton, S., and Chervany, N. C., "Evaluating Information Systems Effectiveness, Part 1: Comparing Evaluation Approaches," *MIS Quarterly*, Vol. 5, No. 3, 1981.

ISRIL, "Indagine Conoscitiva Sulla Informatica (A Survey on Computerization)," Roma, 1979.

King, J. L., and Kraemer, K. L., "Evolution and Organizational Information Systems: An Assessment of Nolan's Stage Model," *Communications of ACM*, Vol. 27, No. 5, 1984.

Kleijnen, J., *Computers and Profits: Quantifying Financial Benefits of Information*, Addison-Wesley, 1980.

Lusa, J. M., and Winkler, R. S., "The Real Truth About DP Salaries," *Infosystems*, Vol 29, No. 6, 1982.

Marion, L., "The DP Budget Survey," *Datamation*, April 15, 1984.

Motta, G., "Trattamento Delle Informazioni Nelle Imprese e Sistemi Informativi: Un Esame di Alcune Teorie Fondamentali (An Examination of Major General Theories on Information Handling and Information Systems)," *Rivista di Informatica*, Vol. 6, No. 4, 1986.

Motta, G., and Novelli, A., "Informatizzazione delle Imprese: Dati Empirici e Schema di Analisi (Computerization of Organizations: Empirical Evidence and Frameworks for Analysis), Convegno Annuale AICA, 1986.

Nolan, R. L., "Managing Crises in Data Processing," *Harvard Business Review*, Vol. 57, No. 2, 1979.

Nolan, R. L., "Managing Information Systems by Committee," *Harvard Business Review*, Vol. 60, No. 4, 1982.

Nolan, R. L., "Managing the Computer Resource: A Stage Hypothesis," *Communications of ACM*, Vol 16, No. 7, July, 1973.

Nolan, R. L., "Steering DP Through a Recession," *Harvard Business Review*, Vol. 60, No. 5, 1982.

Nolan, R. L.,   and Wetherbe, J. C., "Toward a Comprehensive Framework for MIS Research," *MIS Quarterly*, Vol. 4, No. 2, 1980.

Norton, D. P., "The Application Portfolio," in Nolan R. L. (ed.), *Managing the Data Resource Function*, Second Edition, West Publishing Company, St. Paul, Minnesota, 1982.

Olson, M. H., and Chervany, N. L., "The Relationship between Organizational Characteristics and the Structure of Information Systems Function," *MIS Quarterly*, Vol. 4, No. 2, 1980.

Phyrr, P. A., "Zero Base Budgeting," *Harvard Business Review*, Vol. 48, No. 6, 1970.

Strassmann, P. A., *Information Payoff: The Transformation of Work in the Electronic Age*, The Free Press, New York, 1985.

Strassmann, P. A., "Stages of Growth," *Datamation*, 1976.

Verity, J., "The 1985 Budget Survey," *Datamation*, March 15, 1985.

**Economic and Organizational Assessment
of Information Technologies
P. Maggiolini**

"Negotiating a contract means building a formal model of the exhange on which both parties can agree."

INFORMATION SYSTEMS ASSESSMENT
N. Bjørn-Andersen, G.B. Davis (Editors)
Elsevier Science Publishers B.V. (North-Holland)
© IFIP, 1988

ECONOMIC AND ORGANIZATIONAL ASSESSMENT OF
INFORMATION TECHNOLOGIES

Piercarlo MAGGIOLINI

Politecnico di Milano
Milano, Italy

In order to assess the economic and organizational
impact of information technologies, we distinguish
between the utilization of informatics, telematics,
and office automation technology in tasks where
they are used as work tools and those where they
are used in an organizational and mediating role.
The main economic effects of information technologies used as work tools are work time savings
achieved with new systems.

In order to understand the real nature of different
impacts resulting from the application of information technologies in organizations, it is necessary
to understand the different economic and organizational roles of information within them.

These roles are identified in information supporting exchanges (transactions) within and between
organizations. Following this approach, a typology
of economic issues and organizational effects of
information technologies supporting coordination of
transactions is presented.

1. INTRODUCTION

We first distinguish between the utilization of information
technologies (informatics, telematics, office automation technology) in tasks where they are used as *work tools* and those where
they are used in an *organizational and mediating role.*

2. INFORMATION TECHNOLOGY AS A WORK TOOL

What is the impact of information technology (especially computer-
based office technology) used substantially as a work tool? Such
an impact can be summed up as *savings of human work time* (Engel,
et al., 1979; Poppel, 1982; Polak, 1982; Wilson and Pritchard,
1983). How does information technology achieve these economies of
work time? In order to quantify this, it is be necessary to
identify the factors that traditionally "consume" time in the
information activities of the organization. They include:

(1) Many information processes are mainly manual.
(2) They involve the transformation of information from one
     medium to another.

(3)   There are many shadow activities.   These are the unforseen
       and unforeseeable time consuming activities that accompany
       activity but do not contribute to the result.

From this point of view, computer-based information technologies
can influence such factors, improving efficiency, by:

(1)   automating all or some parts of the information processes;
(2)   eliminating some of the transformations of medium;
(3)   eliminating or reducing the shadow activities/functions;
(4)   speeding up information processes.

These increases in productivity (Bair, 1980) result from:

(1)   Automation -- the benefits derived from the substitution or
       elimination of manual procedures; i.e., computer substitute
       for manpower.

(2)   Reduction on transformation of media -- a change of the
       medium that carries the message occurs in going from verbal
       to written, from handwritten to typewritten, etc. Reduction
       in these transformations saves labor.

(3)   Reduction of shadow functions.

(4)   Speed, timeliness -- immediate economies result from the
       reduction of idle or waiting time (labor saving) and thus the
       possibility of greater productivity.   This is extremely
       important because it provides leverage by increasing all
       production factors that depend on "economies of speed." Such
       economies, though they bring a decrease in unitary costs, are
       fundamentally different from economies of scale.   The
       increased total productivity of the factors in the case of
       the economies of speed is not achieved by adding more
       production factors but by speeding up the flow of goods
       through the processes of production and distribution and so
       permitting a steadier, more intensive use of the system
       (Chandler and Daems, 1979).

When computers are used as "work tools" (to efficienty produce and
distribute data and documents), the approach used to evaluate
economic and organizational implications of information technologies is accurate but it is limited.   In fact, it does not permit
us to understand the real reasons that people use information in
the organizations or to understand more generally the role of
information and communication in and between organizations.   This
makes to understanding the real economic and organizational issues
of information technologies difficult.   We must therefore examine
the added value and hidden benefits of information and communication in and between organizations.

3.   THE ECONOMIC FUNCTIONS OF INFORMATION AND COMMUNICATION

In order to identify the real economic and organizational impacts
of information technologies we have to understand the information
dimensions of basic economic functions.   These functions are allocation of resources and monitoring and coordinating economic
activities.   Each economic system requires the resources to be
allocated to the various units, the functioning and the performance of these units to be monitored, and the flow of goods, services, money and information between the units to be coordinated.

Because the transactions (exchanges) between units are of vital importance, the most important function is that of coordination. Any mechanism that improves the efficiency of transaction, speeds up the flow through the system, or allows a more intensive use of production factors is likely to improve the overall performance.

There are various ways of organizing these functions. The best known seems to be the price system (the market). Other ways are the "hierarchies" (the traditional firms), interagency arrangements ("federations") and "clans" (Chandler and Daems, 1979; Williamson, 1975; Ouchi, 1980). The choice between these forms of organization does not depend only on production costs but above all on transaction costs. The economic activity is carried out inside or outside the firm depending on relative importance of the costs of internal and external transactions; i.e., between the costs of internal coordination and monitoring and of the marketplace.

According to some economists (Arrow, 1974; Coase, 1937), information has a strategic role in the evaluation of the limit of economic activity in a market system. The possibility of using the price system to allocate, monitor and coordinate economic activity depends on the access of economic agents to information. When the access differs from one agent to another, the price system presents difficulties. Consequently the markets considered as information systems (and prices considered as transmitters of information) are costly and imperfect: transactions have an information cost. Thus, when "hierarchical" organizational integration reduces costs, the "hierarchy" substitute for the market; i.e., hierarchical organization prevails when it is difficult to exchange on the market because the costs of organizing (exchanges on) the market are too high.

Failures in the market mechanism are due to the difficulty potential sellers and buyers have in finding one another, meeting, agreeing on the terms of the transaction, defining the contract of the sale/purchase, monitoring the execution of the contract, etc. An administrative mechanism is more efficient because it economizes on the processing of the information by absorbing the uncertainty of the exchange.

Coordination, allocation, and monitoring of the resources within the "hierarchy" also has a cost: that of *coordination* (i.e., the cost of transactions within the organization). For convenience, we distinguish the costs of coordination from those of transaction (external exchange with the environment), even if they are of the same nature (Antonelli, 1982). From this point of view, the *coordination and transaction costs* are those of collecting, processing, evaluating, and communicating information regarding the environment (and behavior of the agents) inside and outside, respectively.

4. COORDINATION COSTS

The subdivision of an activity into specialized subactivities poses the problem of coordinating these subactivities to assure execution of the overall activity. Thus, the need is to create mechanisms that permit coordinated actions by a number of interdependent parts.

The various organization coordinating processes have, however, a limited validity and efficiency in the processing of the information needed to coordinate the interdependent roles. Galbraith (1973) hypothesized that "the greater the task uncertainty, the greater the amount of information that must be processed among decision makers during task execution in order to achieve a given level of performance."

If there is good prior knowledge of the task with respect to its development, a large part of the activity can be predefined. If, on the other hand, the task is unknown (during execution more knowledge is acquired), changes must be made to the allocation of resources, etc. This implies a need to process information *during* the execution of the task. By these assumptions, the uncertainty of the task is what determines the information needs. Uncertainty implies a variety of events of states that the decision maker has to face while using a limited capacity for processing information (Simon, 1976).

According to Galbraith's analysis, organizations respond to uncertainty in two ways: either by reducing the requirements of information processing (diminishing the quantity of information), or by increasing the capacity and consequently increasing the quantity of information processed and exchanged (Table 1). We now briefly examine the principal ways in which the two types of behavior can be put into practice.

		1. Creation of slack resources
I.	Reduce the need for information processing	2. Creation of self-contained tasks
II.	Increase the capacity to process information	3. Investments in vertical information systems
		4. Creation of lateral relations

(From Galbraith, J. R., *Designing Complex Organizations*, Addison-Wesley, Reading, Massachusetts, 1973.)

Table 1. Strategies for Reduction of Uncertainty

Reducing the information requirements means reducing exceptions (the unforseen). In other words, there must be a wide margin of slack resources (financial and material, equipment and labor) or they must be organized with respect to their activity to guarantee a certain self-sufficiency (i.e., self-contained tasks). In the first case, the organization is less demanding: later deadlines, high stock levels, and large production capacities allow wide throughput variations, etc. Obviously the uncertainty is paid for by a higher resource cost. In the second case, units are self-sufficient with respect to the output they produce. Typically one can transform a functional organization, oriented towards input resources, into a divisional organization, oriented towards outputs. Scale diseconomies and more specialized professional skills are the prices paid for greater self-sufficiency (and autonomy) with respect to the unforseen.

Increasing the capacity to process and communicate information means either investing in "vertical" information systems or creating roles and organizational structures that facilitate "lateral" processing and exchange of information. Classical management information systems support planning, coordination and control (from production management to warehouse control and so on) in a vertical fashion. In the second case, the organization must create and establish direct lateral contacts, provide liaison roles linking organization units, task forces and teams, and have integrating roles with matrix structures (Table 2). The price to be paid is the greater cost of information processing systems and greater organizational costs (vis a vis greater efficiency in the reduction of uncertainties).

---

1. Direct contacts (between managers who share a problem)

2. Liaison roles (linking organizational units)

3. Task forces (temporary groups created to solve problems affecting several organizational units)

4. Teams (permanent working groups for constantly recurring interdepartmental problems)

5. Integrating managerial roles (e.g., product managers, program managers, project managers, etc.)

6. Matrix organization structures.

(From Galbraith, J. R., *Designing Complex Organizations*, Addison-Wesley, Reading, Massachusetts, 1973.)

Table 2. Lateral Processes

5. INFORMATION TECHNOLOGY SUPPORTING COORDINATION

What are the economic and organizational effects of the use of information technologies in support of planning, coordinating, and control activities? Information technology supporting coordination systems is used to reduce the scope of "bounded rationality" (Simon, 1976) of management, the costs of control, and the necessity to resort to slack resources and delegation of responsibility. This approach favors strategies increasing the capacity to process and communicate information (Type II in Table 1).

As illustrated in Table 3, the "vertical" information systems can render more efficient the functions of allocation (planning), coordination and monitoring within the firm. There is no doubt that the most specific and original telematics and office automation systems (those designed to support communications [telephone-PABX, electronic mail, and the various teleconference systems]) allow the adoption of organizational strategies based on the easiest and most widespread *horizontal* communications and on modalities of self-coordination.

o Possibility of faster planning cycles (faster reaction to
   changes to environmental conditions)

o Identifying and controlling the critical areas (reduction of
   reaction time with correcting actions)

o Simulating alternatives (studying interactions between firm
   subsystems, more accurate forecasting)

Table 3. Effects of Computer-Based "Vertical" Information
          Systems Supporting Planning, Coordination, and
          Monitoring Activities within Organizations

Thus, strategy 4 (creating lateral relations) in the Galbraith
framework would be favored (see Table 1). This strategy consists
of using collective decision making processes that selectively cut
across lines of authority. This strategy lowers the level at
which decisions are taken to coincide with the level at which
information is first available.

Among the lateral processes of Table 2, direct contacts, task
forces, and teams are favored and strengthened by office communication systems. In other words, office communication systems
(local area networks) and telematics reduce the necessity of
intermediaries, either hierarchical or lateral. Summing up, in
these cases the economic and organizational effects derive from a
reduction of *coordination costs.*

6. TRANSACTION COSTS

Transaction costs are costs of collecting, processing, evaluating
and communicating information about the environment external to
the organization. In particular, such information refers to the
condition of the market, the delivery terms of services and goods,
the quality of products, and all the details necessary to define
the obligation of parties in contracts.

More analytically, it can be said that the cost of carrying out a
transaction results in possible losses of resources due to a lack
of information between the interested parties to the transaction
itself.

There are three phases in the process of exchange (Coase, 1960):

(a) *Research.* This involves the activities necessary to produce
     an interaction involving a minimum social unit (the con-
     tracting couple). It includes the exploration and identific-
     ation of the alternatives of exchange, the identification of
     possible reciprocal advantages of the exchange, etc.

(b) *Negotiation.* This involves activities related to the nego-
     tiation of the terms of the transaction and to the conclusion
     of the contract. Negotiating a contract means building a
     formal model of the exchange on which the parties can agree.
     In this model, the price and quality are specified as well as
     aspects of behavior of the parties. The process is described
     procedurally, including an estimate of future events that may

involve the parties during the execution of the contracts, as well as the actions that the parties should take in case certain circumstances arise.

(c) *Control and monitoring.* These include the activities that make the model of the contract effective under conditions of uncertainty (for reaching agreement on adjustments and for putting them into practice). Furthermore, activities for monitoring deviations from the terms of the contract and any sanctions imposed to reestablish conditions must be specified.

The information system supporting transactions can thus be defined as a network of information and communication flows necessary to create, negotiate, monitor and control the exchanges.

7. INFORMATION TECHNOLOGY SUPPORTING TRANSACTIONS

If one considers information technology (in particular telematics and office automation technology) as that which can render information flows and the communication necessary to create, install, control and monitor transaction faster, more regular and more efficient, then benefits derive from the reduction of the costs of transaction. More specifically, it can be said that the transaction costs depend principally on

o the opportunistic behavior of the participants in the transaction;

o the numbers of potential participants;

o the nonperfect and asymmetrical distribution of information between participants (Williamson, 1975).

The use of information technology supporting *external economic transactions* of firms (services with the use of external data banks, electronic mail, public videotex systems, etc.) tends to reduce the information costs of the transaction itself, thus reducing the importance of the factors (opportunism, small numbers, information impact) (see, for example, Ciborra, 1981).

8. NOLAN'S CURVE REVISITED

We do not intend to reexplain Nolan's model (Gibson and Nolan, 1974; Nolan, 1979). Nolan's well-known result correlates the evolution of the data processing budget and numerous other variables with time. In his investigations, the DP budget evolved over time as a double S curve, which has six stages (a result of two successive and partly overlapping cycles of learning and assimilation by the firm). The first cycle is due to *computer technology* (stages 1 through 4) and the second to *data resources technology* (stages 3 through 6). Each cycle goes through four stages: initial, proliferation, control, and maturity.

From our observation of applications by enterprises, public administration and especially by agencies which operate in telecommunication infrastructures and services, we believe that a third cycle of innovation can be foreseen based on communications.

Telecommunications are a large part of future systems. In certain
countries, the data bank markets are growing. Enterprises, especially large ones, have started investing in local and geographic
networks, in electronic mail systems, and in private videotex
systems. Thus, apart from the expansion of the traditional
computer based systems, large investments in telematics and OA
systems are now started or being planned.

First Cycle: COMPUTER TECHNOLOGY

o "Operational" systems (e.g., payroll)

o Computer as "work tool," informatics as "production"
   technology

o Added value: computerizing procedures

o Benefits: reduction of (information processing)
   "production" costs

Second Cycle: DATA RESOURCES TECHNOLOGY

o "Coordination and control" systems (e.g., production
   planning and control)

o Information technology as coordination and organizational control technology

o Added value: electronic memorizing data

o Benefits: reduction of "coordination" costs

Third Cycle: ELECTRONIC COMMUNICATION TECHNOLOGY

o "Transactional" systems (e.g., electronic mail, telematic services, external data bank services)

o Information technology as mediating technology (particularly on the market)

o Added value: computerizing communication

o Benefits: reduction of "transaction" costs

Table 4. Cycles of Investments in Information Technology

We can thus identify a third cycle of investments in information
technology that corresponds to the learning and assimilation of
electronic communication technology and to the use of this to
support economic transactions, particularly between economic
agents on the market. The evolution of the use of information
technology in organizations can be described in the following way
(see Table 4):

o It passes from operational systems to coordination and
   control systems and then to systems supporting transactions,

particularly on the market. It therefore passes from information technology as a *work tool* in production technology to informatics for *coordination and control of information technology* and then to the technology of *electronic communication* supporting transactions and exchanges;

o it goes from planning and managing *computer* resource to planning and managing *data* (data resources) and then to planning and managing *communications*. The emphasis is shifted from procedures and their mechanization to data and its support of electronic filing and automatic retrieval and then to communication and its support (telematic and local area networks);

o to the benefits that derive initially from the reduction of costs of *production* (also administrative "production"). As a result, economies of labor are later added those deriving from a reduction of *coordination* costs (to which will be added those originating more specifically from a reduction in *transaction costs*).

Our reinterpretation leads us to identify three cycles of investment and assimilation of information technology which seems to be confirmed by the most recent empirical data (Nolan, 1981).

REFERENCES

Antonelli, C., "The Impact of Telematics on the Firm: A Tentative Analytical Framework in a Transactional Approach," *Proceedings EEC-FAST Conference on the Transition to an Information Society*, London, 1982.

Arrow, K. J., *The Limits of Organization*, W. W. Norton and Company, New York, 1974.

Bair, J. H., "Economic Payoff: The Productivity Question," in Uhlig, R. P., Farber, J., and Bair, J. H. (eds.), *The Office of the Future*, North Holland Publishing Company, Amsterdam, 1980.

Chandler, A. D., and Daems, H., "Administrative Coordination, Allocation, and Monitoring: A Comparative Analysis of the Emergence of Accounting and Organization in the USA and Europe," *Accounting, Organization and Society*, January 1979.

Ciborra, C., "Information System and Transactions Architecture," *Journal of Policy Analysis and Information Systems*, December 1981.

Coase, R. H., "The Nature of the Firm," *Economica N.S.*, November 1937.

Coase, R. H., "The Problem of Social Cost," *Journal of Law and Economics*, 3, 1960, pp. 1-44.

Engel, G. H., Groppusd, J., Lowenstein, R. A., and Traub, W. G., "An Office Communication System," *IBM Systems Journal*, Vol. 18, No. 3, 1979.

Galbraith, J. R., *Designing Complex Organizations*, Addison-Wesley, Reading, Massachusetts, 1973.

Gibson, C., and Nolan, R. L., "Managing the Four Stages of EDP Growth," *Harvard Business Review*, January-February 1974.

Nolan, R. L., "Managing Crises in Data Processing," *Harvard Business Review*, 1979.

Nolan, R. L., "Managing Information Systems by Committee," *Harvard Business Review*, 1981.

Ouchi, W. G., "Markets, Bureaucrats and Clans," *Administrative Science Quarterly*, March 1980.

Polak, D. L., "Function Analyzer for Office Automation," in Goldberg, R., and Lorin, H. (eds.), *The Economics of Information Processing*, John Wiley, New York, 1982.

Poppel, H. L., "Who Needs the Office of the Future?", *Harvard Business Review*, 1982.

Simon, H. A., *The New Science of Management Decision*, Prentice-Hall, Englewood Cliffs, New Jersey, 1976.

Williamson, O. E., *Markets and Hierarchies: Analysis and Antitrust Implications*, Free Press, New York, 1975.

Wilson, P. A., and Pritchard, J. A. T., *Office Technology Benefits*, National Computing Center Publications, Manchester, 1983.

DISCUSSANT NOTE

On: ECONOMIC AND ORGANIZATIONAL ASSESSMENT OF
      OFFICE INFORMATION TECHNOLOGIES

By: Piercarlo Maggiolini

Discussant's comments by: Michael GINZBERG

Weatherhead School of Management
Case Western Reserve University
Cleveland, Ohio USA

1. INTRODUCTION

There is some ambiguity in this paper as to just what is meant by
"office information technology;" whether it is limited to office
automation or includes all information technology used in an
office (e.g., data processing). In this comment, I have assumed
the author is concerned only with office automation.

2. PRIMARY ROLE

It is hard to disagree with the perspective suggested by Professor
Maggiolini.   The primary role of Office Automation (OA) *is not*
labor savings; rather, it is the support of communication and
coordination among the personnel in the office. If we examine the
users of OA, we find that, to a large extent, they are professionals and managers, and to a lesser degree the clerical workers
who are the primary users of traditional data processing systems.
The purpose of these office systems is to enable these professional and managerial users to do *more* and to do *better* work than
they have previously been able to do.   OA enables them to accomplish things which they could not accomplish without such systems,
and this occurs largely through the communications capability
provided by the technology, the ability for office professionals
to easily and directly contact one another.   Thus, the basic
framework suggested by the author -- looking at information and
communication, viewing the organization as an information processor -- is the right framework to use for assessing office information technology.

3. EVALUATION BASED ON COSTS?

While I agree completely with the author's choice of perspective,
I have difficulty agreeing with where the paper goes from there.
If we accept the organizational communication paradigm, does it
make sense then to evaluate and assess office automation in terms
of its impact on transaction and coordination *costs*?   The issue
here is not the question of transactions and coordination, but the
focus on cost and cost alone.   Considering only cost implies that
the *objective* of these systems is communication or transactions
(exchanges).   In fact, transactions and communications are of

interest only because they support other necessary organizational activities. Our real concern is these *other activities*, not the communications and transactions which enable them to take place efficiently. We should ask, then, how do we evaluate and assess those other activities.

4. FURTHER QUESTIONS

In an important sense, the content of this paper does not live up to the title. The title is "Economic and Organizational Assessment of Office Information Technologies." The focus on transaction and coordination *costs* addresses the economic side, but the organizational side of assessment seems to have been left out. In order to accomplish *organizational* assessment of office information technologies, we need to answer several questions:

o *Who* are the users and stakeholders in office automation systems?

o *What* (in organizational terms) are the system users and stakeholders trying to accomplish?

o *How* does office automation impact their ability to achieve their objectives?

The framework suggested by Galbraith's view of the organization as an information processing system is probably the right place *to start* in answering these questions, but it is just the start.

5. CONCLUDING COMMENTS

Professor Maggiolini's comments concerning the relationship between office automation and the Nolan stage model seem quite reasonable. As he notes, "telecommunications are a large part of the future systems." The integration of communication and computation technologies is much written about and is quite evident in many current systems (in the United States, at least). No doubt, this trend will be felt even more strongly in the next few years. Regardless of what one believes about the Nolan stage model, the result of this trend will likely be a growth spurt in spending for information handling followed by a lull as the new technology is digested and assimilated. This could be viewed as adding two more stages to Nolan's model. Further, this is unlikely to be the last addition to the "growth curve." As new, promising technologies are introduced and organizations rush to adopt them, the pattern of alternating periods of rapid growth and stability is likely to continue.

Channel Disposition Assessment:
Toward the Diagnosis of Information System Utility
E. Burton Swanson

"Such channels are understood to constitute those
established paths by which the user obtains and
receives messages from a system."

INFORMATION SYSTEMS ASSESSMENT
N. Bjørn-Andersen, G.B. Davis (Editors)
Elsevier Science Publishers B.V. (North-Holland)
© IFIP, 1988

CHANNEL DISPOSITION ASSESSMENT: TOWARD THE
DIAGNOSIS OF INFORMATION SYSTEM UTILITY

E. Burton SWANSON

Graduate School of Management
University of California, Los Angeles
Los Angeles, California 90024 USA

Among the techniques of information system assessment are those which assess attitudes of individual
users of information systems. Instruments for the
measurement of user satisfaction are perhaps the
most well known of techniques of this type, which
assume in general that the purpose of the system is
utilitarian and that the individual is the appropriate unit of analysis. More recently, the
measurement of an individual's information channel
disposition has been proposed as another assessment
technique of this same type. In the present paper,
progress in the development of a channel disposition model and assessment instrument is reported
and the underlying assumptions of the work are
examined.

1.   INTRODUCTION

An information system is assessed when a value is placed upon it.
From a systems point of view, this presumes that: (1) the system
is understood to be purposeful; (2) there exists a client for the
system; and (3) a measure of system performance is established
(Churchman, 1971).

Information systems are thus conceived as utilitarian in nature.
Their performance measures seek the value of the system in terms
of the purposeful serving of the client's interest.

Not surprisingly, therefore, the utilitarian conception is
reflected in the Call for Papers to this conference, which "aims
at addressing the crucial issue of evaluating the costs and benefits of information systems from the technical, economic, organizational and societal perspectives."

Ironically, however, though the breadth of this utilitarian
interest is substantial, the stated focus on costs and benefits
would appear to give an upper hand to the economic perspective
among alternative bases for system assessment. The systems
approach thus has its weaknesses, i.e., "enemies," and it is worth
reminding ourselves that systems are not only rational and economic; they are political (possessing community), moral (possessing goodness), aesthetic (possessing beauty), and religious
(possessing faith) (Churchman, 1979). These values are not always
well served by our benefit and cost assessments.

Among the techniques of information system assessment are those which assess attitudes of individual users of information systems. The most commonly assessed of these attitudes is user satisfaction (Bailey and Pearson, 1983; Ives, et al., 1983), which is often held to be a surrogate for system success (the more satisfied the users, the more successful the system is presumed to be). As a surrogate, user satisfaction has been strongly criticized, especially by those who assume that economic utility to the organization is the ideal measure of system performance (Chismar and Kriebel, 1985).

In general, however, the motivation for user attitude measurement in information systems research does not rest upon such a surrogate assumption. Rather, it stems from the desire to understand both the antecedents and consequences of user behavior, on the one hand, and to understand how a user is informed by a system, on the other. Either an implementation perspective or an information perspective, or both, may motivate such research (Swanson, 1982).

In examining the antecedents and consequences of user behavior, an implementation perspective frequently underlies the researcher's inquiry. From this perspective, the basic concern is with the development of an explanatory model in which the user's role in contributing to system success or failure is included. The work of Lucas (1978) is illustrative.

In the case of an information perspective, the emphasis is placed upon an understanding of the process by which users are informed by an information system. Information is regarded as a psychological product and, hence, something to be studied by psychological measurement instruments. Zmud's (1978) attempt to empirically derive the dimensions of information provides an example.

From either an implementation or information perspective, user attitudes are thus measured because individual assessments of information systems are held to matter. That is, whatever the global measure of performance of an information system, in principle, the individual user is assumed to bring his or her own judgments to bear upon the process, in practice. That these judgments are consequential may be to some a matter of faith; to others it is the burden of the research itself.

A recent example of research in this vein is the study of an individual's information channel disposition. (Swanson, 1987). This work is summarized and examined in terms of its underlying assumptions in the following sections.

2.   THE CHANNEL DISPOSITION CONSTRUCT

The concept of an information system user's channel disposition was originally advanced by Swanson (1982). Broadly speaking, channel disposition is conceived as a manifold of valuations about the quality of information and access provided to the user by the information system's channel(s). Such channels are understood to constitute those established paths by which the user obtains and receives messages from a system. Examples include periodic, distributed written reports; interactive terminal-based query and response; and decision-support intermediaries.

While conceived with applicability to formal information systems in mind, the generality of the channel disposition construct is also intended to serve comparable research in organizational communication, where the focus is traditionally on interpersonal channels among individuals. (For a review, see O'Reilly and Pondy, 1980.)

In valuing the quality of information provided by a channel, the user is assumed to be assessing those benefits associated with its use. In valuing the quality of access, the user is assumed to be assessing corresponding costs. Both benefits and costs are assumed to accrue to the user in his or her organizational role. Thus, for example, the user may benefit from an information channel in terms of decision support of a given organizational task at the cost of his or her personal resources in terms of time and effort.

Such benefit and cost assessments are further assumed to reflect in general the user's information opportunities. Thus, for example, benefits of decision support reflect the consequences associated with the absence of such support. Similarly, cost assessments reflect the consequences of using alternative means for obtaining comparable information.

In assessing both benefits and costs, it is assumed that prospective and retrospective elements are combined. Thus, on the whole, channel disposition is conceived as reflecting the net utility of an information channel (or system) to a user. As an attitude, it also suggests incorporation within an expectancy theory of behavior (see, e.g., Robey, 1979).

How is a user's channel disposition consequential? In addressing this question, a model of channel disposition and use is proposed in which: (1) the individual's channel disposition is hypothesized to affect his or her employment of the channel and, thus, use of the information thereby obtainable; (2) an information supply and demand structure in the organization is hypothesized to affect the individual's channel disposition in terms of the assessed quality of information, as well as the individual's consequent use of information obtainable from the channel; and (3) a channel supply and demand structure in the organization is hypothesized to affect the individual's channel disposition in terms of the assessed access quality, as well as the individual's consequent employment of the channel. (For a schematic summary, see Figure 1.)

The information supply and demand structure of an organization is understood as formed by the evidence introduced (supplied) and sought (demanded) by organizational participants for all varieties of informative and persuasive purposes. (For a typology of organizational uses, see Swanson, 1978.) The corresponding channel supply and demand structure is understood as formed by those specific means provided (supplied) and sought (demanded) for the purpose of obtaining needed information. Both structures are understood to be imbedded in an essentially bureaucratic, rather than market, context.

Validation of the channel disposition construct entails an examination of the proposed model in conjunction with the development of an instrument by means of which an individual's disposition may be assessed.

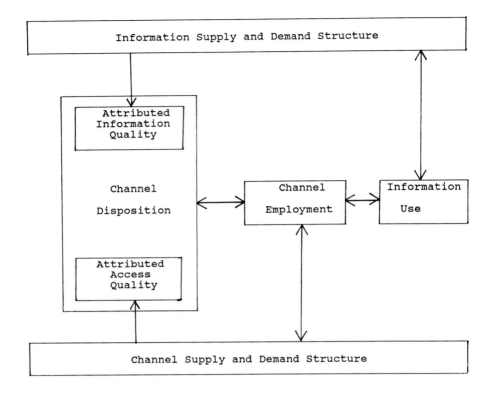

Figure 1:   Channel Disposition Model

3.   RESEARCH PROGRESS TO DATE

The examination of the proposed model and the development of an
assessment instrument with which to measure an individual's
channel disposition is a long-term endeavor.   Here, the progress
to date is summarized.

The first phase of the research has focused upon the conventional
management report as one information channel type.   For data
gathering, a questionnaire has been developed by means of which
the individual user of any management report may provide an
assessment.   Within the questionnaire, a semantic differential
scaling technique is employed to assess the user's disposition
toward the report.   Twenty items are used to assess information
quality; eighteen items are used to assess access quality.   Many
of these items were drawn from past research.

The questionnaire also obtains self-reported data on use of the
management report.   Three items establish the frequency (daily,
weekly, monthly, quarterly, never) with which information from the
report is discussed by the respondent with subordinates, boss, and
others.

Data is also gathered on the background of the respondent (current job position, length of time in the position, and number of subordinates reporting to the position), and on recommended changes to the report, and overall satisfaction with the report.

Ten management reports, three each in three organizations and one in a fourth organization, have to date been evaluated by means of the questionnaire. For each report in each setting, copies of the questionnaire, with supporting cover letter, are distributed to report users by internal company mail. Responses are anonymous and are returned postage-prepaid directly to the researcher, who analyzes the results and summarizes them for the participating organization. (The summaries are intended to be useful for the participating organization, not just the researcher. Several of the reports have, in fact, been modified on the basis of their assessments.)

The composite database of assessments across the ten reports and four organizations now contains a total of 186 individual user responses which have been analyzed as reported in Swanson (1987).

A principal objective of this analysis has been an examination of the dimensionality of the channel disposition construct. To this end, factor analysis has been employed. From this analysis, four interpretable factors have been identified, two of which were found in a subsequent regression analysis to be significantly related to use of information obtained from the channel. The two significant factors, termed "information value" and "information accessibility," correspond closely to the dimensions of channel disposition originally postulated. The structures of these two factors, in terms of the semantic differential items from which their indices have subsequently been composed, are shown in Table 1. Reliable measures of both information value (Cronbach alpha = .83) and information accessibility (Cronbach alpha = .91) have thus been obtained.

Factor 1. Information Value

Semantic Differential Item	Factor Loading
valuable (valueless)	.79
useful (useless)	.75
relevant (irrelevant)	.73
important (unimportant)	.71
meaningful (meaningless)	.57

Factor 2. Information Accessibility

Semantic Differential Item	Factor Loading
unobstructed (obstructed)	.79
untroublesome (troublesome)	.77
unburdensome (burdensome)	.73
unrestricted (restricted)	.70
convenient (inconvenient)	.67
easy (difficult)	.64

Table 1: Significant Channel Disposition Factors

A third factor, termed "information technique" (reflecting information reliability, precision, accuracy, timeliness, comprehensiveness, and conciseness), accounted for a substantial portion of
the variance in the channel disposition construct itself, but
proved little, if at all, related to information use. A fourth
factor, termed "information interest," was also unrelated to
information use, though it was underrepresented among the items of
the questionnaire, and deserves further study, as indicated below.

Two contextual variables, report medium (printed copy or accessible terminal display) and report frequency (daily, weekly,
etc.), both of which represent channel supply characteristics,
also proved to be of significance in the regression analysis of
information use.

In summary, limited evidence in support of the channel disposition
model has been obtained in the exploratory study summarized here.
Further, reliable measures of two channel disposition components
have been developed in support of continued research and application. Nevertheless, caution with regard to the ultimate validity
and usefulness of the channel disposition construct is clearly
warranted.

Of particular importance in the further investigation of channel
disposition will be the development and refinement of the two
contextual constructs -- the information supply and demand structure and the channel supply and demand structure -- incorporated
within the proposed model. These constructs are not well articulated in the present exploratory study, in which the total
explained variance in information use proved to be small (16
percent), though comparable to that achieved by other research
studies of this type.

The development of more sophisticated measures of information use
also looks to be necessary in the long term.

4. DISCUSSION AND CONCLUSION

It may be helpful to consider in some depth the underlying assumptions of the channel disposition model in order to place it in
context. These assumptions may be identified in terms of level of
analysis and perspective on action (Pfeffer, 1982). With respect
to the former, the channel disposition model assumes that individual (as opposed to organizational or subunit) behavior should be
observed and explained.

With respect to the latter, the assumption is that action is
purposive (as opposed to externally controlled or primarily
dependent on process and social construction). The underlying
model may thus be characterized as "micro-level rational action"
(Pfeffer, 1982). Micro-level rational action models are subject
to a number of weaknesses, summarized by Pfeffer (1982). All of
these bear upon the present channel disposition research.

A first difficulty with micro-level rational action models is said
to be a tendency toward tautological explanations. In the present
case, the statement that people use information channels because
they are disposed to do so comes dangerously close to a simple
restatement of the data. The irony in this case, on the other
hand, is that unequivocal support for such a simple and general
restatement is hard to come by. Channel disposition, as presently

assessed, is but inconsistently and weakly related to information usage.

A second characteristic difficulty with micro-level rational action models is asserted to be the common neglect of context in explaining attitudes and behaviors. While the channel disposition model specifically incorporates such a context, as discussed above, this context is underdeveloped in the exploratory report evaluation study, a weakness which appears to show up in the results.

A third alleged problem is the reliance upon "hypothetical constructs that reside largely in people's heads," in Pfeffer's words. This is said to create substantial epistemological diffi-culties for many researchers, who consider constructs such as channel disposition not directly observable, in contrast to overt behavior, considered observable. Without underestimating the difficulties of measuring channel disposition, the view here is that the problem of observability is poorly drawn when thus dichotomized. In particular, the difficulties of observing and measuring behavior in theoretically powerful ways may be underes-timated. In the present research, for example, the problem of measuring information use is at least as imposing as that of measuring channel disposition. Ultimately, validation of the channel disposition construct will rest as much upon the former as the latter.

Another asserted difficulty with the micro-level rational action model is the common assumption that behavior is foresightful rather than retrospectively rational, i.e., that attitudes deter-mine behaviors, rather than the reverse. The proposed channel disposition model seeks to have it both ways, but this admittedly presents substantial difficulties in interpreting the results of any empirical study. These difficulties are compounded in the exploratory study by the gathering of data on both channel dispo-sition and information use by means of the same questionnaire instrument and the consequent common method variance which may thus have been introduced. Because subjects are asked to recall use, for example, a bias toward retrospective interpretation may be inherent in the study.

Still another suggested problem is the reliance by micro-level rational action models on information processing explanations of attitudes and behaviors. Affect and sentiment, rather than cogni-tion, offer alternatives for explaining behavior, it is argued. This problem may indeed be relevant in the present research. The structure of channel disposition was serendipitously found to include an information interest factor, distinct from the other factors, and interpretable as reflecting affect. Though the interest factor was unrelated to use in the present case, this may be due to lack of reliability in the measure, and further study is clearly warranted.

Finally, micro-level rational action models pose the problem of aggregation to achieve explanation of collective or macro-level organization behavior. In the present research, the two contex-tual constructs -- the information supply and demand structure, and the channel supply and demand structure -- constitute such macro-level phenomena, and are themselves worthy of explanation. In principle, these contexts are given shape by the collective effects of individual behaviors. It is by no means clear, how-ever, that a macro-level theory of substance is best developed by pursuing this elementary notion. A reasonable alternative is to build macro-level theory entirely by means of macro-level analysis.

On the other hand, macro-level theory itself poses the corresponding challenge of disaggregation for those interested fundamentally in the explanation of individual behaviors. To illustrate, consider the macro-level view of information systems as "exchange support systems," inspired by transaction cost theory, as suggested by Ciborra (1985). This view would appear to relate directly to the notions of information and channel supply and demand structures advanced here. Its application to the channel disposition model, however, requires that the exchange support among organizational participants be characterized differentially.

In conclusion, the present channel disposition construct and model is subject to a number of weaknesses which are characteristic of micro-level rational action models. These weaknesses do not invalidate the model; they do, however, pose a research challenge to be met.

This challenge is worth meeting. In assessing the overall value of any information system, the client's interest is the standard for any proposed measure of performance, as indicated above. The commitment of the channel disposition construct and associated assessment instrument is to "asking the user" as one means of arriving at such a judgment. The user's answers are presumed informative, if not necessarily authoritative. In practice, a diagnostic purpose is thus served; the user's answers support both the overall assessment and the guidance of the system's continued development.

Whether "asking the user" is necessary or sufficient for information system assessment is no doubt an issue subject to continued debate. Choosing to do so is, however, at least in spirit, user-friendly.

REFERENCES

Bailey, J. E., and Pearson, S. W., "Development of a Tool for Measuring and Analyzing Computer User Satisfaction," *Management Science*, 1983, Vol. 5, No. 29, pp. 530-545.

Chismar, W., and Kriebel, C., "A Method for Assessing the Economic Impact of Information Systems on Organizations," *Proceedings of the Sixth International Conference on Information Systems*, Indianapolis, Indiana, December 16-18, 1985, pp. 45-56.

Churchman, C. W., *The Design of Inquiring Systems*, Basic Books, New York, 1971.

Churchman, C. W., *The Systems Approach and Its Enemies*, Basic Books, New York, 1979.

Ciborra, C. U., "Reframing the Role of Computers in Organizations: The Transactions Costs Approach," *Proceedings of the Sixth International Conference on Information Systems*, Indianapolis, Indiana, December 16-18, 1985, pp. 57-69.

Ives, B., Olson, M., and Baroudi, J., "Measuring User Information Satisfaction: A Method and Critique," *Communications of the ACM*, 1983, Vol. 10, No. 26, pp. 785-793.

Lucas, H. C., "Empirical Evidence for a Descriptive Model of Implementation," *MIS Quarterly*, 1978, Vol. 2, No. 2, pp. 27-42.

O'Reilly, C., and Pondy, L., "Organizational Communication," in Kerr, S. (ed.), *Organizational Behavior*, Grid, Columbus, Ohio, 1980.

Pfeffer, J., *Organizations and Organization Theory*, Pitman, Marshfield, Massachusetts, 1982.

Robey, D., "User Attitudes and Management Information System Use," *Academy of Management Journal*, 1979, Vol. 3, No. 22, pp. 527-538.

Swanson, E. B., "Information Channel Disposition and Use," *Decision Sciences*, Vol. 18, No. 1, Winter 1987, pp. 131-145.

Swanson, E. B., "Measuring User Attitudes in MIS Research: A Review," *Omega*, 1982, Vol. 2, No. 10, pp. 157-165.

Swanson, E. B., "The Two Faces of Organizational Information," *Accounting, Organizations and Society*, 1978, Vol. 3/4, No. 3, pp. 237-246.

Zmud, R. W., "An Empirical Investigation of the Dimensionality of the Concept of Information," *Decision Sciences*, 1978, Vol. 2, No. 9, pp. 187-195.

DISCUSSANT NOTE

On: CHANNEL DISPOSITION ASSESSMENT: TOWARD THE
     DIAGNOSIS OF INFORMATION SYSTEM UTILITY

By: E. Burton Swanson

Discussant's comments by: Rudy HIRSCHHEIM

Templeton College, Oxford
Great Britain

1. INTRODUCTION

Since the role of a discussant is to critically assess the
contribution made by a specific paper, I shall do my best to be
critical of the paper's assumptions and arguments. The discussion, therefore, adopts a largely dialectical position, with a
view of providing an alternative interpretation of the substantive
issues.

The paper in the proceedings postulates that our understanding of
information systems (IS) evaluation might be improved if a
"channel disposition model" of information systems use is adopted.
But what is a channel disposition model? The answer to this
question cannot, unfortunately, be adequately found in this paper.
The reader must go to another paper (Swanson, 1987) where a
detailed description of the model is offered. My comments about
the channel disposition model and its usefulness are, therefore,
based on my reading and understanding of the other paper. I have
chosen to discuss the Swanson paper by, first, summarizing my
interpretation of the channel disposition model (the core of the
paper) and, second, offering some comments about the value of the
model within the context of IS assessment.

2. OVERVIEW OF THE CHANNEL DISPOSITION MODEL

The raison d'etre of the model is to provide a better understanding of the key characteristics of IS use and effectiveness.
The model is an attempt to go beyond the simplistic models in the
field which try to explain the relationship between user involvement, system quality, system use, and user satisfaction. It
postulates an alternative explanation of why people use or do not
use IS. At its most basic level, the channel disposition model
relates an individual's attitude toward a channel to channel
usage, and is composed of two key components: attributed information quality and attributed access quality. Channel disposition
is favorable when both information quality and access quality are
perceived to be high, which should lead to an increased use of the
channel. Unfortunately, prior research results (Allen, 1977;
O'Reilly, 1982) do not support the model in that channel use was
only related to channel accessibility. Such counter-intuitive
results provide the motivation for embarking on an empirical study

to test the validity of the channel disposition model. The results of that study are reported in Swanson (1987).

It is not my intention to describe in detail the results, but it is probably worthwhile to summarize the key aspects of the study. A questionnaire was developed to obtain data about channel disposition and information use. It was distributed to a large number of IS report users in four different organizations; 186 completed questionnaires were subsequently analyzed in the study. Factor analysis was employed to assess the dimensionality of the channel disposition construct. A five-factor solution was generated, leading Swanson to conclude that it "suggests a more complex structure to the channel disposition construct than the two dimensions -- information quality and access quality -- originally posited" (Swanson, 1987). Further analysis employing multiple hierarchical regression using indices representing the three most significant factors resulted in the support of the basic proposition of channel disposition being related to information use. Support for the subordinate proposition relating information use to attributed information quality was also found. Interestingly, however, the additional subordinate proposition relating information use to channel accessibility was not supported. This is directly opposite from that derived by Allen (1977) and O'Reilly (1982). Swanson goes on to offer some explanations on the antithetical conclusion.

3. COMMENTS

I would like to suggest an alternative explanation on the incompatible results; viz, the model is too simplistic. Information use cannot be deterministically understood as this would imply human beings are deterministic, thus denying the existence of free will. The real question is do people really behave in such a way that information use can be explained by a simple causal connection? More fundamentally, is the cause-effect model of human behavior really appropriate here? This of course is a particularly thorny problem, and has been debated at great length in the philosophical literature. It is not possible to explore this difficult issue here, but elsewhere (cf. Klein and Hirschheim, 1985; Mumford, et al., 1985) it has been discussed with particular reference to the IS field. A view adopted by a number of researchers who study the epistemological assumptions underlying IS research is that while causal connections are not possible when the subject of study is the human (social) being, certain generalizations might be possible but with considerable difficulty. (For more information see Hirschheim, 1985.) In the Swanson paper, it is likely that many factors contribute to information use which are outside the bounds of the channel disposition model, or are simply untestable; for example, IS use and its relationship to power, expectations, ritualistic value, channel type, etc.

Further, is it possible to isolate a single channel on its own, and even if you can, does it make the end product totally artificial? Swanson recognizes that there are connections between channels, but still feels that it is possible to study a channel on its own. I question this belief.

Another concern I have relates to Swanson's assumption that while information supply and demand structure and channel supply and demand structure are interlocked, "their contextual impacts upon channel disposition are distinct" (Swanson, 1987). Is this true?

My suspicion is that their impacts are not as distinct as Swanson contends.

Last, I would like to return to my fundamental disagreement with the paper: the adopted epistemological and ontological stance. Swanson notes that "information use is an essentially social phenomenon" (Swanson, 1987) yet treats it, I would argue, in an essentially non-social way. The epistemological and ontological assumptions asserted are not reflected in the methodology chosen. My position is simply this: if information use is a social phenomenon (and I believe it is), then a more phenomenological research vehicle is needed to study it. (This is an issue explored at some length by Boland [1985].) It is my contention that we ought to undertake more phenomenological studies; my belief is that they would provide alternative conceptions of why people use or do not use information systems.

REFERENCES

Allen, T., *Managing the Flow of Technology*, MIT Press, Boston, 1977.

Boland, R., "Phenomenology: A Preferred Approach to Research in Information Systems," in Mumford, E., et al. (eds.), *Research Methods in Information Systems*, North-Holland, Amsterdam, 1985, pp. 193-201.

Hirschheim, R., "Information Systems Epistemology: An Historical Perspective," in Mumford, E., et al. (eds.), *Research Methods in Information Systems*, North-Holland, Amsterdam, 1985, pp. 13-36.

Klein, H., and Hirschheim, R., "Fundamental Issues of Decision Support Systems: A Consequentialist Perspective," *Decision Support Systems*, Vol. 1, No. 1, 1985, pp. 5-23.

Mumford, E., Hirschheim, R., Fitzgerald, G., and Wood-Harper, T. (eds.), *Research Methods in Information Systems*, North-Holland, Amsterdam, 1985.

O'Reilly, C., "Variations in Decision Makers' Use of Information Sources: The Impact of Quality and Accessibility of Information," *Academy of Management Journal*, Vol. 25, No. 4, 1982, pp. 756-771.

Swanson, E. B., "Information Channel Disposition and Use," *Decision Sciences*, Vol. 18, No. 1, Winter 1987, pp. 131-145.

**Flexibility of Software as a Dimension
of Information Systems Assessment
P. Järvinen**

"...a user should be able to adjust interactively the
order of execution of separate functions."

INFORMATION SYSTEMS ASSESSMENT
N. Bjørn-Andersen, G.B. Davis (Editors)
Elsevier Science Publishers B.V. (North-Holland)
© IFIP, 1988

FLEXIBILITY OF SOFTWARE AS A DIMENSION OF INFORMATION SYSTEMS ASSESSMENT

Pertti JÄRVINEN

University of Tampere
P.O.Box 607
SF-33101 Tampere, Finland

Cost of application software is often the dominant cost component of an information system. About 50 to 70 percent of total software costs are for maintenance (repairs and enhancements). Inflexible software costs more to repair and enhance than does a flexible one in response to the changing environment of the information system.

All requirements of an information system cannot be stated precisely at the beginning of the development period. After implementation, the system must often be adjusted and enhanced to satisfy users' actual needs. Flexibility of application software may facilitate implementation of necessary adjustments and improvements. Therefore, flexibility of software relative to maintenance should be a key dimension when an information system is assessed.

In this paper, a scale for flexibility in application software is presented. Some systems are evaluated against this flexibility scale. A model for the evaluation of computer software packages is considered and critically analyzed. It is also applied to a comparison between application-specific and flexible software. The analysis gives more evidence for flexibility as a key factor of an assessment.

1. INTRODUCTION

A user can easily learn to initiate and execute application programs. However, he/she is dependent on functions included in the application programs. In order to have unique, tailored features, a user needs to acquire programming ability. An alternative to user programming is software design to allow users to specify unique features without programming.

The motivation for this alternative is to increase human freedom in computer utilization. Examples are: a user may wish to store a new data item in the database, the rows of a report are to be sorted in a different order, two functions are to be performed in a different order depending on the planning horizon. The changes above require programming work, but a user generally cannot do it, and waiting for the help of a programmer will cause a decrease in user productivity (work per hour -- Boyle, 1984).

We developed earlier (Järvinen, 1985) a six-level model of user computer utilization proficiency (Figure 1).

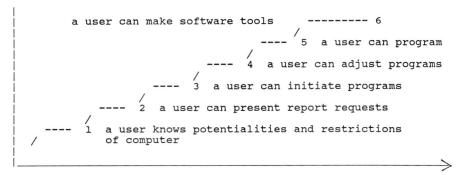

Figure 1: The Six Level Model of User Computer Utilization Proficiency

Here we are interested in analyzing level 4 (the level when a user can adjust programs without computer programming skill).

The phrase "adjust programs" refers to application programs where alternative ways for utilizing them already exist, i.e., the software is flexible in that it has alternatives. Program adjusting can involve data to be processed and/or functions to be performed. Data to be adjusted can be input, stored, or output. Both data values and structures can be adjusted. Hence the gradations on our scale of flexible software (in section 2) will measure the extent to which data (and functions of software) may be adjusted. Some software packages are assessed using this scale. It will be shown (in section 3) that the gradations of the scale are useful and that an assessment can be performed prior to software use.

2. A GRADUATED SCALE OF SOFTWARE FLEXIBILITY

Our purpose is to develop a graduated scale for measuring flexibility of software. Because the research is at an exploratory stage, this report shall concentrate on only very few gradations.

Computers are utilized to enhance human memory by storing data in files or databases. This storing feature needs two subfunctions: input and output. The former is a prerequisite of the latter. But the latter is directly supporting a user in his/her action. With respect to system integrity, output is safer to change than input, because output such as reporting does not change the content of the database. Accordingly, the first gradation on our flexibility scale is a flexible reporting function.

Gradation 4.1: A User Can Adjust the Reporting Function

Flexibility of the reporting function mainly refers to various ways and means of adjusting the report to be produced. It can mean, for example, an opportunity to select the content and the form of the report, the data items to be selected, locations and representation formats in the report (title, headings, footnotes), order of rows, computations (sums, averages) to be performed, etc. Martin (1982, pp 19-25) reports on report generator features.

If (application) software has a flexible reporting function, a user can define an ad hoc-report. To do this, he should know which data items have been stored in the database and how he can describe the content and the format of the report.

In order to define the second gradation on the flexibility scale, there is an assumption that the data items are available and accessible to the report function (gradation 4.1). Accordingly, the next step is to increase flexibility in the input function of a database and at the same time to provide data independence (cf., Date, 1981). This gradation is termed a flexible database maintenance function.

Gradation 4.2: A User Can Adjust Database Maintenance Function

The function contains normal updating subfunctions: changing value of a data item, inserting a new record and deleting an old record. The database maintenance function also allows a user to create a new file, add a new data item to the record, lengthen the field of a certain data item in the record, etc. Most of those subfunctions are included in applications generator (Martin, 1982).

Gradations 4.1 and 4.2 cover most user requirements to manipulate data stored in the databases. We can now proceed to make available other kinds of flexibility. Although the reporting and maintaining functions contain many subfunctions, they are in a certain sense single functions (taking care of output and input relations with the databases).

After users have two or more functions that can be executed, the following questions must be asked. In which order should they be performed? Is it allowable to join two separate functions into a sequence? Are functions always performed in the same sequence and if not, how can a user adjust their performance during run time? We propose that software should allow a user to control performance of separate functions interactively, in other words, a user should be able to adjust interactively the order of execution of separate functions.

Gradation 4.3: A User Can Adjust Interactively the Order of Execution of Separate Functions

At gradation 4.3, the functions are preprogrammed and the user defines the order of execution for a particular run using the software (gradation 4.3). In that definition, user input, part or all of output, and the functions to be called and performed are described. The definition can be stored and invoked for repeated use.

In order to increase a user's freedom to utilize the computer further and at the same time to define the next gradation, the software should allow the insertion of new functions (gradation 4.4).

Gradation 4.4: A User Can Adjust Software by Inserting New
             Functions

Gradation 4.4 refers to the open-endedness of the system. This
presupposes that a user has a programming skill sufficient to
perform insertions. Hence, it does not differ much from level 5
(a user can program). However, the software at gradation 4.4 can
constitute a fairly safe "programming" environment because it
controls the compatibility of the new function with the other
functions of the system.

All the gradations 4.1 - 4.4 defined above represent gradations
on our flexibility scale (Figure 2) for level 4 described in
section 1.

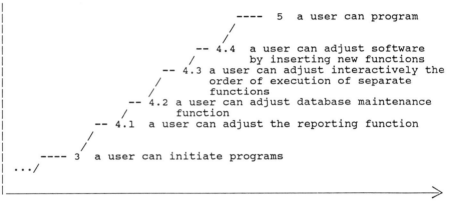

Figure 2: The Graduated Scale of Flexibility in Application
          Software

3. AN ASSESSMENT OF SOME PACKAGES

In this section, some software packages are assessed against the
flexibility scale in order to demonstrate its validity and
usability.

Bass (1985) presented a tool, the Karlsruhe Screen-Based Application Support System, that may be used to define user interaction.
The tool is said to be simple enough so that the end user (or,
more likely, a nonprogramming application manager) can control and
customize dialogue without the help of an application programmer.
The Karlsruhe system includes an editor facility that allows the
specification of screen geometry, input constraints, computation
facilities, and display logic. The system also manages functions
like the grouping of related pieces of information into a display
and the calculation of operators commonly used in report writing
(sums, counts, averages, maximums, and minimums).

A user specifies a screen geometry by using the editor. The
display specification is bound to the application program at run
time: that is, the editor produces a disk file describing the
display, and this file is read in by the application program. The
user can therefore adjust an output form and re-execute an

application. Hence, the Karlsruhe system belongs to gradation 4.1 on our scale.

Our own efforts (Järvinen, 1983) have concentrated on the implementation of a software package, the ABC package, to enable a user to create and maintain a master file and produce various reports. Because an arbitrary data set can be stored as a master file, data items that belong to the record of the master file must be described to the ABC system. A user always specifies and describes the report he/she wants to have. Our empirical experiment (Järvinen, 1984) shows that the users learned to update the master file and to describe and to run output reports almost without any organized training.

Compared with the Karlsruhe system, in the ABC system there is an additional characteristic that a user can create and maintain an arbitrary file. Hence the ABC system belongs to gradation 4.2.

Design of the human-computer interface in an interactive system is a task different from design of algorithmic programs for computation. When implementing interactive software, according to Hägglund and Tibell (1982), we should base our work on language constructs and employ software architectures which recognize these differences. Data abstractions, as well as the idea of schema-driven interpretation of stored representation of data in database systems, illuminates a very important concept; namely data independent of software (Date, 1981). Hägglund and Tibell feel that a similar abstraction facility for the external interface of a human-computer system is very useful. The idea is to separate the description of the content of the dialogue from the decision on how the actual dialogue is to be performed. They can then support multi-style dialogues based on either menu-selection, fill-in-the-blank, or command language (Shneiderman, 1980) using the same underlying definitions of objects and operations. Hägglund and Tibell use the term "control independence" to denote such an organization of software. They describe the IDECS system for dialogue modelling. The system was designed to provide an opportunity to make rapid prototypes of the human-computer dialogue before the final requirements specifications were to be settled.

The IDECS system is based on the concept of a conversation graph, i.e., a directed network where nodes represent message contexts and the arcs correspond to valid transitions between contexts. The graph structure acts as a grammar for message sequences which may be accepted during a dialogue. The IDECS system provides an interactive environment for creation and interpretation of messages and message contexts.

In order to relate the IDECS system to the flexibility scale, the conversation graph was used as a model of dialogue. Depending on an input message and a node (message context) the IDECS system gives a response and moves control to the node specified in the graph. A user can adjust actions of the IDECS system interactively. Hence the IDECS system belongs to gradation 4.3.

Another example of 4.3 is a Decision Support System dialogue generator described by Benbasat and Wand (1982). From a user's viewpoint, a "run" of the system consists of a series of requests for input at which the system awaits some response from the user. As a result of this input ("data" or "instructions") the system takes some action (processing) which may result in information

being displayed.   Such a request and the response to it are
defined as an interaction event.   This is the basic notion in the
dialogue implementation, and the dialogue generator is based on
subdividing an interaction into a specified set of common phases
or a "cycle."   The following basic phases are always present in an
interaction event:

1. Prompt - Indicate to the user that the system expects an
              input
2. Input   - The user provides an input
3. Action - The system takes an action based on the input

An action may be as involved as activating a function or as simple
as storing a value for later use.

The basic set of steps above is, of course, overly simplistic; for
example, it does not provide for input checks.   Also, in many
interactive systems the user may optionally request more explanations regarding the input (a "help" feature).   In addition there
may be a default value to be substituted for the input if the user
gives no response.   Another useful option is for the user to
"escape" from a request for input that was unintentionally
invoked.

Finally, a mechanism is needed to control the dynamic flow or
sequence of events which determines the order of processing.   This
implies that after each event a pointer   should be set to the next
event to be executed (at times, the same event).   To accomplish
this, the event cycle should include a "set next event" phase.
The complete interaction event cycle is now:

1. Prompt
2. Input
3. Escape - if Input = "escape," change next event indicator,
              end event cycle
4. Help   - if Input = "help," display additional information,
              and repeat event cycle
5. Check   - apply input checks; if errors, report errors, end
              event cycle
6. Next   - set "next event" indicator
7. Action

Each event is given a unique identification code (ID) in order to
identify the "next event."   An interaction event may be described,
therefore, in terms of the information necessary to carry out the
seven phases, and the full description of an event is:

        <ID; Prompt; Default; Escape; Help; Check; Next; Action>

The full dialogue description consists of the set of interaction
event descriptions.   The events in this set may be invoked in
various sequences.   The sequence of events may be fully pre-
scribed, partially user-controlled, or fully user-controlled.
Because the latter is possible, Decision Support System belongs to
gradation 4.3.

We are now programming a program modifier package to allow a user
to adjust a structure of a program.   Our idea is quite similar to
the USE methodology (Wasserman, 1985).   A user will specify and
define the state transition diagram describing dialogue of "the
program" and functions to be called in transitions.   Hence, our

program modifier package (and interactive information systems implemented with USE) belong to gradation 4.3.

Palme (1977) developed a prototype version of an application system in which a gradual upward adjustment to adjust to user competence was made possible. Users begin as novice users. As they learn more about the system, they can gradually learn the advanced facilities. On the lowest level, it will be driven by the system, at the next level, driven by user commands, and on the highest level users will be writing their own top-level programs. In the system there are eight levels:

1. Conversation led by questions and menus
2. Help facility
3. Other user commands for interruption
4. Parameters to commands
5. Command-driven user interface
6. Saving series of commands
7. Parameters to user-defined commands
8. Model language

With Palme's system, learning can take place in small steps and each user can select a suitable initial level. The same basic routines can be used both by novices and by experts.

At level 8, Palme's system belongs to gradation 4.4 because the system allows a user to generate new subfunctions to add to the system by using the model language. The system itself interprets expressions written by the model language. At lower levels it is difficult to say whether it belongs to gradations 4.1, 4.2, 4.3 or not for two reasons: the reporting and maintenance functions are not explicitly declared and Palme's system was developed for a budgeting field, not for universal purposes. Therefore it is not independent of data or an application.

In section 2, gradations of flexible software were emphasized such that the usage of a system does not demand programming ability of a user. In addition to the Karlsruhe system, report generators belong to gradation 4.1 and most application generators (plus the ABC system) belong to gradation 4.2. In this section, systems belonging to gradations 4.3 and 4.4 were presented. Hence all the gradations are valid and usable.

4. EVALUATION OF SOFTWARE PACKAGES

A set of programs (or an application software system) is an important component of the information system. The application software can be either tailor-made for an information system or general and intended for many similar information systems applications. The former is necessary in "new" applications and in functions specific for a particular line of business (Järvinen, 1985a). The latter are becoming more popular and therefore their evaluation is important. The general application software (usually purchased from a software house) has general application functions that can be used in many similar applications; it has few application-specific functions. The application-specific software mainly belongs to level 3 in Figure 1 and the flexible application software to level 4 and at the same time to some of gradations of 4.1 through 4.4. Although this section mainly considers general applications software and its flexibility, we want to emphasize that tailor-made software can and should be flexible.

In this section, a preliminary comparison of application-specific and flexible applications software is made. Therefore, some measure or evaluation model for comparison is needed. We shall first take a particular model and relate it to various evaluation approaches and to some general calculation problems. The model contains several factors, and application-specific and flexible software are then compared against them.

Sanders, et al. (1983), developed a model for the evaluation of computer software packages. There are many dimensions to the software selection process. In terms of critical, objective and subjective factors, Sanders, et al., selected the following dimensions for this illustration:

Critical factors

    (1) Hardware compatibility
         If the package won't run on our computer, it is obviously useless to consider it

    (2) Operational compatibility
         If we need a package for financial planning, an auditing package is inappropriate

Objective factors

    (1) Initial purchase cost
    (2) Cost of operation, maintenance, and modification
    (3) Cost of training users and operators

Subjective factors

    (1) Quality of program documentation
    (2) Ease of use by managers and analysts
    (3) Information quality
    (4) Provision of audit trails
    (5) Expandability
    (6) "Track record" of vendor
    (7) Quality of security system

Critical factors may eliminate some packages at the outset. Objective factors are summed up. For each qualitative factor, the model translates nominal ratings into numerical scores and allows the decision maker to express his view of the relative importance of the subjective criteria by weighing them. The sum of objective factors and weighted sum of subjective factors are then "normalized" between 0 and 1. Depending on how the decision maker rates objective factors (X, $0<X<1$) versus subjective factors, the combined measure can be generated by multiplying the former by X and the latter by $(1-X)$.

Ashour (1972) identified three approaches for multiple criteria: (1) composite evaluation approach (weighted sum of single measures), (2) sequential evaluation approach (particular single measures comprising the multiple criterion are ordered with reference to priority; the evaluative process proceeds in such a manner that each measure is treated individually by beginning with the primary criterion), and (3) constrained evaluation approach (optimizing a primary criterion and considering the remaining measures as constraints). The model presented by Sanders, et al., can be said to be a combination of the composite and the constrained evaluation approaches.

In the literature of accounting (e.g., Virkkunen, 1951), four general calculation problems are identified: A) Fixing the limits of relevant items, B) Measurement, C) Valuation, D) Allocation (D1. Allocation to products and departments; D2. Allocation to time periods). Referring to the model presented by Sanders, et al., it can be asked:

(A) Does the model contain the relevant items or factors that influence software selection? For example, should we add a third critical factor, software compatibility? If the package won't run on our operating system or with other systems software, we should either evaluate and add costs of adding systems software or eliminate the package. Relative to objective factors we also ask: should costs of maintenance and modification be separated from the objective factor and made into an independent factor because they are 50 to 70 percent of total software costs (Lientz, Swanson and Tompkins, 1978)?

(B) How can subjective factors be measured? Is the proposed mechanism correct and valid?

(C) How should valuation of single subjective factors be performed? How should subjective factors be weighted compared with objective ones?

(D1) How should common costs such as the computer be allocated to applications or software packages?

(D2) How can the usage period of a software package be estimated ex ante?

The detailed questions above show that the development and application of a model for the evaluation of computer software packages is a very complex and difficult task. All of these questions should be considered carefully when any model is applied to software selection.

Single factors of the model presented by Sanders, et al., will be considered next. From the critical factors, hardware compatibility is naturally valid for both application-specific and flexible software. In sections 2 and 3, data independence was emphasized which at the same time means that in flexible software (gradations 4.1-4.4) names of data items are not fixed and predetermined but a user can define them. However, in application-specific software, names of data items are usually fixed. Therefore, operational compatibility is a more critical factor for application-specific than flexible software.

The objective factors in the Sanders, et al., model [(1) initial purchase cost, (2) costs of operation, maintenance, and modification, and (3) costs of training users and operators] can get smaller values in evaluation of application-specific software than in evaluation of flexible software (for use in a single application). But the result of evaluation can turn out favorably for flexible software if it will be used in more than one application. Similar arguments are also valid for some of subjective factors: (2) ease of use by managers and analysts, and (5) expandability. Some subjective factors like (1) quality of program documentation, (4) provision of audit trail, and (6) "track record" of vendor, are so situational that comparison between application-specific and flexible software is impossible. We can only guess that in

order to cover higher development costs of flexible software a
vendor should pay attention to subjective factors (1), (4) and
(6), and to (7) quality of security system. Concerning subjective
factor (3) (information quality), we can say that in application-
specific software it is predetermined but in flexible software it
depends on how a user utilizes the software.

Returning to question (A), does the model contain relevant items
or factors influencing software selection, we can ask: should the
model or any model contain flexibility as a factor of software
evaluation?   Our comparison between application-specific and
flexible application software suggests acceptance of flexibility
as a long-range aim. There is, however, still one factor which
should be considered: division of labor.

In the introductory section we emphasized the measure "work per
hour" as a basis for flexibility of software. Actually, utilization of flexible software means a change in division of labor
between a programmer and a user. In a conventional case, a
programmer makes changes to application software as requested by a
user.   With flexible software, a user can make her/his own
changes. This reduces maintenance costs. At the same time, we
can avoid an information gap between a user and a programmer and
its negative consequences. Therefore, both economic and operational arguments support flexibility as a dimension of information
systems assessment.

ACKNOWLEDGEMENTS

I am grateful to the editors and to the referee for extensive and
insightful comments on earlier drafts of this paper.

REFERENCES

Ashour, S., "Sequencing Theory," *Lecture Notes in Economics and
Mathematical Systems 69*, Springer-Verlag, Berlin, 1972.

Bass, L. J., "A Generalized User Interface for Applications
Programs (II)," *Communications of the ACM*, 28, pp. 617-627,
1985.

Benbasat, I. and Wand, Y., "A Dialogue Generator and Its Use in
DSS Design," *Information and Management*, 5, pp. 231-241,
1982.

Boyle, B., "Software Performance Evaluation," *BYTE*, pp. 175-188,
1984.

Date, C. J., *An Introduction to Database Systems*, Third Edition,
Addison-Wesley, Reading, Massachusetts, 1981.

Hägglund, S. and Tibell, R., "Multi-style Dialogues and Control
Independence in Interactive Software," Linkoping Institute of
Technology, LiTH-MAT-R-82-40, 1982.

Järvinen, P., "Five Classifications for Varied Tasks in Analysis
and Design of Computing Systems," in Mathiassen, L., and
Lassen, M. (eds.), *The Eight Scandinavian Research Seminar on
Systemeering*, University of Aarhus, Department of Computer
Science, 1985, pp. 140-151.

Järvinen, P., "Levels for Utilization of Computing," *Convention Informatique,* September 14-18, pp. 455-459, Paris, 1985.

Järvinen, P., "The ABC System - a Collection of Research Articles," Dept. of Math. Sciences, University of Tampere, A112, 1983.

Järvinen, P., "Training through Experience: The ABC System," in Rijnsdorp, J. E., Plomp, Tj., and Möller, J. (eds.), *Training for Tomorrow,* IFAC Proceedings Series 4, pp. 155-160, Pergamon Press, Oxford, 1984.

Lientz, B. P., Swanson, E. B., and Tompkins, G. E., "Characteristics of Application Software Maintenance," *Communications of the ACM,* 21, pp. 466-471, 1978.

Martin, J., *Application Development without Programmers,* Prentice-Hall, Englewood Cliffs, New Jersey, 1982.

Palme, J., "A Man Computer Interface Encouraging User Growth," FOA Report C 10073-M3(E5, H9), Stockholm, 1977; see also Landau, Bair and Siegman (eds.), *Emerging Office Systems,* Proceedings, Stanford University International Symposium on Office Automation, 1980 pp. 103-123.

Sanders, G .L., Chandforoush, P., and Austin, L. M., "A Model for the Evaluation of Computer Software Packages," *Computer and Industrial Engineering,* 7, 1983, pp. 309-315.

Shneiderman, B., *Software Psychology,* Winthrop Publishers, Cambridge Massachusetts, 1980.

Wasserman, A. I., "Extending State Transition Diagrams for the Specification of Human-Computer Interaction," *IEEE Transactions on Software Engineering,* 11, 1985, pp. 699-713.

Virkkunen, H., "Teollisuuden kertakustannukset - niiden degressio seka kasittely kustannuslaskennassa" (Initial Costs for Product Types and Lots in Manufacturing as a Cause for Decreasing Unit Costs and their Treatment in Cost Accounting, Summary), Liiketaloustieteellisen Tutkimuslaitoksen julkaisuja 13, Helsinki, 1951.

DISCUSSANT NOTE

On: FLEXIBILITY OF SOFTWARE AS A DIMENSION OF
     INFORMATION SYSTEMS ASSESSMENT

By: Pertti Järvinen

Discussant's comments by: E. Burton SWANSON

Graduate School of Management
University of California, Los Angeles
Los Angeles, California USA

Flexibility of software is proposed by Järvinen as a "key dimension" for information system assessment. But the concept of
flexibility would seem to incorporate at least three distinct
ideas:

(1) *applicability*, i.e. the extent of the software's application
     domain;

(2) *portability*, i.e. the ability to relocate the software, with
     little or no modification, within its application domain; and

(3) *adaptability*, the ease with which the software may be
     modified when it must be modified. It would be useful, I
     believe, to keep these distinct ideas in mind. All contri-
     bute to flexibility, but they do so in quite different ways.

The author's six level model of computer utilization suggests to
me one concern. The model appears in general to equate computer
utilization with computer intimacy. Programming knowledge, for
example, is specifically associated with level of utilization.
But utilization is based more in application than in computing, in
my view. A user may achieve a very sophisticated utilization from
his or her LOTUS software, for example, on the basis of a deep
knowledge of the problem domain, with little or no programming
knowledge as such.

I am therefore also wary of the idea that higher levels of
utilization within the model might be considered inherently better
levels. It is a short step from the attractive feature, "a user
can adjust programs," to the unattractive feature, "a user *must*
adjust programs." With this in mind, I believe the author is on
the right track when he observes later that the economics of the
division of labor between the user and the programmer is a central
issue here.

Another observation pertains to the general notion of software
usefulness. It occurs to me that software may often be made more
flexible by being made less directly useful, but more indirectly
useful. Application generators provide a good illustration. As
applications, they are incomplete, and not directly useful. They
are designed, however, for indirect use across a wide domain, and

emphasize portability and adaptability of application specifications across this domain.

Last, a comment on whether an evaluation model should include software flexibility as a factor. In general, I often find these models rather unattractive, especially when they venture into rather arbitrary and dubious scoring techniques (such as weighting "objective" against "subjective" factors). However, I do believe that the effects of software flexibility (or lack thereof) must be incorporated within any comparative assessment. The opportunity costs associated with software flexibility are indeed substantial, and should not be overlooked, as the author rightly indicates.

PART III
EMPIRICAL INVESTIGATIONS

In-Context Information Systems Assessment:
A Proposal and an Evaluation
G.B. Davis and J.R. Hamann

"It also explains the information systems new
employee search process which looked for persons
who had lived in or had family ties to the area."

INFORMATION SYSTEMS ASSESSMENT
N. Bjørn-Andersen, G.B. Davis (Editors)
Elsevier Science Publishers B.V. (North-Holland)
© IFIP, 1988

IN-CONTEXT INFORMATION SYSTEMS ASSESSMENT:
A PROPOSAL AND AN EVALUATION

Gordon B. DAVIS

Visiting 1986-1987
Shaw Professor, Information Systems and Computer Science
National University of Singapore
Singapore 0511

Honeywell Professor of Management Information Systems
School of Management
University of Minnesota
Minneapolis Minnesota 55455 USA

Jay R. HAMANN

Vice President, Management Information Systems
Schreiber Foods, Inc.
Green Bay, Wisconsin USA

An information systems function and the information
system that it develops and maintains provide computer-based information support for a specific
organization operating in a somewhat unique
environment. The assessment of an information
system or an information system function should
therefore reflect the organizational context. The
paper presents an in-context assessment approach
and describes its development through action
research in a large industrial company.

1. INTRODUCTION

Assessment of an information system or the information systems
function implies the existence of standards against which the
system or the function can be compared. The standards are
typically normative statements that describe features information
systems should contain, how the information systems function
should be organized or operate, and performance expectations. The
difficulty with normative standards is that they do not always
apply; they are too rigid and simple to be used across a broad
spectrum of organizations and conditions.

The paper describes an approach in which the assessment standards
are designed to fit the environment of the information system and
the information systems function. The underlying concept is that
information systems support the other parts of the organization
and therefore should be designed and operated within the context
of the competitive environment, the host organization's characteristics, and the way the organization functions. The in-context
assessment approach is essentially a contingency approach to
assessment in that the assessment standards for information
systems depend on the characteristics of the organization that is
served. The paper focus on the premises of in-context assessment,

the three major areas of context for information systems, and the
steps in implementing the in-context assessment approach.

The in-context assessment approach has been developed and tested
as an action research project in a large consumer foods company.
Some lessons from the development and use of the approach in this
experimental setting provide insight for its general use.

The in-context approach is being documented as a professional
book.   Each part of the assessment has a chapter with general
background, a set of assessment questions for that topic, and a
discussion of the case study.

2.   A DEFINITION OF IN-CONTEXT ASSESSMENT

In-context assessment of an information system is defined as the
evaluation of an organization's computer-based information system
and its information system function within the unique context of
the organization itself.

An information system (IS) is a human/machine system that

o   utilizes   information   processing   technology   (computers,
    telecommunications, and office automation)

o   to   support   the   information   processing   requirements   and
    information access requirements

o   of   the   management   and   the   various   functions   within   an
    organization

An information system exists within a host organization.   The term
"information system" is used to refer to the overall system
composed   of   information   systems   applications   (which   are   also
systems) and databases.   These applications and databases (along
with the humans who are part of the systems) can be specific to
individual organizational functions or can service a number of
different functions.   They can also extend beyond the boundaries
of the host organization as part of inter-organizational information systems.   The information systems function in an organization is the function that designs, constructs, maintains, and
operates the information system.

Assessment   of   information   systems   may   have   different   meanings
depending on the timing, scope, and context of the evaluation.
Six different levels of assessment, ordered from least comprehensive to most comprehensive, show the relative position of the
in-context assessment described in this paper:

1.   *Assessment   of   the   effect   (impact)   of   an   application   at   a
     point in time.*   An example is the assessment at a point in
     time of the impact of an application on the productivity of
     persons who use it.

2.   *Assessment   of   an   application   during   the   development   cycle.*
     This is primarily an assessment of how well the application
     meets user requirements and the quality of the design and
     development.

3.   *Assessment   of   a   set   of   applications   that   interact   together.*
     For example, the set of applications that are used for order

processing may be evaluated relative to the organizational activity (order processing) being supported.

4. *Assessment of processes or subfunctions within the information systems function.* For example, the application maintenance subfunction may be evaluated without evaluating the entire information function. A subfunction may be evaluated relative to the way the subfunction is performed in other organizations or relative to other subfunctions within the same organization.

5. *Assessment of the information system and the IS function relative to norms or standards derived from other organizations or generally accepted practices.*

6. *Assessment of the information system and the IS function relative to the unique context of the organization and environment of the host organization (in-context assessment).*

The paper deals with the highest level of assessment, the assessment of the overall function within the context of its host organization.

Cameron (1980) has identified six critical questions in organizational evaluation. By answering these questions relative to in-context assessment, the nature of this approach is further clarified:

Cameron Question	*In-Context Assessment*
1. What domain of activity is being focused on?	Information system and information system function in an organization.
2. Whose perspective or which constituency's point of view is being considered.	Top management of host organization.
3. What level of analysis is being used?	Macro analysis on one organizational level.
4. What time frame is being employed?	For evaluation, current period plus future plans for three to five years. For context, three to five years of history.
5. What type of data are to be used?	Observations, interviews, documents, and surveys.
6. What referent is being employed?	Several: Normative - relative to a theoretical ideal. Goal-centered - relative to a stated goal. Improvement - relative to past performance. Trait - relative to effective traits.

3. THE NEED FOR AND DANGER OF IN-CONTEXT ASSESSMENT

Although the most common executive request relative to information systems is for some assessment of the performance and value of the function, the rules of thumb that seem to work reasonably well in other parts of the organization do not work as well in information systems. Expenditure levels, for example, differ dramatically for different organizations in the same industry. The reasons for these differences need not be based on good or bad information systems but on different strategic decisions with information systems. In-context assessment is useful because it reveals the underlying assumptions and strategies that motivate some of these differences in information systems.

The alternatives to in-context assessment are assessment based on *general* normative guidelines or assessment without standards. The problem with general normative guidelines is their rigidity and lack of applicability in a specific case. For example, documentation standards are generally considered to be very important, but an organization that purchases most of its software as packages will place less importance on this assessment than an organization doing extensive, large-scale inhouse development. Assessment without standards will use implied standards or examine the efficiency of current activities (rather than their effectiveness). It is also virtually impossible to replicate studies using implied standards since the assessment framework and standards are undocumented.

There are several conceptual and practical pitfalls in an incontext approach which is contingent on the organization. The problems arise because the assessment standards are changed to fit the organizational context. In-context standards may tend to be based on what the organization is doing. Since several alternatives may be "workable," the alternative already chosen by the organization may become the defacto standard for assessment, and other alternatives may not receive adequate consideration. In other words, the danger is that in-context assessment can lead to assessment which explains and justifies existing structures rather than highlighting areas that need to be changed.

The dangers inherent in in-context assessment can be partially overcome by two procedures. The first is to include in the evaluation team an evaluator-consultant from outside the organization. The second is to conduct the in-context assessment over a fairly short period of time (say two to three months); this aids in preventing the assessment team from becoming too comfortable with existing practices.

4. THE CASE STUDY ORGANIZATION

The in-context assessment approach was developed as a general method based on assessment concepts; it was refined through action research in which assessment was performed for a company. The company, referred to as the SX Company, is a large privately-held food company in the upper midwest of the United States. Its products are generally private label (the brand names affixed to the products are those of the purchasing organization). The company headquarters are located in a fairly small city. There are six plants also located in small cities. It is centralized in terms of central control of order processing, scheduling of production, scheduling of shipments to customers, and billing.

At the time of the assessment, the information systems function has a staff of 60. The development staff is smaller than normal for the size of organization because all large applications are purchased from outside vendors. The characteristics of the hardware and software are:

o   IBM 4381 and IBM 4341
o   Operating systems are MVS for the IBM 4381 and VM for the IBM 4341
o   There are ten major groups of applications. IBM's PROFS is used for electronic mail and other office systems support. All major applications are coded in COBOL.
o   There are several hundred terminals or IBM PCs (that can operate either stand alone or as terminals) connected to a wide area network within the office and with the plants.

5.   THE PREMISES OF IN-CONTEXT ASSESSMENT OF
     THE INFORMATION SYSTEMS FUNCTION

The in-context assessment approach is based on several assumptions or premises with respect to organizations and the role of information systems within organizations. Five of the key premises are:

1.   *Organizations are open systems with strong adaptive powers.* This view of organizations supports the principle of equifinality, which in this context means that the same organizational objective may be achieved by more than one organizational form and operational procedures. This does not imply, however, that all forms and procedures are equally efficient in terms of organizational resources or stress and strain on the organization. Two different structures may both achieve the same performance objective, but one may require significantly less organizational resources and cause much less organizational stress.

2.   *The purpose of information systems and the information systems function is to support the other functions of the organization.* Information systems do not have an independent purpose; there is always a host organization to be served.

3.   *The organization and management of the information systems function should "fit" the organization and management of the host organization.* The management information system function may, in some respects, be organized and managed differently than other functions to reflect the unique characteristics of this information support function, but the unique features of the MIS function are constrained, amplified, and modified by the need to adapt to the host organization.

4.   *The effectiveness of the management information system function is measured by its performance in providing computer-based information processing to meet the information needs and information priorities of the organization.* The information needs of an organization have a time-horizon hierarchy of transaction processing, short run reporting, and longer term planning and decision making needs. These needs have different priorities (that reflect the impact of not doing them). A management information system function which fails to perform transaction processing and basic reporting in an accurate and timely fashion is rated poorly on effec-

tiveness, even though it provides other sophisticated support.

The most effective information system is one that not only performs basic transaction processing and reporting but also provides for innovative additions to basic functions and has capabilities for extensive analysis, retrieval and reporting functions. These capabilities support organizational strategies, competitive advantage applications, and higher-level management activities.

An information system function can be evaluated by its effectiveness in delivering information across the entire range of organizational needs in approximate priority order as defined by the host organization.

5. *The efficiency of the management information system function is measured by the resources required to provide a given level of information support.* The internal organization and management of the information system function and the technology used for it will determine the efficiency with which resources are utilized in providing information service. The resources to be considered are not only the financial and personnel resources but also the stress placed upon the organization by the structures used.

6. THE THREE MAJOR CONTEXTS FOR ORGANIZATIONAL
    INFORMATION SYSTEMS

The information systems function serves a host organization that (1) exists in an industry with a competitive environment; (2) has a specific organizational structure, management style, and culture; and (3) has specific information requirements. These three features of industry, organization, and requirements of the host organization define the contexts for assessment.

6.1 The Context of Industry and Competitive Environment

Information systems are affected by the industry and the competitive environment of the host organization. The McFarlan-McKenney strategic grid is a useful classification to define three types of information environments that exist because of the industry and competitive environment (McFarlan and McKenney, 1983):

1. *Support.* Information systems are used for back office transaction processing and managerial reporting. Applications are oriented to recordkeeping and accounting. A failure of information processing will be an inconvenience but will not cause operations to cease.

2. *Factory.* Information systems are used in customer service and other operational activities. A failure of information systems will affect the operational effectiveness of the organization and may cause operations to cease.

3. *Strategic.* Information systems are used to create new services and create competitive advantage.

The existing industry context and competitive environment define what is expected of information systems at the current time; new applications and new information products may be used to change the industry structure and achieve competitive advantage. In other words, the industry and environmental contexts do not provide a static context; the assessment question is not only how well information systems meet the industry and competitive environment norms for information systems but also how aggressive the information systems function is in identifying opportunities to achieve competitive advantage by using information systems to change the way the industry operates.

The Porter framework for strategic analysis (Porter, 1980) is useful in this context. The basis for competition is defined as cost, differentiation, or a market niche. The basis for competition of the host organization suggests information system support needs. For example, in the case study, the basis of competition was found to be cost; there was little product differentiation. However, the information system was very poor with respect to cost reporting. The analysis of the competitive environment highlighted this deficiency during assessment.

6.2 The Context of Company History, Culture, and Organization

Organizations differ in the way they approach problems and the way they respond to competitive pressures. These differences are reflected in the organizational structure, culture, and management style of the organization. This context is important in an assessment of how well information systems fit the host organization as it currently exists; the assessment can also identify changes in information systems that are necessary to support strategic changes in culture and organization that are planned or desired by management.

The literature of organizational design is not well formulated for use in contingency analysis of organizational culture, organization, and management style, but several broad classifications are possible. They provide sufficient overall context-setting for in-context assessment. As an example, the Nolan Stage model of technology diffusion and organizational learning is explicitly a contingency theory. However, in practical use, it is a directional theory explaining broad movements (King and Kraemer, 1984). For in-context assessment, the Nolan model is useful in explaining the current situation and identifying directions.

Three examples from the case study illustrate the value of understanding the cultural and organizational context.

1. The company had a culture emphasizing volume and market share. The current executives were working to make a change and establish a culture that emphasized profitability and recognized constraints to volume and market share. The profitability constraint culture established new information requirements.

2. The company culture reflected its geographic and small town location. There was an emphasis on integrity and loyalty. This was reflected in stability in employment and programs to remedy personal and managerial deficiencies in employee behavior rather than terminating employment. It also explains the information systems new employee search process which looked for persons who had lived in or had family ties to the area.

3. The company had a centralized organization. There was
    centralized scheduling of production and centralized order
    processing. Shipments from plants were scheduled from the
    main office. This organization reflected the technology
    being used and the centralized nature of the purchasing
    function of its major customers. This organizational context
    provided a setting for the organization of information
    systems as a centralized function with a heavy use of
    communications.

6.3   The Context of Information Requirements

Since information systems provide information services and information needed by the organization, information requirements are a
measure against which current and expected performance can be
measured. Information requirements are interpreted broadly to
include information for operations, strategy, planning, managerial
analysis and decision making. They include the requirements of
information systems for competitive advantage and systems that
support both clerical and knowledge work activities of employees.

7.   AN OVERVIEW OF THE PROCESS OF IN-CONTEXT ASSESSMENT OF THE INFORMATION SYSTEMS FUNCTION

The process of assessment begins with identification of the
industry/competitive, organizational, and requirements contexts
for information systems. These contexts are used to evaluate
current and future information systems support. This assessment is
followed by an evaluation of the effectiveness and efficiency of
information systems as an organizational function.

The assessment of the management information system function can
be divided into three major stages with eleven logical steps.
("logical" in "logical steps" is used in the computer system sense
of steps that are logically defined as independent steps but may
be combined differently when they are physically performed.)

STAGE ONE: ANALYSIS OF HOST ORGANIZATION FOR THE INFORMATION SYSTEMS FUNCTION

> *Step 1: Analyze the Industry and Competitive Environment
> for the Organization.* In this step, the domain in which
> the organization operates is analyzed. The technology
> of the industry and the competitive structure define the
> environment for the host organization. Factors such as
> high or low technology, rate of technology change,
> nature of competition, and fierceness of competition are
> examples of environmental factors to be evaluated. The
> factors critical to survival, success, and competitive
> advantage in the industry are identified (Rockart,
> 1979).

> *Step 2: Analyze the Historical Development and Culture
> of the Organization.* The purpose of this step is to
> establish the historical precedents which affect the
> current organization and to define major elements of
> organizational culture. An understanding of the history
> and culture are important because information systems
> may be designed to support existing culture or may be
> used as a mechanism for change (see Step 8).

Step 3: Analyze the Host Organization and the Factors which Determine its Organizational Structure. Using organizational theory, the reason for the overall organizational structure and significant organizational mechanisms are analyzed. This provide a basis for measuring how well the information systems function fits the host organization or identifying ways information systems may be used to effect change.

STAGE TWO: ASSESSMENT OF INFORMATION ARCHITECTURE

A detailed study of information needs and support needs is a major undertaking. However, a fairly high level analysis that is satisfactory for assessment can be performed within the constraints of resources normally available for information systems evaluation.

Step 4: Determine Information Systems Support Needed for Competitive Strategies and Competitive Advantage. This step identifies both information requirements needed to support competitive strategies of the organization and information systems that provide competitive advantage.

Step 5: Determine Information Needs of Management in Each Functional Area or Major Organizational Unit. The objective is to identify higher-level information needs, map them to critical success factors, problem solving, and measures of effectiveness and efficiency for management of each function. The process is also applied at the top management level (Davis and Olson, 1985).

Step 6: Identify Necessary Transaction Processing and Important Operational Control Information for Each Function and Organizational Unit. The objective is to document the transactions that must be processed in order for the organization to serve customers and perform necessary support functions. Another objective of this step is to identify the necessary operational reports for management to perform scheduling and operational control.

Step 7: Make an Assessment of Extent to which Current and Planned Information Architectures Satisfy the Information Requirements for Competitive Strategies, Organizational Management, Operational Scheduling and Control, and Transaction Processing. The information architecture consists of the set of databases, the portfolio of current applications, and the interrelationships among them. The architecture of existing databases and applications defines what is currently being done to provide information processing and to meet information requirements; when combined with plans for databases and applications, the planned architecture establishes future information capabilities. The architecture should support all basic transaction processing and routine reporting. The assessment should not ignore these requirements, but the emphasis will generally be upon assessment of the architecture with respect to information systems to support organizational strategies and promote competitive advantage and information systems that support management information needs (especially beyond traditional routine reports).

STAGE THREE: ASSESSMENT OF STRUCTURE AND ACTIVITIES WITHIN
THE INFORMATION SYSTEMS FUNCTION.

*Step 8: Evaluate the Organizational Fit between the Host
Organization and the Information Systems Function.* This
evaluation includes factors such as centralization/de-
centralization, formalization, management style, stage
theory fit, and mechanisms for allocation of information
systems resources. Evaluate whether information systems
should "fit" the existing organization or should be used
as a change agent to alter the organization and its
culture.

Step 9: Evaluate Information Systems Planning. This
assessment includes the information systems planning
process, the use of the plan for management of information resources, and the specific area of technology
tracking and capacity planning. The evaluation of
processes and performance in information systems
planning and capacity planning provide an indication of
information systems management ability to do strategic
and tactical information systems planning.

*Step 10: Evaluate Information Systems Activities and
Functions.* The major activities and functions to be
assessed are application development and maintenance,
database administration, system software management,
quality assurance, end-user support, office automation,
and information systems operations. The various activities and subfunctions within information systems each
have factors critical to their success and management
processes that can be evaluated.

The amount of detail that is included in the assessment
of each activity or subfunction will depend on the
assessment being performed. In general, however, the
in-context assessment can evaluate organizational structure for the activity, policies, general flow of work,
and indicators of performance without significant analysis of detailed records. For example, if application
development management structure, methodology procedures, and quality assurance procedures are evaluated as
satisfactory and adequate conformance to procedures is
indicated by reports and other evidence, then detailed
analysis of conformance by individual programmers is
generally beyond the scope for an in-context assessment.

*Step 11: Evaluate Information Systems Personnel Manage-
ment.* The processes for recruiting, training, assigning, and retaining information systems personnel are
assessed within the context of the overall organization,
the information systems industry personnel market, the
information systems organization, and the mission
assigned to the information systems function.

8.   AN ACTION RESEARCH CASE EXAMPLE OF IN-CONTEXT
     ASSESSMENT OF THE INFORMATION SYSTEMS FUNCTION

The in-context approach to assessment of the information systems
function was first outlined conceptually using principles from the
organizational and assessment literature. The approach was then

developed and refined through an action research project in which in-context assessment was performed in an organization.

8.1 Time Required for In-Context Assessment

The assessment was performed over a five-month period as a joint consulting-research project by a university researcher and the vice-president for information systems (who has a Ph.D. in management information systems). The university researcher spent the equivalent of 60 work days on the project; the co-researcher within the company spent approximately 12 days. The time spent was allocated approximately one-third to the specific assessment of the company and about two-thirds to more general research, development of the approach, and research writeup. There was a benefit to the company from the assessment itself. Also, the research process provided a richer assessment than is normally provided by consultants.

Based on this project, the assessment activity time budget for an in-context assessment of the information systems function can be estimated. It assumes a medium sized company and an assessment team organization of three persons (one consultant from outside, one person from information systems, and one person from another function such as planning). This team composition is different than the one used in the action research but one that is common to organizations. It reflects not only the need for representation from information systems but also the need for team members from other parts of the organization and from outside.

Assessment Activity	*Project Team Work Days*
Analysis of host organization and its competitive environment	10
High level analysis of information requirements	25
Assessment of structure and activities of information systems function	50
Report preparation and presentation	25
Total project team work days	110

These estimates do not include the time taken by persons interviewed by the assessment team, or time to prepare special analyses required for assessment. This probably brings the total work days to do an in-context assessment to about 200.

8.2 Experiences and Lessons from the Case Study Assessment

Some experiences from the case study research illustrate both the advantages and power of in-context assessment and also some of the problems.

o The study of the competitive environment and the organization's competitive strategy pointed very clearly to the need for a very good cost system. This had been on the planning agenda but had not yet been implemented.

o The study of the composition of the portfolio revealed an
   emphasis on providing extended transaction processing and
   basic financial reporting.   All major systems were being
   redone to provide excellent operational support.   Most
   innovative managerial reporting requirements were being
   delayed until the basic systems were completed.

o Information systems were being used to support some corporate
   strategies (such as good customer service) but not others
   (such as emphasis on profitable volume rather than volume per
   se).   Inter-organizational systems to allow customers to
   order directly were in the schedule but had not received
   adequate resources.   There was a need to have strategic
   planning exercises with key executives to identify and rank
   alternatives for using information systems for competitive
   advantage.

o The information system organization fit the centralized host
   organization.   Various mechanisms to decentralize computing
   such as end-user facilities and an information center were in
   place and operating satisfactorily but at a fairly low level
   of support.

o Various other areas seemed to be satisfactory and to fit the
   host organization.

   - Hardware technology and software at an appropriate level
      of stable state-of-the-art

   - Good stable staffing and motivation

   - Development strategy of buy versus make for large
      applications

   - Most significant transaction systems at state-of-art

o There had been maturation of the information system function,
   and the managerial functions within it were operating quite
   well.   There were areas for improvement:

   - The information systems planning process was ad hoc and
      incomplete. The company planning process was undergoing
      change, so information systems planning will be a part
      of this general planning improvement.

   - Diffusion strategy for end-user computing needed
      improvement.

   - Backup and recovery system for operational problems and
      disasters was inadequate. This contrasted with a marked
      increase in exposure as extensive computer transaction
      support was being provided for all major functions.

   - Databases to support more integration of applications
      and more ad hoc retrieval needed improvement. A project
      was in process.

   - Information technology scanning and capacity planning
      needed improvement. A person had been assigned fulltime
      to these duties, whereas in the past it had been an ad
      hoc process.

The assessment at the case study organization did not reveal any major weaknesses that were not known, but the systematic quality of the assessment provided strong justification for the assessment of strengths and weaknesses. Reasons for changes in priorities were provided. The processes such as requirements eliciting from functional executives heightened their awareness of the potential for information systems for their functions. Assumptions were challenged and alternatives were considered; this might otherwise not have happened.

8.3 Observations on Getting Assessment Data Through Interviews

Everyone in the case organization was open and provided information if the right questions were asked. This supports the use of a systematic questionnaire or question outline. Even when the "right question" was not asked, clues were usually available. Much of the valuable information for assessment came from following up clues based on casual questions about "how long" something had been used, asking to "see" results from processes said to be in effect, and asking personnel about their perception of problems with information processing operations or applications that related to their jobs.

8.4 The Need for Instruments for Assessment

One of the results of the study was a heightened awareness of the lack of good measuring instruments for assessment. Questionnaires were developed for each topic; these aid systematic collection of observations and opinions, but analysis of the responses is very judgmental. The questionnaires will be published in the book describing the method.

An existing instrument for analysis of job satisfaction of information systems personnel (the Couger-Zawacki information systems job satisfaction instrument) was administered and seemed satisfactory in this organization (Couger and Zawacki, 1980). The instruments and scoring are available for a fee through Couger and Zawacki (University of Colorado, Colorado Springs).

User satisfaction instruments were found to be less satisfactory in this setting. The Ives-Olson-Baroudi short form information satisfaction instrument, available from Professor Jack Baroudi at New York University Graduate School of Business was administered to users of major applications (Ives, Olson, and Baroudi, 1983). This instrument presents adjective pairs and the respondent indicates strength of agreement based on a seven-point scale. The most serious objection came from plant personnel who said they did not understand some of the adjectives. A modified instrument was administered to users of end-user computing. Wording of questions was modified to reflect the end-user environment; the results were supportive of end-user satisfaction in the case study organization, but the modified instrument needs improvement and testing.

9. SUMMARY OF RESULTS

In summary, the in-context assessment approach for information systems is an improvement over normative evaluation or evaluation with unspecified criteria. The process has the danger of justifying the current structure and operations, but this did not appear to be a major problem in the case study.

The approach has been refined in an action research setting. The in-context assessment approach is defined in terms of three stages with 11 steps. The three stages are:

o   Analysis of the host organization of the information systems function

o   Assessment of information architecture

o   Assessment of organizational structure and activities within the information systems function

The results of the assessment action research provided strong evidence for the usefulness of the in-context approach.

REFERENCES

Cameron, Kim (1980), "Critical Questions in Assessing Organizational Effectiveness," *Organizational Dynamics*, Autumn 1980, pp. 66-80.

Couger, J. D., and R. A. Zawacki (1980), *Motivating and Managing Computer Personnel*, Wiley, New York, 1980.

Davis, G., and M. Olson (1985), *Management Information Systems: Conceptual Foundations, Structure, and Development*, Second Edition, McGraw-Hill Book Company, New York, 1985, pp.443-471.

Ives, B., M. Olson, and J. Baroudi (1983), "The Measurement of User Information Satisfaction," *Communications of the ACM*, 26:10, October 1983, pp. 785-793.

King, J. L., and K. L. Kraemer (1984), "Evolution and Organizational Information Systems: An Assessment of Nolan's Stage Model," *Communications of the ACM*, 27:5, May 1984, pp. 466-475.

McFarlan, F. W., and J. L. McKenney (1983), *Corporate Information Systems Management: The Issues Facing Senior Executives*, Richard D. Irwin, Homewood, Illinois, 1983.

Porter, Michael E. (1980), *Competitive Strategy*, Free Press, New York, 1980.

Rockart, J. F. (1979), "Critical Success Factors," *Harvard Business Review*, March-April 1979, pp. 81-91.

**Retrospective Appraisal of Information Technology
Using SESAME
T. Lincoln**

"A SESAME study seeks to identify the full costs associated with each system under review."

INFORMATION SYSTEMS ASSESSMENT
N. Bjørn-Andersen, G.B. Davis (Editors)
Elsevier Science Publishers B.V. (North-Holland)
© IFIP, 1988

RETROSPECTIVE APPRAISAL OF INFORMATION TECHNOLOGY
USING SESAME

Tim LINCOLN

Senior Consultant
IBM United Kingdom, Ltd.

This paper is concerned with one dimension of
system evaluation -- establishing the actual
financial returns obtained from an established
computer system. The paper is based on a series of
studies in which IBM has worked with a number of
other organizations to appraise rigorously the
financial returns achieved from information
technology investments. Using a standard methodology called SESAME, over 150 applications across a
range of industries have been reviewed to date.
This paper reviews the SESAME methodology, discusses some results of individual studies and
summarizes the general conclusions emerging from
this work.

1. INTRODUCTION

A computer system is a complex entity and a thorough evaluation
will consider many dimensions. This paper is concerned with only
one of these dimensions -- the quantifiable financial performance.
The justification for focussing on this aspect is that senior
executives faced with potentially large investment decisions very
often ask the question "Have we obtained reasonable benefits from
our existing investment?" Although this is a difficult question
to answer, and probably impossible to answer with complete
accuracy, it is not an unreasonable question and it is one to
which systems professionals should make every effort to respond.
Experience has shown that, despite the wide use of cost-benefit
forecasting to justify proposed system investments, executives
still remain skeptical of the level of benefits actually achieved.
This can be explained partly by the uncertainties inherent in
cost-benefit forecasting. User's reluctance to commit to future
savings, previous large cost overruns, arbitrary estimates of
system life, risk, and inflation rates all erode the credibility
of forecasts. However, in addition, DP managers must bear part of
the blame. All too frequently there is a lack of financial
discipline applied to the system development process and it is
often unclear who is accountable for benefit achievement. It is
rare to find a DP plan integrated with business plans. User
benefits are frequently declared as "intangible" and rarely post-
audited.

Such a situation reinforces suspicion in executives' minds that
benefits from computer systems are highly speculative and probably
marginal. Increasingly we see a reluctance to invest further
until concrete evidence is available that existing system investments have produced reasonable financial returns.

This conclusion is supported by a recent report sponsored by the
Department of Trade and Industry (1984) reviewing the barriers and
opportunities associated with information technology.   It concluded that "the main barriers (to the further use of information
technology) are the lack of appropriate cost-benefit techniques
and the need to consolidate previous investments."   Previous
analysis of such barriers within individual companies in the
mid-70s (Lincoln, 1976, 1980) led to the establishment of a long-
term program, termed "SESAME," designed to explore technology
investment appraisal issues.   This paper will describe the SESAME
program, review some of the results achieved, and outline some of
the overall conclusions which are now emerging.

2.   SESAME

2.1   SESAME Approach

The SESAME program started as a series of individual cost-benefit
post-audits, with the first study being conducted within British
Aircraft Corporation in the mid-70s (Hall and Lincoln, 1976; IBM
Report GE15-6141-0, 1979).   It has now evolved into a coordinated
attempt to build a database of proven financial returns from the
use of Information Technology.   A SESAME study focuses on systems
that have been implemented for at least 12 months and identifies
in considerable detail the full costs and benefits experienced to
date.   Once these are established, projections will be made over
the expected system life to a maximum of five years.

SESAME is therefore a bottom-up approach, based on individual case
studies, as contrasted with top-down studies of the business
impact of information technology (Cron and Sobol, 1983; Strassman,
1984).   Both approaches should produce consistent conclusions;
however, because of the few published top-down analyses, checks of
this sort are not possible at this stage.

A cost-benefit analysis is essentially a comparison between two
states.   Proposed new system costs and benefits are usually
compared with current systems whether they be manual, partly
computerized or fully computerized.   Post-audits of established
systems, however, do not have such an obvious basis for comparison.   While many possibilities exist, experience has shown that
the comparison of most general value to senior executives is to
compare an existing computer system against a realistic manual
alternative.   There are, of course, objections to this approach.
In some cases, people are reluctant to consider a manual alternative system as a practical possibility and therefore have difficulty in seeing the relevance of SESAME results.   However, difficulties arise with any general basis for comparison and alternatives, e.g., typical mainframe systems, mini-based systems or
commercially available software prove to have greater problems.

Moreover, comparison against a manual alternative system provides
a number of positive advantages.   It provides a bedrock comparison
which is consistently applicable to most situations and can be
viewed as the systems equivalent of zero based budgeting.   It
clearly highlights those computer applications whose objectives
could be met at less cost by a manual alternative system.
Finally, the approach has the pragmatic advantage of having been
used over a number of years in many different companies and has
provided insights to senior executives which they found valuable.

2.2 Cost Allocation

A SESAME study seeks to identify the full costs associated with
each system under review.   Cost categories typically include
system development, operation and maintenance; user analysis,
training, data input and data analysis; management time directly
associated with system development and operation; and all related
overheads.

There are, of course, situations where accurate records have not
been maintained, but it is usually found that base records (e.g.,
time sheets) and careful estimating enables an acceptable cost
profile to be built up.   The difficulties of precise cost allocation are well known, especially where a common resource is involved.   This is particularly true if allocation within arbitrary
boundaries (e.g., organization) is required.   SESAME studies, however, are concerned with overall cost-effectiveness and it is
usually possible for system boundaries to be defined which are
meaningful to management and allow fairly straightforward cost
allocation.

2.3 Benefit Identification

The SESAME approach identifies benefits by asking users to consider how they would meet their current objectives without the
help of the system under review.   This is done via extensive user
interviews in which every attempt is made to ensure that users
seriously think through the implications of their answers.   The
user interviews employ standard questionnaires covering the
following areas:

o System usage, importance, satisfaction
o Development and operational costs
o System problems
o Achieved benefits
o Expected growth
o User requested enhancements
o Comments/quotes concerning system performance

Interviews are documented and users asked to review the documentation, amend it as necessary, and to sign-off that it represents
their considered views.

Experience has shown that it is very rare for users to be unable
to identify a credible alternative manual system and to specify
the impact on resources that such a system would have.   Multiple
interviews provide a check on individual assessments and reviews
with senior management ensure that unrealistic estimates are
challenged.

The resource implications of a manual alternative system depend,
of course, on the use being made of the computer system.   In a few
cases, users are confident that they could switch from computer to
manual system with little increase, and sometimes even a reduction, in resources.   In the majority of cases, however, users feel
that the introduction of a manual system would require more people
and would be accompanied by additional disbenefits.   Typical
examples of these are reduction of competitiveness, increased
inventories, additional scrap, etc.   Users are asked to quantify
the impact of these additional disbenefits separately from the
headcount implications, using past statistics (e.g., inventory

levels) wherever available and these estimates are subject to considerable analysis and senior management review before they are
accepted.

2.4 Analysis and Presentation

Experience has shown that no single financial measure adequately
describes the full financial performance of a computer application. SESAME studies generally quote the break-even point, mean
benefit/cost ratio over system life and internal rate of return
for all applications reviewed.

The output from a full SESAME study will typically be a presentation to the Board of Directors covering the following:

1. Detailed analysis of systems cost and benefits profile over
    the expected life of the system and under alternative growth
    scenarios as appropriate.

2. User assessment of the system's effectiveness with key
    problem and critical success factors analysis.

3. User requested system enhancements with "first cut" future
    costs and benefits forecasts.

4. Hardware and budget implications of predicted growth and
    future enhancements.

5. Management recommendations designed to optimize the return
    from their computing investment.

2.5 Studies Conducted

To date, SESAME studies have been run in 18 organizations. These
can be classified into three major types covering 162 individual
applications (see Figure 1).

                                              Applications

         A. Large Integrated Systems
                 Aerospace   13
                 Banking   14
                 Newspapers   7

         B. Large Stand-Alone Systems
                 Local Authority   5
                 Brewing   6
                 County Council   6

         C. General Facility/Service
                 Telecommunications   9
                 Oil   11
                 Insurance   11
                 Public Transport   14
                 Manufacturing   12
                 Insurance   15
                 Chemical   8
                 Local Authority   10

Figure 1. SESAME Studies To Date

Type "A" studies conduct a detailed review of all applications being run within a installation. Such studies typically will take four weeks to complete and will employ a team of four to six people. Type "B" SESAME studies review very large stand-alone systems, for example, a library system within a local authority or a distribution system for a large brewery chain. These studies typically take two to three weeks with a team of two to three people. Type "C" studies cover general facilities or services such as an information center, personal computing and end user computing facilities. These studies typically take one to two weeks for two to three people.

As can be seen from Figure 1, SESAME studies have been conducted in a wide range of organizations and industries. Experience now suggests that the SESAME technique can be applied in any organization or industry type.

3. EXAMPLE OF COST BENEFIT PROFILES

Within the limits of confidentiality, many studies have been described in individual reports[1] (Tyrell). It is not the intention here to illustrate all of the types of analyses which a SESAME study would produce. However, examples of typical cost benefit profiles are given in Figures 2, 3 and 4.

3.1 Merchant Bank

Figure 2 provides an interesting illustration of the dramatic growth in benefits which can occur for a personal computing application. The application in this case provides computer support to foreign exchange dealers within a Merchant Bank. The cost profile shows that a considerable period of "research and development" was required before the application was usable by the dealers. However, once implemented, the benefits grew very rapidly and exceeded the costs by a considerable margin.

The benefits in this case were overwhelmingly concerned with increased revenue and profit generation rather than cost reduction. By providing foreign exchange and bond dealers with decision-making aids to support market transactions, the bank's executives were confident that a dealer could transact more deals and that these deals would, on average, be more profitable. In addition, it was felt that such dealing aids allowed dealing with new financial instruments (futures, options, etc.) which, in their early life, tend to be more profitable than conventional instruments. Finally, it was felt that the ability to deal profitably in a variety of markets brings further advantages when marketing the bank's services to prospective clients.

Even allowing for a comparatively short expected life of this application, the internal rate of return generated was approximately 400 percent per annum and the mean benefit to cost ratio was of the order of 15.

---

[1] Case study reports issued from time to time by the Systems Management Consultancy Department, IBM United Kingdom, Ltd.

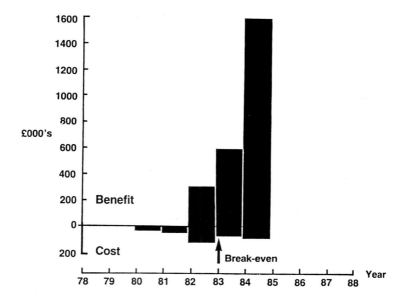

Figure 2. Cost Benefit Profile -- Dealing Aids

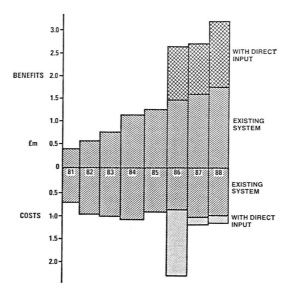

Figure 3. Cost Benefit Profile -- Integrated Newspaper System

3.2 Newspaper Production

Figure 3 shows the cost benefit profile of an integrated set of applications concerned with the production of a daily newspaper. The applications covered sales, finance, production, editorial and location services.

The analysis identified a base cost-benefit profile of existing systems, and a superimposed profile of additional costs and benefits associated with "direct input" of advertising copy. The major benefits of the existing systems are associated with pricing, advertising accounts, commercial and advertising administration and production labor. The additional benefits associated with direct input are primarily in the production area but with significant additional advertising revenue.

While not as spectacular as the results shown in Figure 2, this cost benefit profile is still very healthy. For an overall investment of between 7.3 and 9 million pounds, the return on investment achieved is in the range of 30 percent per annum, for the existing applications, to 42 percent per annum when taking into account direct input. These returns show the significant impact that changes in working practices can have on financial returns and therefore on willingness to invest further.

3.2 Local Government

Figure 4 provides an example drawn from a local government borough. The borough in question tends to be very motivated towards cost-effectiveness and computing is seen as a means of providing services at minimum costs consistent with management objectives. The application in this case was developed initially to exercise control over housing rents but was extended as its value was proven.

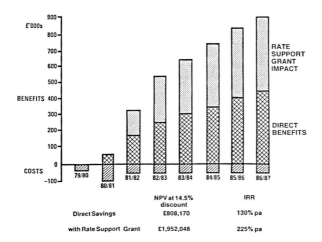

Figure 4. Cost Benefit Profile -- Housing Rent System

At the time of analysis, the system controlled a fortnightly collection service, managed the arrears process and controlled voids (empty houses), sales of properties and homeless persons. Further planned enhancements included control of repairs and maintenance. The system is almost totally online with user departments providing all input data.

The cost benefit profile shows a very healthy buildup of benefits greatly exceeding projected costs. For clarity, the effect on benefits of expected government grants are identified separately. The internal rates of return for this application were approximately 130 percent per annum without government grants, rising to 230 percent per annum with government grants. The impact of such high returns on senior management's perception of computer systems was very significant and was described in some detail in a subsequent talk given by the DP Manager (Cowton).

3.4 Winners and Losers

With such a wide range of applications reviewed with the SESAME technique it is possible to identify the best major investments and the worst. Figure 5 provides such a breakdown.

It is noticeable that the same industry and organization types appear as both winners and losers and it is clear that no one industry has the recipe for producing maximum returns from information technology. It is quite common to find, in the same organization, applications producing spectacularly high returns and applications which are a dismal financial failure. Almost always this can be shown to result from a lack of an effective financial appraisal and control process applied to computer systems. Management judgment, even steering committee consensus, is not a substitute for formal analysis.

1. Best Major Investments (IRR [100% p.a.])

Stock Management	– Aerospace
Dealing Aids (DSS)	– Merchant Bank
Library Management	– Local Authority
Marketing (DSS)	– Oil
Revenue Planning and Control	– Public Transport
Housing Rent Control	– Local Authority

2. Worst Major Investments (IRR-ve)

Corporate Reporting	– Banking
Parts Control	– Manufacturing
Establishment Control	– Public Transport
Distribution	– Brewery
Personnel Reporting	– Oil

Figure 5. Winners and Losers

4. OVERALL SESAME RESULTS

It is only comparatively recently that sufficient SESAME studies have been undertaken to allow meaningful statistics to be produced on financial performance relating to information technology.

These analyses are shown in Figures 6, 7 and 8 and they relate to the total population studied. The size of the population is currently too small to allow deeper analysis, for example by system type or industry, but as more SESAME studies are conducted such analyses will be possible.

Figure 6 illustrates the break-even point distribution found amongst the applications analyzed. We see, for example, that approximately two thirds of all applications reviewed break even in less than one year after implementation. Such rapid break-even points can come as a surprise to Financial Directors accustomed to the more leisurely break-even points of industrial investments.

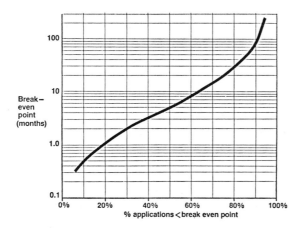

Figure 6. Break-Even Point Analysis

Figure 7 shows the mean benefit/cost ratio analysis and Figure 8 the internal rate of return analysis. Both analyses dramatically demonstrate the outstandingly good financial performance available from information technology. Average benefits exceeding costs by a ratio of two to three are very common. Internal rates of return in the hundreds of percent per annum are the norm rather than the exception.

When evaluating these figures, it should be borne in mind that SESAME adopts prudent and cautious accounting principles, and users generally accept that SESAME results tend to understate the available return on investment. The results shown, therefore, in Figures 6, 7 and 8 can be taken as baseline performance. Figure 9 summarizes the overall financial picture drawn by SESAME studies and this picture looks exceedingly healthy.

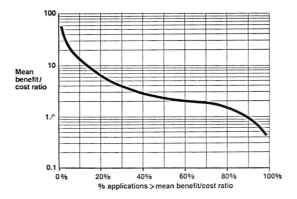

Figure 7. Mean Benefit Cost Ratio Analysis

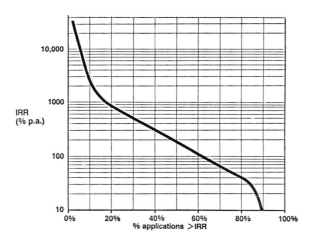

Figure 8. Internal Rate of Return Analysis

1. Break-Even Point
    o   Median five months
    o   50% between 1 - 21 months
    o   77% two years

2. Mean Benefit/Cost Ratio
    o   Median 2.4
    o   50% between 1.7 - 4.8
    o   88% at 1.0

3. Internal Rate of Return
    o   Median 190% p.a.
    o   50% between 50% - 650% p.a.
    o   81% at 40% p.a.

Figure 9. Financial Performance of Information Technology

Once sufficient statistics are available it is possible to look
for correlation between key financial parameters.   Figure 10
illustrates this by plotting internal rates of return against
development costs.

As might be expected, the results are scattered and must be viewed
with caution.   In particular, at the higher development cost
range, the sample size is small and conclusions must be drawn with
care.   However, it does appear that the vast majority of applications reviewed fall between two boundaries.   The lower boundary
occurs at about 25 percent per annum internal rate of return and
is independent of development costs.   The upper boundary, however,
appears to vary with development cost as shown.

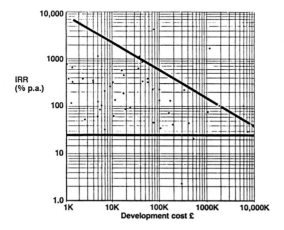

Figure 10.   Development Cost versus Internal Rate of Return

At lower levels of development cost, a high variability of
internal rates of return is perhaps not unexpected. Applications
developed in this range are primarily personal computing or end
user computing applications. Such applications often access databases of operational data which have been developed previously to
support "core" systems and thereby "add value" to them. It is not
surprising, therefore, that very high internal rates of return can
be generated under the right circumstances. However, such applications are not in general kept under tight control and large
variations in IRR can be expected. At the other end of the
development cost scale, however, we are dealing with very large
systems which frequently break new ground. Research and development costs associated with these types of applications can be
large and, because of the size of the investment, project management is usually very thorough. Accordingly, where development
costs are high, one would expect the risk to be reduced, possibly
at the expense of limiting the overall returns available. Even in
this range, however, return on investment can still be expected to
be between 40 percent and 100 percent per annum.

Over the period in which SESAME studies have been conducted, the
author has tried to find similar financial post-audits against
which these results could be compared. Some individual application audits have been found, although these are rarely published,
but no comparable statistical base has been identified.[2] However,
figures do exist originating from two very thorough cost-benefit
forecasting techniques used by IBM consultants. The "Application
Transfer Team" approach has analyzed very large numbers of applications over the last few years and in most cases predicted
detailed costs and benefits. These results have recently been
summarized (Hogbin) and the ATT forecasts are in line with SESAME
results. Similarly, a methodology for forecasting information
technology cost/benefit ratios for complete corporations (EPDP),
developed by IBM-Canada (IBM Report No. G509-2189) has recently
produced statistics which are within 20 percent of the SESAME
median results.

5. SUMMARY

The SESAME results described in this paper illustrate the very
attractive returns on investment which can be achieved through the
use of information technology. Eighty percent of all applications
reviewed were showing positive returns. In most cases, the return
on investment was above 100 percent per annum and in some cases
exceeded 1000 percent per annum. However, it should be borne in
mind also that one in five of the applications studied were not
showing sufficient financial returns to justify the original
investment.

Analyses of this sort have proved very valuable for senior
management. They enable them to feel more confident about the
financial returns available from technology and thereby allow a
more rational investment policy to be developed. Equally, such
analyses enable senior management to weed out those applications
which are not financially viable and thereby enhance the overall
return on investment available from technology.

---

[2]The author is indebted to Michael Earl of Templeton College
for pointing out that a recent dissertation on personnel information systems concluded that post-audits were very rarely conducted.

In addition to evaluating existing applications, such results also enable targets to be set for new development. Hitherto, standards have been available covering efficiency of computer applications, for example response time, availability, maintenance load, etc. Now, however, the opportunity arises to establish standards for effectiveness of applications in terms of return on investment. These targets can be ambitious compared with the returns available from other industrial investments.

The SESAME program has shown that it is possible to post-audit the financial returns of computer systems. While many organizations do perform post installation audits of major applications, it is unusual for these audits to evaluate thoroughly the benefits achieved in addition to the costs. The absence of such hard post-audit financial data has worked against the interests of both technology professionals and the organizations in which they work. Many discussions with senior executives has convinced the author that all major computer applications should have clear cost-benefit targets established as part of the planning process and should be automatically post-audited.

The database of financial results described in this paper will be enhanced by conducting further studies. The SESAME methodology will be used in these studies to ensure consistency of results and it is hoped that in this way standards will be developed to allow objective measures of financial success and failure. It is believed that the availability of such a database will answer some of the legitimate concerns of senior management who will thereby be encouraged to invest further in those areas where proven returns can be achieved.

REFERENCES

Cowton, D., "The Cost Effectiveness of the Kensington and Chelsea Housing System," presentation to the IBM Local Government Computer Users Association.

Cron, W. L., and Sobol, M. G., "The Relationship between Computerization and Performance: A Strategy for Maximizing the Economic Benefits of Computerization," *Information and Management,* Vol. 6, 1983, pp. 171-181.

Department of Trade and Industry, "The Barriers and the Opportunities of Information Technology: A Management Perspective," The Institute of Administrative Management, A. T. Kearney, Ltd., October 1984.

Hall, P. G., and Lincoln, T. J., "A Cost Effectiveness Study of Production and Engineering Systems within a Tightly Integrated Management Environment," *Management Datamatics,* Vol. 5, No. 6, 1976.

Hogbin, G., "The Decision to Invest -- Cost Justifying Information Technology and Systems with ATT Studies," Field Marketing Support, IBM United Kingdom, Ltd.

IBM Report GE15-6140-0, "Computer Systems Profitability Assessment in Manufacturing," 1979.

IBM Report G509-2189, "Value of Data Processing," Del Smith, Consulting Marketing Representative, IBM Canada.

Lincoln, T. J., "Information Systems Constraints -- A Strategic
    Review," IFIP Congress, 1980.

Lincoln, T. J., "Information Systems -- The Future Constraints,"
    The Oxford Centre for Management Studies Top Management
    Briefing Report, 1976.

Strassman, P. A., "Information Technology and Productivity,"
    PITCOM, Vol. 3, No. 1, 1984, pp. 1-19.

Tyrell, J., "SESAME Information Centre Study Reports," Systems
    Marketing, IBM United Kingdom, Ltd.

DISCUSSANT NOTE

On: RETROSPECTIVE APPRAISAL OF INFORMATION
      TECHNOLOGY USING SESAME

By: Tim Lincoln

Discussant's comments by: D. A. WASSENAAR

Twente University
The Netherlands

1.   IN GENERAL

Empirical research such as the contribution by this author is very
important.   This quantitative research can be a starting point for
more qualitative research.   I ask questions such as: Why are
there both excellent and poor financial performances of computer
systems in the same industry?   What are the reasons for success or
failure?

2.   POINT OF VIEW

Appraisal of information technology using SESAME represents the
specific point of view of the senior manager and not a societal
point of view.   From a societal point of view, the total (social)
costs can be higher than the economical costs.   For example,
computerization can affect the rate of unemployment and can result
in significant uncalculated social costs.

The danger of pure managerial economical cost benefit analysis is
that we do not incorporate the external (dis)economies in our calculations.   A good example is the very complex Dutch tax regulation which has only been possible using extensive computer
systems, since it would not be possible to perform the complex
regulation manually.   However, at the moment, people -- com-
plaining about very complicated tax legislation -- are asking for
a more simplified legislation.   In this case we have seen the risk
that supply (of technology) creates autonomous computer applications with external diseconomies.   This trend can be flavored by a
bounded economical rationality.

3.   METHOD OF STUDY

The SESAME study was focussed on computer systems used for a
period of at least 12 months.   The question is how representative
the sample of this study is.   Obviously it is not failing computer
applications that have been cancelled before the 12 month period.
So the study sample represents the most successful applications,
touching up the rate of returns.   The second point I want to put
forward is the reliability of the data collected from the users in
their role of owner of the applications.   I am wondering whether
they can objectively evaluate their own application.

4. SCOPE OF THE APPROACH

The approach is based on comparing the existing costs with the
opportunity costs of the applications. The existing costs are
considered as the costs and the opportunity costs as the benefits.
Therefore, in my opinion, it is worth making a distinction between
the two types of applications:

o   *Applications based on process innovation.* These applications
    support the data processing for an existing product activity
    in the company. Computerization in this case means substi-
    tuting labor with formalized information systems consisting
    of hardware and software.

o   *Applications based on product innovation.* In this case, a
    company introduces (often) totally new (information inten-
    sive) products or services on the market. These products
    would not be introduced at all if there were no new oppor-
    tunities of information technology.

The opportunity cost approach is only relevant for the first type
of applications; it is irrelevant for the second type of application, because producing new (information intensive) products or
services would not be considered at all if these products and
services had to be produced manually.

The high returns on investment for applications could (only) be
due to successful introduction of new products and services, as
the unsuccessful products which were abandoned within 12 months of
introduction are excluded from the sample. It is for this reason
that the results of the study could be said to have been touched
up.

Post Implementation Assessment of Information Systems Applications:
Notes from Personal Experiences
L. Capper

"In one organization, the number of clerical workers
was reduced so greatly that one office block was
shut, the cost of which alone had been greater
than that of the DP installation."

INFORMATION SYSTEMS ASSESSMENT
N. Bjørn-Andersen, G.B. Davis (Editors)
Elsevier Science Publishers B.V. (North-Holland)
© IFIP, 1988

POST-IMPLEMENTATION ASSESSMENT OF INFORMATION SYSTEMS
APPLICATIONS: NOTES FROM PERSONAL EXPERIENCES

Leonard CAPPER

Division of Computer Science
Hatfield Polytechnic
PO Box 109
Hatfield, Herts AL10 9AB England

In an attempt to learn from the past, a number of
post-implementation assessments of IS applications
were examined. From this analysis it could be
concluded that the efficiency of the application
system was seen to be of importance, but other
factors appeared to merit equal or greater consideration. Any new application must not make
demands upon users that are beyond their capability, nor must the new system eliminate the opportunity for staff to gain the experience and knowledge that is essential if the application is to be
used correctly. But demanding of greater consideration appeared to be the effectiveness of any new
system, as perceived by powerful groups and individuals within the organization.

It appears, therefore, that the political factors
involved within the organization also need to be
investigated if worthwhile assessments are to be
made and lessons learned that can help in the
development of new and improved IS.

1. INTRODUCTION

In the search to develop information systems more suited to the
needs of the user, attempts have been made to evaluate existing
manual and computer-based systems. The reasoning behind this move
was to use the criteria for defining what was good and what was
poor about past systems to improve the design of the next generation of information systems. It is assumed that the assessment of
past systems helps with the design of future systems, and that the
objectives of any new design, and hence the terms of reference of
any future assessment, are an essential element of a Requirements
Specification. To the author this was to involve, in particular,
the appraisal of particular enterprise modelling methods and the
possible construction of improved models.

It was decided to examine data collected over a number of years
and use the results of this analysis to prepare and plan a future
course of action. This exercise, therefore, was aimed at the
following:

o   examining a number of information system applications

o   identifying the reasons for their development

o assessing the relevant impact of the application systems upon
   the different host organizations

o examining the available information assessing the application
   system

o describing the reasons for the cessation of operational
   running of each application system, where appropriate

Despite the apparent paucity of data, much of value did follow
from this examination. It provided a basis for future investiga-
tory work into the variables affecting information systems and
their possible measurement.

This paper describes some of the systems investigated, the assessments, the results obtained, and the conclusions. But as much of
the detail (e.g., cost reductions) is too voluminous, irrelevant
and, usually, confidential, it has been omitted.

It is also hoped that the case notes will be useful, providing
additional documented material to other workers who are concerned
with the poor performance of past and present generations of
information systems.

2. THE SYSTEMS EXAMINED

Over a period of twenty years, information systems in the following application areas have been investigated in varying degrees
of detail:

o physical distribution and the associated accounting systems
   (although certain parts of such systems may not be considered
   by some to be information systems) in the toiletry/pharmaceu-
   tical and oil industries

o wholesale/retail audits for consumer goods essentially from
   one organization

o indirect materials control and salesmen's stock control in an
   organization manufacturing toiletries

o production control and costing in light engineering, consumer
   goods, fine chemicals and toiletries

The information for this analysis came from the author's own work
as an analyst, as a manager of analysts, and from the work of his
students employed on in-company projects. Very little came from
his own personal research.

In addition, because suitable data was not available, a brief comparison was made with the internal assessments of two organizations of their use of, in one case, a fourth generation language
and, in the other, standardized and company assembled microcomputers.

3. OBJECTIVES FOR SYSTEMS DEVELOPMENT AND ASSESSMENT

In very simple and summarized terms, it appeared initially that
the development of the systems were triggered, all within profit
orientated organizations, by one or more of the following:

o   a drive to reduce the cost of operating an information system

o   a perceived need to have the required output sooner

o   an ill-defined but strongly felt need for better information

The term "better information" proved difficult to define in the context of these investigations.   But interviews with users, mostly managers, during the early stages of the life cycles and after implementation enabled a list of criteria, summarized for this paper, to be developed.

o   The information produced and its layout were more suited to the various users' needs. This required that the information was relevant and comprehensible to individual users, and that the interactions with the computer-based application systems could be performed easily and accurately by the users.

o   The output could be changed more easily and quickly to meet changing needs, where possible, by the users themselves.

o   Having output that is accurate and available on schedule, perhaps aims not normally associated with "better information."

(Note: "output" includes printed reports and VDU displays, interactive and non-interactive.)

Although not as comprehensive or as detailed as later work (Ives, et al., 1983), it was thought that these aims would provide a suitable basis for analysis in organizations where there is a continuing drive to improve competitiveness.   But it was frequently found that the causal relationships between the given or perceived needs and the requests for new IS or changes to existing IS were either tenuous or obscure.   It was soon realized, therefore, that the reasons openly given or specified could not be the only triggers to the development of IS, or to their abandonment. The users' needs were in some ways being obscured.   In order to break through such barriers, the following argument was developed. It was assumed that if a system is rated highly, then it must meet the needs of the users; equally, the reverse should be true.   By examining the rated performance of a number of information systems, i.e., their post-implementation assessments, it would seem possible to judge how well the achievements of the systems map onto the aims and hence the needs of the users.   From these comparisons and the resulting variances, conclusions as to the needs of users could then be drawn.   These conclusions should then be of use in improving the design of future information systems.

The case histories outlined below form neither a random nor a large sample.   They have been selected from the experiences of one man through his own personal involvement or that of his staff or students.   Nevertheless, it does appear that one major conclusion can be drawn from this experience that can in turn be exploited in the development of new information systems: namely, the criteria for assessing systems have to be established at, at least, three levels and with which parallels can be drawn with other areas of Computer Science and other work (Bemelmans, 1983) in this area.

3.1 Operational and Technological

Essentially concerned with the technical and resource efficiency, there appears to be a set of criteria (Ives, et al., 1983) concerned with the reliability, accuracy, costs and timeliness, for example, of systems.

3.2 Usability

All information systems are used by people and, therefore, all systems must function within the limits set by the capabilities of those who will use them in the future under operational conditions (Nicholson and Molnar, 1986).

3.3 Political and Organizational

The information provided must help people to perform their work and improve managerial efficiency and effectiveness. But this could conflict with the political aims of individuals and groups. The importance of political factors has been well established, e.g., Markus (1983) and Bjørn-Andersen and Pedersen (1980), and there is a necessity to ensure that the desired role or purpose of any system as seen by the users is met.

In the experience of the author, this level has been ignored by technologists but not by successful DP managers, who see their major task as determining the role or purpose of any information system in terms of political or organizational needs, and ensuring that the implemented systems meet those requirements. They assess systems informally in this manner, carefully and continually, ensuring that the applications are and remain effective in the eyes of the powerful users.

4. CASE STUDIES

A number of post-implementation assessments of different applications are discussed in the context described above with each example illustrating one or more of the factors, a stated goal, a hidden goal, and a lesson that could be learned.

4.1 Physical Distribution and Associated Financial Systems

            Stated Goal - cost reduction
            Lesson   - loss of training and career development

The outputs from the totally manual or business-machine-based Physical Distribution and Accounting Systems were satisfactory and no new information was required. The trigger for development was a perceived need to reduce the costs of operating these systems. Over a period of a decade, to achieve this objective, computer-based systems were gradually introduced and costs compared before and after each change. Because the quality of the analysts and programmers involved was high and the system's requirements were well understood, the work performed was of a high standard and the computer sub-systems worked well and efficiently. Unfortunately, the operating systems used at that time were frequently not fault free and problems were created in very many installations, including this one.

It was calculated that the savings in wages, office space, and furniture were much greater than the cost of hardware, software, and training. The operating costs were reduced by a factor varying between two and four (confidential internal reports of the three organizations operating such systems). Learning costs were not included, but this experience in computer usage, once obtained, was believed to be generally beneficial as further computer-based systems were introduced.

In one organization, the number of clerical workers was reduced so greatly that one office block was shut, the cost of which alone had been greater than that of the DP installation.

Based upon accounting principles, such cost/benefit assessments are comparatively simple to carry out and give results that are well received by management. Efficiency in terms of reliability, timing, and security, for example, was expected to be good and considered to be the responsibility of DP management; if poor, it was their fault and a reflection on their total performance regardless of the poor operating systems. Few formal assessments of the software and hardware were performed, except to count the number and type of errors and breakdowns and to plot these over time.

One important factor escaped notice in the short-term departmental drives to reduce costs: the total elimination of the training ground for the clerical managers and clerks. For example, the jobs for a wages manager and a credit control manager in one organization remained although the tasks did change. But no junior supervisory positions remained whereby the jobs could be learned and a stand-by for holidays and sickness provided. In addition, no clerical posts remained from which the selection of candidates could be made. The Chief Accountant responsible chose to ignore the situation as any remedy, he explained, would involve additional costs. He has since become Financial Director.

In another organization, this loss of a training ground was further aggravated in one area of activity when all the able clerks were either moved or made redundant (voluntary and eagerly accepted redundancy). The remaining inexperienced clerks did not understand the complexities inherent in the system (and not due to the computer) and were not, therefore, able to operate it satisfactorily. The systems analyst project leader had to spend some two to three days a month overcoming the problem until suitable clerical labor was eventually made available. Senior management did not appear to see this situation as being difficult and undesirable, believing that the cheapest labor available should be used. The project leader was blamed for designing a computer-based application system that could not cope with this level of complexity without the use of skilled staff (to have done so would have required the system to process knowledge) and it was initially left to him to do the clerical work as his time was costed to a different center.

These situations indicate certain of the dangers inherent in using short term cost reductions as the only or major aim. If the ability, knowledge, skills, and career development of the people involved are not considered, adverse effects must occur.

The author's recent experiences with a utility billing system providing information on bad payers suggests that the elimination of a training ground would have severe and adverse impacts: the clerical users/operators who mainly learn by "doing" did not understand the system and its interfaces and did not use it correctly. With a manual system, such people could have learned the whole process as they saw it happen. This is no longer possible as the processing is essentially hidden. As a result, the number of errors being made by the on-line and other users appeared to be high. But as the computer was treated as a black box and blamed for errors, nothing was done to rectify the situation. Because of the nature of the system, the onus of correcting errors could be passed on to the consumers.

4.2 Wholesale/Retail Audits

```
        Stated goals - reduction in lead time
                     - cost reduction
        Hidden goal  - expediency of staff reductions
```

Many information systems are too expensive and slow, producing output after an unacceptably long period of time. The earlier availability of information as well as cost reduction appears to be the triggers for development because it is believed that this will be of benefit to the organization. Two case studies reflect this situation.

The original manual system using a large number of part-time female clerks with a number of full-time supervisors produced the output monthly some 25 working days after the end of the calendar month. A technically competent, efficient, and easy-to-use computer-based system producing very similar output reduced the lead time to about five working days. The reduction in costs to produce the output was calculated, but not considered that important either by the marketing or production management. The earlier output gave the organization at that time a competitive edge because it could react more rapidly to the consumers' changing demands. With fast moving "me-too" consumer goods this is important. The production staff also believed that they could, on average, hold one month's less stock, the cost of which could be calculated.

In the opinion of the analysts involved, which included the author, this system provided the marketing staff, and hence Production Control, with their most useful information. It was also apparent at that time that it was expedient for each manager to be seen to reduce the number of people within his own department.

The benefits, other than of reduced costs, could not be estimated as the rate of satisfaction of customers' (customers as distinct from consumers) orders was affected by many factors. Nevertheless, the marketing management, a powerful body in a marketing oriented company and the main users of the system, was so pleased with its performance that no further assessment was permitted.

Within a comparatively short time, the use of computer-based systems became widespread and generalized software packages were soon appearing in the market. Fear of competitors getting useful information earlier than this company ensured the continued running of the system with weekend operations on overtime rates being encouraged to speed the output.

Finally, some years later, this company ceased to run its own wholesale/retail audit system, buying the information from specialized companies who could, with greater resources and expertise, use larger samples and process the data more efficiently. But the triggers for the change were an apparent reduction in costs and the elimination of the "bother" of maintaining and managing specialized teams of auditors. Some loss of flexibility resulted, but the timing remained unchanged.

Further informal probing showed that it was still politically advantageous to decrease the head count and reduce the wages bill at that time. Managers had to be seen to reduce the number of staff they employed. Total costs to the organization were not seriously considered.

4.3 Stock Control

> Stated goal - reduction in lead time
> Lesson - politics of undesirable information

A manufacturing organization maintained very high levels of indirect stock items that were both costly and grossly inadequate. Where a required item was not available, somebody had to "pop out" quickly to buy it locally. The usage also seemed incredibly high. A small and apparently efficient computer-based system was developed and installed to overcome the inadequacies; it produced the same simple information but very quickly. It was thus hoped that stock levels, stock-outs, and, hence, costs could be reduced. The costs of producing the information would not be greatly affected.

It was suggested that the system and its impact be assessed some months after commencing operations. This suggestion was not accepted and one year later the system ceased operating. It was stated that a computer-based system to control the stock and usage of such systems as "broom handles," "rags" and "jars of jam" was extravagant. The importance of certain items held in these stores, for example, machine oil and light bulbs, whose stock-outs could affect production, was ignored. Although each item may not have been expensive, the total value of the stock was high as the number of items held was very large.

Much of the stock held in this store was of the type worth stealing. But as it appeared that the availability of some items for personal use was considered one of the perks, how could managers, with better information, stop it? Indirect Stores and its stock control was not considered an important area; its manager was in a very junior grade and this was no power base. A system for aiding its management that could upset many people was expendable.

An almost identical situation occurred with a system designed to improve management of the stock held by salesmen, their managers, and marketing managers for replacing damaged goods and for giving gifts to important customers. This system was disliked and rejected without any formal assessment taking place, or even being permitted. This system provided information that was "positively" not wanted.

The importance of the information to help junior managers to reduce costs and raise efficiency appears secondary within these organizations, secondary to some other stronger power.

4.4 Production Costing -- Consumer Goods

          Stated goal - better (more relevant) information
          Hidden goal - information for organizational power

An analyst was instructed to develop a new production costing
system as the existing system was no longer considered to be an
acceptable model (the author's choice of words) of the changed
production processes. The request came from the cost accountants,
who were to be the sole users of the system. Production Management and Control were to continue using the existing system, a by-
product of the production control system. Better information was
wanted, but by only one group.

The accountants wanted the system installed very quickly -- within
three months -- and were to be the only people to be consulted.
This situation placed the analyst, a chartered engineer and qualified accountant who had originally moved to Accounting from Engineering and Production, in a difficult political position. Being
in his middle 40s, he was not that able to change employment and
he believed himself to be vulnerable. He therefore acted with
extreme caution, successfully, and survived.

A suitable high level language was used to produce a prototype
which was accepted after a few changes. The analyst then attempted to assess the quality of the output but was quickly
prevented from doing so. "Don't waste time evaluating a highly
valued system, get on with your next job" he was told. The system
itself was efficient and easy to use.

From conversations, it appears that the system was developed to
meet the needs of a group of individuals within an organization to
fight a battle for power. The content and format of the output
was paramount; it had to suit the group needs showing that a
particular course of action would be beneficial to the company.
Tighter financial and cost control was the reason given for
requiring new information; the underlying cause was probably the
need by the accountants for ammunition to fight for further power
in a highly profitable but technically orientated company.

Two facts emerged during the following year.

    o The production was rationalized, some products being switched
       between factories in different countries while others were
       dropped. One processing plant closed.

    o Plans to expand and develop production on the main United
       Kingdom site, where the analyst worked, were dropped and the
       local council warned that the too strict planning regulations
       in their mainly residential area would result in the closure
       of part or all of the factory.

No further information could be obtained.

4.5 Production Costing -- Fine Chemicals

          Stated goal - better information
          Hidden goal - information for political power
          Lesson   - a need for management leadership

Production management collected and analyzed data showing that production efficiency and hence costs for a range of important products varied with a number of external factors that were beyond their control, e.g., batch of raw materials, humidity. From this basis it was argued that there was a need for capital investment, not just in a better plant, but also for better control techniques.

The Costing Department totally disregarded this information in an attempt to prevent capital investment in a new plant, saying that the poor efficiency was due to poor production management. Their system showed that the variations were random with efficiency improving during those periods when a member of their own staff was in evidence auditing the stock and hence in a position to watch the operators working.

These two systems were manual, this case history dating from the late 1950s, with each department having developed its own information system for which the motivations were easily seen. The accountants regarded the chemists as shop-floor technicians and not as managers; the chemists regarded the accountants as clerks. There was a power battle for the ear of the chief executive in a company where most of the directors were nearing retirement. Unfortunately, the political battles ended when the chief executive, who was the major shareholder, sold the company as it drifted into bankruptcy.

4.6 Production Control -- Light Engineering

> Stated goal   - better information
> Hidden goals - political power and prestige
> Lesson   - wrong problem tackled

A phased, extensive and advanced system for production control was developed over a number of years by an engineering organization with the help of consultants and the hardware manufacturers. It was to replace an existing manual system which could best be described as "Management by Chaos." The information currently available was inadequate.

Unreliability of standard and application software did play an important part in what was to prove an unsatisfactory system. But even a reliable system would have proved unsuitable. Using the assessments of Ives, et al. (1983), for example, with the user management would have probably provided a high positive score as the fault lay with management itself and their inability to manage. Installing a sophisticated computer-based system in that organization was equivalent to adjusting the carburetor when the timing chain is slack. An exception report, for example, showed that between 80 and 90 percent of all batches were part of the backlog of work and running late, reducing the value of many of the planning reports, ideal in other situations, to almost nil. This application system was not suitable for this management, but its development did not stop.

The very sophisticated computer-based system was developed because, in the view of the project leader, it appeared glamorous and prestigious. It was wanted by Production Planning to improve their image and raise their prestige to show that they and not Production Management should control this technical and production oriented organization whose products were, and are, of high qua-

lity, but whose deliverables were lamentable. This organization
needed, and finally got, a new and vigorous approach to management.

4.7 Production Control -- Toiletries and Pharmaceuticals

        Stated goal - better information
        Lesson   - centers of power and problem not per-
                       ceived by salesmen

A salesman from a computer manufacturer presented a production
control software package to a group of senior and middle managers,
describing it in glowing terms as an essential tool in the drive
to reduce production costs. This he supported with a convincing
demonstration -- a badly oriented but good presentation of a good
package. As a result, no sale was made, even though such a
package was badly needed to provide the information required to
ensure a better, smoother flow of production that was more responsive to sales.

At that time, the level of inflation in the country was low, the
economy buoyant, and the standard of living rising; sales were
good and increasing. For this company, the average work's cost
was ten percent of the consumer price. Therefore, the drive to
reduce production costs was not great and any package that could
lower the work's cost of any product by ten percent, a very big
reduction, would have negligible effects. The big need was, and
is, to get what is essentially a "me-too" product onto the shelves
for the consumer to buy as and where that consumer wants it.

A "Bill of Materials" production control package was installed as
the inflation rate rose, unemployment rose, raw material prices
rose, and consumer spending appeared to be dropping. Whether
right or wrong, the management saw their needs for information
changing as the environment within which the organization operated
changed, changing the buying habits of its consumers and the
purchasing style of the customers' buyers, increasing the costs of
raw materials and reducing their own profitability.

The production control package would have satisfied all their
needs, but senior management in a marketing oriented company had
not perceived this and were unwilling to accept advice from the DP
technologists following the poorly oriented presentation of the
software.

The perceived needs of the powerful marketing group within this
organization -- the organization described in section 4.2 above--
directed the development of the information systems into the
directions, essentially concerned with marketing and sales, they
said would benefit the organization.

4.8 Comparisons

        Stated goal - provide a better central support service
        Hidden goal - satisfy the powerful directors in the
                       profit-making divisions

Employees of one organization were briefly asked a number of questions about their use of 4GL (fourth generation languages), and in
a second organization why they used their own standard, but com-

pany-assembled, microcomputers. In particular, they were both asked how they had evaluated the use of these tools. In both cases, no formal assessment had been carried out, being considered unnecessary and not worth the labor.

The 4GL had enabled the analysts to meet the systems users' demands more rapidly and more precisely. The standard microcomputers had enabled the users to develop their own systems with good central DP support. The users in both cases were members of the profit-creating operating divisions. Their satisfaction meant that, with tough financial constraints, the central DP personnel were more secure and less likely to be made redundant; they were seen to be worth their costs. A formal assessment could produce information that was adverse and therefore why spend time and money taking risks that were not required? The parallels between this situation and that described above are obvious: the overriding power of certain groups within the organizations and the resulting political and financial (the words used by the interviewees and not this author's) pressures they can exert on the way information technology is used.

5. CONCLUSIONS

Based upon analysis of the case studies outlined above, and against a background of other experiences and much published work, it is possible to draw a number of conclusions. The conclusions must, at this stage, be both tentative and preliminary.

o In terms of efficiency, e.g., accuracy, reliability, costs, it is possible to establish a set of aims and hence assessment criteria at an operational and technical level. These may well be measurable. But being at this level will ensure that although these factors may be important, other criteria will be given greater consideration by the more senior and powerful members of the organization.

o Application systems must not create demands beyond the capabilities of present or future users. Nor must any new system reduce or eliminate the means of maintaining and developing those capabilities for the future. What variables are involved and how or if they can be measured is largely unknown, so that designers have to rely upon intuition and experience. Although important, it did appear again that other criteria would be given greater consideration by senior management; but in these case studies, no senior or powerful managers were prime users of any system.

o Information systems must be effective, that is, supply information that is required to help people perform their daily tasks. It follows, therefore, that such information should raise the performance of individuals and groups and in turn improve the performance of the organization. But this picture is clouded by the aims and ambitions of individuals and groups and by what they see as effective.

These last two points raise the following question: If power lies with those groups and individuals who are seen as being able to cope with uncertainty (Duncan, 1972), and if such groups also rely upon information as one source of that power, how much should the design and assessment of the IS be influenced by political factors?

From the small number of cases described above, it appears that, however efficient or usable a system is, to be successful it must be seen to be effective in the eyes of the users or it will be discarded.

The author suggests that assessments must cover such factors as:

     o efficiency
     o usability
     o effectiveness

But, for assessments to have real meaning and be of use in the design of new systems, it must be possible to specify the variables using units of measure. Without these, comparisons cannot be made across applications and time.

REFERENCES

Bemelmans, Th. M. A., "Systems User-Friendliness in Organizations," in van Apeldoorn, J. (ed.), *Man and Information Technology: Towards Friendlier Systems*, Delft U.P., 1983, pp. 99-106.

Bjørn-Andersen, N., and Pedersen, P. H., "Computer Facilitated Changes in the Management Power Structure," *Accounting Organizations and Society*, Vol. 5, No. 2, 1980, pp. 203-216.

Duncan, R. B., "The Character of Organizational Environments and Perceived Environmental Uncertainty," *Administrative Science Quarterly*, Vol. 17, No. 3, September 1972, pp. 313-327.

Ives, B., Olson, M. H., and Baroudi, J., "The Measurement of User Information Satisfaction," *Communications of the ACM*, Vol. 16, No. 10, October 1983, pp. 785-792.

Markus, M. L., "Power, Politics and MIS Implementation," *Communications of the ACM*, Vol. 26, No. 6, June 1983, pp. 430-444.

Nicholson, D., and Molnar, B., "Advanced Help Through Plan Instantiation and Dynamic Partner Modelling," paper submitted to ECAI '86.

DISCUSSANT NOTE

On: POST-IMPLEMENTATION ASSESSMENT OF INFORMATION
     SYSTEMS APPLICATIONS: NOTES FROM PERSONAL
     EXPERIENCES

By: Leonard Capper

Discussant's comments by: Piercarlo MAGGIOLINI

Politecnico di Milano
Italy

1. INTRODUCTION

In his paper, Leonard Capper presents some useful results about
ISA based on his personal experience.

These experiences concern:

o the aim of the IS assessment

o the IS dimensions to be assessed

Regarding the first point, Capper sees ISA not primarily as an
investigation in order to improve the specific system assessed,
but as a way to accumulate ex post knowledge in order to design
better systems.

Regarding the second point, Capper mentions three sets of dimensions of IS assessment:

o The *operational and technological aspects*. These dimensions,
   which are usually considered the principal ones in ISA, are
   not very important.

o The *usability* dimensions.

o *Organizational and political dimensions*. These are, in fact,
   the most relevant: effectiveness vis-a-vis the aims of the
   organization, on one hand, and effectiveness vis-a-vis the
   specific aims of various powerful groups on the other.

In focusing on these dimensions, we should remember that IS are
weapons in the struggle for power inside the organization and IS
assessment is also a political tool.

2. CONCLUSIONS FROM THE PAPER

We can summarize the conclusions of the paper:

o organizations seldom assess their IS

o   the economic dimension (i.e. cost-benefit analysis) of IS is
    seldom relevant

o   we can usually assess organizational and political dimensions
    (as well as usability) *qualitatively*. In order to do this,
    we have to rely on the intuition and experience of the
    analyst.

3.   EVALUATION OF THE PAPER

It would be useful to have answers to the following questions:

o   Is it possible to conceive of and define techniques and
    methodologies which make it possible to systematize the
    assessment experience and to socialize it?

o   Why are important political issues usually neglected in IS
    assessment and design methodologies (and literature)?

o   What are the important social dimensions of IS?

o   How can we take into account the political and organizational
    dimensions of IS in building more formalized methodologies
    for IS assessment (and design)?

o   If ex post ISA is useful for the design of other IS, can we
    conceive of an ex ante assessment of usability, organiza-
    tional, and political dimensions of IS?

In my opinion, it is difficult to assess IS from an organizational
and political point of view using existing methodologies because
they are based on an a *conflict* model of IS in organizations.

According to this model, organizations need faster and more
precise information, *better information for better decisions*, and
so on, but what about *opportunism* and *conflict* (and *cooperation*)
and the opportunistic use of information?

Starting exclusively from a theoretical and formal model of
organization as *networks of exchange* between opportunistic agents
cooperating and conflicting according to their objectives, values,
etc., and taking into account the relative costs of exchange, we
can build more realistic, effective and less idiosyncratic
methodologies for organizational information systems assessment.

**Information Systems Assessment
as a Learning Process
P. Etzerodt and K.H. Madsen**

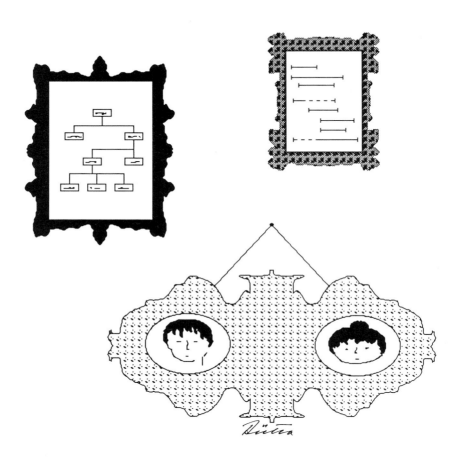

"...and using specific techniques to uncover and
contrast different framings of situations in the
organization."

INFORMATION SYSTEMS ASSESSMENT
N. Bjørn-Andersen, G.B. Davis (Editors)
Elsevier Science Publishers B.V. (North-Holland)
© IFIP, 1988

INFORMATION SYSTEMS ASSESSMENT AS A LEARNING PROCESS

Preben ETZERODT
Kim Halskov MADSEN

Computer Science Department
Aarhus University
DK-8000 Aarhus, Denmark

In this paper, we emphasize the cognitive and
learning aspects of information systems assessment.
In doing so, we step away from what we consider as
the conventional framework.

We elucidate the cognitive and learning aspects by
presenting a specific project on information
systems assessment. In this project, the basic
means for fostering a learning process among the
participants have been: working groups, focusing
on experiences gained by individuals using the
information system, using unstructured descriptions
to clarify and interpret situations, and using
specific techniques to uncover and contrast
different framings of situations in the organization.

1. INTRODUCTION

Information systems assessment activities are certainly not new
within the field of systems development (see, for instance, Mumford, et al., 1978). But it is only recently that the literature
on systems development has generally recommended formal procedures
for information systems assessment, (see for instance Capron,
1986; Leslie, 1986; Nordbotten, 1985; Senn, 1985; Zmud, 1983). In
the prevalent tradition, different techniques for gathering and
processing information concerning the performance of the system
and the organization are proposed with the purpose of determining
whether the new or changed system has met its objectives. The
collected information is seen as an important basis for the subsequent maintenance or adjustment of the system.

The acknowledgment of assessment as an important part of the life
cycle of an information system is valuable progress. However, it
is regrettable that assessment has been based on the same set of
assumptions over the years. The general wisdom has been dominated
by a very narrow understanding of success or failure of an information system: e.g., "The most fundamental concern during post-
implementation review is determining whether the system has met
its objective. That is, analysts want to know if the performance
level of users is improved and the system is producing the result
intended. If either is not, one may question whether the system
can be considered successful" (Senn, 1985). Determining the success or failure of an information system has, in general, been
seen as a matter of measuring the gap between the stated goals and
the actual performance of the system, e.g., "Therefore, the

primary objective of an evaluation of a system is to determine the extent to which the system and/or proposed changes to it fulfill the goal statement" (Nordbotten, 1985). In the more extreme cases much effort has been put into the development of sophisticated mathematical techniques for transforming non monetary values, e.g., user confidence, into monetary values in order to set the costs against the benefits of the information system.

We do not deny the need of organizations to control the costs and benefits of major investments such as computer systems. But our point is that the conventional techniques for objective measurement of a fixed set of system values tend to obscure the valuable experiences of the members of the organization. The insight gained by the actors involved in the development and use of the system, be they users, managers or computer professionals, is in general not given great importance and hence often lost. The crucial point is that this knowledge could be a basis for a better utilization of the resources spent on the development of the system, which is far beyond what the conventional techniques can offer. If this knowledge is brought to the surface it would help the actors in improving their understanding of the situation in which they are involved, and ultimately it would improve the ability of the actors to identify and solve problems emerging as a consequence of the information system in the organization. Our point of view on this issue is very much in accordance with the findings of the MARS project, a Danish research project on systems development in practice (see, for instance, Lanzara and Mathiassen, 1984).

The considerations above indicate our intention in this paper. We emphasize the cognitive and learning aspects of information systems assessment, to some extent leaving other aspects in the background. Information system evaluation should be seen as a process where the actors involved learn from their own experiences and not just as a process of measuring a fixed set of system values.

We draw on experiences from a two year information systems assessment project at the Danish university libraries. The project has been driven by the notion of information system assessment seen as a learning process and it has aimed to foster a process where the employees are given the skill and knowledge necessary for assessing present information systems as well as visions of future computer applications. The project has been organized around working groups at three selected libraries, where employees from the library work together with external consultants. In the following, we draw on experiences from one of the working groups by referring to specific examples and situations. The working group in question is located at one of the major Danish university libraries that has used computers intensively over several years.

Each of the following four sections covers a different aspect of the library project: the organization of the project, the focus of attention within the project, the basic tools and the basic techniques. As a way of presenting the characteristics of ISA (Information Systems Assessment) as a learning process we often contrast with what we call "the conventional framework of ISA." To clarify our message, we draw, from time to time, a somewhat simplified picture of "the conventional framework of ISA."

2. ORGANIZATION

Within the conventional framework of ISA the subject-matter is
approached from outside. The assessment activities are carried
out by a small group of experts detached from the development of
the system as well as detached from its daily use. Usually the
group is made up of experts in assessment associated with the
computer department or of external consultants. In some cases, it
is recommended that the users take part in the assessment, but it
is important that the persons involved have an objective perception of the system, e.g., "A disinterested party is best, because
this person has no preconceived notion or vested interests"
(Capron, 1986). As the result of the assessment, the experts are
supposed to deliver a document containing their judgment and
measurements of the system and its performance.

The assessment activities within the library project have been
organized in accordance with our notion of ISA as a learning
process. The assessment activities have been carried out from the
inside, in the sense that external consultants have been engaged
with the purpose of supporting the members of the organization in
assessing the information systems used at their work-place. It
has been the intention that exactly those members of the organization who have interests in the information system should be
engaged in the assessment.

When the library in question was chosen as one of the participating libraries, a working group was established. The working
group is made up of a sociologist, a computer scientist, and six
members of the staff. The work within the group has been organized around group meetings approximately every third week.
Except for an overall coordination with similar working groups
established at the two other participating libraries, the group
has been in control of its own work and only responsible to the
library in question, i.e., the existing committees at the library
made up of representatives from the staff and the management.

One of the first experiences -- which we actually had taken into
account but underestimated in the overall planning of the project
-- was that the conditions for carrying out assessment from the
inside were not present beforehand. These conditions had to be
created before any assessment activities could be undertaken. The
essential issue was that the members of the group had very different backgrounds. Besides the two consultants coming from outside, the group was made up of clerical workers and librarians.
Almost every department had a representative.

The first three months were spent establishing the local part of
the project at the library in question. During that time the
working group reached a consensus on the domain to be investigated
and on what the group was aiming at. Moreover, a common understanding of the conditions that the group was working under was
reached.

The group intended to start out by uncovering the impacts of the
circulation control system on the conditions of work as well as
its impact on the work in general. Moreover the intention was to
uncover possible domains of actions, i.e., clarifying desirable
and realistic changes and ways of achieving them. On the other
hand, the group realized that it did not have the resources to
intervene radically into the existing development and use of
computers, for instance, by creating alternative designs. The

present computer system, long term contracts, the existing power structure were conditions or obstacles impossible to overcome immediately.

During the following assessment activities undertaken by the working group, the outside consultants played various roles: They supported the group members coming from the library in uncovering and highlighting problems concerning the use of the computers. They played different roles, such as that of "experts" having a theoretical background in computer science and in sociology, as advisers having experiences with similar kinds of co-operation with users, and as critics having their own opinion about the situation at the library.

As we shall describe in greater detail in the following sections, the investigations made by the working group often had the following course of action: Most of the investigations were not planned in detail in advance. The motivation for doing the specific investigation often emerged from the insight gained by previous investigations. At such occasions, it was the task of the consultants to choose and present appropriate methods for carrying out the investigation. After the group members had decided to use a particular method, the group often planned a pilot project where the group members tried out the method by making observations during their own day of work or by describing a small part of their own work. The purpose of performing these pilot projects was mainly to make the group familiar with the method. Afterwards, when the investigation was carried out in full scale, some of the group members from the library often had the responsibility for carrying out the investigation, while the consultants played the role of advisers or critics.

It is important to notice that the group members from the library (i.e., the staff) could not have carried out the assessment activities completely on their own. They needed the help from the outside consultants and their theoretical and practical background. It is important to stress, however, that the staff had the decisive word on which activities should constitute the assessment at their own place of work. Moreover the staff performed the assessments.

3. FOCUS OF ATTENTION

Within the conventional framework of ISA, the technical-oriented "bird's eye view" of computer based systems is used. The organization is seen from above and the focus of attention is primarily on system performance and on information and data processing capacity of the organizational unit using the information system, e.g., "The concerns raised during analysis and design about the accuracy of information, timeliness of presentation, completeness, and appropriateness of format continue to indicate systems quality" (Senn, 1985). The main concern is to determine to what extent the system fulfills the technical and economic goals stated at the beginning of its development.

Within the library project, the use of the information system has basically been considered from the point of view of the individuals using the system. Various aspects of how the use of computers influence the situation of work for the individual as well as the organization as a whole have been considered. Focus of attention has especially been put on how individuals perceive their own situation of work. The intention has been to uncover individual points of view on what constitute the problems concerning the use of the information system. As an example, let us consider the following course of action within the library project.

The early investigations of the project, one of which we will return to in section 4, had uncovered certain changes in the way various tasks were done after the installation of the circulation control system, e.g., changes in the technology and in the organization of the work.

Though a consensus was reached about these issues, it was not at all a trivial task to agree on the impacts of these changes on the work situation, e.g., the kind of problems and uncertainty faced in the daily situation of work and the service offered by the department.

It was clear that the question of judging the above mentioned changes, to a large extent, was a question about which values and views were brought to the situation. For instance, the quality of service could be seen as a matter of "time taken to get hold of a book" or "that there should always be someone to guide and help the borrowers."

On an earlier occasion, the working group had planned to complement the previous investigations with interviews of the different groups of users with the purpose of revealing different perceptions of how the computer system had affected the daily work situation. The importance of these interviews was strengthened by discussions within the group about how to interpret the uncovered changes in the work.

From the knowledge gained so far, the group prepared a number of themes and more detailed questions to guide the interviews. In accordance with the overall aim of the local project, the group members agreed that it was important during the interview session to put emphasis on problems faced during work and causes or explanations that the workers could give to these problems.

The interview session revealed a great variety of problems and individual experiences. The following is an account of how one of these experiences was revealed and pursued: The majority of the people involved in the interview session concurrently expressed that the new computer system had left them in a position often not in control of "things." The problems were, of course, expressed differently by different people. One person said that the computer system had made her dependent on younger colleagues who knew the system better. Another said that she did not feel the same control over the tools as when she was working with the manual card index. Others expressed that they felt a lack of qualification to fulfill their job, and some pointed out examples where they, due to mistakes or failures, had been blamed by borrowers or colleagues. Some of the problems seemed to have become more and more important as time went by. There was an expectation that everybody would get used to the new routines, but what happened instead was that everybody seemed to put more and more effort in hiding their uncertainty, first of all from the borrowers, but also from their colleagues and their leaders. When seeking causes to the problems, there was some variation in the explanations given.

Among *the staff of the department* there was some variation, but
quite a lot expressed a dissatisfaction with the training programs
offered before the computer system was introduced, and some
pointed out the very abrupt change to the new and not sufficiently
tested system as an important cause of the problems.

The management recognized that the revealed problems were present
in the department. But they did not accept the given explanations, like the offered training programs, etc., as reasonable
causes of the problems. Instead they pointed out a very low
degree of motivation among parts of the staff towards new challenges as the main cause of the problems. They stressed their
opinion of the situation by examples such as: "During the last
years the staff had several times been invited to join courses of
different kinds. But it was always the very same few enthusiasts
who actually applied."

The technicians of the EDP department recognized that there were
serious problems in the department, but they denied that the
causes of the problems had anything to do with the new computer
system. Though there had been some technical problems during a
transitional period of time, they argued that the problems should
be found elsewhere. Instead they pointed out "poor leadership"
and "bad social relations" as the causes of the problem.

Evidently, the various groups of individuals had interpreted the
same situation in rather different ways. The process of exploring
the individual experiences has not just been a process of collecting and structuring information with the purpose of giving an
account of these experiences. During the interview sessions, the
different explanations or interpretations of the problem have been
discussed. This in itself can be seen as an important contribution to a better understanding of the individual's, or group's,
conception of reality and how they, explicitly or implicitly,
justify their actions.

During the interview session and the succeeding discussions of the
working group, emphasis was consciously put on elaborating and
clarifying the individual and sometimes conflicting interpretations of the impacts of the circulation control system on working
conditions.

The intention was to bring to the foreground the experiences
gained by the individual using the computer system. The important
point is that communicating and bringing to the foreground this
kind of knowledge is essential in improving the understanding
among the actors of the situation in which they are involved, and
ultimately in improving the ability of the actors to identify and
solve problems emerging as a consequence of the information system
in the organization.

4. BASIC TOOLS

Within the conventional framework of ISA, descriptions are being
used as the basic tool for documenting and making representations
of the situation. Descriptions are made with the purpose of communicating the result of the assessment. The basic concepts are a
fixed set of system values or categories, e.g., "Depending on the
system characteristics being evaluated, a number of separate measures may be used. The most common is a monetary measurement,
giving each system characteristic a price or dollar value. Other

measures used in system evaluation include processing times, counts of goals served or users supported, and assignment of scores of subsystem quality," (Nordbotten, 1985).The meaning of concepts like "response time" are formally or clearly defined. Misunderstandings are considered as failures and should be avoided. No attention is paid to the use of language itself.

Within the library project, unstructured descriptions have been used as a tool for clarifying and interpreting the situation at the library. Describing has been a cognitive activity and a way for the staff to learn from their own experiences. The attention of the group members has been guided by some overall themes, e.g., "the organization of work." The meaning of concepts used in descriptions of the situation at the library has often been questioned. Misunderstandings have been seen as important and fruitful indications of relevant issues to be discussed. Special attention has been given to the language itself.

As an example, consider the following course of action from the very first part of the project when the group had decided to uncover the impact of the circulation control system: An obvious precondition for gaining insight into the impact on the work was an understanding of what the work itself was all about. Some of the members of the group were actually working in the circulation department, but the rest of the members had only an overall understanding of the work.

As a first introduction to the circulation department, two members of the group working in the department gave a presentation of the department. The first one, a librarian, gave a presentation of the circulation control system. She presented the history and components of the system and demonstrated the various types of dialogues on a terminal. The second one, a clerical worker, went through the tasks of the department before and after the system was introduced.

As the two persons introduced the group to their work, they often showed us what they did, or made drawings on the blackboard visualizing the scenery of the department and the changes made as the system was introduced. As they talked about their work, they did it in terms of concepts from their daily work. They used some formal terms, such as "counter duty" very often referring to physical locations and used in the official or formal planning of work. They used a lot of informal terms, such as "dispatch of batch messages" used by smaller groups in the coordination of their daily work.

The observations made above are very much in accordance with observations made by Andersen and Holmqvist (forthcoming): It is important to note the differences between the language inside and outside the work situation. Two characteristics of the language used in the work situation are of special importance in our case: It is impossible to understand the language of the work situation without the knowledge of actions undertaken in the work situation, and the language of the work situation focuses on concrete actions that have to be done and not on results and abstract actions. For group members who were not working in the circulation department, it was often difficult to understand the presentation of their work when explained in a language similar to the one used in the work situation. Although the concepts used were meaningful and useful in the work situation, they were almost meaningless when used about the work detached from the concrete work situation.

Another kind of explanation may be given by referring to Heidegger. According to Heidegger's philosophy, the fundamental state of being is to have access to the world through practical involvement: one is acting unreflectingly without having representations of phenomena; the situation is ready-to-hand. Object and properties are only inherent in events of breaking down in which they become present-at-hand. The point is clarified by one simple example (originally from Heidegger, but here quoted from Winograd and Flores, 1986, p. 36):

> One simple example he gives is that of a hammer being used by a person engaged in driving a nail. To the person doing the hammering, the hammer as such does not exist. It is part of the background of *readiness-to-hand* that is taken for granted without explicit recognition or identification as an object. It is part of the hammer's world, but it is not present any more than are the tendons of the hammerer's arm. The hammer presents itself as a hammer only when there is some kind of breaking down or *unreadiness-to-hand*. Its hammerness emerges if it breaks or slips from grasp or mars the wood, or if there is a nail to be driven and the hammer cannot be found.

Turning back to the investigation of the circulation department, we can note that the staff do have knowledge of their own work but in a state of readiness-to-hand. In the daily work situation, they do not have to talk about what they are doing; only in situations of breakdown do objects and properties come into existence. The statement "language need express only what is not obvious" (Winograd and Flores, 1986, p. 74) contains the key point in one sentence.

Motivated by a need for a better understanding of the work in the circulation department, we decided to make various kinds of unstructured descriptions of the work. One of the descriptions made was based on a time structure investigation aiming at documenting issues such as "the amount of time spent at terminals," "the distribution of work among the employees," "the variation in the work," etc. Although this was the major aim of the time structure investigation, the investigation turned out to contribute decisively to the establishment of a better understanding of the work.

An important part of the investigation was the identification of the functions of work in the circulation department. At a group meeting, we presented a general set of categories of functions of work such as "planning functions," "control functions," etc., which we used in the generation of a set of specific functions carried out in the circulation department. For instance, we had identified the control functions as being "control of returned books," "control of requisition forms," etc. During the group meeting, some minor modifications of the specific set of functions were made. The next step was to perform a pilot project only involving the three working group members from the circulation department. During a three day period the three working group members registered what they were doing in terms of the various functions. To get a detailed picture of the time structure, the three group members filled out a time schema during the working day. The schema was made of the various functions along the rows and time periods along the columns.

During the pilot project, it became evident that the meaning of the various functions was unclear and hence had been interpreted differently by the three persons involved. It was decided to form a subgroup which would be responsible for revising the set of functions and giving a thorough explanation of their meaning. Furthermore, the group was responsible for the introduction of the method to the staff in the circulation department as well as for the conduct of the investigation.

During the time structure investigation, various unstructured descriptions of the distribution of work, the time spent at the terminal, etc., were made. These descriptions were, in themselves, of great value. But more importantly, the process of making the descriptions was a learning process making the individual members of the group more qualified at talking about the work in the circulation department. The ability to talk about the work on a functional level was improved, making it possible to talk about other aspects of the work, such as in which situations of work the circulation control system actually is used. Moreover, the meaning of concepts like "interruption" and "variation" of the work were clarified.

Not only the descriptions made during the time structure investigation, but also other kinds of descriptions made at later stages of the library project, have been used within the group as tools to develop and bring to the foreground experiences gained by individuals in the daily use of the circulation control system. Describing has been a cognitive activity and a way for the staff to learn from their own experiences and thereby making them more qualified at discussing the impact of the circulation control system. Descriptions have reflected the knowledge of the group and made it possible to build up further knowledge.

5. BASIC TECHNIQUES

Within the conventional framework of ISA, assessment is basically seen as a matter of gathering and processing information about the new or changed information system, e.g., "Evaluators will need to gather statistics and do some interviewing and observation in order to assess system functioning and user satisfaction" (Capron, 1986). For this purpose various techniques are recommended, e.g., questionnaire, interview, observation, sampling, record inspection.

Within the library project, we aimed at fostering a learning process among the members of the organization using the information system. The techniques reflect the basic assumption that different people interpret reality differently. We have focused on techniques for bringing out the individual experiences concerning the use of the system, as well as techniques for clarifying the way the situation was framed, i.e., by which views and values the situation was arranged by different groups of members of the organization. The intention was, through uncovering and contrasting different and sometimes conflicting framings of the situation, to develop a better understanding. We have not intended, nor has it been possible, to create a fully shared understanding among the different groups of members of the organization.

Seen from this point of view -- viewing frames as important for how one understands phenomena -- reframing becomes important as a technique for gaining a better understanding. Reframing can be considered as a matter of drawing boundaries for the domain of our attention and seeing a situation as another situation. There is no general rule on how to reframe problems experienced. Different kinds of problems need different kinds of treatment. The following is an account of how the kind of problems mentioned in the section 3 were treated.

It was obvious that the technicians saw the situation in the circulation control department from outside, feeling no responsibility for what was happening. They belonged to the newly established computer department and their only responsibility was to keep the computer running. The management saw the situation from outside too, explaining the problems as personal characteristics. They had, with no success, tried to change the situation by offering courses. They strongly believed that it would only be possible to change the situation radically when the elderly part of the staff retired. Among the staff, the situation was obviously seen from inside. But the problems were mainly seen as problems of the individuals, for instance by explaining the problems as lack of qualifications.

The working group decided to challenge the embedded frames that were crucial for how the different parties addressed the situation and the problems in the department. The basic technique was to set up other frames and to examine the consequences of viewing the situation and the experienced problems from new points of view. The intention was to create an interpretation of the situation in the department that would include a better understanding of how the experienced problems were related to the use of the computer. The idea was to make the management and the technicians, together with the staff, part of the present situation in the circulation control department. Instead of seeing the problems as problems of the department, we intended to see the problems as problems in the system development process.

Based on the experiences brought out during the interview sessions, the members of the group agreed on three themes that should be of special interest during the historical investigation:

o   the communication during the development process, especially between the persons engaged in the process and the staff at the library;

o   the decision making during the development process, especially the influence of the staff on the decisions made;

o   the change made of the library during the development process, including the introduction of the system and the offered training programs.

The historical investigation was carried out in two steps. The first step consisted of collecting and uncovering the various public as well as private notes and documents concerning the development of the system. Based on this uncovering of scattered information, formal as well as informal, the group created a first overall, but still insufficient, description of the development process. The description identified and structured important events in a time sequence and related these events to actions undertaken during the process and to conditions for the process. The description acted as a common frame of reference for the group and, as such, it was an important part of the preparations for the second step of the investigations. During the second step of the investigation, the group arranged hearings of representatives from the management, the staff, and the technicians who had been engaged in the development of the system. As a result of the historical investigation, the members of the group wrote a working paper made up of fourteen small stories about important events during the development process, structured in a chronological time sequence.

The process of reframing the experienced problems -- seeing the problems of today as problems in the development process -- have been fruitful in clarifying dilemmas and in gaining a better understanding of the situation in the circulation department. The stories mentioned represent the grounds for other settings of the experienced problems than the ones given during the interview sessions. Instead of seeing a problem like a widespread feeling of uncertainty or lack of control among the staff primarily as a matter of personal characteristics or poor leadership, another domain of possible sources for the problems was brought to public awareness:

o   the lack of information from the project group to the future users;

o   the absence of possibilities for the users to influence the project before the very last part of the development process;

o   the abrupt introduction of the system in the department;

o   the changes to the system that were undertaken due to technical problems;

o   demands that were not fulfilled.

Bringing these possible sources of today's problems to the foreground not only created a better understanding within the group but also a greater consensus among groups of individuals in their judgment of possible and feasible domains of action. Not only the historical investigation aimed at reframing the experienced problems but so did the other investigations made during the library project.

6.   SUMMARY

The previous sections have promoted the idea of ISA as a learning process. The basic idea is to consider ISA as a process where the members of the organization learn from their own experiences and not just as a process of measuring a fixed set of system values. We have elucidated and made the notion of ISA as a learning process concrete by presenting four different aspects of the library project.

The working group based organization has been an important precondition for ISA as a learning process. The assessment has been carried out by the members of the organization who actually use the information system. The external consultants have acted as advisors and critics.

Focus of attention has been the experiences gained by the individuals using the information system. An important point is that this kind of knowledge is very valuable not only to the specific

organization or employees in question, but also to employees at
other organizations and perhaps using a different information
system. We believe that communicating and bringing to the foreground this kind of knowledge is of greater value than a more
general set of statements when employees in other organizations
are working at influencing the use of computers.

Unstructured descriptions have consciously been used as a tool for
creating awareness of the situation in the organization. The use
of language for making descriptions has been a cognitive process
and a way for the members of the organization to learn from their
own experiences and hereby making them more qualified at assessing
the information system. The language of the members of the
organization has reflected their knowledge and made it possible to
build up further knowledge.

The basic technique has been reframing in order to create better
interpretations of the situation in the organization. Behind the
idea of using different frames are the assumptions that understanding (i.e., assessing) is a matter of interpretation, and that
the situation in the organization may be interpreted in more than
just one way.

We have set up an alternative to conventional ISA. Although
unusual, our project is not unique. Within Scandinavia a number
of similar projects, e.g., DUE (Kyng and Mathiassen, 1982),
FLORENCE (Bjerknes and Bratteteig, 1987), UTOPIA (Bødker, 1987)
have been undertaken during the last ten years. These projects
have been based on a democratic view on working life: All parties
involved should have the resources and the rights to influence the
development and use of the information system in accordance with
their own interests.

REFERENCES

Andersen, P. B., and Holmqvist, B., "Work Language and Information
    Technology," *Journal of Pragmatics,* forthcoming, North-Hol-
    land, Amsterdam.

Bjerknes, G., and Bratteteig, T., "FLORENCE in Wonderland--
    Systems Development with Nurses," in Bjerknes, G., Ehn, P.,
    and Kyng, M. (eds.), *Computers and Democracy -- The Scandina-
    vian Challenge,* Gower, London, 1987.

Bødker, S., et al., "A Utopian Experience," in Bjerknes, G., Ehn,
    P., and Kyng, M.(eds.), *Computers and Democracy -- The
    Scandinavian Challenge,* Gower, London, 1987.

Capron, H. L., *Systems Analysis and Design,* The Benjamin/Cummings
    Publishing Company, Inc., Reading, Massachusetts, 1986.

Kyng, M., and Mathiassen, L., "Systems Development and Trade Union
    Activities," in Bjørn-Andersen, N. (ed.) *Information Society,
    for Richer, for Poorer,* North-Holland, Amsterdam, 1982.

Lanzara, G. F., and Mathiassen, L., "Mapping Situations within a
    System Develop ment Project," Mars-report No. 6, Aarhus
    University, 1984.

Leslie, R. E., *Systems Analysis and Design: Method and Invention,*
    Prentice-Hall, Englewood Cliffs, New Jersey, 1986.

Mumford, E., Land, F., and Hawgood, J., "A Participative Approach to the Design of Computer Systems," in *Impact of Science on Society*, Vol. 28, No. 3, Paris, 1978.

Nordbotten, J. C., *The Analysis and Design of Computer-Based Information Systems*, Houghton Mifflin Company, Boston, 1985.

Senn, J. A., *Analysis and Design of Information Systems*, McGraw-Hill Book Company, New York, 1985.

Winograd, T., and Flores, F., *Understanding Computers and Cognition: A New Foundation for Design*, Ablex Publishing Corporation, Norwood, New Jersey, 1986.

Zmud, R. W., *Information Systems in Organizations*, Scott, Foresman and Company, Glenview, Illinois, 1983.

DISCUSSANT NOTE

On: INFORMATION SYSTEMS ASSESSMENT AS A
      LEARNING PROCESS

By: Preben Etzerodt and Kim Halskov Madsen

Discussant's comments by: Ananth SRINIVASAN

Indiana University
Bloomington, Indiana   USA

1.   INTRODUCTION

The main issue to be addressed in a paper such as this is the
level of contribution made by the descriptive report of a case
study where a particular process of system implementation is
described.   While there exist several examples of debates that
address this issue, it is my opinion that the information systems
(IS) field benefits greatly from such studies.   Typically, such
reports are interesting to the IS researcher because they provide
micro-level details about an implementation situation that otherwise would remain unnoticed if the data were aggregated into a
larger pool and analyzed.   Such studies also enable IS researchers
to test, in a limited way, the predictive ability of IS proposi-
tions that exist in the literature.

2.   THE PROCESS SCHOOL

Although the authors state repeatedly that their paper takes a
radically new approach to IS implementation and assessment, the
ideas expressed in their work have been articulated by several
system implementation researchers.   Specifically, the process
school of thought among IS researchers has, as its core, the
following tenets:

o   Implementation should be viewed as a *process* of activities
    and not merely in terms of system installation.

o   System users should be included in the process during early
    stages of system development.

o   System users should have adequate influence on the develop-
    ment process.

o   System users should have a sense of ownership over the
    system.

What makes *this* paper interesting is that many of these ideas have
actually been incorporated in the development of the library
system.

3. OUTCOMES

A key question that remains inadequately addressed in the paper pertains to the *outcomes* of the assessment that took place. How did the results of the assessment process affect the systems that had already been implemented? Were the assessment results incorporated into the design of systems being planned? Were system resource allocation decisions changed or otherwise affected? In general, were there any policy level impacts on system implementation practices that came about due to the assessment process?

These questions are extremely important in assessing the value of pursuing this particular assessment approach.

4. ACCEPTABLE SUBSET?

Whenever users are directly involved in any system related activity (in this case, assessment of a particular system), the question arises as to whether one should include all the users or some subset of the users. If the former approach is rejected due to feasibility considerations, then the question is reduced to one of what is an acceptable subset. It would be interesting to find out how this issue was handled in this research. How did the researchers determine that user representation on the working committee was adequate? A more fundamental issue is how can such adequacy be defined? I am also slightly concerned with the level of influence the external consultants had on the activities of the users on the working committee. This is primarily due to the fact that the users are, to a large extent, dependent on the technical advice of the external consultants. If such influence is significant, then the main thrust behind this approach is defeated.

5. CONCLUDING REMARKS

Finally, I am curious about the ability to extend this work. What kinds of system environments are most conducive to using such an assessment strategy? Is there something unique about a library environment (Danish libraries?) that makes such an approach suitable? The authors would do well to elucidate to make the study and the results more interesting to a larger community.

Theory and Practice in Evaluation:
The Case of the New Information Technologies
F. Blackler and C. Brown

"While cost benefit analysis based on labor savings can be used
to partially justify this technology, almost all researchers in this
area and many of the people who participated in the survey stressed
that the benefits of CADCAM lie in long term downstream benefits."

INFORMATION SYSTEMS ASSESSMENT
N. Bjørn-Andersen, G.B. Davis (Editors)
Elsevier Science Publishers B.V. (North-Holland)
© IFIP, 1988

THEORY AND PRACTICE IN EVALUATION: THE CASE OF
THE NEW INFORMATION TECHNOLOGIES

Frank BLACKLER
Colin BROWN

Department of Behaviour in Organisations
University of Lancaster
Lancaster   LA1 4YX
United Kingdom

This paper relates the debate on the nature and
adequacy of evaluation research to the findings of
a survey recently concluded into the nature of
current British practices in the evaluation of
information technologies.

The paper is organized into five sections: an
introduction; a description of the current status
of evaluation research and a resume of "crises"
associated with it; an overview of the results of a
survey of evaluation practices with British work
organizations; a review of the "crises" in the
light of the survey; and conclusions.

1.   INTRODUCTION

The aim of this paper is to relate debates on the nature and
adequacy of evaluation research to the findings of a survey
recently concluded into the characteristics of current British
organizational practices in the evaluation of Information Technologies (IT).   There are some good reasons to think that the
ability to satisfactorily evaluate technological innovations is an
important factor in the decision to implement.   Over the past
decade, a number of studies of the uptake of Computer Numerically
Controlled (CNC) equipment and office automation technologies have
reinforced this point.   Bhattacharya (1976) showed that the
inability of British management to satisfactorily evaluate and
hence justify investment in Numerically Controlled (NC) and CNC
equipment was a major reason for firms rejecting the technology.
Putnam (1978) reported an exactly similar position in the United
States.   Nasbeth and Ray (1974) comparing United States and
European uptake of NC equipment found related effects.   In the
case of office automation, Strassman (1985) reports the conclusions of studies by the American Productivity Center and the White
House Conference on Productivity.   Both studies emphasize that a
major obstacle to "information technology investments" was the
inability to measure productivity gains.

This is an important and disturbing state of affairs given that
governments,   throughout   advanced   industrial   societies,   are
committed to policies which are designed to encourage the uptake
of information technologies across all major sectors of their
economy.   In the United Kingdom, for example, the last five years
have seen the launching of several awareness schemes (e.g., the

Department of Trade Industry's CADCAM, CADMAT and Office Automation programs) as well as programs of technological development
such as Alvey.   That such government policies have attributed
little or no significance to evaluation as an issue in uptake
might be considered surprising.   Yet, as the authors have argued
before (Blackler and Brown, 1985; see especially Wilkinson, 1983),
such Government policies are based upon a deterministic view of
the technologies which assumes that benefits almost automatically
accrue from usage.   This contrasts with the widely accepted
suggestion from social scientists (for example, Buchanan and
Boddy, 1982) that a variety of alternative approaches to IT
utilization exist with a range of potential effects.

In approaching the issue of IT evaluation, we have found it
helpful to draw on the literature on evaluation research.
Research techniques that have been developed for the evaluation of
social change programs are likely to need modification before they
can be applied to IT evaluation.   But it is our suggestion that
debate about problems within this field is instructive and, in the
light of current approaches to the practice of IT evaluation,
offers important pointers for the future.

2.   THE CURRENT STATUS OF EVALUATION RESEARCH

Although many different definitions have been offered as to the
nature of evaluation research, we follow Wortmann (1983) in
characterizing the area as a multidisciplinary activity united by
a concern for appropriate methodologies that can be used to obtain
valid information concerning the degree to which some specified
activity achieves some desired effect.   From a slow and uncertain
beginning in the mid 1960s, the field is now growing very fast.
By way of example, reference to the current catalogue of a major
U.S. publishing house (Sage) shows three separate journals and no
less than 38 books specifically devoted to evaluation issues.
Most of the literature on evaluation research relates to educational and social program assessments; little is specifically
concerned with the evaluation of information technology (although,
as we comment below, changes can be expected here).   Nevertheless,
the amount of available material is impressive and the growth over
the past decade spectacular.

No doubt there are many reasons for this but two seem particularly
pertinent here.   The first factor, and one which is directly
relevant to the context of technological usage, is the change in
economic circumstances over the past decade.   Economic recession,
initiated in part by the energy crisis, have led to circumstances
of inflation, unemployment and bankruptcy.   The optimism based
upon the possibilities for economic growth of early decades has
been replaced by "a climate of retrenchment and cutbacks, of
justifications and accountability" (Legge, 1984).   Kaplinsky
(1984), commenting upon the impact of these changes on management
in Western democracies, shows how they have led to an emphasis
upon the management of scarce resources, the reduction of costs
and a growing demand for evidence of value for money in both
private and public investment.   In such a climate, the opportunities and rewards for effective evaluation are clear and this has
led to growing employment opportunities for social scientists.
Legge (1984) has characterized evaluation research as the province
of professional groups drawn from academia or consultancy.   In the
United Kingdom, resources for research over the past decade have
increasingly been directed towards policy issues and the resolution of practical problems (for example, Bell's 1984 account of

developments at the Social Science Research Council). Under these circumstances, social scientists have reacted to the growing blockages to a traditional pure academic research career by moving into more applied areas. Such developments are not unique; there are many similar examples in the history of social science (see for example Ben David and Collins [1966] on the origins of psychology in 19th century Germany or Boakes [1984] on applied psychology at the turn of the century).

A second factor relevant to the growth of evaluation research is more recent and is directly related to the growing use of the information technologies themselves. Several authors have pointed to the pervasiveness of these technologies (e.g., Leontieff, 1982; Kaplinsky, 1984) in that they are applicable to the full range of manufacturing and service organizations. In manufacturing, examples include CNC tools, robots, computer aided design (CAD), flexible manufacturing systems (FMS), integrated CAD and computer aided manufacturing (CADCAM), process control, and computerized stock control and warehousing. In the field of organizational administration examples include word processors, electronic mail and filing systems, video conferencing and teletext, information and decision support systems, expert based systems, information satellites and networks, electronic point of sale systems and electronic funds transfer.

As was noted earlier, characteristics of policy initiatives in the United Kingdom have been based on assumptions that the use of these technologies will automatically lead to benefits for the organization. Such an approach carries with it the implication that careful evaluation of impacts is neither essential nor problematic. For such an approach to retain credibility there must be little or no controversy as to the range and type of impacts. As Johnston (1984) has observed, demand for evaluation data in education began only when controversy arose over the Head Start Program in the United States. In the case of information technologies, we are past the early euphoric phase and corporate budgets for IT are growing under the influence of the "automate or liquidate" imperative. Reports of failures and disappointments are now appearing in the literature (e.g., Butera and Thurman, 1984). In the office automation area in the United Kingdom, the widely publicized Department of Trade and Industry's projects yielded ambiguous and disturbing results which prompted demands from potential users for more specific evaluative information. Thus a combination of factors involving the pervasiveness of the technology and the growing realization that successful use is not automatic may be expected to lead to an increase among practitioners in the perceived relevance of systematic evaluation of information technology applications.

Doubts persist as to current value in spite of the increasing popularity and growth of evaluation research. Mandell (1984) points to the "performance gap" in evaluation between sophisticated methodologies on the one hand and the failure to affect policy making on the other. Joyce (1980), among many others, points to the disputes in evaluation over what is to count as appropriate method. Weiss (1975) has shown how the results of evaluation seldom disturb the status quo. Gottfredson (1984) has argued that evaluations seldom contribute to social theory since most change programs have vague or poorly articulated theoretical rationales. The most systematic examination of the state of the art has been provided by Legge (1984; see also Gowler and Legge, 1984).

Legge argues that evaluation research is characterized by a state
of crisis which may threaten its very survival. The crisis has
three aspects. First, there is a *crisis of methods or verification* which centers upon the validity of positivistic research
methods and the adequacy of alternative interpretative or process
orientated methodologies. Second, there is a *crisis of utilization* since the results of evaluations are often not utilized by
decision makers. Many explanations for this state of affairs have
been offered (Patton, 1978), some of which link this difficulty
with inappropriate methodology. Finally, according to Legge,
there is a *crisis of accreditation,* which arises from the liberal
bias of much evaluation research, and bias which may threaten its
credibility in the eyes of "conservative" administrators. This
often places evaluators in a cleft stick, either they lose
credibility with decision makers for being too radical or they
seek to maximize the acceptance of their findings and in so doing
adopt an inherently conservative position that is supportive of
the status quo. Legge has much to say on the nature of these
crises and concludes her work by seeking to resolve or at least
ameliorate them "by undertaking a matching process to achieve
compatibility between evaluation functions sought and evaluation
design employed."

This paper seeks to examine this proposal. The results of a
recent study of evaluation practices relating to information
technologies are reported. In the light of those results, the
crises postulated by Legge as characteristic of the field are
re-examined.

3. A STUDY OF CURRENT PRACTICES IN BRITISH WORK ORGANIZATIONS FOR THE EVALUATION OF INFORMATION TECHNOLOGIES

At the start of the research, four possible approaches to the
evaluation of information technologies were identified:

(i)   *Cost substitution:* the relative costs of the old and
        new system are compared utilizing quantitative cost
        benefit or cost effectiveness approaches (see Input,
        1983).

(ii)   *Value added:* qualitative and quantitative comparisons
        are made on issues such as improved service to custo-
        mers, product quality, or flexibility. Strassman (1985)
        has provided the most comprehensive and impressive
        advocacy of this approach.

(iii)   *Organizational evaluation:* the impact upon hierarchies
        of control, work organization, the design of jobs, and
        user attitudes are relevant. Many organizational
        theorists have stressed the relevance of such factors to
        successful outcomes (Buchanan and Boddy, 1983).

(iv)   *Process evaluation:* the focus here is upon an evalua-
        tion of the processes through which the new systems are
        designed and introduced. Quality of project management,
        participation, and end user support and development are
        the key issues (Blackler and Brown, 1986).

The original intention was to identify case examples of different
evaluation practices and to set such findings against the debates
current in the field. This strategy proved unworkable since early

site visits showed current practice, as far as formal evaluation was concerned, was very poorly developed. The approach was therefore broadened and a range of well informed "opinion leaders" were selected. Such people were sought from particular interest groups (management, trade unions, government agencies, manufacturers, consultants, academics) and of the different sectors of the economy most affected by the new information technologies (manufacturing, banking/insurance, education, health, local government, retailing, telecommunications, transport). Fifty four semistructured interviews were conducted with such representatives covering (1) a description of the impacts to date and likely future impacts of the technology; (2) a description of current evaluative practices, including their aetiology and perceived adequacy; (3) exceptional cases of particular interest, including their judgments of "best practice"; (4) the existence of available "off the shelf" evaluation packages; (5) ideas for change and development in evaluative approaches. While this interview program was the backbone of the methodology, various other activities were undertaken. These included: (a) visits to organizations which were engaging in evaluation activities of particular interest; (b) examination of relevant academic and consultancy reports; (c) discussion with various academics in the United Kingdom and Western Europe; (d) the organization of a workshop to feed back the results of the research to respondents and other interested parties; and (e) regular contact with individuals at the Department of Trade and Industry following the progress of the government awareness schemes and Office Automation projects.

3.1 Overview of Results

The research yielded results of a wide-ranging nature which enabled us to consider evaluation in a broad organizational context. For example, in the attempts to identify and define "best practice," evaluation was highlighted as a vital ingredient in project management, both as a means of involving different interest groups in the innovation process and as a technique for the provision of feedback in a series of incremental and evolving stages. Karl Weick (1984) has talked of this approach to social problems in terms of "small wins....complete outcomes of moderate importance that build a pattern that attracts allies." The interviews suggest that, in the United Kingdom, the standard of project management was not high, with understanding of how the use of technology can improve an organization's competitiveness being at a low level. The implications of these results are discussed elsewhere (Blackler and Brown, 1986) and here we shall concentrate solely upon the evaluation issue. Three aspects of the results are relevant: evaluative strategies for the prior justification for the purchase of technology, strategies for post event evaluation, and strategies for the evaluation of a specific form of the technology (CADCAM).

3.2 Prior Justification

There was considerable emphasis upon prior justification. Apart from some casual one-off purchasing of stand-alone personal computers in some larger companies, respondents stressed the necessity for proposals for technology purchase which were realistic in the particular organizational context. In a great majority of cases, what counted as realistic was a cost subs-

titution approach utilizing cost benefit techniques to justify the
purchase over a relatively short time period. The assumptions
behind the approach have been neatly summarized by Strassman
(1985):

> The most frequently used methods for evalua-
> ting the effects of information technology
> investments are characterized by the attitude
> that work does not change. The purpose of the
> investment is to increase output. As a
> consequence a smaller number of workers will
> be needed to perform existing functions. In
> addition the purchase of new machines is
> justified by the argument that no additional
> personnel need be hired [p.114].

However, within this general perspective certain sectorial differences were noted. In manufacturing, the demand for cost substitution type approaches was more often emphasized to us than in
office applications. For example, interviewees suggested that
expenditure on production and cost control equipment was justifiable over approximately two years, CAD in three or four, and
robotics over eight to ten years. In office applications, we did
hear of tight controls on cost reductions in certain areas where
studies of clerical work are used (especially in banking and
retailing). Additionally, staff savings are sometimes promised in
organizations when word processing systems are being considered.
But the relative cheapness of many new office technologies seems
to ease the need for cost benefit justification in many instances,
while advanced management information systems were seen as
notoriously difficult to justify in short term cost reduction
terms. Several respondents noted that CADMAT systems, and some
CADCAM systems, were increasingly being recognised as essential
while flexible manufacturing systems (FMS) can be impossible to
cost justify as the pay-back period may be as long as ten to
fifteen years. It seems that the new technologies are often
initially introduced with cost savings in mind. The search for
better organization, performance and services follows later.
Several of the interviewees referred to an initial period of fami-
liarization with the new technologies in their organizations
(through, for example, "stand alone" PCs) which can be followed by
broader work changes as more sophisticated systems are tried
(e.g., integrated work stations).

Some of the people surveyed were highly critical of the emphasis
that they felt is placed on prior justification through short term
cost benefit calculations. It was argued that, in many instances,
the principal benefits of the new technologies lie in the "value
added" benefits they can provide or in the novel business opportunities that they can facilitate. While it was emphasized to us
that good task/systems analysis is necessary for the optimum use
of the new systems, the mere automation of existing practices can
amount to a misuse of the technology.

In this vein, certain of the interviewees argued that the technologies require "an act of faith," "vision," or a "guiding philosophy" for their justification. A supplier of office equipment
even argued that "while our customers often do try to cost justify
their plans, this is always artificial, a facade." Indeed a
feature of some of the accounts of the introduction of new work
systems that we heard about were references to the "political"
tactics that their proponents adopted to overcome the restraining

pressures that an emphasis on short term cost can provide.
Examples included accounts of exaggerated claims that:

o   substantial manpower savings would result from the new
    systems

o   orders had already been lost because the proposed new
    system is not already in place

o   competitors already have the equipment

o   a substantially increased exchange of information across
    the organization is becoming a business necessity

As a general rule, if there is any chance of justifying the new
systems in a conventional way, this tends to be attempted.
Sometimes this may involve proponents "quantifying" the intangible
benefits (see Gerwin, 1984). Only where this is not feasible does
it seem that value added/organizational benefits tend to be
highlighted.
The results here confirm the point made by Blumberg and Gerwin
(1981) when they noted

> managers do not have the expertise to second
> guess the judgments of technical experts when
> evaluating whether or not to purchase equip-
> ment. Consequently, they tend to employ
> mainly financial criteria in judging requests.

3.3 Post-Implementation Evaluation

In contrast with the effort put into the justification to purchase, post-event evaluation seems to be much more poorly developed. Indeed, apart from certain government funded demonstration
projects, examples of attempts to undertake systematic post-event
evaluation were difficult to find. In terms of the four types of
evaluation noted earlier, conclusions were:

(a)   If systematic post-implementation is undertaken at all, it is
      likely to be concerned with cost benefit analysis, excepting
      technical assessments. Cost benefit evaluation may occur,
      for example, if staff losses have been involved.

(b)   "Value added" evaluation is often recognized as important by
      the people involved, although its systematic assessment
      appears uncommon.

(c)   Some attempts to gauge the ergonomic acceptability of
      equipment and user reactions to software were reported but,
      excepting these, psychological and organizational consequ-
      ences of the new equipment are rarely assessed systematic-
      ally.

(d)   No examples were reported where a prime concern of systematic
      evaluation has been the manner in which the new systems have
      been designed and introduced.

Various reasons for the general lack of concern with evaluation
were suggested. Concerning the ease with which evaluation may be
effectively done, comments included:

o   you usually cannot get the right sort of information
    from the accountants

o   what you want to achieve, i.e., preferred end states,
    are difficult to specify; in reality you have a moving
    target

o   separating out the effects of the new systems can be
    very difficult to do; there are invariably multiple
    causes for important developments

However, the technical difficulties of evaluation are not the main
issue.   Common explanations of why post-implementation evaluation
commands so little attention were:

o   if the system works O.K. then that is enough

o   in this organization there is a lack of any need to
    demonstrate success

o   reward systems are not geared to evaluation

o   top management are not interested; you cannot get them
    to value indirect benefits

o   resources were not made available for evaluation

o   senior people appear to think that evaluating pilot
    studies is enough

o   people are not used to the idea of audits of user accep-
    tability

o   there is always the danger that evaluation may show a
    non-cost effective result

o   after the decision to invest cognitive dissonance sets
    in and people do not want doubt cast over the wisdom of
    the action taken

o   it can take a long time to get a system working, by
    which time new issues and problems have come to demand
    attention

o   there can be an element of careerism with the new
    systems; the original driving personality behind the
    innovation may move on

These results strongly suggest that evaluation fulfills a number
of overt and covert functions in organizational life.   Many
conventional accounts of evaluation stress the benefits that can
result from proper practices, such as aiding future decisions,
providing learning through feedback, or complementing the inevi-
table subjective judgments of organizational members (Peccei and
Guest, 1984).   Yet the reasons given above for the failure to
evaluate point to the existence of both structural blockages and
the contrary personal purposes of key individuals.   It appears
that the organizational context is the most important determinant
of actual practice.

3.4 The Case of Computer Aided Design and Manufacture (CADCAM)

CADCAM is selected as an example of the technology to illustrate some specific issues in evaluation concerned with the balance of short and long term benefits and the importance of the organizational context in which the technology is used. Other examples could be used to the same effect (in particular, advanced management information systems).

The impacts of the CADCAM systems on organizations are many and varied. There are problems to solve because the technical integration between CAD and CAM is very difficult to achieve at present (see Primrose, et al., 1984). But over and above the technical issues there is the question of how to develop the organizational integration between design and manufacture. Respondents pointed out that existing practice was often poor with design engineers utilizing as their main criteria performance and reliability as well as making inappropriate assumptions about manufacturing processes, whereas production engineers emphasize criteria of costs and timing and have to accept designs that are sub-optimal in manufacturing terms. Added to this is a status differentiation in some companies which strongly favors the designers. Wolfe (1985) has noted that "engineering designs the product and then throws the drawings over the wall for manufacturing to make the product."

However unsatisfactory this state of affairs might appear, especially as a basis for automation with the attendant formalization of the dysfunctional relationship between design and manufacture, such considerations are seldom relevant to current evaluation practice. Rather, short term labor saving benefits are sought and found. Arnold and Senker (1982) note that saving on labor was the justification in 25 out of the 34 establishments where cost justification was attempted. Kaplinsky (1984), reviewing a number of studies, showed that, on average, there was a three-fold increase in productivity for CAD and that a further justification for some firms was that the technology had been an essential rather than just an optimizing tool for certain applications.

While cost benefit analysis based on labor savings can be used to partially justify this technology, almost all researchers in this area and many of the people who participated in the survey stressed that the benefits of CADCAM lie in long term downstream benefits. Better products, less wastage, more satisfied customers, and better delivery performance are all probable consequences of proper application. Such advantages are strategic, essential in all probability to medium and long term development of the organization. Yet to obtain these benefits it will be necessary to examine and modify the context (at the very least the relationships between departments) in which the technology is placed. It follows from this that evaluation should include the relevant contextual developments as well as setting the predicted medium and long term benefits within the strategic decision making of the organization. However, current practice remains orientated to the short term cost reduction approach. Primrose, et al. (1984), accept the limitations of such an approach and go on to specify a 45 item check list, many of which are impossible to quantify. This only has advantage if placed within the broader context of strategic decision making. The general point here is that, for certain advanced applications of the technology, the full material and social benefits depend upon the context and strategy of implementation. Specific effects are not determined by the nature of the technology. As Ettlie (1984) has concluded in reviewing the results of manufacturing innovations, the most important predictor of utilization success is likely to be the implementation process. Evaluation must therefore focus on the evolution of that process and upon the significance in strategic terms of the longer term downstream unquantifiable benefits.

The final and most general conclusion from this research is that current British evaluative practices indicate the severe limitations of the rhetoric of technological determinism, since the effects of the technologies are various and dependent upon organizational context for all but the most simple applications. This highlights the need for the development and use of evaluation practices which complement a more strategic, incremental, pluralist and participative approach to innovation and implementation (see Blackler and Brown, 1986).

4. THE THEORY AND PRACTICE OF EVALUATION

The research summarized here has implications for the analysis of the current state of evaluation offered by Legge (1984) and others. It was noted earlier that Legge conceives of evaluation research as a professional activity carried out by academics and consultants. Although in our research we found that the most sophisticated attempts at evaluation often emerged from such sources (i.e., the Economic Intelligence Unit evaluation of the Department of Trade and Industry projects, or CCTA's 1984 package), the vast bulk of evaluation and justification was carried out by non-specialized management. Thus the majority of the evaluation literature focuses upon the problems of "expert" evaluators from a prescriptive perspective rather than upon the actual evaluation practices adopted by non-specialists.

4.1 The Crisis of Method

For Legge, the battle lines drawn between the positivistic and interpretative evaluators are unresolved and troublesome. Our results indicate that there is indeed a crisis of method, but it is largely focused on the nature of cost benefit analysis (CBA) and its inadequacy as applied to information technologies. Current practices draw heavily upon this set of techniques, to the exclusion of nearly everything else, at both the pre- and post-implementation phases. Borovitz and Neumann (1979), Input (1983), and Huany and Ghandfovoush (1984) all advocate the use of the technique to evaluate the new technologies. To account for this state of affairs, we have concluded that two factors are central. Anglo Saxon financial management techniques lay heavy emphasis upon cost audit and return on investment techniques. Armstrong (1985) has provided a valuable historical analysis of why this is so, citing the development of British industrial organization and the post-War impact of American financial management techniques as crucial. Senker (1984) pointed to the prevalence of discounted cash flow methods which, in combination with a profit center control system, leads to managers seeking short term profit performance (see also Sheridan, 1985). Mitroff (1984) utilizes quotations from several heads of large corporations in the United States to emphasize the same trend. A second major influence here is the "world views" and practices of systems designers. Floyd (1985) has shown how complexity is tackled by fragmentation and simplification in a process strongly reminiscent of Taylorism. Long term unquantifiable benefits are of little relevance in such a perspective with its concern for formal specifications and logical consequences. While there is reason to believe that there is some realization among British management that information technologies will have long term consequences for the future of their organizations and that CBA is not helpful in planning that future, in the absence of alternative economic methodologies there is a strong tendency to relapse into the familiar. A more rational response might be to recognize the limitations of economic evaluations for the development of strategy formulations such as gaining a competitive edge and seek to evaluate along a range of dimensions relevant to broader strategic considerations.

It should also be noted here that while the research reported here has indicated the limitations of CBA to the evaluation of information technologies, several authors have pointed to the inadequacy of the technique in more general terms. Copp (1985) examined the underlying rationale, including the Hicks-Kaldor choice rule, from an economic and philosophical perspective and found it seriously wanting. Jameson (1981) examined the effects of the use of the technique in the United States Agency for International Development and noted that there was a considerable gap between theory and practice in CBA, a gap he sees as based upon the use of arbitrary procedures, organizational obstacles and lack of appropriate resources. Both Dean (1968) and Twiss (1982) studied the use of CBA in research and development project selection and concluded that analysis was impeded by a severely restricted use of appropriate criteria.

There are good reasons then to doubt the general appropriateness of CBA in organizational terms as well as its specific application to information technology. In relation to information technology, CBA fails because it is partial and incomplete and cannot deal with non-quantifiable and indirect aspects of the new technologies, which is often where the main benefits lie (see Hirschorn and Farquhar, 1985; Nahapiet, 1984). In addition, CBA is likely to focus upon specific benefits of particular interest to managerial groupings. Profit, return on investment, or cost reduction are not likely to be the main concerns of trade union groupings, supervisors, or other groups inevitably involved in implementation. As Keene (1981) has shown, such groups faced with a change designed to achieve benefits in others' interests are likely to resist, either by adopting a variety of counter-implementation strategies or with apathy and lack of involvement. Evaluation methods which fail to reflect the plurality of interests in an organization are thus likely to be counterproductive. It can be concluded therefore that the crisis of method in practice centers upon the uses and abuses of cost benefit analysis.

4.2 The Crisis in Utilization

For Legge as well as Rossi, et al. (1979), Patton (1978), and others, the failure of much evaluation research to influence policy making is of central concern. Various remedies are proposed to make evaluation more responsive to policy making needs, although Patton sees the danger that evaluation is often only effective when it supports what policy makers already believe. The results summarized here highlight a different aspect of the links between evaluation and policy. A general tendency to treat evaluation in isolation seemed evident; it is only rarely

related to corporate policy. There is a lack of strategy for
utilizing the technologies, with purchasers often just looking for
"a better mousetrap." Thus, even where evaluation was conducted,
the results were not utilized to aid long term organizational
objectives.

There were, however, a few exceptions to this. A large retailing
organization utilizing office automation justified its investment
in terms of the likely long term competitive position in the
industry. Given a coherent corporate strategy, this company
discovered that cost benefit analysis did yield information of
some value, but it should be pointed out that in this application
end user attitudes were not central to success. Another example
in manufacturing involved a shift from conventionally arranged
design and manufacture towards a system built around a small
central staff team supported by machine operators employed on a
contract basis. Such examples were rare and the general picture
strongly supported in the United States by Strassman (1985) is of
failure to link use and evaluation of new technologies to corporate strategy.

A second aspect of the utilization of findings concerns the issue
of congruency between styles of evaluation and organizational
decision making. Rossi (1981) and others have argued that, if
congruence is absent, evaluation will be ignored, unresourced, or
stillborn. In the earlier discussion of CADCAM, it was suggested
that effects are likely to be long term, downstream, indirect and
non-quantifiable. Furthermore, there is good reason to think that
changes will occur in an evolutionary fashion, in such a manner
that it is not possible to initially specify the desired end
state. Hall, et al. (1975), have shown how educational programs
are seldom implemented as their designers intend and, after
several years, the innovation is of a form that was not originally
intended by the designers. In a study of video conferencing,
Rice, et al. (1984), make a similar point showing how, over time,
user attitudes change and develop and that from an organizational
viewpoint the impacts and benefits will also evolve. One of the
crucial roles for evaluation is process orientated, aiming to
identify appropriate changes and to facilitate the desired
evolution. Difficult though it may be to achieve, we conclude
with Legge (1984) that effective evaluation must be congruent both
with a viable model of how technology will impact on the organization and with an appropriate incremental decision making procedure
(see Blackler and Brown, 1986, for more on this).

4.3   The Crisis of Accreditation

For Legge there are systematic pressures in conventional evaluation practice which tend to give a conservative bias. The use of
experimental design with their neglect of contextual factors, the
fact that it is the instigators rather than the receivers of
change who act as the evaluators' client, and the desire to be
practical or effective are all relevant factors. As a result of
our research two further observations on this dilemma can be
offered.

First, the preferred method of evaluation, cost benefit analysis,
emphasizes cost reduction and substitution, top down authoritarian
design and implementation procedures with a bias against human
social and organizational factors. It is, therefore, congruent
with the interests of those in control. As Noble puts it:

While the new technologies and theories, formally deterministic and intrinsically compelling, compounded the
traditional compulsions and enthusiasms of the scientific community, they reflected also the needs of those in
command, adding immeasurably to their power to control.

Hoos (1985) suggests that with economic rationality, and hence CBA
at its core, systems methodology has served as "the unchallenged
decision making apparatus for more than a quarter of a century."
She characterizes this approach as intolerant of unquantified
variables, excluding long run considerations, biased against
social factors, driven by technical optimism, and with an ethic
of the marketplace. Cost benefit analysis is the preferred
technique and the inherent status quo orientation on this analysis
is clear to see.

But there is a second aspect to this question. It was suggested
earlier that, in the case of management information systems and
CADCAM, effective use of the technology to secure maximum material
(and other) gains entails consideration of the expectations of
different interest groups apart from top management. Design
implementation and evaluation under these circumstances must be
incremental and participative and process orientated. While the
outcome of such a process would certainly be "rationally efficient" and thus supportive of the status quo in one sense, the
democratization and competence raising aspects of such a process
would not be. This point is similar to the approach developed in
organizational change in Scandinavia in the late 1970s, where
competence raising and "learning to learn" emerged as a prime
objective in change programs (see Elden, 1983). There is no
necessary connection between evaluation and conservatism, but
certain methodological procedures serve to maintain such a connection.

5. CONCLUSIONS

Evaluation research has become distanced from actual evaluation
practice, at least in the case of the new information technologies. The concerns of Legge and others are not mirrored by
managers and policy makers. Instead a different set of issues,
not surprisingly rather more pragmatic and geared to the particular questions raised by trying to utilize information technologies, predominate. The following suggestions are offered to
guide the future practice of evaluation and the theory of evaluation research.

(1) Evaluators, social scientists and others should vociferously
     criticize the rhetoric of technological determinism, since it
     clearly implies that once the technologies are in place,
     benefits will automatically accrue. This perspective renders
     evaluation largely irrelevant.

(2) At present, in British organizations, there is a low level of
     awareness among key professional groups of the social and
     organizational consequences of the use of the new techno-
     logies. As a result, important choices are presently being
     made by default.

(3) Rather than concentrate upon bringing evaluation research up
     to scratch, effort should be directed at how best to in-
     fluence the bulk of evaluators, namely non-professional

management. Compelling arguments should be developed to demonstrate how cost benefit approaches will divert attention away from indirect and long term benefits. It is these that are characteristic of many applications of the technology.

(4) There is a pressing need to develop an alternative set of method guidelines which concentrate upon the value added and process impacts on the organization. The most significant and impressive development to date has been Strassman's (1985) work on effectiveness measurement and value added productivity measurement in relation to office automation.

(5) Evaluation procedures and outcomes should be linked to broader corporate policy and to the processes that are necessary for successful innovation. This would necessitate analysis of the conditions under which full benefits are likely to be realized and the development of evaluation procedures to gauge whether these conditions are increment-ally achieved.

(6) It should be recognised that post evaluation exercises require significant resources and may themselves be subject to a variety of counter-implementation strategies if any interest groups are excluded. All obstacles to proper evaluation should be set against the likely value of feedback to future organizational decision making.

REFERENCES

Armstrong, P., "Accountacy in British Wartime Controls of Industry and the Progress of the Profession in Industrial Management Hierarchies," paper presented at the Aston University/UMIST International Conference on the Labour Process, Manchester, England, March 1985.

Arnond, E., and Senker, P., "Designing the Future: The Implica-tions of CAD Interactive Graphics for Employment and Skills in the British Engineering Industry," *E.I.T.B.* occasional paper No. 9, 1982.

Bell, C., "The SSRC Restructured," in Bell, C., and Roberts, H. (eds.), *Social Researching,* R.K.P., London, 1984.

Ben David, J., and Collins, R., "Social Factors in the Origins of a New Science: The Case of Psychology," *A.S.R.,* Vol. 31, 1966.

Bhattacharya, S. K., *Penetration and Utilization of NC/CNC Machine Tools in British Industry,* University of Birmingham, Depart-ment of Engineering Production, Birmingham, England, 1976.

Blackler, F., and Brown, C., "Alternative Models to Guide the Design and Implementation of the New Information Technologies into Work Organisations," *Journal of Occupational Psychology,* Vol. 59, 1986, pp. 287-313.

Blackler, F., and Brown, C., "Evaluation and the Impact of Information Technologies on People in Organisations," *Human Relations,* Vol. 38, No. 3, 1985, pp. 213-231.

Blackler, F., and Brown, C., "Qualitative Research and Paradigms of Practice," *Journal of Management Studies*, Vol. 20, No. 3, 1983, pp. 349-366.

Blumberg, M., and Gerwin, D., *Coping with Advanced Manufacturing Technology*, International Institute for Management/Labour Policy, Berlin, 1981.

Boakes, R., *From Darwin to Behaviourism*, C.U.P., London, 1984.

Borowitz, I., and Neumann, S., *Computer Systems Performance and Evaluation*, Lexington Books, Lexington, Massachusetts, 1984.

Buchanan, D., and Boddy, D., *Organizations in the Computer Age*, Gower, Aldershot, England, 1982.

Butera, F., and Thurman, J. E. (eds.), *Automation and Work Design*, North Holland, Amsterdam, 1984.

Central Computer and Telecommunications Agency, *Method for Evaluating the Impact of New Office Technology Systems*, H.M.S.O., London, 1984.

Copp, D., "Morality, Reason and Management Science: The Rationale of Cost-Benefit Analysis," *Social Philosophy and Policy*, Vol. 2, No. 2, 1985, pp. 128=-35.

Dean, B. V., "Evaluating, Selecting and Controlling R and D Projects," *Research Study 89*, American Management Association, Inc., 1968.

Elden, M., "Three Generations of Work Democracy Experiments in Norway," in Cooper, C., and Mumford, E. (eds.), *The Quality of Working Life in Western and Eastern Europe*, Associated Books, London, 1979.

Ettlie, J. E., "Implementation Strategy for Manufacturing Innovations," in Warner, M. (ed.), *Microprocessors, Manpower and Society*, Gower, Aldershot, England, 1984.

Floyd, C., "Towards a Paradigm Change in Software Engineering," paper presented at the Conference on Development and Use of Computer-Based Systems and Tools, Aarhus, Denmark, August, 1985.

Gerwin, D., "Innovation, Microelectronics and Manufacturing Innovations," in Warner, M. (ed.), *Microprocessors, Manpower and Society*, Gower, Aldershot, England, 1984.

Gottfredson, D., "A Theory-Ridden Approach to Program Evaluation," *American Psychologist*, Vol. 39, No. 10, 1984, pp. 1101-1112.

Gowler, D., and Legge, K., "The Democratisation of Evaluation Research," *Personnel Review*, Vol. 13, No. 3, 1984, pp. 3-13.

Hall, G. E., Loucks, S. F., Rutherford, W. L., and Newlove, B. W., "Levels of Use of Innovation: A Framework for Analyzing Innovation Adoption," *Journal of Teacher Education*, Vol. 26, No. 11, 1975, pp. 52-56.

Hirschorn, L., and Farquhar, K., "Productivity, Technology and the Decline of the Autonomous Professional," *Office: Technology and People*, Vol. 2, 1985, pp. 245-265.

Hoos, I. R., "Backward Through the Looking Glass," *Technological Forecasting and Social Change*, Vol. 28, 1985, pp. 287-295.

Huany, P., and Ghandfovoush, P., "Procedures Given for Evaluating: Selecting Robots," *Industrial Engineering*, April 1984, pp. 44-48.

Input, *Methods of Cost/Benefit Analysis for Office Systems*, Input, New York, 1983.

Jameson, K. P., "Implementing Benefit-Cost Analysis: Theory Meets Reality," *Journal of Management Studies*, Vol. 18, No. 4, 1981, pp. 411-422.

Johnston, J. (ed.), *Evaluating the New Information Technologies*, Jossey-Bass, San Francisco, 1984.

Joyce, L., "Developments in Evaluation Research," *Journal of Occupational Behaviour*, Vol. 1, 1980, pp. 181-190.

Kaplinsky, R., *Automation: The Technology and Society*, Longman, Harlow, England, 1984.

Keene, P., "Information Systems and Organizational Change," *Social Impacts of Computing*, Vol. 24, No. 1, 1981, pp. 24-33.

Legge, K., *Evaluating Planned Organisational Change*, Academic Press, London, 1984.

Leontieff, W. W., "The Distribution of Work and Income," *Scientific American*, September 1982, pp. 100-112.

Mandell, M. B., "The Design and Selection of Evaluation Studies," *Knowledge: Creation, Diffusion, Utilization*, Vol. 5, No. 4, 1984, pp. 419-445.

Mitroff, I., "Two Fables for Those Who Believe in Rationality," *Technological Forecasting and Social Change*, Vol. 28, 1985, pp. 195-202.

Nahapiet, J. E., "Assessing Costs and Benefits in Systems Design and Selection," in Otway, H. J., and Peltu, M. (eds.), *The Managerial Challenge of New Office Technology*, Frances Pinter, London, 1984.

Nasbeth, L., and Ray, G. F., *The Diffusion of New Industrial Processes*, C.U.P., London, 1974.

Noble, D., *Forces of Production*, Knopf, New York, 1984.

Patton, M. Q., *Utilization-Focus Evaluation*, Sage Publications, Beverly Hills, California, 1978.

Peccei, R., and Guest, D., "Evaluating the Introduction of New Technology: The Case of Word-Processors in British Rail," in Warner, M. (ed.), *Microprocessors, Manpower and Society*, Gower, Aldershot, England, 1984.

Primrose, P. L., Creamer, G. D., and Leonard, R., "Identifying and Quantifying the 'Company Wide' Benefits of CAD within the Structure of a Comprehensive Investment Program," in Rhodes, E., and Wield, D. (eds.), *Implementing New Technologies*, Basil Blackwell, Oxford, 1985.

Putnam, G. P., "Why More NC Isn't Being Used," *Machine and Tool Blue Book*, 1978, pp. 98-107.

Rice, R. E., and Associates, *The New Media: Communication Research and Technology*, Sage Publications, Beverly Hills, California, 1979.

Rossi, P. H., Freeman, H. E., and Wright, S. R., *Evaluation: A Systematic Study*, Sage Publications, Beverly Hills, California, 1979.

Senker, P., "Implications of CAD/CAM for Management," *OMEGA*, Vol. 12, No. 3, 1984, pp. 225-234.

Sheridan, T., "Financial Management and Innovation: The Need for Change," from the Spring Convention of the Royal Aeronautical Society on The Effective Management of Technological Change, 1985.

Strassman, P. A., *Information Payoff*, Free Press, New York, 1985.

Twiss, B. K., *Managing Technological Innovation*, Longman, Harlow, England, 1980.

Weick, K. E., "Small Wins: Redefining the Scale of Social Problems," *American Psychologist*, Vol. 39, No. 1, 1984, pp. 40-49.

Weiss, C. H., "Where Politics and Evaluation Research Meet," *Evaluation*, Vol. 1, No. 1, 1973, pp. 37-43.

Wilkinson, B., *The Shopfloor Politics of New Technology*, H.E.B., London, 1983.

Wolfe, P. M., "Computer Aided Process Planning is the Link between CAD and CAM," *Industrial Engineer*, August 1985, pp. 72-77.

Wortmann, P. M., "Evaluation Research: A Methodological Perspective," *Annual Review of Psychology*, Vol. 34, 1983, pp. 223-260.

DISCUSSANT NOTE

On: THEORY AND PRACTICE IN EVALUATION: THE CASE
     OF THE NEW INFORMATION TECHNOLOGIES

By: Frank Blackler and Colin Brown

Discussant's comments by: Love BHABUTA

Systems Designers PLC
Camberley, Great Britain

1. INTRODUCTION

A brief account of the paper is presented with attention drawn to
the significant issues. This is followed by a commentary on the
implications and issues arising from the research findings of
Blackler and Brown, as well as the observations of other researchers engaged in evaluation studies.

The paper by Blackler and Brown offers a valuable contribution to
the debate on evaluation research. It achieves this by focusing
on:

o approaches to evaluation of information technology in Britain

o setting the practice within the context of the theory of
   evaluation

o examining the state of practice against the concerns and
   exhortations of researchers and evaluation specialists

The greater proportion of the paper is concerned with a descriptive analysis, with a small part addressing prescription. This
blend adds weight to the arguments presented and strengthens the
prescription.   The paper can be divided into three parts, as
follow:

o why undertake evaluation

o how can it be done and how it has been done

o what are the implications

2. RATIONALE FOR EVALUATION

The rationale for evaluation and evaluation research are treated
synonymously. Current interest in evaluation stems primarily from
two developments:

o pervasive use of IT in manufacturing and service industries
   as well as government services

o economic circumstances of recent years have led to increased focus on value for money in both public and private investments

Further, contrary to some institutional belief about the automatic benefits of IT, failures and doubtful analysis have necessitated evaluation.

3. THEORY AND PRACTICE OF EVALUATION

The strategy adopted by Blackler and Brown was to review candidate approaches to evaluation and then conduct a survey into the actual practice of evaluation in Britain. The survey strategy had to be modified because only a subset of the candidate approaches were used in practice.

The four approaches considered were:

o cost substitution: a comparison of relative costs of old systems versus new system

o value added: qualitative and quantitative comparisons of improved service or quality, increased flexibility

o organizational evaluation: impact on organizational structure, work organization, job design, user attitudes

o process evaluation: evaluate processes employed in affecting transition

The intention of locating case examples for these four approaches failed because formal evaluation is currently more commonplace than post-implementation justification. The favored approach is "cost substitution," with production equipment justifiable over two years, CAD in three to four years, and robotics over eight to ten years. Office applications and systems (e.g., word processing, electronic mail, work stations) are easier to justify owing to their relative cheapness. New technologies are introduced initially with regard to cost considerations only, with a search for better performance and service following only later. Value added analysis is attempted in cases where cost substitution cannot be justified.

In the main, however, despite the limitation of cost-benefit analysis, it remains the most utilized approach because

> managers do not have the expertise to second guess the judgments of technical experts....Consequently, they tend to employ mainly financial criteria in judging requests.

Post-implementation evaluation: in contrast to the above, systematic attempts at this kind of evaluation are rare. In the few cases where it has been attempted, the application of the four approaches is as follows:

o cost-benefit analysis most likely

o value-added analysis recognized as important but uncommon in practice o   organizational evaluation and user attitude analysis is rare

o   process evaluation -- none; no example found in any analysis
    focusing on the way/manner in which systems have been
    designed/introduced.

A number of political reasons are given for the unpopularity of
post-implementation evaluation. Two which summarize the arguments
are:

o   resources are not made available for evaluation

o   it can take a long time to get a system working, by which
    time new issues and problems have come to demand attention

The case of CAD/CAM was chosen as an example to illustrate some
specific issues in evaluation. It is a particularly interesting
case in that it highlights the limitations of cost-benefit
analysis and the need to appreciate the organizational context.
CAD/CAM systems pose two principle difficulties: (a) the technical integration between CAD and CAM, and (b) the organizational
integration between manufacture and design. The latter is of
relevance to evaluation because the utility of CAD/CAM systems
lies in the support they provide for the transition phases between
design and manufacture.

Participants in the survey, as well as researchers, stress that
the benefits of CAD/CAM lie in the long term -- in the likely
provision of better products, better delivery performance, reduced
operational costs. Yet, to obtain these benefits, it will be
necessary to modify the organizational arrangement (structure and
information exchange) within which the organizational impacts are
realized and view the benefits within the context of strategic
planning over a medium/long term. However, in current documented
practice, focus is on short term labor savings.

It is argued (though without any supporting evidence) that, for
certain advanced applications of technology, full material and
social benefits depend on the context of the strategy of implementation. The most important predictor of utilization success is
likely to be the implementation process.

General conclusions from the research are that the effects of
technologies are various and dependent on the organizational
context for all but the most simple applications. Therefore, some
general predictor or association of same technology impacts in
other organizations are meaningless.

5.   IMPLICATIONS AND CONSEQUENCES

The practice of evaluation and evaluation research are beset with
some serious challenges and problems. The greater proportion of
evaluation is done by non-specialists, yet the literature is
biased towards problems of "expert" evaluators. Further, prescription dominates with little account of actual practice of non-
specialists.

Cost-benefit analysis prevails as the method of evaluation because
managers rely upon it in the absence of alternative economic
methodologies. This is despite the realization that the method
cannot deal with the non-quantifiable and indirect aspects of new

technologies, where the main benefits lie. Also, non-management groups are less interested in the return-on-investment and more with the quality of working life. Therefore, methods which fail to reflect plurality of interest in an organization are likely to be counter-productive.

The results of evaluation are seldom used. Links between evaluation and corporate strategy are rare. Results are not utilized to aid the formulation of long term organizational objectives. (This is most probably due to the absence of organizational impact analysis in evaluation studies.) The situation is also compounded by the bias of policy makers in rejecting views and evidence which does not support their beliefs.

6. DILEMMAS AND PARADOXES

The preceding analysis and observations by Blackler and Brown are well researched and argued, so as to leave little room for challenge. Indeed, their conclusions and recommendations would carry the support of researcher and practitioner alike when they propose that:

o the concerns of the expert evaluators are not mirrored by policy makers

o awareness of social and organizational consequences is poor among key professional groups; important choices are made by default

o evaluation procedures and outcomes should be linked to broader corporate policy formulations and implementations

o there is a need to develop alternative method sets which focus upon value added and procedural aspects

o efforts should be made to influence the bulk of non-specialist evaluators rather than develop more sophisticated tools for the expert

To these recommendations, we can add accounts from other sources which highlight the division between "what out to be" and "what is."

In a survey conducted by Galliers (1986) during 1985/1986 on the "state-of-practice of strategy planning for IT," where the respondents were asked to rank factors they considered critical to successful IS planning, the following findings are of relevance to evaluation of IT:

o IS managers ranked "review of IS plans" at number 5, with the top four factors being the commitment and involvement of senior management

o IT strategy consultants ranked "review of IS plans" at number 7, after "outcome of ISP well supported by IS management" (ranked at 6)

This evidence comes from a population of 130 organizations including management consultancies. Despite this ranking, the number of respondents who undertook a formal review of the process and outcome of IS planning amounted to eleven percent; this figure drops to six percent if the respondents from consultancies are excluded.

The notable conclusions that can be drawn from this survey are that:

o   while the need to review (and therefore evaluate) the outcome of plans against actual practice is considered to be a significant issue, such evaluations are so uncommon as to be "hardly ever."

o   consultants (who are assumed to be more informed and inclined to formal evaluations) are in fact less disposed towards evaluation than are the "non-experts."

Thus far, from preaching and educating the "non-expert," there is an equal need to educate those experts engaged by organizations to advise on IT strategies.

The failure of organizations to undertake evaluation/assessment of the impact of existing (internal) IT strategies and the potential opportunities afforded by IT has led to a myopic vision on the part of policy makers.   Thus, the lack of adequate feedback from the effects of IT has resulted in most policy makers treating IT as a necessary "evil."

It needs to be spelled out that organizational learning and aware-ness require a link between "action" and "reflection."   Since not all actions are successful/purposeful, reflection serves the pur-pose of a "corrective mechanism."   Failure to reflect (i.e., evaluate/assess) leads to lack of understanding and appreciation.

The poor links between IT and business policy can be attributed to absence of organizational learning (gained through systematic reflection).

The importance of these observations is brought into focus by a survey and study undertaken by management consultants A. T. Kearney in the United Kingdom on behalf of the Department of Trade and Industry (United Kingdom government) and the Institute of Administrative Managers in 1984.   The survey involved 235 mana-gers, of whom 87 percent held general management positions.   The findings and conclusions of the study are:

o   The majority of senior management recognize IT as a strategic and operational opportunity which pro-vides competitive advantage in areas of reducing costs and improving customer service.   Yet, few companies have taken full advantage of IT and most fail to treat IT as a normal investment.   Few com-panies align their business IT strategies and most relegate IT to providing a reactive service for middle management.

o   The greatest barrier to the further use of IT in industry and commerce is management itself.

o   Although there is a genuine and clear need for cost-justification techniques and tools, the main need is to gain the interest and commitment of management to make use of IT within the business. [Kearney, 1984]

Are the exhortations of Blackler and Brown practical, or are those of Kling (the advocacy that IS assessment should be done from the perspective of those impacted by technology, rather than the powerful stakeholders)? The question is whether policy makers should be made to realize the consequences of their actions and inaction.

There are two main barriers to this laudable recommendation. First, accessibility to appropriate levels of management, who are likely to be supportive of the aims of such research and investigations. Policy makers are ill-disposed towards organizational sociologists. As Haga (1976) points out,

> corporate managers make rather poor partners for sociological research. Managers at the top invariably know the location of problems in their organizations. The problems are "down there" among the little people in an organization. Top managers are predictably hesitant to concede that the organization's problems stem from their own behavior or the way they have structured work relationships.

Assuming that this hurdle can be overcome, the next major barrier lies in obtaining acceptance of proposals/findings. It has already been reported that "findings which challenge the beliefs of policy makers will be ignored." This failure to accept data which challenges beliefs can be interpreted in terms of "organizational and individual morale."

Evidence which suggests that previous policies and decisions were at fault can have the effect of undermining the morale of the policy makers and those affected by the policies. This in turn makes management difficult. Thus, when findings threaten to undermine the wisdom and judgment of decision makers, it is logical to refute or ignore them.

As Gambling (1977) argues,

> The most desirable sort of accounts seem to have the facility of appearing dead right when the model works, but infinitely capable of producing other answers under pressure!

> Few people are ready to admit Napoleonic convictions about what ought to be done, but prefer to present some formal, preferably quantified model with highly supportive data. This is not necessarily irrational behavior, to the extent that those of us who are not Napoleons are frequently called upon to justify our decisions before and after the event. The irrational element enters here: we are most unscientific in our approach to these data. When they favor our cause we accept them as deterministic, but when they do not, we not only forcibly draw attention to their unreliable nature and origins, but extract contrary readings from the same sources and argue for their deterministic validity.

Are the concerns with methodological rigor and epistemological validity misplaced, given the gulf between theory and practice?

ould management scientists instead concern themselves with only
the pragmatic dimension, where prescription is realized in
practice?

Theory and prescription which do not bear upon practice have an
important role to serve for the practitioner. They serve as
symbolic constructs which enable practitioners to interpret the
significance of their own actions and those of others to make
sense out of their practical experience (Astley, 1984).

We conclude that while evaluation research and practice is
purposeful when it results in appropriate action, it is also
worthwhile when it has no apparent impact on direct practice, for
it serves as a normative model.

REFERENCES

Astley, W. G., "Subjectivity, Sophistry, and Symbolism in Management Science," *Journal of Management Studies*, Vol. 21, No. 3,
July 1984, pp. 259-272.

Galliers, R., "Information Systems Planning in the UK: The State-
of-the-Art," Working Paper, London School of Economics and
Political Science, 1986.

Gambling, G., "Magic, Accounting and Morale," *Accounting, Organizations and Society*, Vol. 2, No. 2, 1977.

Haga, W. J., "One Sociologist's Reply to Wieland's Review Essay,"
Academy of Management Review, January 1977.

Kearney, A. T., Management Consultants, "The Barriers and Opportunities of Information Technology: A Management Perspective," London, 1984.

Citizen Benefits from Information Systems
K. Lange and F. Sippel

"If tax and insurance premiums have not been paid,
the motor vehicle will be withdrawn from traffic."

INFORMATION SYSTEMS ASSESSMENT
N. Bjørn-Andersen, G.B. Davis (Editors)
Elsevier Science Publishers B.V. (North-Holland)
© IFIP, 1988

CITIZEN BENEFITS FROM INFORMATION SYSTEMS

Klaus LANGE
Frank SIPPEL

Institute for Applied Information Technology
Gesellschaft für Mathematik und Datenverarbeitung mbH
P.O.Box 1240
D-5205 Sankt Augustin 1

A case study on the introduction of an information system in a motor vehicle registration office showed that the quality of service offered to citizens increased with computerization. This result contradicts the state-of-the-art in our research field: computer use in public administration is said not to be citizen orientated and of no benefit to citizens. In order to verify our case study results, we carried out a national evaluation survey among all registration offices in the Federal Republic of Germany.

The survey showed that computerized offices have a higher quality of service than non-computerized ones. We also found a high variance in the quality of service among computerized offices which could not be explained by the quantity of resources, i.e., manpower, technical equipment, and office space. Citizen orientation and professionalism of the management seem to explain the high variance in the quality of service.

When information systems are introduced, opportunities arise to alter the work process. We found that most of the managers did not use these opportunities to significantly increase the quality of service. Thus, they missed a chance for using modern information technology as a vehicle for citizen oriented administrative reforms.

1. CASE STUDY, SO WHAT?

It is popularly believed that the use of information systems in public administration will alienate the administration from the public (Lange, 1983). Scientific research seems to support this belief:

o Case studies on public administration in the Federal Republic of Germany show that the use of information technology is more to the citizens' disadvantage than benefit (Brinckmann, 1981; Lenk, 1979).

o A cross-national study with eight European countries shows that electronic technology has had only marginal effects on the quality or kind of service (Blennerhasset, 1985).

o   The very comprehensive study on computerization of local
    government, the URBIS study conducted in 1975, concluded that
    computing is mainly oriented towards governmental efficiency
    and not towards service quality (Danzinger, 1982).

We conducted a case study on the development and introduction of
an information system in a motor vehicle registration office (see
description below) to investigate the impact of this innovation on
the quality of service. In intensive talks and discussions with
developers and organizers of the project, as well as with the
managers and the clerks of the office, we traced the development
and implementation history. Our research showed that the development of the information system was orientated towards citizen
interests and that the quality of service increased with the
implementation of the system. Our research also showed that the
technological possibilities of the information system were
utilized only suboptimally for improving the quality of service.
Our respondents explained these suboptimalities as due to scarce
manpower, technical equipment, and office space. There were hints
that these suboptimalities were not only based on scarce material
resources but also on the professionalism and citizen-orientation
of the office managers. They would not or could not modify the
work process such that the features of the information system
produced a high quality of service.

The results of our case study were dissatisfying in two respects:

o   We felt unsure whether we could generalize our result (that
    information system use improves the quality of service) to
    all computerized motor vehicle registration offices.

o   We were unsure about the relationships of material resources
    to the production of a high quality of service.

With a single case study, we could neither analyze the explanatory
power of scarce resources nor explain the contradiction between
our findings and the general state-of-the-art. In recognition of
the controversy about the value of case studies and qualitative
data (Miles, 1979; Yin, 1981), we extended our study by a representative survey with quantitative data. In this research, case
studies and surveys or quantitative and qualitative data are not
mutually exclusive but are complementary (Miles and Hubermann,
1984).

Thanks to the support of a central authority (Federal Office for
Motor Traffic at Flensburg), we were able to conduct a postal
survey among all of the motor vehicle registration offices in the
Federal Republic of Germany. The office managers answered a
questionnaire with 85 questions. About 80 percent of the mailed
questionnaires were returned by the beginning of 1985. We could
not find systematic differences between respondents and non-
respondents with regard to variables such as county, business
volume, and use of computers. Therefore, our data appear to be
representative. We were able to compare 83 registration offices
using a computerized information system with 305 offices without
computer automation.

2.   COMPUTER USE IN MOTOR VEHICLE REGISTRATION OFFICES

A description of the functional scope of the motor vehicle
registration offices and the history of computerization in this

area provides a background for understanding the results of the study.

In the Federal Republic of Germany, motor vehicles must be registered by motor vehicle registration offices. For registration purposes, citizens must submit an application and present proof that they have contracted for liability insurance. The citizen is assigned a registration number for the licence plates. After having the plates made and having paid a handling fee, the citizen receives registration papers and the licence plates. The motor vehicle registration office informs the insurance company concerned, the tax office, and the Federal Office for Motor Traffic about the registration. If tax and insurance premiums have not been paid, the motor vehicle will be withdrawn from traffic.

In the Federal Republic of Germany, there are about 480 registration offices, with nearly one out of three currently using an information system. The introduction of information systems in registration offices began in the early 1970s when the number of registrations rapidly increased. The number of installations increased significantly by the late 1970s when systems became available on the hardware of the market leader. Implementations accelerated again when distributed data processing (DDP) became available. Until DDP, the registration offices had been totally dependent on the central computer of a computing center. The introduction of DDP enabled the registration offices to handle all business with the citizens by means of a subsystem installed in the office; data updating and data communication with other authorities and organizations was carried out in a so-called night circuit on a host computer. Recently an information system has been introduced which handles all tasks of a registration office on a stand-alone system installed in the office. Currently, eight different information systems are used in the Federal Republic of Germany. Three of these systems, developed for the hardware of the same manufacturer, share more than 80 percent of the market. Apart from their basic concepts (centralized, partly independent, stand-alone), the systems differ primarily by the amount of printer facilities provided. All systems will be upgraded, especially with respect to paperless data exchange with other organizations, word processing, and handling of rare events.

Computerization increased the efficiency of registration offices considerably by:

o   computerized completion of the registration papers,

o   independence of paper files in face-to-face contacts with the citizens, and

o   paperless data exchange with other authorities and organizations.

Computerization increased the flexibility of the offices with respect to the organization of the work process because, basically, any event can be handled at any terminal if a printer is available.

3. SERVICE DELIVERY IN MOTOR VEHICLE REGISTRATION OFFICES

Dealing with authorities implies many problems for the citizens, i.e., long distances, long and uncomfortable waits, feeling strange in the office building, and confusion about how to complete the forms. Based on the information furnished in the returned questionnaires, we divided the registration offices into three groups with a low, average, and high quality of service.

Offices with a high quality of service have the following features:

o   short periods of waiting and handling
o   long open hours
o   open hours in the afternoon
o   large and comfortable waiting areas
o   completion of application forms by means of a printer

A cross-tabulation of the quality of service with the fact of being or not being computerized is shown in Figure 1.

We recognize a significant correlation: Computerized registration offices offer a high quality of service more frequently than non-computerized ones. Nevertheless, 12 percent of the non-computerized offices show a high quality of service and 19 percent of the computerized offices show a low quality of service.

The higher quality of service of the computerized registration offices cannot be explained solely by reduced waiting and handling periods and completion of application forms. There are also improvements induced indirectly by the use of technical equipment. The implementation of information systems was accompanied by the following changes:

o   29 percent of the registration offices extended the waiting zones

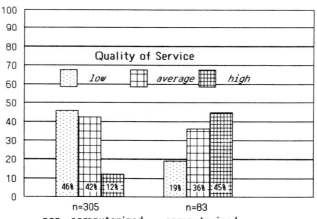

Figure 1. Information System Use and Quality of Service

o 47 percent made the waiting zones more comfortable
o 18 percent extended the open hours in the morning
o 27 percent introduced open hours in the afternoon

The results show that the implementation of an information system was used to improve the quality of service on dimensions which are relatively independent of the information system itself. The described improvements are, however, indirectly connected with the implementation; for example, the introduction of open hours in the afternoon has become possible through labor saving electronic data exchange with other authorities.

More surprising than the above results is the high variance in the quality of service among the computerized registration offices. Even when we controlled for the type of information system (centralized versus partly independent), we found clear differences in the quality of service.

4. EXPLANATORY POWER OF SCARCE RESOURCES

In our case study, the management of the office explained the suboptimal quality of service by references to scarce manpower, technical equipment, and office space apart from legal regulations on the state or federal level. If we regard service quality as a good produced with scarce resources, it seems logical that more resources allow a higher quality of service. In our single case study, we could not examine this relationship; in our representative study, we could.

We examined the explanatory power relative to service of the quantity of manpower, technical equipment, and office space. Therefore, we built different measures: we divided the number of cars which are registered at an office by the number of clerks, the number of terminals and printers, and the number of square meters of office space and cross-tabulated these measures with the quality of service.

4.1 Manpower

The surprisingly high variances in manpower employment (one clerk registers 5,000 to 10,000 motor vehicles) do not explain the variances in the quality of service. There are registration offices with subaverage manpower employment which rated very high with respect to service quality. A possible explanation is that inflexible allocation of labor often counteracts a possible positive effect of above-average manpower employment. This might be due to resistance on the side of the personnel, insufficient qualifications, and rigid pay schedules. This suggests that needed modifications of the work process have often been neglected. Damanpour and Evan (1984) describe a similar phenomenon in their theorem of "organizational lag."

4.2 Technical Equipment

The number of terminals installed in a registration office could positively correlate with its general and service-specific efficiency. Identical information systems show great differences in the amount of technical equipment installed: one terminal for one or two clerks, one printer for 10,000 or 20,000 registered motor vehicles. We were not able to discover a systematic relationship between the quantity of technical equipment and the quality of service. However, this can be explained by the fact that hardly any registration office uses the facilities provided by technology for service optimization, especially in application form printing and word processing. Labor intensive control procedures are continued even though automatic error checks are provided. A high degree of division of labor is maintained though the information systems would allow a complete delivery of service by a single clerk. All in all, the flexible utilization of the technology was unsatisfactory. Therefore, we concluded that the type of information system has no direct influence on the quality of service.

4.3 Office Size

The size of the available office space can not explain the quality of service either. Though some registration offices have three times more space than others, they do not offer greater waiting zones or comfortable service delivery at desks in single rooms. Only if the implementation of an information system was accompanied by greater alterations of the office building was high service quality often achieved, especially if the complete office was rennovated. Therefore, funds for basic rennovations are the only quantitative resources that have a provable influence on the quality of service in the case of computerization.

Since scarce quantitative resources do not explain the variance in the quality of service sufficiently, we must investigate other possible causes.

5. CITIZEN ORIENTATION AND PROFESSIONALISM OF ADMINISTRATORS

Kraemer (1980) assumes that citizens derive benefits from information system use in public administration if

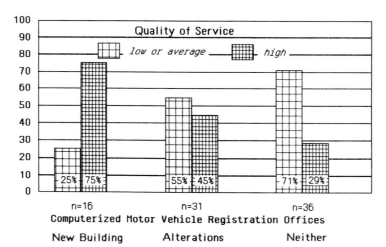

Figure 2. Building Alterations and Quality of Service

o the autonomy of local government is great
o available funds for experimental applications are large
o the utility of citizen orientated applications in proximate
   authorities is demonstrated
o users and developers of technology work in close proximity
   and have intensive communication
o the involvement of citizens in the system development is high
o the development process is performed iteratively
o the implementation process is accompanied by reorganization
   measures
o professionalism and citizen orientation of management (and
   computer specialists) are high

In our study, some of these factors proved to be irrelevant or not
measurable. For example, participation of citizens in system
development and implementation did not occur. The degree of
autonomy of the registration offices differs insignificantly since
all registration offices are integrated into the respective local
authorities in the same manner. The intensity of communication
between administrators and computerists does not play a central
role since the highest quality of service is not delivered by the
pilot users where the communication between administrators and
computerists is naturally most intensive. Reorganization is not
enforced by information technology but results from adequate
insight by management. We have seen that scarce resources contribute little to explain the variances in the quality of service.
Therefore, the professionalism and citizen orientation of management seem to be prime moving factors for a high quality of service
of a registration office.

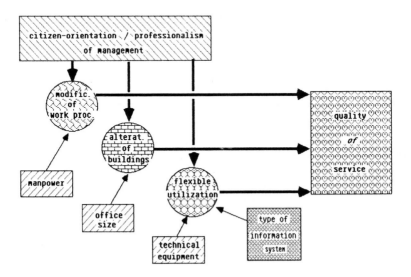

Figure 3. Frame of Reference

If an office manager does not use the introduction of a labor-saving and labor-facilitating information system for extending open hours, this action may be explained either by his insufficient citizen orientation, the missing insight into the citizen orientation of such a measure, or insufficient power to make adequate modifications of the work process accepted within his office. Insufficient resources do not justify this shortage since some registration offices offered open hours in the afternoon even before computerization and other offices introduced them in spite of a certain manpower reduction after computerization.

The above is speculative since citizen orientation and professionalism of administrators cannot be measured directly. Every administrator will say that he is citizen oriented. In our postal survey, more than 90 percent of the office managers stated they introduced the information system because of the long waiting time and handling periods. Professionalism appears only in the way the managers fulfill their functions. In our case study, we considered citizen orientation and professionalism only indirectly by indicating reorganization measures with impacts for service quality which had or had not been performed. So far, we have only conducted a limited test for the relationships in the above frame of reference.

6.   COMPUTER USE AND ADMINISTRATIVE REFORMS

The contradiction between our results and the results of most other studies cited above can be explained by the state of technological development. "Old" data processing technology was centralized, not dialogue-oriented, and supported batch processing of large data volumes rather than communication within authorities. "New" information technology supports decentralization by enabling the clerks to handle problems completely at their workplaces and supports not only communication with authorities but can also improve communication with the citizens. Interests in maintaining bureaucratic procedures which are not oriented towards citizens are increasingly difficult to justify by technical-financial restrictions in view of the possibilities of advanced information technology. Centralized administrations can hardly be advocated convincingly since information technology allows the provision of administrative services in the immediate neighborhood of citizens, e.g., in branch offices. Moreover, the complicated completion of forms by citizens has become obsolete. In the early phases of registration office computerization, it was not feasible to relieve the citizens from completing the application form since the printers then available were too inflexible and expensive. Today, computerized application form completion is almost natural in view of the state of technological development. In our study, the registration offices with the "oldest" information system show less service quality than offices with "newer" ones.

Rationalization and control interests of administrators insufficiently explain the actual impacts of computerization projects. If authorities who are confronted with similar efficiency problems introduce information systems twenty years earlier than others, the explanatory power of rationalization interests must be questioned. Furthermore, in Danzinger's (1982) "manager rationalism," rationalization interests and citizen interests can well coincide.

Information technology offers many opportunities to alter anti-quated administrative structures and processes. Therefore, information technology may become a vehicle of administrative reforms (Reinermann, 1985) and, as a consequence, increase the quality of service.

We are far from proposing that the introduction of information technology in public administration will always result in higher service quality. Offices with similar tasks show a different mixture of resources and interests and these affect information technology utilization and its impacts. Weltz and Lullies (1983) state this in their theorem of "intra-organizational action pattern." Much more research must be done and extended to other domains of public administration such as the social welfare authorities (Kaufmann, 1979) where citizens may have quite diffe-rent interaction problems with authorities than in the branch we investigated.

REFERENCES

Blennerhasset, E., "Information Technology and the Public Service: Organizational, Human and Client Service. Implications of a Cross-National European Study," paper prepared for EIPA Seminar: "Information Technologies and their Utilization by Sub-central Government: Local Government Management with Information Technology," Eupen/Maastricht, May 6-8 1985.

Brinkmann, H., et al., "Automatisierte Verwaltung. Eine Empirische Untersuchung über die Rationalisierung der Steuerverwaltung," Campus, Frankfurt/New York, 1981.

Damanpour, F., and Evan, W. M., "Organizational Innovation and Performance -- The Problem of 'Organizational Lag'," *Adminis-trative Science Quarterly*, 29, 1984, pp. 392-409.

Danzinger, J. N., *Computers and Politics -- High Technology in American Local Governments*, Columbia University Press, New York, 1982.

Kaufmann, F. X. (ed.), *Buergernahe Sozialpolitik. Planung, Organisation und Vermittlung sozialer Leistungen auf lokaler Ebene*, Campus, Frankfurt/New York, 1979.

Kraemer, K. L., "Proposals for Research on Citizen Outcomes from Information Technology in Public Administrations," proposal for the Institute for Planning and Decision Systems of the Gesellschaft fur Mathematik und Datenverar beitung, St. Augustin, 11.11, 1980.

Lange, K., "Das Image des Computers in der Bevölkerung," GMD-Stu-dien Nr. 80, St. Augustin, 1984.

Lenk, K., "Computer Use in Public Administration -- Implications for the Citizens," in Mowshowitz, A. (ed.), *Human Choice and Computers 2*, North-Holland, Amsterdam, 1979, pp. 193-212.

Miles, M. B, "Qualitative Data as an Attractive Nuisance -- The Problem of Analysis," *Administrative Science Quarterly*, 24, 1979, pp. 590-601.

Miles, B. M., and Hubermann, A. M., *Qualitative Data Analysis*, Sage, Beverly Hills, California, 1984.

Reinermann, H., "Öffentliche Verwaltung und Informationstechnik," ÖVD/Online, 1985, pp. 77-82.

Weltz, H., and Lullies, V., "Innovation im Buero -- Das Beispiel Textverarbeitung," Campus, Frankfurt/New York, 1983.

Yin, R. K., "The Case Study Crisis -- Some Answers," *Administrative Science Quarterly*, 26, 1981, pp. 58-65.

DISCUSSANT NOTE

On: CITIZEN BENEFITS FROM INFORMATION SYSTEMS

By: Klaus Lange and Frank Sippel

Discussant's comments by: Frank BLACKLER

University of Lancaster
Great Britain

1. INTRODUCTION

This paper is of undoubted interest where, as Lange and Sippel indicate has happened in West Germany, widespread criticisms have been voiced about the quality of service associated with computerized information systems in the public sector. Their study illustrates the positive benefits that computerization may bring: citizen oriented rather than administration oriented information systems can indeed be developed within the arena of public administration.

My own interest in the case stems from a related concern. The tasks computerized in the vehicle registration offices Lange and Sippel studied are exactly of the type where, a priori, it is reasonable to expect that improved customer services should be obtained. The information systems in this case are used to collate and check fragments of information, to pass routine data to other agencies, and to provide personalized printouts of application forms -- operations well suited for automation. Rather than being surprised that an improved service to the public was achieved in this case, my concern is: Why is it that such an outcome is not more commonplace?

2. ANSWERS

The Lange and Sippel paper is helpful in answering this question. By comparing the performance of a range of registration centers all using essentially similar information systems, they were able to identify variations in the quality of services provided. Their study showed that several possible explanations of this phenomenon were not, in fact, correct. Thus, the suggestion that the better service provided by certain offices was due to a higher quality of staff did not stand scrutiny; nor were differences in the numbers of terminals available directly related to indicators of service quality. Similarly, factors that management theorists have suggested are related to the quality of service provided by computer systems in the public sector did not apply to this case. Especially, neither the involvement of end-users nor the involvement of representatives of the public in the design of the systems described here were relevant factors. What *was* crucial, as Lange and Sippel point out, was the ability of local management to exploit the opportunities created by the introduction of new office procedures. The crucial factor, in other words, was the standard of management within local offices.

3. KEY IMPLICATIONS

While this point is well made within the paper, certain of its key implications are not discussed. Lange and Sippel are, of course, correct in pointing out that earlier information processing technologies tended to be centralized and, while well suited to handling large batches of data, could easily be used to facilitate novel changes in the broader pattern of communications within an organization. However, it would be misleading to imply (as the authors come perilously close to doing in the final section of their paper) that applications of micro-electronic based informa-tion technologies necessarily lead to decentralization and to improvements in organizational communications. In recent years, there has been significant research interest in the organizational effects of the new technologies, but research in this area has been singularly unsuccessful in identifying consistent trends. In some instances certainly the technologies have been associated with increased decentralization, but in others (for example in the system operating at the National Driver and Vehicle Licensing Centre at Swansea in the United Kingdom), an increase in centrali-zation and bureaucratization has been the result. The new information technologies *can* be used in an unconventional way to decentralize, to improve communications, to facilitate a wider participation in decision making, to provide a better customer service, but there is no inner logic about them to ensure that they must be used in such a fashion.

The most distinctive feature of the new technologies is their versatility. In any particular application, choices exist con-cerning, for example, which of their characteristics could be exploited, what particular benefits are sought, who will gain and who will loose, how the application should be planned and deve-loped, and what behavioral assumptions should be used to inform the process. It is not enough, however, simply to point out that choices such as these need to be faced. The fact is that, typi-cally, pressures exist within organizations to use the techno-logies in particular ways, in most cases to use them in a minima-list and conservative fashion.

Only rarely is the range and nature of policy options created by the new technologies fully appreciated by top management. Many senior managers are not familiar with the new information pro-ducts; policy in the area of systems development tends to be strongly influenced by short term financial considerations; and there is a tendency to rely too much on technology specialists who, while well trained in their own fields, are generally rather poorly equipped to understand the behavioral implications of the work that they do.

4. CONCLUSION

It is because of such considerations that I am of the opinion that, as a matter of priority, research is needed into ways in which the organizational effects of information systems can be better understood and managed. The more detailed account of the work by Lange and Sippel that is shortly to be published in book form will help alert public opinion to the positive benefits that computerized systems can, in theory, bring to public administration.   Yet, provocative though their methodology proved to be in comparing different offices, and useful as their summary concepts of "professionalism" and "citizen orientation" most certainly are, more needs to be done.

It is urgent that ways be found to improve the general standard of management practices in this field.   There is no substitute for detailed case work to help in this.   At the start of their paper, Lange and Sippel criticize qualitative data as an attractive nuisance.   But it is only through "story telling" that the web of pressures which support the dynamic conservatism of organizational life can be fully understood.   This research report would have been strengthened if insights had been offered into the reasons *why* some managers perceived the organizational opportunities that others did not and *why* some were successful and others failed in their attempts to handle the change process.   It is only through evaluation studies which focus on issues of this kind that methods to facilitate innovative and effective uses of the new technologies will be developed.

Constructive Technology Assessment:
Social Assessment of Technological Innovation
A. Simonse and S. Dijkstra

"Our diagrams have been kept simple."

INFORMATION SYSTEMS ASSESSMENT
N. Bjørn-Andersen, G.B. Davis (Editors)
Elsevier Science Publishers B.V. (North-Holland)
© IFIP, 1988

CONSTRUCTIVE TECHNOLOGY ASSESSMENT: SOCIAL
ASSESSMENT OF TECHNOLOGICAL INNOVATION

A. SIMONSE
S. DIJKSTRA

Institute for Social and Industrial Psychology
University of Amsterdam
The Netherlands

In 1984, an inventory was made of research on the
social aspects of office automation in the Netherlands (Barkema and Dijkstra, 1985).   Twenty-four
programs of socio-organizational research were
inventoried.   The majority were case studies
describing the *social consequences* of new technologies after their introduction; in other words, *ex
post* descriptions of the negative and the positive
consequences of technology innovation.

In contrast, Technology Assessment (TA) represents
the development of methods for *prediction* of social
consequences of different technological options at
an early stage of decision making and for *steering*
technological options into a socially desirable
direction after weighing the consequences.

The first phase of our TA research program, carried
out through 1984 and 1985, has focused on the development of approaches for predicting social effects
of new technologies and the criteria to be used.
To this end, an ex post method of research has been
developed and applied in five case studies.   The
second phase of our study is designed to test
approaches and criteria in a "real life" situation.
A number of automation programs will be followed
from start to finish.   We will do this in longitudinal case studies partly by action research.   The
third phase consists of experiments with the design
of new technologies, directed by criteria based on
predictions of expected social consequences.

1.   TECHNOLOGY ASSESSMENT: BACKGROUND AND DEFINITION

Technology Assessment is the main issue in the policy memorandum
of the Minister of Education and Science.   On page 6 of this
memorandum, TA is defined as follows:

all activities and all measures used to study
at the earliest stage the various aspects and
consequences of a technological development
for (different groups in) the population, pre-
ferably in their interrelationship, for the
sake of social applicability of the techno-

logies in question. [Ministerie van Onderwijs
en Wetenschappen, 1984]

This definition follows the views on TA in the United States,
where the Office for Technology Assessment, commissioned by
Congress, studies the effects on society of new technologies on
behalf of political decision making (Hetman, 1973; Wissema, 1977).

The Dutch TNO Centre of Studies for Technology and Policy did
preparatory studies for this memorandum (TNO/STB, 1984). TNO
concentrated on large-scale technological development with a
variety of societal implications, such as media technology, a
television cabled network experiment in the province of Limburg,
medical technologies and computer technology in education. TNO
considers TA procedures first of all as a medium to feed political
discussions around such developments.

A preliminary study of the Institute for Social and Industrial
Psychology focused on the relationship between technology and
labor and the steering of technological innovation at enterprise
level from the social point of view. Technology Assessment is
here defined as the *steering* of selection, design, and introduction of new technologies in a (labor) organization, based on the
weighing of alternative technological options through *predictions*
of expected social and societal implications (in addition to the
usual weighing of expectations with regard to efficiency and
improvement of profitability).

This definition of TA emphasizes:

1. The introduction of social criteria in the process of
   decision making on technology at the enterprise level and,
   therefore, social responsibility in the organization's
   decision making;

2. The possibility to choose from several alternative technological options. If this is not the case, and the study is
   focused on the identification of the consequences of one
   specific technological option, we call this Impact Analysis
   (IA). If it is only a matter of determining the expected
   negative consequences, we call it Risk Analysis (RA). TA,
   therefore, explicitly presupposes a selection from several
   options.

3. The assessment of relative importance of the expected effects
   on employees inside (and outside) the enterprise and subsequently steering the selection, development, and implementation of new technologies.

1.1 A Model of Constructive Technology Assessment

Constructive TA should be set up in such a way that the social
consequences of technological innovation are taken into account
during all phases of the decision making process. Therefore, we
should look into decision making and planning procedures within
organizations.

Of primary importance in all organizational planning is the
strategic (long-term) planning. All subsequent decision making is
constrained by limitations and restrictions laid down in this
phase.

Alternatively, socially desirable options should be considered in this phase. Strategic planning is of the utmost importance for every organization. Ill-guided selection of priorities or too limited a range of selected (technological) possibilities can lead to costly changes and organizational problems in later phases.

From this point of view, strategic planning has a bearing via medium-term planning (tactical planning) on the operational system. This is represented in Figure 1.

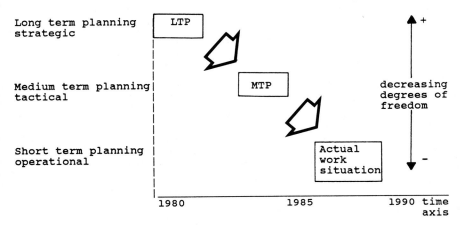

Figure 1. Phases of Decision Making in Technology Development

Figure 1 stresses the limitations and restrictions earlier phases put on later planning phases. Figure 1 is, of course, a simplification of the complexity of planning, but the phasing is a commonly used representation of organizational decision making (Snellen, 1985; Van Binsbergen, 1985).

The time span covered by strategic management, tactical management, and operational management depends on what is planned. For planning and building a house a total period of two years should suffice; the planning and building of a nuclear plant takes about fifteen years. In the case of a nuclear plant, there should be early surveys of locations and available nuclear techniques. Examples of early strategic surveys were also found in networks for electronic transfer of funds in Case 1 and in the mail handling systems of the PTT (the Dutch postal and telephone company). Planning of the first phase of technological innovation should have a strong accent on surveys or a strategic reconnaissance of possibilities.

The strategic planning leaves several options for the development of technology. Options should be selected on the basis of social criteria as well as efficiency and economic criteria. Constructive TA in this phase should lead to the design and/or recommendation of socially desirable technological alternatives (Malotaux and in't Veld). For example, the role of labor and capital in the future organization should be determined, the effect of an aging population, the intended level of qualifications of the workforce, and so forth. We call this *pro active decision making.*

Technological innovation often starts with phases like problem
survey and problem definition which then provide the basis for
functional and logical design. The orientation in these phases is
mainly technical, but there is a definite tendency to view automation as a form of organizational change. In that case, technology, organization, and labor should all be subjects within the
strategic decision making. As to how far the stakeholders within
an organization are able, or willing, to give equal attention to
the factors of labor and organization remains an unanswered question. Social advisors and/or worker-representatives could play an
influential role in predicting (negative and positive) effects of
alternative technological options.

In the medium-term (tactical) planning, a choice is made from
strategic options which culminates in design. The broad margins
from the earlier phase are considerably reduced. The steps in
systems design such as functional, technical, and software design,
have often taken place without participation of social staff and
advisors to ensure the realization of optimal social conditions.
The influence of workers during this phase is often minimal.

Constructive TA in the medium-term should lead to prevention of
undesirable outcomes. Giving direction to the design of technology on the basis of social criteria is an important goal of
constructive TA. Impact Analysis (IA) and Risk Analysis (RA)
should indicate the consequences and risks of design options for
the organization and the work force. This should lead to structural (re)design or changes in organizational and/or technological
design. When the moment of implementation approaches, the degrees
of freedom are very limited.

During the short-term planning (operational management), the
organization is being made ready for implementation of the new
technology. The latitude for changes in technology and organization is completely reduced. By carrying out a last-minute Impact
Analysis or Risk Analysis, some marginal adjustments may be possible, but in most cases it is up to the employees to adjust to the
new requirements in some other way.

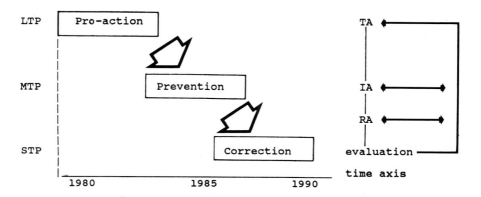

Figure 2. TA, IA, and RA and Pro-Action, Prevention and Correction

After implementation, correction of apparent faults or persistent problems may occur. Evaluation can feed strategic and tactical management with clues for considering social aspects in decision making on future technology. Figure 2 illustrates the role of TA, IA, RA, and evaluation in the organizational planning process.

The overall principle of constructive TA should be that by the long term planning, structural adjustments within the medium term planning are made unnecessary. Forestalling necessary corrections on an operational level is an essential principle of medium term planning.

The above illustrates the coherence of TA activities in the successive policy domains. Together, TA, IA, and corrective measures make it possible to design technology on the basis of social criteria.

Our diagrams have been kept simple. Far more complicated diagrams of decision making are conceivable (Nederlands Genootschap voor Informatica, 1983). In automation programs, elaborate models are used with preliminary studies, definition studies, logical designs, technical designs, etc. Practical introduction will have to be adapted to the organization's current method of technology development. However, the essence of what has been said so far is:

o   selection from several options = TA
o   selection within one option   = RA
o   decision making at earlier stages imposes limits on social policy at later stages (Pot, 1985).

Criteria for quality of work are being widely discussed. An approach was developed within the socio-technical experiments in the 1970s in which the quality of work is broken down to the structure of jobs, tasks, and the layout of the work site. One example of this approach is the study carried out at the University of Nijmegen in cooperation with Philips (Eijnatten, 1985). Sometimes the criteria includes research on attitudes towards automation (Wentink and Zanders, 1985). Within TA, criteria for the quality of work are closely related to the objectives of employers and employees in the organization (Kerkhoff, 1982; Fruytier and Ter Huurne, 1983).

For employers, the objectives and revenues of technology innovation are well defined. Management or employers aim at improved revenue *through* technological innovation. Improvement of revenue may appear in different forms, including cutting down labor costs, improvement of efficiency, consolidation or strengthening of the competitive position, product innovation, etc. A second objective or revenue of technological innovation which is often mentioned is improvement in the management of the organization.

In the course of this study, the objectives of management with the introduction of new technology will have to be checked in each project. For now, we will only state that, from its function in the organization, management will first try to maintain or improve revenue and then obtain supervision and control of production processes. It is also important that management, as the initiator of most organizational action, is strategically ahead of the employees in the organization.

The objectives and revenues through technological innovation for
employees are not as clear. Social scientists often define the
revenue for employees in terms of job satisfaction, motivation,
social needs, etc. In the current labor market, however, it is
obvious that employees first of all work for income security.
Technological innovation from the point of view of the employee
will therefore have to be assessed on instrumental revenue, such
as employment, pay, and work security.

The analysis by Kerkhoff (1982) mentions, as a second criterion
for the quality of work, the employees' strength of negotiation
within new technologies. This is easily understood as being
counter to management's objectives of supervision and control. We
had some problems with operationalizing this criterion. We limit
ourselves now to the predictable effects of technology on specialization and qualifications, centralization, supervision, and
isolation of employees (isolated work sites).

Within constructive TA, the most important criteria for the
quality of work as a consequence of technological innovation are:

1. the instrumental revenue for employees

2. strength of negotiation for employees resulting from techno-
    logical innovation and differences that may arise among
    groups of employees

We believe that these are the most important criteria in strategic
decision making. It will also be obvious that these criteria for
constructive TA may be at odds with management's objectives. The
essence of constructive TA is to allow for a fair balance between
social and economic objectives at a moment when several technological options are still possible.

Within government organizations, such weighing of social criteria
against economic criteria ought to be a matter of routine in strategic decision making (Hagen, 1985). In contrast to the situation
in private enterprise, there should be no question of clashing
interests between management and employees (civil servants). A
government organization should strive for optimal social service
in terms of optimal work conditions for employees. Both intra-
organizational and societal consequences are at stake here. Two
case studies presented in section 2 deal with government organizations.

The decision on design and implementation of the new technology in
the phases of tactical and operational planning add predictions on
the following criteria:

3. the physical-medical effects on employees (visible indicators
    such as recognized unfitness for work, prolonged illness,
    etc.) resulting from the burden of the work load and work
    conditions

4. the task-related effects, such as obsolescence of qualifica-
    tions and a decrease of flexibility and versatility (visible
    in turnover and absenteeism)

5. psycho-social (behavioral) patterns, such as motivation, job
    satisfaction, estrangement, and apathy

Within these predictions, a constructive contribution to design and implementation of new technologies should be possible.

Figure 3 shows the five fields of criteria for quality of work combined with the phases in decision making as described previously (Dijkstra, 1985).

	Instrumental revenues	Strength of negotiation	Medical/ physical work conditions	Task related effects/work work structuring	Psycho-social effects
LTP					
MTP					
STP					

Figure 3. Term and Fields Covered by the Predictions in Constructive Technology Assessment

The crossed fields in Figure 3 indicate points when reliable predictions cannot be made.

1.2 Research Program on Constructive Technology Assessment

The research program on Constructive Technology Assessment (CTA) has been set up with caution. Nourishing too high of hopes in the short term may lead to failures, as happened with earlier social innovations such as organizational democratization and social indicators (Kleinendorst and Kerkhoff, 1982). The research on CTA is divided into three phases, each phase dealing with one specific problem.

In the first phase, predictive power with respect to social consequences of recent technological innovations is assessed. This is the main topic of this article.[1] The predictive ability of social specialists (researchers, advisors, staff members) is assessed through an ex post study.

The subject of the ex post study is a recently introduced automation project in a clearly defined section of an organization; for instance, a department or an office. From documents and interviews, an accurate description is made of the situation of that particular section of the organization *before* introduction of the new technology. Information is gathered about the organization's important lines of policy (specifically the automation policy), work conditions, social management, organizational development, and environmental influences (government regulations, competitive position, labor relations). This information, together with a global description of the new technology, is presented to a number of social experts.[2] These are requested to formulate, with the aid of Figure 3, predictions on the effects of technology in the organization as described. This simulates an Impact Analysis or a Risk Analysis. Next, the predictions are compared with the real outcomes of the automation project.

The importance of this phase is in the determination of the strong and weak points in predictions with respect to the social consequences of recent technological innovation. At the same time, it supplies insight into the information required to formulate the predictions and the questions to be put to the predictors.

The second phase, planned for the period 1986 through 1989, focuses on predictions in current automation projects. In a longitudinal study, a number of projects are being followed through their actual course. During the project, predictions are formulated of the social consequences of decisions on selection, design, and implementation of the new technology. After its introduction, the actual outcomes are compared with the predictions given in the various phases. From this comparison, the development of predictions against actual outcomes can be determined.

This phase shows at which moment reliable predictions on social criteria can be formulated (see the fields in Figure 3). At the same time, the predictions are determined in a situation in which there is less structured information available than in the artificial ex post situation. The longitudinal study allows for two variations. In the first variation, the study runs alongside the project, but predictions *are not included* in the decision making. Methodologically, this yields a very accurate assessment of predictions. The second variation is action research in which the predictions *are included* in the decision making process, which may induce adjustment of technological choices. If that is the case, the predictions cannot be determined objectively. On the other hand, action research supplies more information on the introduction of social criteria in strategic and tactical decision making. Both strategies are conceivable, and it is probable both will be used.

The last phase covers experiments with alternative technological designs. From phases 1 and 2 we expect to gather sufficient insight on the effects of technological innovation to formulate suggestions for alternative technological options towards optimal social outcomes.

2.   THE PREDICTION BY SOCIAL SCIENTISTS IN FIVE CASE STUDIES

2.1   Introduction

All five case studies follow an ex post design in which:

1.   An outlined part of an organization and its activities is being described, including the introduction of a new technology (automation) and the relevant decision making.

2.   Based on this information, a group of social scientists makes predictions on the social effects after automation according to the criteria for quality of work as described in Figure 3.

3.   The predictions are compared with the situation as it has developed after automation.

The five case studies describe the following automation processes:

Case Study 1   The introduction of counter terminals in a branch office of a cooperative bank

Case Study 2   Automation of a butter production line in a cooperative dairy factory

Case Study 3   Introduction of automatic mail handling systems in the PTT

Case Study 4   Introduction of semi-automated points of payment in two offices of a commercial bank

Case Study 5   Automation of the card index system in the branch offices of a public service institution

The ex post design imposes restraints on the prediction's time limits. In all five cases, the new technology had been introduced recently (a few months to a maximum of two years). The periods for which the predictions can be tested are therefore limited. Only short term effects can be tested.

In this research situation, therefore, the subject is the short term effects of a single technological design. This means it is not really a matter of Technology Assessment, because this extends over a long period and presupposes alternative technological options. Rather, it is a matter of Impact Analysis and Risk Analysis. For the determination of know-how required for TA, we have limited ourselves in this phase to examining the predictions of social experts on a limited scale.

A number of researchers at the Institute for Social and Industrial Psychology at the University of Amsterdam were invited to predict the following points from the case description:

o   Instrumental Revenue
       - short term (size of work force, new jobs, legal status)
       - medium term (trends in turnover, segmentation)

o   Strength of Negotiation
       - short term (the effect of centralization and formalization on the organization)
       - medium term (development of qualifications)

o   Physical/Medical Effects
       - short term (working conditions directly impairing health and safety)
       - medium term (conditions influencing prolonged sick leave)

o   Task-Related Effects
       - short term (work pressure, monotony, autonomy)
       - medium term (congruence of task contents and qualifications)

o   Psycho-Social Effects
       - short term (stress, job satisfaction)
       - medium term (mobility, flexibility)

The researchers were asked not only to give concrete predictions on the influence of the technology in question on the selected criteria, but also a motivation of their predictions and possible outside interfering influences. By specifying whether the predicted effects would affect all the employees or only subgroups in various degrees, the predictions could be detailed.

Medium term predictions will be less specific and will appear as
trends with a margin of uncertainty as a consequence of other,
possibly adverse, developments inside or outside the organization.
Therefore, a broad outline could be given of the field which is to
be considered fit for predictions by social experts. Finally, the
predictors were invited to report missing data for the prediction
of specific criteria. In view of the limited experience with
prognostication, expectations were not high.

2.2 Results

A number of striking results of the ex post case studies in each
field of prediction, as presented in Figure 3, will now be discussed. In all five cases, predictions were made of changes in
the volume of the work force as an indicator of the instrumental
revenue. In spite of the fair insight of the predictors in the
volume of disappearing tasks and newly created jobs, predictions
on the volume of the work force appear to be rather unreliable.
This is chiefly due to a number of factors which are difficult to
calculate:

a. *The often unclear relationship between the volume of the work
    force and the volume of tasks to be performed.* Overstaffing
    as well as understaffing is possible. In Case Study 2, the
    number of employees on the butter production line was con-
    stantly subject to change, mainly through temporary transfers
    of employees from other sections and seasonal influences. In
    addition, employees often worked overtime. The actual size
    of the work force could not be derived from personnel files.

    In public service (Case Study 5), time became available for
    long neglected inspection of returns. In the two banks (Case
    Studies 1 and 4), more attention could be paid to commercial
    tasks (marketing, for instance) after automation of clerical
    tasks.

b. *In addition to automation, reorganizations were put through.*
    In Case Study 2, the butter production was centralized in the
    automated department and removed from smaller departments
    elsewhere. In Case Study 4, regional data processing centers
    were closed down when a data network was set up between
    branch offices and the computer center. The branch offices
    took over a number of regional tasks.

These and similar issues can be accounted for through detailed
system descriptions and data collection on future organizational
change. The following points, however, are almost impossible to
account for.

c. *Delayed or obsolete planning of introduction.* In several
    cases, the planning stretched over a long period with
    frequent adjustments in the course of time.

d. *The work force (staff size) is often a source of controversy.*
    Differences appear between predictions and actual outcomes as
    a consequence of compromises resulting from negotiations.
    This was especially noticeable in Case Study 3, the automa-
    tion of mail sorting, where the Postal Service's own prog-
    noses differed radically from the actual effects.

Predictions on the volume of the work force, therefore, need accurate information on current management of work processes (tasks, priorities, neglected tasks, and work load), the "commercial" policy (new tasks), the organizational policy (concentration, elimination, merging, etc.), and reliable calculations of work force. Even then, predictions leave a considerable margin of doubt due to unpredictable influences.

Predictions of changes within the work force were, in almost all cases, focused on specific categories of personnel and on ensuing changes in the composition of personnel. Quantitatively, these predictions reveal the same shortcomings as those mentioned above. Qualitatively, however, the predictions were fairly reliable. In all cases, personnel categories can be indicated on which the cost of technology weighs heavily. Clerical tasks disappeared in Case Study 1. The consequences for the (female) clerical employees were, as predicted, compensated for by transfers to other departments and through natural turnover. Heads of clerical departments saw their tasks being minimized (as predicted). Correction was attempted afterwards through the creation of a function vaguely described as "information supply."

This had not been predicted, but could in fact have been foreseen for years. Therefore, meaningful implementation of the "information function" could have been prepared many years before and would have been a good deal less frustrating for the employees in question.

In the butter production case (Case Study 2), the effects became apparent in the staffing of the packing department where unskilled immigrant workers were employed. The predicted and actual "solution" was a "return to the homeland" premium.

In Case Study 5, a decrease of low-qualified clerical tasks had been predicted, as had an increase of higher qualified supervision tasks. The training policy in question did not, however, allow for promotion from clerical to supervisory responsibilities.

All cases show examples, especially of older employees, low-skilled, and female workers, who have come to bear the burden of technological innovation. Since no attention is paid to early estimation of these effects, the "solutions" always appear to stimulate turnover, including provisions for early retirement.

Predictions on segmentation have gradually come to rest on fairly good insight in the consequences of new technologies for the composition and stratification of the work force. These effects are closely related to the situation on the labor market, which at the moment offers every possibility for hiring and firing at low, medium, and high levels of skill (with the exception of specific functions).

These causes also affect the predictions on legal status and pay, the last, frequently used indicator of "instrumental revenues" in all five ex post cases. Often the predictors foresaw changes in legal status through an increase of part time contracts, short notice contracts, temporary employment, and lower initial salaries. Salary raises were predicted and realized for a smaller part of the work force, often to compensate for heavier responsibilities and risks. The butter makers in Case Study 2 were assigned to higher salary brackets. In Case Study 3, the disputed

point was whether operating the sorting machine was to be upgraded.

Under the heading "strength of negotiation," we shall come back to
the effects of segmentation with respect to qualification development. For the heading "instrumental revenues," the conclusion is
that further elaboration in longitudinal case studies seems warranted.

Under the heading "strength of negotiation," three indicators were
used:

1. Effects of the new technology on employees' qualifications

2. Effects on the organization in terms of structural charac-
    teristics such as centralization, formalization, and hier-
    archy (bureaucracy)

3. New systems of control

(1) In several cases, a polarization trend was predicted between
     functions comprising new tasks and functions designed to
     disappear sooner or later. In Case Study 3, the predictors
     foresaw a polarization trend between hand indexing and
     remaining tasks (operating the sorting machine, supervision,
     and maintenance). Hand indexing is mostly done by women in
     part time employment. Turnover is high and is handled
     through internal transfers and external recruitment. Stan-
     dards of qualification are minimal and the necessary dex-
     terity is easily learned. The remaining duties more or less
     imply development of quantification. Experience is gained
     with automatic procedures and training courses are given on
     the spot. The qualification development may be rather speci-
     fic, but at the same time the employee in question becomes
     more valuable to the organization. Maintenance personnel had
     to be recruited from outside because the required qualifica-
     tions were not available inside the company. Scarcity and
     value of qualifications will, of course, have an effect on
     the employees' strength of negotiation and future opportuni-
     ties for work.

An important question in Constructive Technology Assessment is to
what extent segmentation and polarization are unavoidable or
follow, per definition, from technological innovation. At this
early stage of our study, a conclusive answer cannot be given. We
do suppose, however, that technology development will continue to
tax employees. We believe that, through Constructive Technology
Assessment, adjustments in personnel management (training programs, for instance), and selection of different configurations
adverse effects may be counterbalanced.

Secondly, the labor market should be considered. Important
changes are to be expected on the medium term in labor supply in
the Netherlands. After 1990, young people will become scarce on
the labor market, as is already the case in West Germany and
France. Organizations will have to practice a more constructive
policy with respect to employment of women and older workers (35
and up) who, at this moment, are mainly called upon to fill the
gaps.

(2) For alternative system configuration, predictions on the
     effects of organizational structure are of major importance.

Predictions on this issue were, in all cases, succinct and generalized. We will not discuss these predictions in detail but will mention that they lacked an underlying theory. There exist vague notions on the relationship between technology, standardization, and (de)centralization of work. These notions will, however, have to be further developed and made more concrete (see Section 3, Conclusions).

(3) On the predictors with respect to our last point, we may again be brief. The cases revealed many forms of automated systems of control (such as registration of errors and mistakes, attendance, etc.). Research on the consequences of these issues is scant. Attention is paid to the subject in an independent study on employee monitoring systems and their possible impact on employees' privacy (Pruis, 1985).

On the physical/medical effects, predictions were made on changes in working conditions and consequences such as sick leave and physical complaints. The predictors limited their prognoses mostly to data entry tasks. Predictions were made of monotonous work, strain, and intense concentration causing fatigue, headaches, and frequent short periods of sick leave. In some cases, corrective measures, such as work breaks, maximum working hours, and job rotation were introduced. These predictions appeared to be fairly reliable. However, there is a problem arising from predictions limited to data entry tasks. With increasing use of automated equipment in clerical jobs, insight in risks outside data entry is indispensible. In the Netherlands, some research is currently being done on software ergonomy and human-machine interaction (NGI Proceedings, 1985). Whether this guarantees sufficient insight to locate physical/medical risks is not yet clear.

Task related effects cover all predictions on changes in work content, task characteristics, and their effects on employees such as obsolescence of qualifications, mobility problems, early retirement, turnover, and absenteeism. In this field, the predictors made fairly rough prognoses in the first cases (1 through 3). In Case Studies 4 and 5, the predictors were explicitly made aware of a number of specific task characteristics. This inducted detailed predictions on changes in responsibilities, autonomy, isolation, and interaction. In most cases, corrective measures were proposed in the socio-technical design of the work situation, such as job rotation and enrichment (work structuring). In some cases, such initiatives had already been taken by the organizations themselves, primarily as a corrective measure. Explicit criteria for work structuring beforehand were rare. One outstanding example appears in Case Study 2, the automation of butter production. The company had carefully prepared the introduction of new machinery with special training of the butter makers, design of the new process control panels, and structuring of functions. After consultation with the employees, a number of tasks were not automated so as to avoid monotony and loss of concentration. In the same way, a control panel was put up on which the entire production process could be followed. These changes combined with an improvement of working conditions caused sick leaves in the butter department to drop dramatically.

We conclude with predictions on psycho-social effects on employees. In some cases, changes were predicted in motivation, job satisfaction, insight into the work process, stress, status, and similar experiential indicators. The predictions, however, showed irregular use of indicators (stress and motivation were most

frequent).   These shortcomings are partly due to the ex post
design.   Ex post cases are not suitable for attitude research in
advance.   In this field, however, we lack a scientific tradition
for the prediction of behavioral reaction patterns.   Most research
in this area is done by post hoc questionnaires, which provide no
basis for predictive research.

For the assessment of indicators of psycho-social patterns, independent of experiential research (or in combination with it), a
separate study has been initiated (Jansen and Kerkhoff, 1984).

3. CONCLUSIONS WITH RESPECT TO PREDICTIONS AND FURTHER
    DEVELOPMENT OF CONSTRUCTIVE TECHNOLOGY ASSESSMENT

With respect to the ex post cases, some general observations can
be made:

1. Predictions are not yet sufficient but can be further deve-
    loped.

2. Improvement of predictions requires sounder substantiation of
    criteria and indicators.

3. Improvement of predictions requires a different type of
    research.

4. Prediction should be based on a multidisciplinary approach.

5. An expedient method for preventive social policy in automa-
    tion should be developed in continued studies.

6. Especially for public service, this method may be of utmost
    importance in the near future.

4. NOTES

(1) As appears from the results, the available predictions are as
    yet imperfect.   Considering the fact that in social sciences
    there is limited experience in predictive research, it is not
    altogether disappointing.   There are indicators on which
    prediction is adequate; in other fields, the know how fails
    to achieve better results.   This can be improved, however,
    through specific research (Pruis, 1985; NGI Proceedings,
    1985; Jansen and Kerkhoff, 1984).

(2) The case studies illustrate that predictions not only depend
    on the know how but equally on the substantiation of crite-
    ria.   The best example is the domain "strength of negotia-
    tion."   This requires further exploration theoretically and
    needs to be made more concrete.   The notion that this is an
    important criteria seems right, but predictable indicators in
    this domain are vague.

    In addition, the effects of work on behavior and attitudes
    require predictable indicators.   Moreover, improvement of the
    data collection on the organization and its environment with
    clearer directives to the predictors may further improve the
    predictions.   These suggestions are further discussed in the
    final report on the case studies (Simonse, et al., 1986).

(3) If predictions are to be further developed, a different research set up will be necessary. Automation is a form of organizational change. At stake is a dynamic process which, in an ex post study, is made static. Predictors gain no insight in the process in which automation is developed and this strongly limits their predictions. In the second phase of the research program, longitudinal case studies will be used.

(4) From the results, it appears that the team of predictors needs expansion. In view of the relationship between expertise and correctness of prediction, inclusion of other disciplines in addition to the present social scientists (personnel managers, worker representatives, social advisors, technical experts) is recommended for future research.

(5) Insight into social consequences of automation in organizations and socially acceptable technology designed on the basis of this insight would be highly desirable in many organizations. In the third phase of the study, socially desirable and effective alternatives should be developed based on substantiated predictions of the social effects of several options.

(6) We assume that the social (and societal) issues in new technology will become increasingly important, especially in public service. The social effects of new office and administrative technology in government organizations will eventually translate themselves back into their own services. For instance, physical/medical effects will translate themselves into health care; large labor turnover will translate into costs of social security; automation without assessing societal effects will translate into dysfunctioning of organizations and inadequate services.

Strategic planning and decision making with respect to automation and optimization on social grounds of a selected automation system provide important cues for making social policy more concrete. Constructive Technology Assessment aims at developing a method to this end.

REFERENCES

Barkema, A., and Dijkstra, S., "Sociale Aspecten van Kantoorautomatisering: Een Inventarisatie van Onderzoek," publicatie van het Ministerie van Onderwijs en Wetenschappen, Den Haag, Januari 1985.

Dijkstra, S., "Sociale Technology Assessment: Verslag van het Deelonderzoek naar de Invoering van Automatische-Postverwerkende Systemen in het Postdistrict 's-Gravenhage," Werkstuk Vakgroep Sociale en Arbeids & Organisatie-Psychologie, UvA, 1985.

Eijnatten, F. M., "STTA, Naar een Nieuw Werkstructure Ringsparadigma," Philips Eindhoven, 1985.

Hetman, F., "Society and the Assessment of Technology, Premises, Conceptions, Methodology, Experiments, Areas of Application," OECD, 1973.

Fruytier, B., and Ter Huurne, A., "Kwaliteit van de Arbeid als
     Meetprobleem, een vergelijkende literatuurstudie," IVA-Tilburg,
     October 1983.

Hagen, T. F., "De gemeente en haar personel," Informatie en Informa-
     tie-belied, No. 10, pp. 44-51, 1985.

Jansen, J., and Kerkhoff, W. H.C., "Mental Habits of the Aged Worker-
     Psycho-Social Patterns of Behavior as Indicators of the Quality
     of Working Conditions," ISBP/UvA, Amsterdam, 1984.

Kerkhoff, W. H.C., "De Kwaliteit van de Arbeid: Verhoudingen en
     Criteria," WRR Rapport V27, Staatsuitgeverij, Den Haag, 1982.

Kleinendorst, B. F. M., and Kerkhoff, W. H.C., "Sociale Indicatoren:
     Terug naar af?", Achtergrondstudies Maatschappij-en Gerdrags-
     wetenschappen, 1 Staatuitgeverij, Den Haag, 1982.

Malotaux, P. Ch. A, and in't Veld, J., "Inleiding in de Bedrijfsfeer,
     College Hoofdfuncties een Onderneming," T. H. Delft, vakgr.
     Bedrijfsleer en Industriele Oganistie.

Ministerie van Onderwijs en Wetenschappen, "Beleidsnota Integratie
     van Wetenschap en Technologie in de Samenleving," publicatie van
     het Ministerie van Onderwijs en Wetenschappen, Den Haag, 1984.

Nederlands Genootschap voor Informatica, "Methodieken voor Informa-
     tie-Systeem Ontwikkeling," Uitgave 3a van het Nederlands
     Genootschap voor Informatica, Amsterdam, 1983.

NGI Proceedings C-12, "Programmatuur naar Meselijke Maat. Cognitieve
     Ergonomie van Mens-Computer Systemen," Amsterdam, 1985.

Pot, F., "Automatisering en Vakbondsbeleid," Intermediair, 1 Februari
     1985.

Pruis, M., "Volgsystemen en hun Mogelijke Invloed op de Privacy van
     Werknemers," ISPB/UvA, 1985.

Simonse, A., Dijkstra, S., and Kerkhoff, W. H.C., "Constructieve
     Technology Assessment Vanuit Sociale Waarderingsgrondslagen,"
     Deel 1: Retrospectieve Toetsing van Voorspelde Sociale Gevolgen
     van Nieuwe Technologie, ISBP, Oktober 1986.

Snellen, I. Th., "Benadering in Strategieformulieren, een Bijdrange
     tot de Beleidswetenschappen," Alphen aan den Rijn, Samson, 1985.

TNO/STB, "Technology Assessment: Op Zoek Naar een Bruikbare Aanpak:
     1. Mogelijkheden en Beperkingen," Staatsuitgeverij, Den Haag,
     1984.

Van Binsbergen, P. R. M., "Productie-Automatisering 10, Computer
     Integrated Manufacturing: Een Strategische Benadering,"
     Informatie, jrg. 27, 1,5, 11, pp. 929-1032, November 1985.

Wentink, T., and Zanders, H., "Kantoren in Actie," Kluwer Deventer,
     1985, pp. 43-44.

Wissema, J. G., "Technology Assessment," Aspectenonderzoek in Het
     Spanningsveld Tussen Technologie en Samenleving, Kluwer Deven-
     ter, 1977.

PART IV
WORK GROUP REPORTS

INFORMATION SYSTEMS ASSESSMENT
N. Bjørn-Andersen, G.B. Davis (Editors)
Elsevier Science Publishers B.V. (North-Holland)
© IFIP, 1988

WORK GROUP A

Reporter: Leonard CAPPER

1. INTRODUCTION

It appeared from the wide brief that one or more of the following
questions could be discussed:

o into what area should research be directed?
o how should the research be carried out?

The group did not see any need to concentrate upon the issues
covered on IS assessment, but sought rather to examine a much
wider field to cover the development, use, assessment, and impact
of IS.   The diversity within the group, which included both
practitioners and researchers, imposed a diversity of approaches
upon the group discussions.

The following points summarize the discussions.

2. USER ORIENTATION

The approach to the development of IS, including research, should
be user oriented. An IS is like any other product: it is to the
user a means to an end and not an end in itself. Any product that
is market oriented should be more closely tuned to the user's
needs. Assessment and feedback is essential to ensure that the
product is suitable.

2.1 The IS Environment

In order to meet the aims described above, researchers need to
develop a better understanding of the world/environment in which
IS operate. If IS are used to provide information to help people
manage a part of the world, and if the IS purports to map that
part of the real world that users are attempting to manage, then
systems analysts need to know more about:

o the variables in the world, their impact, and how those
   variables and their impact can be measured.   IT and its
   effects are among those variables.

o the relative importance of the variables, which may not be
   constant, to the many people involved.

o how users use IS and the information produced.

To meet these needs requires the development of predictive models
for use in:

o the life cycle of IS
o the data processing functions of IS

2.2 IS Assessment

Assessment is the product; an IS must play a role in all stages of
its life cycle, requirements specification, design, construction,
operational running and enhancement. For the different activities
in the life cycle, and in particular for the pre- and post-
implementation stages, assessment may have different goals,
triggers and methods. But feedback and subsequent action must
occur following all assessment procedures.

3. RESEARCH AREAS

To improve the capability of systems analysts, research must be
directed into a number of different yet related areas:

   o   modelling of systems
   o   determination of environmental variables
   o   development of experimental and pilot methods
   o   managing the process of change

3.1 System Modelling

Better systems modelling methods and models must be developed for
use in an evolutionary and organizational context, in contrast to
the more widely used, static and, hence, more limited approach,
for example, of Checkland (1981).

3.2 Environment Variables

The variables in the environment must be specified and, as far as
possible, suitable metrics developed for each. Without these
standards, the results flowing from diverse and empirical studies
cannot be correlated.

3.3. Experimental and Pilot Studies

The technology and its use must be developed to improve experimental (prototyping) and pilot techniques, and more extensive and
effective use made of them. These advances will enhance the
capability of systems analysts, practitioners, and researchers to
implement real world experimental and pilot systems where the size
and applications area included may be limited without limiting the
scope.

3.4 The Process of Change

Even if not designed as a deliberate instrument of change, new IS
may have an impact which cannot be predicted with any degree of
certainty. There is a need, therefore, to understand more of the
change process and the effects IS can have in diverse situations.
This increased understanding will in turn assist in the management
of the process of change.

4. RESEARCH METHODS

The development of many of the factors outlined above necessitates an improvement in our research methods. Two methods were selected as being of prime importance:

o longitudinal studies
o experiments

However, unless such studies assist in the development of metrics (cf. Section 3.2), correlations and basic underlying theories will not be forthcoming.

4.1 Longitudinal Studies

There is a need for good, detailed and usable data that longitudinal studies alone can provide. These studies must be carried out across a wide spectrum of applications, enterprises and cultures.

4.2 Experiments

Most managers are forced to experiment in novel situations, learning from example and experience how to progress in small, easily reversible stages. Given the development of prototyping tools, similar methods must be developed in the IS area. The real world social experiments will also supply a body of knowledge (cf. Section 3.3).

5. ROLE OF IFIP WG 8.2

Due to the very limited time left to the group, the discussion was very short. Nevertheless, it was possible to make and report the following brief points

o advisory
o leadership
o coordination

on a world-wide scale.

These activities should be directed into:

o funding of projects

o dissemination of information to researchers and practitioners, the latter to ensure that advances are taken up and used

o cooperation with people in other disciplines and other areas of computerization

REFERENCES

Checkland, P, *Systems Thinking, Systems Practice*, Wiley, New York, 1981.

MEMBERS OF THE WORK GROUP

J. Achterberg   S. K. T. Boersma
H. Albas   A. de Bree
N. Bjørn-Andersen   M. Broch
T. Bemelmans   C. A. Brown
L. Bhabuta   L. Capper (Chair)
F. Blackler   M. W. F. J. Creusen
A. Blokdijk   H. A. M. Daniels
D. von Bodegraven   E. B. Swanson

WORK GROUP B

Reporter: John HAWGOOD

1. INTRODUCTION

The following text contains the topics of discussion presented by
the working group.

2. FIRST DAY

The first day was mainly spent in getting to know each other and
asking two basic questions:

o Why should assessment be "soft" for information systems when
   it is "hard" for other investment appraisal?

o Should we assess information systems at all, when in reality
   both feasibility-oriented go/no go decisions and post-implementation reviews are based on "power politics" in the organization, not on assessments?

The first question was not answered. Perhaps the reason for this
was the hope that the organizational culture might change toward
accepting assessment. The second question was answered in the
affirmative.

It was also agreed on day one that cost estimation is not easy but
is more often done than benefit estimation because it is useful,
for example, for manpower planning as well as for system assessment.

3. SECOND DAY

On the second day, we buckled down to the set task of defining
important research topics for IFIP WG 8.2 within the ISA area.
Before actually defining tasks, the preliminary points were made
and (on the whole) agreed:

A. We must distinguish *data* from *information* (the former is
    input to an IS, the latter an output *with* *value* to reci-
    pient).

B. We must distinguish *hard* facts and figures from *soft* opi-
    nions, attitudes.

C. Assessment and development should be integrated.

D. We should know *why* assessment is done, *when* it should be
    done, *who* should do it on behalf of *whom*, before asking *how*.

The proposal research topics were not agreed by all:

1. (Two people)   First ensure that hard facts and figures
    available on costs and benefits are actually used in deci-

sions about information system development and in guiding IS improvement. This implies clear recognition of the fact that those gaining and/or losing only need to do assessment when it can affect a decision.

2. (Two people) Create a climate of acceptance of the principle that the quality of information systems should be assessed *both subjectively and objectively*. In any case, it should be done *continually*.

3. (Three people) Concentrate first on guidelines rather than on techniques or formal methods. This could apply for either of the proposed topics and should in particular say *why*, *when*, *by whom*, and *for whom* assessment should be done.

4. (One person) Suggest a CRIS-like enterprise for IFIP WG 8.2 in the form of carrying out an assessment in a real life situation using different methodologies.

MEMBERS OF THE WORK GROUP

J. Gricar
L. Gyllstrom
J. Hawgood (Chair)
F. Heemstra
R. Hirschheim

W. van der Houwen
J. Hørluck
D. Ibsen
K. H. Madsen

WORK GROUP C

Reporter: Paul MANTELAERS

1. STRATEGY

Before describing the ideas of working group C, two important decisions regarding the approach that was followed during the sessions have to be mentioned.

The first decision was to accept the topic of the discussion as it was formulated by the Program Committee. We deliberately wanted to avoid:

o spending (too much) time on discussions regarding questions such as:

-- what is research
-- research by whom
-- what is assessment

(without denying the importance of these questions)

o ending up with the conclusion that the topic was not phrased in appropriate terms.

The second decision was the selection of an approach intended to optimize equal participation of all group members. How this participative approach was realized will be reported in the next sections.

2. MILESTONES

For each session the group defined a milestone:

o Identifying (clusters of) research topics within the area of information systems assessment with relative priorities assigned to them.

o Indicating for research areas with a high priority

-- activities that should be performed
-- criteria for the assessment of the quality of the research

It was clear from the beginning that the second milestone was rather ambitious. However, its formulation might help to prevent the discussions from drifting off into generalities.

3. TAKING STOCK

As a start, the members of the group were asked to write down one or more relevant research topic. This was to be done on the basis of the perception ("gut-feeling") of each member individually. Altogether, 25 topics were mentioned and made available to the group.

4. CLUSTERING

Because several topics referred to similar aspects, the group decided to cluster the topics. The procedure we used for this purpose was rather informal. The resulting eight clusters of research topics were:

1. The assessment of information systems design methodologies: to what extent are actual information systems influenced by the supporting methods and techniques?

2. Who assesses what aspects: the role of the individual stakeholders.

3. Stimulating acceptance and use of assessment: scenarios for unfreezing, changing, and freezing (the different stakeholders within) an organization.

4. Assessment from an economic viewpoint. Some of the topics mentioned here are:

   o impact on unemployment
   o standard accounting framework for IS-economics
   o induced costs of information systems
   o benefits of information systems
   o how to integrate efficiency, effectiveness and quality in ISA
   o whether cost/benefit analysis really is important

5. Assessment from a social point of view

6. Differentiation of assessment methods as to

   o type of IS (DSS, MIS, etc., i.e., type of application)
   o type of organization (public or private, office or factory)
   o "cultural" differences between countries or enterprises

7. Impact on education

8. Impact on management style

5. ASSIGNING PRIORITIES

To determine the perceived importance of the individual clusters, each group member cast three votes, allowing a maximum of two votes for each person on one cluster. The result was:

Cluster	Votes
1	-
2	3
3	-
4	9
5	4
6a	1
6b	1
6c	-
7	3
8	-

Having done this, the question was raised whether the group it was correct to use these priorities as a basis for defining new research projects. Wouldn't it be better to take into account the research effort that already has been going on in certain areas? As one of the participants put it, information systems assessment from an economic viewpoint received the highest priority, but should one put additional effort in an area in which so much already has been invested in the past?

Some group members argued that because of this our attention needed a shift to new areas. Others pointed out that, although so much already had been done in this field, the results were still insufficient.

From this discussion two conclusions were drawn:

o   There was a high correlation between the research interests of the individual group members and the priorities they had assigned to the research areas. This meant that we did not concentrate on what we perceived to be important research topics from a general point of view; the research interest and present research commitments of the individual group members was used instead (and the group implicitly admitted that there was a gap between the two). Three of the group members presented papers at this conference relating to economic aspects in information systems assessment!

o   It is difficult to answer the question "what research should be done" without knowing the type and the quality of the research capacity. (Who is going to do it?)

6.   REVISION OF PRIORITIES

The group decided to use another approach for priority assignment. This meant that the previous decision criterion ("perceived importance of a topic") was decomposed into three other criteria:

1.   *Importance:* how important is it to do additional research in a certain area?

2.   *Quantity:* how much research has already been done in that field?

3.   *Quality:* what is the quality of research performed?

We also decided that a topic that scored high on the "importance" criterion and low on the "quantity" and "quality" criteria deserved the highest priority. This is obvious because it is an important subject on which there has not been much research and the research that is being conducted is not of high quality. Judgment of each criterion should again take place on the basis of perception based on the expertise and experience of each indivi-dual.

For each criterion, we used a three-point scale. The results are presented in Table 1.

During the process of priority assignment, we decided to take clusters 7 and 8 together because they are strongly related.

Cluster	*	Importance	Quantity	Quality	*	Priority
1	*	1.3	1.3	2.0	*	
2	*	2.3	1.0	2.2	*	4
3	*	1.1	1.3	2.5	*	
4	*	2.6	2.6	1.7	*	2
5	*	2.2	1.4	1.4	*	3
6	*	1.2	1.2	1.1	*	5
7	*	2.6	1.2	1.2	*	
8	*	2.5	1.2	1.5	*	1

Table 1

Comparison of this list with the previous one shows that there is not too much difference. There is a resequencing of topics that were already considered to be important. Furthermore, cluster 7/8 is now on poll position, but cluster 4 is still second.

7. CONCLUSIONS

The conclusion of Working Group C is that the impact of information technology on educational systems is the most important research topic for the next decade. Research in this area should answer such questions as:

o   What kind of training should we provide to young people in general to prepare them to live with technology in a changing world (the information society)?

o   Which curricula should we present to our students to prepare them for meaningful functions in the area of informatics?

o   What type of education and training should be provided for future managers in general?

MEMBERS OF THE WORK GROUP

M. W. F. J. Creusen
S. Hagelund
D. F. Lekanne
T. J. Lincoln

P. Maggiolini
P. Mantelaers (Chair)
G. Motta
A. H. Nettenbreyer

WORK GROUP D

Reporter: Hans-Erik NISSEN

1. INTRODUCTION

The discussion of the first meeting started by asking the practitioners present (four out of twelve) what they expected of assessment of information systems. Other group members then entered the
debate.

2. ISSUES

The main issues covered can be summarized in the following way:

- o Many problems --> assessment
- o Luck (in developing good IS) --> knowledge
- o Opportunities to improve (to be created by assessment)
- o Business <--> information systems (mutual support)
- o IS potential and contribution
- o Generate new ideas and products
- o Increase/maintain competitiveness
- o Proactive role of ISA

Why assess?
- o to make an analysis of strength and weakness
- o to answer the question "Where do we stand?"
- o to compare performance or application portfolio with others

What to assess?

- o a particular information system
- o the information system function
- o part or all of an organization

Who does the assessment?

What measures and criteria can be used?

Who takes action upon the results of an assessment?

On the issue "Why assess?", one participant stated that he
routinely asked: "Do you want me to assess this information
system as a success or as a failure?" In case the respondent
sidestepped the question, he repeated it.

3. PROCESS OF SELECTING TOPICS

The discussion of the second meeting started with an attempt at
finding a few important topics for future research within the
area. At first, convergence on a few such topics seemed to progress.

Two dominating topics could be:

o Transparency of assessment (to all groups of people affected); i.e., how do various degrees of transparency to
   different groups of people influence assessment, action taken
   upon it, and effects ensuing?

o Power and assessment, i.e., how do variations in power
   between groups of people affected by assessment influence the
   assessment, actions taken upon it, and ensuing results?

In both cases important subtopics in characterizing assessment in
a particular case would be:

o measurement criteria employed
o who will do the assessment
o why assess
o when assess (including when formally and when informally)

A check, however, indicated that the group did not agree upon
these points. Raising the issue of power seemed to divide the
group. Some proposed that research to find objective measures
would resolve power conflicts. Others pointed to the fact that
resolution of conflicting interests between various stakeholders
belonged to the normal tasks of management. Finally, some
proposed that research on "power and assessment" should not be
confined only to these two traditional methods of resolving
conflict. (This represents the chairman's interpretation of what
happened after his proposal to put forward the above as shared by
the members of the group.)

4. RELEVANT AREAS FOR ISA RESEARCH

The group then decided to let everyone propose an important topic
for ISA research. This resulted in the following thirteen potential topics for research produced by the twelve members. The
topics have subsequently been grouped into four subgroups.

1. Topics concerning multiple, partly conflicting interests and
    perspectives:

    o How can we make assessment transparent to all groups of
       people affected?

    o How can we expand our current assessment process and
       product so as to adequately represent multiple perspec-
       tives and interests?

    o How can we resolve or integrate the different perspec-
       tives represented by the multiple stakeholders to ISA?

    o Who resolves or integrates the different perspectives?
       Should we let stakeholders decide? If yes, how?

2. Topics concerning measurement, their reliability and gener-
    ality:

    o Effect of individuals in the assessment group (statis-
       tical reliability of assessment according to one method
       but undertaken by different people).

o Relationship between assessment and culture (both national and organizational).

o Possibility of developing an objective and generally applicable set of measurement criteria/standards for doing a problem-driven ISA, i.e., problems of measurement, comparison and interpretation issues such as:

-- which questions to ask
-- which data to gather
-- to what extent data gathered are comparable
-- what types of conclusions can be drawn

3. Topics concerning the purpose and timing of assessment:

o When to assess. Possible moments for assessment could be:

-- information policy selection
-- information planning
-- before development of (particular) system
-- during development of system
-- after development of system
-- during system use (both a particular IS and the IS function)

o Purpose(s) of ISA at various moments.

o Types of measures at various moments.

4. Topics concerning the relation of assessment to action taken

o What lessons can stakeholders obtain from assessment?

o Relation of assessment to the process of understanding and to "carefully" considered action.

o Link between assessment practice and assessment methodologies

-- the sociology of assessment
-- formal and folk assessment

MEMBERS OF THE WORK GROUP

L. Davies
G. B. Davis
F. Delholm
G. Dijkstra
B. Due-Thomsen
R. U. Dumdum, Jr.

P. Etzerodt
H. de J. A. Fluiter
C. L. P. Gerverdinck
L. A. Gimbel
M. J. Ginzberg
H-E. Nissen (Chair)

WORK GROUP E

Reporter: Hans J. OPPELLAND

1. INTRODUCTION

This is the summary of the work sessions of Group E, which tried
to sketch the main aspects for a research project focusing on the
assessment of information systems and their development process.

2. OPPORTUNITIES AND PROBLEMS

The group work addressed primarily the opportunities and problems
related to the assessment of information systems and their
development process. The following items were discussed.

(1) Reason(s) for ISA

    o Why do organizations or persons in organizations
       initiate and perform ISA?

        -- What are the expectations of the organization or
            the initiating person(s)?
        -- How important is ISA for the organization or the
            initiating person(s)?

(2) Planning for ISA

    o When is ISA done or when should it be done?

        -- Regularly scheduled performance, as part of the
            normal "production" or development activities
        -- Special event performance which makes it necessary
            to have a special agreement or decision

    o What should be assessed?

        -- Information systems (result of IS development
            process)
        -- Information system development process
        -- Information management/information quality
        -- Job/work design

(3) Conditions for ISA

    o What are the (changing) conditions under which ISA will
       be done or can be done in a specific organization?

        -- Conflicting parties?
        -- Time and budget restrictions?
        -- Organizational culture with regard to ISA (conser-
            vative or innovative)?

    o Participants should reflect (assess) the conditions
       under which they take part in an ISA process

(4) Methods or methodologies for ISA

- o What are available (reliable) methods, methodologies, frameworks, or procedures for ISA?

    -- Formal/informal approach
    -- Qualitative/quantitative approach

- o Are ISA methods/methodologies related/restricted to certain problem aspects of ISA?

(5) Assessors and their roles

- o Who are the possible "assessors" in ISA?

    -- Stakeholders, for instance
      - users
      - designers/developers of the information system
      - managers
    -- Professionals (occupational types), for instance
      - secretaries
      - nurses
      - doctors

- o Which role do "assessors" in ISA play?

- o How do "assessors" perceive their role?

(6) Consequences of ISA

- o What happens with the ISA results?

- o What are the consequences?

    -- Unexpected/expected results
    -- Unintended/intended consequences

(7) Conceptualizing and theorizing

- o How can results from ISA be used to foster development of concepts and theories for ISA?

MEMBERS OF THE WORKING GROUP

H. J. Oppelland (Chair)
P. van der Poel
S. Prestegaard
T. Rohde
G. Sandström

A. Schweitzer
G. Schaefer
Ph. S. Seligmann
C. Sennov
A. Simonse

WORK GROUP F

Reporter: Daniel ROBEY

1. INTRODUCTION

The working group attempted to learn more about information
systems assessment by conducting personal, informal assessments on
systems that the members used themselves or with which they were
intimately familiar. Systems included word processing, automatic
teller machines, electronic mail, automatic bill-paying systems in
banks, electronic bulletin board for communications between
professor and students enrolled in a class, and a system for
scheduling work in a house. Analyzing the benefits of these
systems was fairly predictable, with aspects such as speed,
efficiency, accuracy, cost reductions, and so on, being the
typical benefits. The negative effects of system use were much
more difficult to assess. In many cases, the negative effects
were not specific to the particular computing application, but to
the way the application interacted with the organization setting
(for example, with existing work rules). The conclusion was that
negative impacts are less predictable than the positive effects of
computer-based systems.

2. IMPLICATIONS

The implication of this conclusion is that assessments that adopt
formal methodologies, derived from prior expectations about
positive and negative impacts, are likely to overlook potential
negative impacts unique to a given setting. Therefore, the group
stressed the value of retaining *informal* assessment as an essential ingredient to a *complete* assessment. To the extent that
formal assessment methodologies are based on checklists derived
from convergent models and concepts of offices and organizations,
they are not able to anticipate divergent thinking about impacts.
The informal assessment, conducted outside of formal modelling
efforts, has a better chance to catch unforeseen impacts unique to
situations.

3. CONDUCTING PROCESS

The working group also focused on the *process* of conducting an
informal assessment, feeling that the mental processes involved in
thinking about organizational and social impacts might involve
some special expertise that could be modelled. The prospect of
building an "expert system for IS assessment" was abandoned,
however, in favor of more group-oriented processes that would
honor diversity of interest and perspectives among participants.
It was expected that a group of workers, led by a process consultant, would be better able to generate and understand potential
impacts of the systems they use than any single expert. Such
processes have been described by Hirschheim as hermeneutic
.exercises, and they are useful, if not fully "scientific," ways
to understand the impacts of systems on the workplace.

4. IMPLEMENTATION

To implement these ideas, "assessment teams" could be organized in the same fashion as "quality circles." The group agreed that such teams should be used during the design and implementation stages of system development in addition to the period after the systems being assessed have been used for some time. In this sense, the working group rediscovered participative system design, which the group found to be a good idea.

The group disagreed on the issue of comparative assessments. Some members felt that assessments of information systems should be compared to old manual systems or prior automated systems so that comparisons would be more fair. Others felt that this comparison would be unfair in the sense that systems should not be compared with past practices but rather with what is currently possible. This latter group felt that systems should be made as good as possible, not just better than what was done before.

5. CONCLUSIONS

The group generated no research agenda in the classic sense. Rather, it felt that the goals of ISA could be met more directly by organizing informal assessment teams as a demonstration project and evaluating their functioning. This could be reported as a series of intensive case studies, much in the same way that experiments in the quality of work life movements have been conducted. Given the unpredictable nature of the outcome of informal assessment, such a demonstration project would be useful in showing the types of impacts that this informal methodology could yield. It would also be beneficial to study the use of informal assessment in conjunction with various formal methods for assessing IS.

MEMBERS OF THE WORK GROUP

N. Pliskin
D. Robey
F. Sippel
S. Smithson
H. G. Sol
M. Souza

A. Srinivasan
L. Thoisen
I. Turk
M. van Vechgel
V. Verheul
G. M. A. Verheyen

WORK GROUP G

Reporter: Steve SMITHSON

1. INTRODUCTION

The work group decided, in the light of the papers presented at
the Conference, that a key requirement in the field of information
systems evaluation was an overall model, or framework, through
which to view the various lines of research.

Different researchers seem to be investigating particular concepts
within the area and it is not immediately obvious how these
concepts fit together.   For example, the papers by Iivari and
Dickson, et al., are mostly concerned with evaluation methods,
whereas the papers by Robey, et al., and Davis and Srinivasan
focus more upon the stakeholders and their values. A start at
building a comprehensive framework has been made in the paper by
Ginzberg and Zmud, but they were unable to include the proposals
of other papers. The work group resolved to construct a framework
to capture the key relationships between the concepts involved.

2. THE MODEL

The model produced by the group, shown in Figure 1, is a static
one, based on the notation employed in the extended relational
model RM/T (Codd, 1979). From this, process or flow models could
be developed at a later stage. A brief description of the model
follows. It is assumed that the reader is familiar with the basic
entity-relationship concepts (including many-to-many and one-to-
many relationships); the only construct that may be unfamiliar is
the diamond shape, which represents an associative entity. This
is a many-to-many relationship among a number of entities; the
exact meaning of which should be clear in the context of information systems evaluation.

At the top of the diagram are shown the stakeholders (different
groups of users, developers, etc.) with their values and interests
and rationale.   The rationale entity is shown with a reflexive
relationship indicating the different levels involved (e.g., overt
and covert, objectively rational and political). Stakeholders are
concerned with a particular scope, by which is meant both the
level of analysis (individual, departmental, organizational or
societal) and the setting of boundaries around the system to be
evaluated.

Evaluation methods are shown linked to particular time frames
(past, present or future) and their nature (summative or formative
-- see the Ginzberg and Zmud paper in this volume).   At the
center, represented by an associative entity, lie the criteria of
evaluation. By criteria, it is meant "what" is being measured or
assessed, e.g., costs, user satisfaction. The importance of the
criteria to be used for an evaluation has been emphasized by many
of the papers at the Conference, in particular by Hirschheim and
Smithson and Ginzberg and Zmud.   Thus, evaluation methods are
applied to certain criteria, within a particular scope, on an

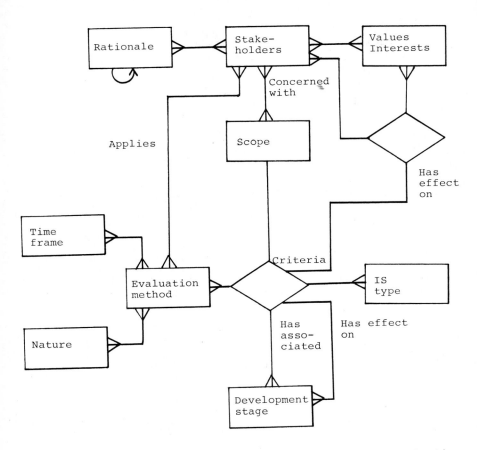

Figure 1: Category Model for Information Systems Evaluation: CAMISE

information system of a particular type, at a certain stage in its development.

The development stage refers to the stage the information system has reached in the traditional systems life cycle, e.g., feasibility study, post-implementation evaluation, regular operational evaluation. The inclusion of the information system type in the model reflects the emphasis upon it as a variable in the evaluation process, documented in the paper by Hawgood and Land.

3. RESULTS

Due to the limited time available for group discussion, the resultant model may be somewhat incomplete and further reflection might lead to a refinement of both the entities and relationships identified. However, it is felt that the model represents a useful tool for the unification of diverse research threads enabling researchers in the area to link their work with those of others. It may also be appropriate as a form of completeness check for anybody planning research.

REFERENCES

Codd, E. F., "Extending the Database Relational Model to Capture More Meaning," *ACM TODS*, Vol. 4, No. 4, December 1979.

MEMBERS OF THE WORK GROUP

S. Smithson (Chair)   R. Welke
C. H. Visser   C. E. Wells
B. de Waal   L. Y. Woo
F. Warrant   M. I. Younis
D. A. Wassenaar

HUMOR TO BE PRESERVED

A group of Danish students participated in the conference and composed the following text:

1. What did you learn at the conference today
   Dear little analyst of mine
   What did the speakers tell you today
   Dear little analyst of mine.

   I learned that assessment is problemland,
   And that professors do not understand
   Why business people live in numberland
   And think they are in wonderland.

   Chorus: That's what we learned at the conference today
             That's what we learned today.

2. What did you learn at the conference today
   Dear little dutchee of mine
   What did the speakers tell you today
   Dear little dutchee of mine.

   I learned that the conference wasn't in Rotterdam
   And "Rot ver dam" not even close to Amsterdam
   But anyway now can everyman
   Say "I've been in Netherland!"

   Chorus: That's what we learned at the conference today
             That's what we learned today.

3. What did you learn at the conference today
   Dear little analyst of mine
   What did the speakers tell you today
   Dear little analyst of mine.

   I learned that the result of the conference can
   Help everybody in every land
   To work and form a better plan
   Hey - evaluation and assessment man!

   Chorus: That's what we learned at the conference today
             ASSESSMENT IS THE WAY